FAREWELL AFRICA:
The Tramp Comes Home

David Lessels

First published in Great Britain by Pen Press

All paper used in the printing of this book has been made from wood grown in managed, sustainable forests.

ISBN13: 978-1-78003-280-1

Printed and bound in the UK
Indepenpress Publishing Limited
25 Eastern Place
Brighton
BN2 1GJ

A catalogue record of this book is available from the British Library

Cover design by Jacqueline Abromeit

Acknowledgements

My thanks to Maureen, my wife, without whose help and support this book could not have been written and my pleasure at being able to present this book to our daughters, their husbands and grandchildren.

My thanks also to those who have been kind enough to speak well of and recommend my book.

About the Author

 David Lessels was born into a mining family, the youngest of five children, in Torryburn, Fife. At the end of the Second World War he went into the Army and was sent to Kenya, where he fell in love with Africa. After his demob, he returned to Africa under his own steam and travelled the long road – the length and breadth of the great continent – a journey lasting five years. Farewell Africa: The Tramp Comes Home describes the lengthy return journey, homeward bound. Until retirement, David was a Lecturer at Portsmouth College of Art and when not writing, he and his wife enjoy spending time with their four daughters and their families.

Introduction

The story of my journey back through Africa in the 1950s is intended as more than a travel tale. The completion of my dream when standing at the Cape had been realised and, although I had first thought of a journey from Scotland to Cape Town, the return journey to see more of Africa had overtaken me and become paramount. The sights and sounds of Africa were magical to me and the chance to see more of that wonderful continent was irresistible. There were friends too whom I would like to meet again, but a different route through the country would offer more experiences; such is the wealth of variety of peoples and customs and so fascinating the history.

So, my mind was made up. Never mind the times of hunger and weariness when the savage tearing of my rucksack straps into tired shoulders made me wonder if I had made the right decision. I was sure I was heading north for more exciting times – a journey that would take me another two and a half years, but my mind was set.

Author's note

Just as with the prequel *A Tramp In Africa*, this book represents diary extracts and experiences from my time travelling throughout Africa in the 1950s. The language used reflects the standard vernacular of the day. Every generation has its own language – the words by which we are classed and defined – and one can often guess a person's age purely by their choice of words and expressions. Just as many words have entered the English language since these pages were written, so too have many since passed from general use.

Terms, considered stuffy or archaic, or even offensive by modern standards, were widespread at that time. However, I would not be describing the correct scenes and flavour of my story if I were to attempt to rewrite it within the construct of modern semantics and put contemporary jargon into the mouths of those I met on my travels in the mid-1950s.

So if at times my words grate on some modern ears, I do apologise but beg tolerance. I was a man of my time writing of the people of my time and so to not misrepresent them and for the purposes of authenticity, such terms are retained here. However, no offence or upset is intended by their inclusion.

Contents

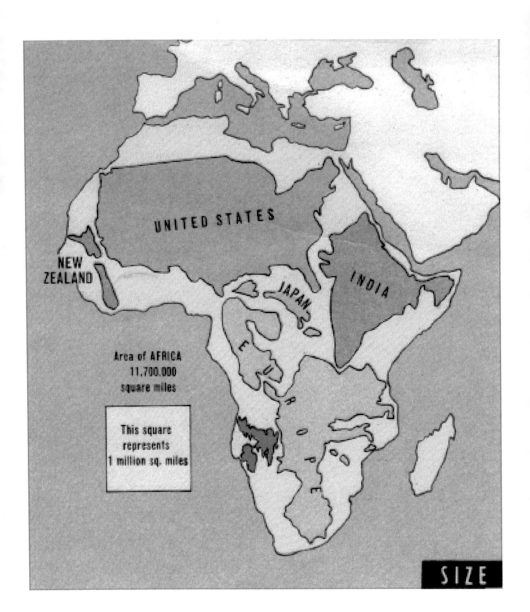

UNITED STATES

NEW ZEALAND

JAPAN

INDIA

Area of AFRICA
11,700,000
square miles

This square
represents
1 million sq. miles

SIZE

A TRAMP IN AFRICA

The Outward Journey

-------------- The Homeward Journey

Tewkesbury Road

It is good to be out on the road and going one knows not where,
Going through meadow and village, one knows not whither or why;
Through the grey light drift of the dust, in the keen cool rush of the
air,
Under the flying white clouds and the broad blue lift of the sky.

And to halt at the chattering brook, in a tall green fern at the brink
Where the harebell grows and the gorse and the foxgloves purple
and white;
Where the shifty-eyed delicate deer troop down to the brook to drink
When the stars are mellow and large at the coming on of the night.

O, to feel the beat of the rain and the homely smell of the earth,
Is a tune for the blood to jig to and joy past power of words;
And the blessed green comely meadows are all a-ripple with mirth
At the noise of the lambs at play and the dear wild cry of the birds.

John Masefield

(Reproduced by kind permission of the Society of Authors – literary
representatives of the Estate of John Masefield.)

IN THE BEGINNING ...

A short résumé of the first half of my journey on
foot from Scotland to Cape Town and my thoughts
when leaving South Africa on the second leg of my
long way home through the African continent.

It had been a long road to this lonely, beautiful spot in South Africa. In 1950, I left my home village, Torryburn in Fife, Scotland, to see as much as I could of Africa. I had come under its spell during two years' army service in Kenya just after World War II. I set out from home determined to travel on foot, walking or hitch-hiking, over the length of Africa to Cape Town and had achieved my objective.

The desire to return by sea was great. I had been away so long and missed my family and home. But, towards the end, the feeling had grown in me that my journey was not yet complete. No matter that I had traversed the great continent and seen so much of it, I realised that there was so much more I wanted to see and know of it. Moreover, since I had left East Africa the Mau Mau uprising had begun in Kenya and that land was now torn with war. It was there I had been introduced to Africa and although the whole continent had become part of me, Kenya was still my first love and I wanted to go back there to 'do my bit' to end the struggle, no matter how small that input might be.

And that was not all. There was something else ... an inexplicable, indescribable longing that made me want to wander on. Had I been asked then what it was that I was seeking I would have remarked what a daft kind of question that was. But was it...? It had happened before.

Way back aeons of years and miles ago, in the very embryo of my journey, a little old man, an Italian with whom I shared deck space on a ship plying between Genoa and Alexandria, had asked me that very question. I had mumbled some inane reply about wanderlust and such like, which

Grasso Stellario cut through with a long, heavy sigh, dismembering my postulations as neatly as a surgeon's scalpel would a body. He went on to say he had watched me during the past few days of our voyage and he had concluded that I had a yearning that would stay with me until I had fulfilled whatever it was that I sought.

"You will remember my words long after you have forgotten me," Grasso had said. This was not quite true because the old sage had popped up in my mind on one or two decisive occasions during the past years of my travels. What was true was that his words had never dimmed, although he remained in the distant shadows of my mind, passive, unobtrusive, but always ready to step forward when I faced a crucial, life-changing decision. I was grateful for his counsel in times of great stress and need.

Now, the decision made, I prepared to set foot on the long road back through Africa. I chivvied up my tired equipment, all of which had been looking forward to retirement. Every piece had done me proud over the past years and now I was expecting it all to start over again and look after me without complaint over the long journey home. My rucksack had a piece of heavy canvas stitched over its frayed bottom and some straps renewed. The old 'Blacks of Greenock' little bivouac tent, 6' x 4' x 3' high, limp thin and sun-wearied, had been stitched in many places and reproofed. My old boots, tired old friends I could expect no more from, had had to be laid to rest and replaced by those I now wore. These were South African Army boots and how I had acquired them is an outrageous tale that has been told elsewhere.

On my way south I worked at times in any way I could to earn my keep. In Aden, I was a painter with an Arab gang and also a building foreman; Kenya saw me in the East African Railway workshops in Nairobi. In Tanganyika, I went mica mining in the Bundali Mountains and hunted crocodiles for some months on rivers that flowed into the northern end of Lake Nyasa. In South Africa, I was employed some time in OK Bazaars, a large emporium in Johannesburg, and I gleaned some more cash from articles I wrote for newspapers and from talks I gave on South Africa Radio, Cape Town. But I was not flush, even by my standards, and knew I would have to get some work in the not too distant future.

Entering South Africa after the roving years in the wild north was like stepping ashore on a fertile island from a tempestuous sea. Here was order amid the calm, social lives of families stretching back countless generations, going about their working lives in idyllic scenery and surroundings, each enjoying quiet evenings on their *stoep,* confident of tomorrow. The whole country had a charm of its own, distinct from the rest of Africa.

This view, of course, was rose-tinted, a surface-deep comparison of the relative differences between the untamed land to the north and South Africa's development over two or three hundred years of white settlement. Over the next few months I learned that my fuzzy, Utopian, dreamlike scenario of the South African way of life was not entirely accurate. There were already fissures in the concrete and tarmac that had been rolled over the Earth's surface by way of advancement that would eventually split asunder and cause a cataclysm. But in the meantime, life in the Union was sweet and prosperous … for the whites at least!

And now, eight months later, I was in reverse mode. I looked back wistfully on new friends made, friends who would remain lifelong with correspondence and exchanges between our children of the next generation, and losing them made me feel sad and lonely. I would miss them. I would miss too the easy life, the towns and shops, the European-ness of it all in comparison to the relatively spartan north. But really, within me, I knew it was time to be gone. Lately, secretly from all, perhaps even myself, I had grown tired of much of the settled, easy life and had begun to yearn for 'Africa', the raw, native Africa that had drawn me to its heart in the first place.

It had all been so different when I entered the 'white' south those months ago. How I enjoyed the company, the conversation, the laughs and flirtation, the good food, the newspapers, the homeliness and kindness of modern society. South Africa was a strikingly beautiful country and a wonderful place to live, but it wasn't the old Africa. Lately it had begun to pall. Not suddenly, not for any particular reason or person. I just gradually knew I had to go.

Before leaving, however, I paused to recollect some memories and moments of fulfilment that marked my time there. At the Cape was that wonderful moment, which marked the end of my journey as it was intended. Through those years of travel and travail I had now arrived. Journey's end, as it was then – a dream come true.

Yet, before I moved on to begin my journey home, I paused. Dreams may fade, but memories don't. There is no doubt that South Africa was indeed a pivotal point in my life. That feeling of having achieved what I had set out to do was like passing through a door beyond which lay maturity, or at least another stage on my journey towards achieving it. Of course, it was not just like that. No passage through life is. We only realise with retrospective, over-the-shoulder memory views that past events along the way had changed and developed our lifestyle, and it is with hindsight we see the milestones that we hadn't noticed passing at the time. And so it was with me. Now, on the second leg of my journey I knew I was a different person, more self-assured, less concerned with what might lie ahead, more certain of what I wanted to do.

A lot of my developing self-assurance had come about when I passed my 25th birthday and knew that my one good eye was likely to see me all through life. That had given me an enormous boost, with the realisation of what could be possible now that the threat of losing my sight had passed. To explain this I have to say that my early life in the army in Kenya had given me a legacy I will carry to my grave. My right eye had been badly damaged by the sun and I was hurried back to Scotland to have it removed. I was told that my left eye had also been affected and the prognosis was not good. I was twenty years old at that time and would have to wait until my maturity at twenty-five to know the outcome. I cannot put into words how I felt when that weight, far greater than that of my rucksack on my back all those years, came off my mind. So, stepping out from Cape Town on my way north through Africa was indeed a Rubicon which I crossed with more assurance and confidence than I had possessed when lighting out on my way south.

Reading my diaries, which had lain in boxes on shelves for over forty years and only brought to the light of day when, having retired from lecturing at Portsmouth College of Art, I decided to write my story, I recognise a different, changing hand on the pens and pencils I had used along the way. The writing becomes firmer, the ideas and composition more professional and mature. I now know, on the threshold of my journey north, where I am going and why.

I have quoted before the words of Richard Burton on this subject, but I think they are worth repeating, for once again they sum up my mood.

Captain Sir Richard Burton, a man with an extraordinary gift for Oriental languages, was the first Englishman to enter the forbidden city of Mecca and the first Christian to write a detailed account of the Muslim pilgrimage. Burton did that journey in 1853 and now, exactly one hundred years later, in April 1953, I started my journey out of South Africa to wend my way up the long, long trail back to Scotland. In his book, *Pilgrimage to Al Madinah and Meccah* he wrote this:

The thoroughbred wanderer's idiosyncrasy I presume to be a composition of what phrenologists call 'inhabitiveness' and 'locality' equally and largely developed. After a long and toilsome march, weary of the way, he drops into the nearest place of rest to become the most domestic of men. For a while he smokes 'the pipe of permanence'* with an infinite zest; he delights in various siestas during the day, relishing withal deep sleep during the dark hours; he enjoys dining at a fixed dinner hour and he wonders at the demoralization of the mind which cannot find excitement in chit-chat or small-talk, in a novel or a newspaper. But soon the passive fit has passed away; again the paroxysm of ennui comes by slow degrees, Viator loses appetite, he walks about his room all night, he yawns at conversations, and a book acts on him as a narcotic. The man wants to wander, and he must do so, or he shall die.

[*The long pipe an Arab uses at home in place of the shorter 'chibuk' used on the road.]

Perhaps it was an exaggeration to say Viator would die if he stayed around 'easy street'. But he certainly needed to wander back into his old domain for the good of his mental wellbeing.

So… you have browsed so far with me and not laid my book aside. Come then, journey with me through Africa. The trail will be long and hard and yes, dangerous, but I promise you will never be bored. Live the life of the people, learn their ways and their customs and histories. Sit by my campfire at night and I will tell you Scheherazade stories while lions growl in the darkness and tiny bushbabies call loudly, plaintively, pitifully to twist your heart strings.

Read on and share my adventures and life…!

CHAPTER 1

WHERE EAST IS RIGHT AND NORTH A LONG WAY HOME

What qualities there are in silence. Even in the loneliest woodlands or savannah there is the creak of foliage or the swish of grass. Here in the Great Karoo there is nothing: nothing to move, nothing to make a sound when you stand alone. And yet … there is something! A sighing in the still air, an aura of past memories, of still voices, of lost people. Mine is an empty world dissected by a long, lonely road, straight as an arrow's flight that disappears in the haze of long distance.

I am travelling that road. The only person in the world. I wear my battered, old bush hat, a khaki shirt and travel-worn Black Watch kilt, old friends of many, many miles together. On my back, like a tortoise, I carry my house and all domestic accessories in my much mended and adapted rucksack. On my feet is a pair of new boots, still not broken-in, replacements for a string of worn out old, precious friends who died along the way.

One new friend which has joined me gives me added confidence and wellbeing and is very welcome on board. It is a Smith and Wesson, .38mm police revolver, slung with a lanyard on the left side of my belt for easy cross right-hand draw. All legally obtained and carried, a present from a Member of Parliament of South Africa who had been an old friend of my father. I hope I never need to use it.

It is hot in the Karoo. Hot for living. Even hotter, very much so, for walking. I hunch my shoulders to better balance my pack and thrust my thumbs through the straps, my natural position on the move. Even today, half a century later, I find myself unconsciously crunching with my fists the lapels of any jacket I may be wearing as I am standing in company.

There is a strangeness about walking in southern Africa, no matter that I have traversed it these past few years, with which I still feel out of kilter. As a Northerner I grew from birth to assume, take for granted even, that the sun rises in the East, which is on the left hand, and sets in the West, which is on the right. But here in the Southern Hemisphere it's all back-to-front.

East is right and I'm all wrong. Well, there's not much I can do about it, so I'll just have to get on with it. Strange though!

Perhaps a car or lorry might come along and perhaps it might stop and offer me a lift. But I will never rely on that. If it comes, it comes. If it doesn't, I'll walk. I am content. I am on my way home.

In this silent world my boots rattle their rhythm on the road and I let my mind wander to forget the grind of the march. I had left Cape Town with a memory of a bustling and vibrant city. Friendly people, interested to know where I had been and keen to give me hospitality. But what of its history? I had spent time in the library and talking to people, expanding my knowledge of its early beginnings. History had always fascinated me and I wasn't disappointed.

In 1488 the Portuguese navigator Bartolomeu Dias, with three very small ships, rounded the cape and named it 'The Cape of Good Hope'. Ten years later his countryman Vasco da Gama also went round, but he carried on to reach India in 1498. Thereafter, the East India trade was established and for a hundred years the Portuguese had the monopoly. Despite the name given to the Cape, the Portuguese found it a wild and stormy place and were glad to give the land a miss on their journeys east and west.

By the end of the sixteenth century the Portuguese monopoly on the trade route was being challenged by the Dutch, who made treaties with Sultans and land owners from Sumatra and Malaya to islands round the Java and Timor Seas. The Dutch East India Company, commonly known as the VOC (Vereenigde OostIndische Compagnie), was formed and eventually knocked the Portuguese off their perch and the men from Holland became the supreme traders with the rich Far East countries.

Although the Portuguese had long used the Cape to collect fresh water, they found the indigenous people there too primitive and wild to be of any trading value, so they never put down roots to colonise it. The Dutch did.

At first they too entered the great natural bay there, later to be known as Table Bay, to put in for fresh water. But when one of their ships sank in the bay the survivors built a fort and thereby started the colony.

At first there was no intention of branching inland. The purpose was to establish a base where some land could be cultivated to produce meat, vegetables and fruit to revictual their ships. Without knowing it the Dutch had made a very wise move. A century later, in 1753, a Scottish naval surgeon, James Lind, showed the world that lemon and orange juice could cure scurvy, the seamen's dreaded curse of long voyages.

Five years after the sinking of their ship in Table Bay, a small band of seventy burgers, under the command of the first governor, Jan van Riebeck, whose statue proudly stands to this day in Cape Town, arrived in 1652, exactly three hundred years before I entered that country in 1952.

In the past, when European countries opened up trade routes to foreign lands, the people who went there, apart from the sailors, would be business men, entrepreneurs, men of substance and the like and their stamp would form the ambiance of their way of life. The Dutch Cape Colony was different to all others. To Holland, this was only a staging post on the way to the rich trade pickings in the Far East. Had the Dutch only known they were sitting on a land with a trading potential, such as gold, diamonds and more, beyond the dreams of anywhere else in the world. But they didn't know and at that time it was farmers they needed more than anything else.

So the government put it to the farming community in Holland that there was a life for them in Africa. At first there was only a trickle, but the numbers swelled and the community prospered. *'Boer'* in Dutch means 'farmer' so the immigrants from Holland were naturally called the Boers. A great boost to the population came some thirty years later, in 1688, when a large contingent of French Huguenots arrived. They were Calvinist Protestants and their religion conformed with the Boers' religion, so their integration went easily.

Huguenot was not the real name of their nationality. That had gone in the mists of time. This was a derogatory pseudonym given to them by the Catholic French and like so many nicknames, it stuck. The Huguenots were highborn, their upper crust vied with top French families, such as the Guise and Medici and others, for the Crown of France. Through it all was religion. Christian religion. The ruling Catholics declared Calvinism a heresy, punishable by death, banishment and confiscation. Many wars were fought over the century, with many people slaughtered. In the end, some 200,000 Huguenots fled their homeland to escape a tyrannical Catholic government hell-bent on massacring them.

All in the name of Christ. All of them Christians, each side trying to prove that theirs' was the truer faith. Dear, oh dear! How He must look down with anguish and frustration with all His family feuds and squabbles. But wait, He couldn't have orchestrated the infighting and slaughter by way of punishment? No, surely not!

Those who fled dispersed to Holland, England, America and 200 of them to South Africa. The Huguenots were an asset to all their adopted countries. They were merchants, businessmen, wonderful wine-makers and excellent skilled craftsmen and all were hard workers. They were, however, extremely individualistic and forthright in their manner, caring little for the ways and thoughts of those who had given them succour. In short, difficult people. The resident Dutch governor, Simon van der Stel, and no doubt the majority of the Boer population, did not take to the French immigrants readily, because they were "aliens and for the trouble their uncompromising independence gave them". He saw to it that the Huguenots were scattered among the Dutch community so their group would, and did, lose their cohesion and with it, their identity and language. Within a short time they were indistinguishable from the Dutch people.

The Huguenots may have lost their French ways, but the names of their forebears have passed down through the centuries and are still there today. The Reys, Du Toits, Marais and Du Plessis are all there, all mixed up with the Van de Mervas and the like. Some French words did survive and, though strangled and mutilated, were incorporated into Cape Dutch, all of which took the Boer language further away from that of their mother tongue and country. Later, much later, their language, habits and way-of-life were so vastly different from those of the 'Old Country' they dropped 'Dutch' as their nationality and language and became 'Afrikaners' who spoke 'Afrikaans'. But not all liked the name. Some still saw themselves as Dutch, even though they referred to new people straight from Holland, not as Dutch, but as *'Hollanders'*, meaning 'not really one of us'.

If Van der Stel was not very well pleased with the Frenchmen his government sent over, he must have been really chuffed for his people when the next lot of migrants from Holland, and on an ongoing basis, were parties of young girls from orphanages.

Female company apart, the new settlers desperately needed workers for the fields, builders and all manner of people to create a civilised community. The Bantu were too fierce and Bushmen too primitive to be taught to work. The solution lay in the East. The Dutch imported large numbers of slaves from Madagascar, Ceylon and the rest of their East Indian empire, where the people were more advanced and civilised. The mixed races from the Far East were collectively referred to as *Malays*. Overall they were lighter in skin colour to the Africans and the olive-coloured women were very attractive to the men from Holland who eagerly took them as concubines but rarely accepted them as wives. Over the years a community of mixed blood grew and generally remained an individual entity. This group of people became known as *Coloured,* or more officially *Cape Coloured*, with Afrikaans as their adopted language.

I left the Cape via De Toit's Pass over the 'Hottentot Hollands' mountains, a memorable road that often jumped back in memory's focus long after I had passed that way. A few short lifts and some walking saw me through the rich vineyard and orchard lands that produce the legendary Cape wines and fruit, passed the town of Paarl (Pearl) and on to Worcester, an important town in a dream setting, ringed with majestic mountains of every hue. Every mile of the way is delightful and eye-catching. But for sheer, breathtaking scenery you must go up the Hex River Pass with no expectations and be met with the sudden, stunning view on the other side. Before your eyes is the land that is called the Karoo desert. The impact of the instant metamorphosis from the lush and verdant Garden of Eden to the wilderness is like looking suddenly into a strange new world.

The Karoo covers nearly a third of the whole landmass of South Africa and in its natural state once supported huge herds of antelope and other wild beasts. The local residents, the little San people, or Bushmen, lived in harmony with the ecology of the land that had been theirs since the beginning of human time. But when the big people, the black tribes from the north and the white immigrants from the south, arrived with their pastoral lifestyles the Bushmen and the wildlife were slaughtered and the land then was allowed to be overgrazed by the domestic herds. From this the desert was born.

But it would be wrong to call the Karoo a desert, for although it shows little or no surface water, it grows sparse patches of rough but nutritious grass that supports sheep. Indeed, sheep farming is the main industry within its bounds, even though the land can support only one sheep per acre.

Millions of years ago the Karoo was an inland sea, but aeons of global warming evaporated the water to form a great swamp where prehistoric crocodiles and their like lived and died and left their petrified bones in the sediment, which gradually solidified into rock. Eventually the last vestiges of water dried up and the land as we know it today developed.

As I toddle on my way I am aware of the dramatic beauty all around and am aghast at people who say the Karoo is crushingly boring, a place to put the foot down and get through as quickly as possible. Yet, though the road is a ribbon rolled out over a flat land that just goes on and on like that, there are nearly always mountains on the side horizons and *kopjes* (small hills usually with round tops and steep sides) scattered around the landscape that break the monotony.

As I walk and look back over my left shoulder I see a long massif that is continually changing colour, blue and grey and red and more, as the sun moves the shadows in the gullies and rock folds. I am fascinated and moved by the ongoing picture and strangely drawn to that horizon, as I am to all mountains. My map tells me that it is the Hexriverberg with what looks like the Hottentotskloof behind it, a reminder that it was the Hottentots who gave their name to the Karoo.

But who were these strange people, the Hottentots, who flit through the history of South Africa but now seem to be a lost race? There is no tribe or group of people in South Africa today who are called Hottentots and yet their name crops up so often, sometimes as a derisory or mocking remark, but more often in the names to mountains or places. I had spoken to many people on this subject and read everything about it I could lay my hands on and one of the interesting things I gathered from it all was how little many South Africans knew about these people.

There is little doubt that the people who came to be known as *Hottentots* owe their beginnings to the greatest human migrations in African history. This was the great drift of the Bantus from the land we know as Nigeria and other West African countries. This began about the time of Christ, though some claim it was earlier. *'Bantu'* is the name given to a whole range of diverse Negro tribes who share a common linguistic bond, even though their speech may differ remarkably. Rather like many diverse European languages that sound foreign to each other but all owe a common bond to Latin.

Over a thousand years the Bantu tribes creepy-crawled from West Africa to the Indian Ocean. Prior to their arrival, the whole land from modern Kenya to the tip of South Africa was inhabited by the little people we know as the Bushmen and to those more in-the-know, the San. It is thought that the Bushmen were among the very first people on Earth and had hardly changed in all that time. They lived the most primitive lives, hardly more than that of animals, and to most of those who met them, they were regarded as such. Their language was completely unintelligible to all and most regarded it as no more than the barking of dogs.

It is almost certain that the Bushmen were pre-Stone Age people who never developed beyond their early station. They did not learn to hew or shape stone to make weapons. What they did learn to do, in very clever form, was to invent little, childlike bows and arrows, which suited their size, and discover the way to make such exceedingly potent poisons that the tiniest scratch from their arrow could bring down a beast in minutes. Poisons that did not render the meat a danger to humans.

Why the Bushmen never developed through the Stone and Metal Ages is hard to understand. Perhaps as little, elfin-like people they lived in a children's world and had no desire to enter the big people's world of trouble and strife. Child or animal-like they may have appeared to the big people, but there was one facet of the Bushman's make-up that showed that they belonged to neither of these categories and that they really were very intelligent people. The proof of this lies in the beautiful rock-paintings executed by the Bushmen that have survived for thousands of years in cave walls and ceilings and on mountain rock overhangs. These I saw when climbing in the Drakensbergs (Dragons Mountains) of Natal and was deeply moved by the skill and detail and movement displayed in the paintings. Nearly all depict the hunt, and what an eye the artists had for capturing the power, the anatomy of the animals, their muscle structure and the whole atmosphere of the scene.

In art one can often tell the time, the era, to which the painting belongs, by something in the style of the artist. And do you know, from what I saw of the rock sketches in South Africa I likened, very much so, to the photographs I'd seen of similar cave paintings done in France and Spain. From this, could we dare to suggest that the people we call Bushmen once inhabited Europe, or at least southern areas of our continent?

These then were the people who had inherited nearly half the land mass of Africa and lived in it and regarded it as their own for, to their knowledge, they were the only people on Earth and had been since human time began. Then the Bantus came.

The two peoples could not have been more different. The Bushman, so small and thin, with light yellow-brown skin, and the Bantu, so big and heavy, with black skin and often heavy features. The Bantu were pastoral people while the Bushmen were hunters – and herein lies the demise of the Bushmen…and the birth of the Hottentots.

Although the Bantu tribes had crossed the whole of the African continent in their migration, they were not nomads. They lived by their cattle and their farms, built decent grass houses for their families and lived simple, stable farmers' lives. But in the next generation there would always be those young ones who had the desire, the need, the thrill of moving a little bit further on, away from the crowd and into the empty land, to have their own place to raise their children.

In comparison, Bushmen lived by hunting, built themselves the most primitive arbours for a few days and were constantly on the move. When they came upon the Bantus' docile cattle they claimed them as easy-meat, far from the rigours of the long hard chase of wild animals. When the Bantu found the remains of their dead animals and knew who had killed them, they regarded the little yellow men as vermin and like farmers throughout the world who guard their animals from predators, they killed them.

The Bushmen, however, were not the only predators. Wild beasts also killed cattle, so the Bantu killed them too. Faced with the depleted wildlife, there came the time when the Bushmen had to kill farm animals to live … and die. Wherever they found the little yellow Bushmen the Bantu slaughtered them. But not all of them. They took the female children and young women as slaves and concubines.

The people of their union were taller and bigger-boned than the elfin people. From the Bushman they acquired a lighter, more olive-coloured skin than the Bantu people, so the race that developed was quite distinct from both the progenitors.

The distinction, however, was not confined to size or the skin colour, but to other features as well. What was obvious was that the mother genes carried much of the facial characteristics of the Bushmen, notably the high

7

cheekbones and small, narrow chin that gave the face a triangular shape. These then were the people who came to be known as the *Hottentots,* though the name was not coined until a century or so later.

Eventually, over the centuries, the San Bushmen were wiped out from all the land north of what we now call South Africa. About this time the Bantu drift was creeping nearer and nearer to the Southern Ocean. So far, they had had it all their own way from West Africa. But now they were going to hit big trouble, for about the same time as the Bantu tribes first dipped their toes in the Antarctic Ocean, the white Man arrived and took up residence in the place they would later call Cape Town.

With the arrival of both black and white migrants, the halcyon, dreamlike days of the Bushmen, which had gone on for aeons, were over. With the arrival of the migrants a community of mixed blood grew and generally remained an individual identity. Over the years the Hottentots developed a natural affinity with the growing Coloured 'tribe' and were eventually absorbed into it and more or less lost. Thereby hangs the tale of the lost tribe of Hottentots.

But perhaps they did leave a legacy. It is in the physiognomy of the coloured people that the mark of the long lost Hottentot remains. Many have the high cheek bones and angular chins of the Bushman people, a trait by which the Hottentots and the Bushman people can never be forgotten.

CHAPTER 2

ALL THAT WERE LEFT

On the side of a lonely, rock-strewn hill near the centre of the Great Karoo, I found the grave of one of the Black Watch regiment's finest soldiers – Major General Andy Wauchope – who was killed at the Battle of Majesfontein during the Boer War. In his poem 'The Soldier', written in the trenches in 1914, Rupert Brooke wrote:

> If I should die, think only this of me;
> That there's some corner of a foreign field
> That is forever England ...

Brooke's words were indeed premonitory for he died of fever at Gallipoli in 1915 when he was twenty-seven. Had he been asked at the time of writing, I'm sure Brooke would have extended his sentiments to all British soldiers. I know when I found the grave of General Wauchope (pronounced Waacope) I felt I had discovered a little corner of Africa that would forever be Scotland.

Graves don't come much lonelier than this one. It lies in a little cemetery just off the road and you go through a creaky iron gate to enter. The Karoo desert rolls away empty in all directions. The long, straight, ribbon road disappears into infinity ahead and behind. Powder-puff clouds dapple the endless blue sky. And it is silent. There is only the sound of the wind sighing through patches of tussocky grass, playing a lament to the sleeping souls.

Although General Wauchope has a special place to himself on a little hill, with a monolith pillar to mark the spot, he is not alone. His resting place, some seven miles from the village of Matjiesfontein, is shared by another eminent Scot, James Logan, founder of the village, who came to this lonely place and remained forever. All his family are also buried there.

Standing in that little corner of Scotland I wanted to know more about this most eminent soldier. After all, it is not often a General dies in battle. They usually command from the rear and live to a ripe old age before drifting away on a sea of memories. When I was called-up for the army during the last few weeks of World War II, it was the Queen's Barracks of the Black Watch regiment at Perth that I was commanded to attend for my initial training. I did not remain in the regiment, being posted to a depot of the Royal Army Ordinance Corps at the end of my training, but I always retained an affinity with it and it was the Black Watch kilt I had worn during all my way south through Africa and now was still proud to sport on the way home.

Some years later, after my return home to Scotland, I kept my promise to delve into the history of the Boer War battle that claimed the life of a British General. The opportunity came when I found on the dusty shelves of an antiquarian bookshop, Louis Creswicke's eight volumes of *South Africa and the Transvaal War* and there it was, a whole chapter on the Battle of Matjiesfontein (also quoted elsewhere as Magersfontein) together with a full page picture of Major General Wauchope.

It was midnight of Sunday 10th December, 1899 that this awful event began. Major-General Wauchope led his Highland Brigade in pitch darkness and driving, morale-sapping, soaking rain across squelching veldt to be in position to surprise and engage the enemy by first light. In addition to the Black Watch regiment, the force was made up with battalions of the Seaforth, Argyll and Sutherland and Gordon Highlanders together with the Highland Light Infantry. The soldiers proudly wore their red coats and many died because of this.

What the British did not know was that the Boers were well aware of their intentions and a force of 12,000 South African Dutch were already entrenched and waiting behind a barbed-wire fence on the side of a drift, through which the Highlanders had to pass. This lack of secrecy with British plans was not surprising, for in those early days of the Boer or South African War the British army had often to rely on local people for information on the terrain and sometimes even recruited scouts who were sympathetic to the enemy. Little wonder that in the early phase of the war the British army had few successes.

And so it was that epic day. From the dim light of early dawn and all through the day, the Boers, all excellent marksmen who had grown from birth with a rifle in their hands, cut the Highland Brigade to ribbons. Against the sand-coloured earth and green grass those red coats were more clearly seen on the battlefield than targets on a rifle range. Bloody chaos was the order of the day, with orders and counter-orders shouted that were mostly drowned by gunfire. Even so, the brigade fought back bravely, if only in uncoordinated places. General Wauchope, gallant, multi-medalled hero of so many campaigns, wounded in many, led a charge at the Boer entrenchments and was one of the first to die. That charge almost reached the enemy line, but those Highlanders who got that far were impaled on the barbed-wire entanglements and cut down. It was one of the worst disasters the British Army suffered throughout that war. Luckily for the British army later in the Boer war, someone invented 'khaki' dye, the colour of the African terrain, so that the uniform hid, rather than revealed, the wearer.

The slaughter went on most of the day until a battery of British field guns was brought up. These blasted the Boer positions causing many casualties, whereupon these household soldiers drifted away as only they could do, leaving the battleground for the British to clear up. One soldier badly wounded that day was picked up from the field and lived. He was Lieutenant Wauchope of the 2nd Royal Highlanders, the General's son.

Many years later I wrote an article on this subject and had it published in *Red Hackle*, the Black Watch regimental magazine. Following its publication, I was invited to visit the little museum in the barracks at Perth. How proud I was to be given this private tour, remembering my young, rookie days with the regiment. Most poignant to me was a large painting which took pride of place on the wall. I first saw a print of it in Louis Creswicke's book and it riveted me then and churned my emotions, but now the original was absolutely arresting and took me far away, still and silent, to that awful morning in the Karoo. Entitled "All That Was Left of Them", it was a most emotive painting of a few Highlanders in kilts and sun-helmets, many with terrible wounds, under a dramatic, glowering dawn sky.

The curator, who showed me round with obvious reverence of his treasures, was named Wauchope.

A few miles on from that lonely cemetery and a little off the main road is the village of Matjiesfontein, founded by a Scot, James Logan, the self-styled Laird of Matjiesfontein, who lies with General Wauchope. He came here in the 1880s, a natural entrepreneur who had mercurial success, became a Member of Parliament, and built a string of railway tea rooms from the Cape to Bulawayo; the one at Matjiesfontein he made his home and expanded it to include a health resort, the air there being recognised as extremely pure.

Walking into Matjiesfontein was like going onto a film set for the early South African era. Like hitting an oasis in the desert, the road suddenly jumps from the rutted sand onto a tarmac stretch barely a couple of hundred yards long and drops off into the sand again and continues as a track into the blue. Along this brief stretch of metalled street is built the village, petrified as at its birth at the turn of the nineteenth century. Along the street at intervals stand tall, heavily ornate, Victorian lampposts and the hotel has fort-like crenellated ramparts. In the comfortable station tearoom Coloured waitresses in early twentieth century period costume wear black dresses with white, frilly bonnets, collars and pinafores. I imagined the surprised pleasure of bored train passengers who alighted at this waterhole in the desert, in the same way as I was captivated by the wonderful, old-world charm of the place.

You step off the film-set stage of Matjiesfontein, walk a few hundred yards and you are back in the real world, oven-hot, dry and empty. But it was not always so. As with many deserts in the world, this one was man-made. That would be before Man came into the paradise and destroyed it. Once elephant, lion and buffalo roamed here in the Karoo, and that was not long ago – within living memory of my time there.

A hundred and fifty miles further on from Matjiesfontein lies Beaufort West, the biggest town in this part of the Karoo. I arrived after a couple of lifts and quite a bit of walking and camping by the roadside at nights. After the desert heat and loneliness, it was a pleasure to walk along the broad, pear tree-shaded streets and drop into a café and enjoy half an hour of blissful company and normality. And it was in conversation with this one and that, that I learned how different the Karoo had become in the span of a single lifetime.

I was told that in the town, there were old people who could remember a time in the distant past when a migration of wildlife ran passed the town. As far as the eye could see, in all directions, the land was black with the multitude of wildebeest and antelope, eland and springbok, zebra and quagga. The animal mass came with the distant sound of a strong wind that heralds a storm and took three days to pass. The Karoo then, in the second half of the nineteenth century was alive, teeming with wild game. Seventy or so years later, when I passed that way, there was not a single wild animal to be seen. All slaughtered by rifle and spear to make way for pastoral flock grazing.

Mention of the quagga is a case in point of Man's rapacious nature and threat to wildlife throughout the world. Some said the quagga was a kind of zebra with no stripes on its hindquarters. Others would have it that it was more horse than zebra. Whatever, they ran easily with zebra herds but were distinctly different. But by the early 1870s they, like the dodo of Mauritius, were extinct and only a few stuffed ones remain in some museums to prove that they ever existed.

Along the road of evolution, species could take millions of years to decline and disappear due, perhaps, to changes in temperature and climate or gradual decline in their necessary food and so on. By the middle of the twentieth century, with the birth of high-powered rifles and other guns, whole species could be annihilated, wiped off the face of the Earth for ever, within the space of one generation of mankind.

Such is progress!

12

CHAPTER 3

DIAMONDS ARE FOREVER

It started to rain that morning as I prepared to move on from Beaufort West, a sure sign that winter has come from the Cape. Luckily, I had my tent rolled up and my equipment packed ready for the road before the rain started

Wednesday 8th April 1953

I got a lift to Colesberg. The driver of the car was a soil preservation expert and goes around instructing farmers on how to prevent soil erosion. His conversation was really interesting and informative. That is the best thing about this way of travelling. I meet so many different people who have something different to tell

Colesberg, a beautiful little town overlooked by enchanting mountain scenery, was built way back in the early 1800s on the site of an abandoned London Missionary Society establishment. I could have stayed longer there but was eager to get on my way to Kimberley and the diamond mines there.

Thursday 9th April 1953 Bloemfontein, Orange Free State
I camped last night on the veldt. It was quite cold. Today I walked about twelve or thirteen miles to the Orange River, where I am camped.

Here was a landmark indeed for me. The Orange River, the greatest river in South Africa, was once the Rubicon of that developing country. 'Over there' was the land beyond the pale, the edge of civilisation, the home of the Hottentots and wild African tribes, where only fools, hunters and missionaries were brave enough to go. At that time, and for long after, it was known by its Hottentot name '*gariep*', meaning simply 'river'. Later, in 1779, it was officially named after the Prince of Orange.

It was dark and miserable when I was dropped off in the streets of Bloemfontein, the capital city. The travelling salesman, who had brought me the last fifty miles, was pleased to hurriedly slam his car door to shut out the cold wind and drizzle from his warm interior. I shrugged on my heavy rucksack and walked briskly round the streets, going nowhere.

Passing the police station suddenly gave me an idea. If this was the Free State perhaps they would give a bona fide tramp a free night in a cell. I was aware that the really professional way to do this, the method followed by the Knights-of-the-Road back home, was to heave a hefty brick through a plate glass shop window, then stand and wait for a policeman to come along. As one of no fixed abode, the State would make sure that you would be taken into custody and given a comfortable bed and good meals. With luck, when you're time came up, the magistrate would give you three months or maybe four or six if you were a habitual offender. Of course, since your sentence started from the day of your remand, your 'punishment' could be more than halfway done. With a month's remission for good behaviour inside, that would nicely cover one over the wintertime, leaving one healthy and fancy-free to toddle on one's way again, down the open road to new adventures, with a warm ditch and shielding hedge to look forward to at nights and serendipitous mornings full of scintillating surprises. Freedom!

In today's world, of course, there aren't many of us professional tramps around and those who do follow the 'profession' must find it far more difficult to eke out a decent livelihood. You see, with the overcrowding in modern prisons, magistrates and the like must be under severe jurisdiction to cut, by at least half, any sentence they might have deemed appropriate for a particular crime. On top of that, the prisoner is then released, after serving only half his given sentence, in order to clear the prisons so as to accommodate the great queues of offenders who can't wait to get in. That again, with remission for good behaviour, which, of course, is endemic in we professional tramps, can find a decent chap back on the streets again come January, with the prospect of having to sleep on wet or even frosty grass for a month or two. The poor fellow has, by necessity, to find himself another large brick and go through the whole process again.

Looking back to my days on the road, things were a bit more stable than that of today. Everyone knew their place, so to speak. This kind of behaviour between the law and the tramp was the real bones of a truly civilised society and naturally, one was pleased and grateful to be part of it.

Unfortunately, I had a feeling that South Africa was not as civilised as one would have hoped at that time. Indeed the *back-veldter* of a policeman at the desk was not one bit civil. In heavy Afrikaans-English he told me I could go to the place where they keep the Burning-Fire going all the time for the likes of us. That, before I had even said a word. No doubt he was used to getting hordes of 'poor-whites', the dregs of South African society, continually looking for shelter.

I lied when I said I didn't want to sleep in the Station but only wanted to know where I could camp, and for that, I suppose, I deserved the fate he had proscribed for me. However, a Sergeant with more between his ears came from a back room, having heard the rumpus. You could see why he had risen from the ranks, for he took in the situation at a glance. *Winos* don't carry their kitchen sink on their back, nor are they likely to have their breakfast in their pack. I got my cell for the night with a good bunk, although it was only a wooden board, together with breakfast and coffee thrown in. Not literally!

I didn't stay long in Bloemfontein. As capital of the Free State it looked quite a fine town, but I was keen to get on the road for Kimberley. I wanted to see the diamonds and the Big Hole.

Had I been merely heading up and out of South Africa I should have stayed on the main road to Johannesburg. Going to Kimberley took me more to the northwest and, as far as I could see from my map, there was one good motoring road and a maze of little ones which I hoped to miss. But as luck would have it, when, after a few miles walking, a vehicle did come along and stop for me, I was dropped off in a far more difficult position than if I had kept walking along the main road. Now I was in the mesh of minor roads that dissipated what little traffic there was. But, as so often happens, the worst turns out to be best, for if the little roads had not delayed me for a couple of days or more, I might not have met a wonderful couple who were like a ray of sunshine in a black storm. How did I meet them? I will explain later.

The first lift I got that day was from a farmer of French or Belgian extraction. His was an old, battered truck and he would persist in taking both hands off the wheel to gesticulate when he found a sentence difficult to express in words. An interesting man, he dropped me off before turning into a track that obviously led to nowhere. I pulled on my pack and walked on for the next three hours.

Between Bloemfontein and Kimberley, as I have said, there are a million roads. At least, that's what it seemed like to me. The roads – tracks would be more accurate – criss-crossed like the runnels on an old face that has seen hard work in strong sun over many generations. This maze of roads tells the very history of South Africa

***

The story begins near the Orange River on a hot, dusty day way back in the 1860s. A Hottentot boy gathering stones to play a game with friends picked one up that had a different look to the others. The odd stone caught a neighbour's eye and he showed it to the children's mother, Mrs D. J. Jacobs.

She, in turn, gave it back to the man with no more ado. That stone passed through various hands, each time increasing in value, until it rested with Sir Phillip Wodehouse, Governor of the Cape. By now it was a well-known diamond, weighing 24.25 carats and worth £500. It was named 'Eureka'.

What a stroke of luck that was, all starting from a children's game. But more was to come, much more, and yet when it did, it was as nothing to what was found later. Eureka was an alluvial stone, rounded and shaped by ageless time in the waters of the Orange River. Soon, large numbers of hopeful prospectors hurried to the area, while others went further to search the land as far as Vaal River. More and more of the hopefuls were becoming successful, but it was a Griqua farmer tending his sheep near the Orange River who hit the jackpot. He picked up a diamond that was nearly four times bigger than the Eureka. Someone gave him a span of oxen and a few hundred sheep for his find.

That diamond was later named the 'Star of Africa'. It was sold for £11,200 and later, in London, for more than twice as much, £25,000, to the Earl of Dudley. In the 1860s that was a fabulous amount of money. All that, however, was as nothing compared to the luck of two brothers a few years later.

To understand the sheer luck of the brothers, one has to understand that diamonds do not occur naturally as single stones in the ground or on the surface, as had been discovered so far in South Africa. Diamonds were made at the very beginning of time, in the innermost core of the planet when it was in the making. Of all the stones made at the time of Earth's beginning, the diamond was the hardest and, when polished, the most brilliant.

Unlike other, common stones, diamonds did not work their way gradually to the surface. They came from their creation bed with a cataclysmic force that blew a hole or pipeline right through the planet and erupted out of the surface. The diamonds found in far-off river beds or open veldt were the loose ones, the first ones out of the hole and so propelled with such force they landed many miles away.

Now for the luck! When, in 1860, the brothers Johannes and Diederik de Beer bought a piece of arid land from the government for £50 intending to make a farm, they did not know they had hit the jackpot of all jackpots.

In the beginning they created their farm, but the land was poor and their work was not very productive. Then, in 1875, came Fleetwood Rawstone, a man with an eye for diamondiferous earth structure and a team of men to dig and prove his hunch. His interest was a little, rocky hill, or *kopje* as they are known in South Africa, on the farm. With permission, he had the top of the hill removed and what do you know! That peak proved to be the cork at the top of the long pipeline down to the molten Earth centre. Down the pipe were diamonds beyond the dreams of the most optimistic prospector.

News of the discovery flew round the world and the mad rush started and grew to fever pitch. Hordes of hope-crazed diggers with diamonds in their eyes came by every means. Frenzied men, singles, partners, groups, whatever, raced each other to stake their claims. By every mode of transport they came: horses, buggies, trek-wagons, foot, some following existing roads, others tramping out their own paths, which others followed. The paths became tracks that grew into roads. So it was by that fortunate lift from the no-hands driver that I was led into the maze that delayed my passage to Kimberley.

Round the mine, tented camps spread overnight like virulent skin rashes. As time went by these were gradually replaced by corrugated iron and rough wood shacks in some order of streets, out of which a town grew up. A pitiless, bawdy town, rough and tough. With the prospective miners there came the wily opportunists, the shysters who knew how to skin the simple diggers of their hard-earned wealth as easily as a skilled hunter would a hare; the hard-faced landladies, the liquor kings and brothel queens, professional gamblers and common rogues and thieves. Not a very nice place!

But for some it was Heaven. Wealth beyond their wildest dreams fell into their laps … but rarely without incredible hard work and immense danger. The Kimberley diamond field was unlike any other in the world. Most mines of any sort go down in shafts, but here the gems were sometimes there for the lifting, barely more than a few spades' depth down. The area was measured out and quartered, each portion numbered and licensed. New diggers eagerly bought a portion or more to make their claim as suited their needs and purse.

In the early days there were few problems with this; miners worked their claims side-by-side over the whole field, some luckier than others. As time went by though, the outer portions became barren. The owners left, only to be followed in time by those on the next outer edge. It was obvious that the hole was funnelling down towards a centre core. That became evident when the outer claims ceased to dry up and the whole mine dramatically became sheer–sided and the great hole developed into a gigantic drainpipe.

The deeper the shaft went down, the greater the problems and dangers. Claims being worked by plentiful manpower, or by those more industrious, went down quicker than others – in many cases very dramatically so. As the speedy ones went down, they left the slower ones high above. Those slower ones worked their claims teetering, as it were, on top of lonely pillars, some hundreds of feet above the others.

There were few safety precautions, no rails to stop a careless, backward step plummeting a man into eternity and taking with him another whom he may have landed on. All this with spiderwebs of wire-hawsers, pulleys and buckets flying overhead, carrying away the waste, as well as the workers to and from their platforms. The whole business was chaotic and incredibly dangerous in the extreme.

This picture was painted in words for me by an old miner who worked his claim in that 'Big Hole' as it was called, back in the 1890s. I was in the main hospital in Durban having an operation for varicose veins and he was in the bed next to me. Alas, his illness was more serious than mine and he died within a few weeks of our meeting.

Our conversation enthralled me. I plied him with never-ending questions and I'd like to think, to hope, that my interest gave him a rosy glow as he relived his memories. I know that his tired old eyes took on a glint when my questions sparked off those faraway days.

"It was Cecil Rhodes who ended it all, you know! Just a lad he was, but he ran rings round all of us. We only saw our own little bit, but he could see that the whole place had to be run as one and he set about being the one to do it. I remember him coming to our shack, offering to buy our claim. A very quiet fellow he was, young, as I said, but older than his years, a lot older. He knew what he was about and was determined to have his way. He made an offer, quite a good one as it was, for the mine was in recession and we didn't know if it had bottomed-out or not. But we resisted. He never said a word, but he made no move to leave and just talked on. He had a bottle of liquor, I remember, but I can't remember if he had any of it himself. Maybe he just had some in a glass to make it look that he was with us. Anyway, it went on and on into the night and in the end he had his way. He went off with the deeds and in a way we were happy. And that's how it all went.

"In the end he owned the whole place, he and his partner, Barney Barnato. Later they were joined by Sir Ernest Oppenheimer. Of course, the whole place changed after that. The rush was over and so were those death-trap claims hanging like flies on the face of a precipice. The new mine was first named 'De Beers New Rush', but that was later changed to De Beers Consolidated Mines. The area, which developed into a town, was named to honour the British Colonial Secretary, the Earl of Kimberley.

"I was sorry in a way that we lost our claim, but it was all for the best. Anyway, looking back, I'm glad to have been part of it all. They were great times and it makes you feel you were part of history."

***

The Orange Free State is almost as desolate outside the towns as the Karoo, except that there is much more grass. Just miles and miles of rolling grass plains. It is remarkable how the country changes into good grassland immediately you cross the Orange River.

It was growing dark when I arrived in Kimberly. I had some tea in a café while I wondered where to sleep. I still hadn't decided when I had finished the tea and walked the streets for a while. I didn't want to go to the police station. That time at Bloemfontein was the first time I had tried that stunt and I hadn't liked my reception. I couldn't pitch my tent in town and I didn't want to tramp away into veldt. So I decided to wait until it was dark and then just go round the back of some building to sleep the night.

I had done that many times before in different towns, but it was never an easy or safe option. In the town at night I was a common tramp. In the bush or veldt I was an honest traveller. Moreover, the animals in the towns were far more dangerous than those in the open plain. Plains animals have a fear of man. The very smell of a human is enough to make most wild predators keep their distance. Town scavengers have no fear of tramps. Town predators, rats and rogues, are only too pleased to find a solitary sleeping body. Nevertheless, there were times when I felt I had no option but to slink into a dark corner behind some building and take my chances.

10th April, 1953, Kimberley

I was standing in a shop entrance waiting for the darkness to get more intense. It was a miserable night. A drizzling rain had started to fall and a stiff breeze blew. A doctor, who came out of his consulting room across the street, saw me and asked if he could help. When I told him my plans he was horrified and invited me home with him. His name is Vaughan-Jones. It was very kind of him. So now I'm very comfortable in a bed with a reading lamp. A bit of a difference from my intended fare.

Dr and Mrs Vaughan-Jones were wonderfully kind people who made me feel instantly at home. Nothing was too much trouble to them and they insisted I stay with them for a few days. In next to no time they had prepared an itinerary of all the things they thought I should see and some more for good measure.

The doctor was well acquainted with the people in De Beer's diamond mines and so was able to arrange a special visit for me. Mrs Vaughan-Jones drove me down. With full V.I.P. treatment – no tourist queue-shuffle for me – I was taken on a one-to-one tour. I was taken through the entire process of extracting the diamonds, right from moment the rock was dug out of the ground to the pile of diamonds on a table, which I actually handled and photographed. The day's takings were valued roughly at £10,000 to £12,000 and this was at 11.00 a.m. A great deal of money in those days!

Even so, I was informed that those diamonds I saw were low carat and were destined to be industrial types. Indeed, this quality comprised 80% of all diamonds mined. At this I was foolish enough to ask what the difference was between those working-class diamonds, intended to toil out their lives in grinding machines or watches and other such things, while other high carat types would nestle in a Queen's bosom, a King's crown or a Rajah's turban. With this question my guide went into overdrive. Gone was the blasé, run-of-the-mill dialogue. Now we were on a kaleidoscopic journey to the very beginnings of civilised man. Primitive though that time may have been, when 'towns' no more than today's villages were rated as cities, there were diamonds. Early man, not long off the trees it would seem, recognised the value of precious metals and stones.

It was in the time of Homer's Troy in Asia Minor (now Turkey) some 5,000 years ago, that an attempt was made to classify the quality of gemstones within a gradation scale according to weight, when each article was measured against a certain number of seeds. This arbitrary test, defined in units of 4 grains (Troy), lasted for thousands and thousands of years, long after the city's nine lives had ended. Julius Caesar came as a tourist to see the mound of earth where cities, each built on top of the previous rubble, had lived and died. 'Grains (Troy)' was only superseded during the twentieth century in the USA, where a new system was devised and which is now recognised throughout the most of the world. The American method recognises that one carat equals 0.20grams in weight and the ultimate quality in diamonds is 24 carats. Any diamond containing extraneous matter that reduces the pure carboniferous content is classified as such: 18 carat, 14 carat, etc., i.e. 18/24th's and 14/24th's, etc. The term 'carat' is believed to come from the old Greek *keration,* or the Arabic *qirat.*

Later, following my visit to the working mine, I went to the site of the old one, now known as the 'Big Hole', the biggest man-made hole in the world. Work stopped there in 1914 or so and now it lies there, a gigantic monument to man's industry, ingenuity and endeavour. I believe that now a great tourist industry has grown up around those old workings of a long gone era. This is good for it will insure that the site will be preserved for posterity. But I wonder if those visitors get the thrill I did as a lone person with the whole, silent place to myself. Only a strand, or maybe two, of barbed wire fence told me not to try walking down the steep slope of shingle and rubble to attempt a better view over the sheer sides of that awful (I mean that in the sense of inspiring the full majesty of awe) pit, the biggest, deepest in all the world. What an amazing feat it was considering it was dug without any modern equipment; picks and shovels were all those diggers had. How they must have worked!

The hole measures a mile round the perimeter and is 1,600 feet deep. It was more than half-filled with water. Even at that level, when a boulder was rolled down the slope and disappeared over the side it took ages to fall and when it eventually struck the water, there was an explosion like several big guns going off. A most weird phenomenon that echoed and reverberated in a deep 'boooom', far beyond anything one would expect from a small object.

After listening to this experience a few times, a thought came back to me from schooldays. I left our school in Torryburn when I was fourteen – thirteen really, for I started my apprenticeship as a painter and decorator two weeks after my fourteenth birthday. How I wished I could have gone on to higher education, but that meant uniforms and bussing to Dunfermline, five miles away. Deep into the war, with my two elder brothers in the army, I thought I should be out working rather than going on to The High School. So with youthful, wartime verve, when the opportunity was offered, I said I didn't want to go. Looking back, how I wished so often things had been different. Still, I have much to be grateful for. Torryburn Public School had a great deal to commend it. In retrospect, I am often amazed at the breadth of education and knowledge our teachers passed on to us in that relatively short span of our schooldays.

All this reverie was brought on by a gem of information that came back to me as I stood by the edge of the mighty Kimberly hole. At our school, phenomena were not divided into different disciplines. Every study of motion or perception came under the broad umbrella of 'Science'. So it was that I suddenly recalled a statement made by the science master to the effect that "All falling bodies travel at the same speed".

Surely I must have it wrong. A big stone must fall faster than a little one! I set about proving this to my own satisfaction. This, however, was easier said than done.

To throw a stone into the hole took some doing. It wasn't that difficult to throw one that bounced once or twice down the slope and then fell over the sheer wall to then splash into the water accompanied by the now familiar boom. What was difficult was to power a stone far enough that it cleared the side and carried on with an unrestricted trajectory, which conveys the size of the hole and the distance involved. Even with my natural size and, dare I say it, strength, developed by the life I had led for the past few years, I did not find the throw by any means easy. I had to have several attempts before I mustered my full power and developed the knack. And that was the easy part.

To prove the theory, one way or another, I had to throw two stones of different size at the same time. So I looked around for a number of round, smooth stones, half of them at least twice the size of the others. I wanted them as round and smooth as possible. I did not know if the shape – flat or irregular – would make any difference in my experiment. At the sea it would have been easy with lots of pebbles, water-washed through millennia (*chuckie-stanes* we called them in Scotland). At last I had two piles. To test the water, it could be said, I fired off two, one after the other. By now I was fairly slick at getting the missiles over the edge of the rim. Sure enough, two booms, one after the other

Now the difficult one: to throw two simultaneously, both placed side-by-side in the palm of my hand. In tandem, one behind the other, would not do. Even with the earlier practice it took me several goes to get both stones in flight over the funnel rim. But at last I did it. I waited. And waited. A long time. At last it came. Just one mighty *boooom*.

Much later, I was told by someone far more knowledgeable than I, that it is a fact that all falling bodies, irrespective of their weight or size – but not feathers or other projectiles lighter than air – travel at 23 feet per second. What a blessing to be taught such wonders, but how much more fun to empirically work it out for one's self.

One last little story on this experiment: when I came to write of this incident fifty years after the event, time had dimmed my memory and once again, I was wracked with doubt. Could I really be sure that a light object would travel at the same speed as a heavier one? Once more, I set up my stage before writing the event into my story. I pushed a large, two-part ladder 25 feet up the side of our house, and set it at a dangerously acute angle in order to get maximum height. I then climbed it precariously to the last two, nail-biting rungs and hung on with one lot of fingertips, while in the other hand I held two *chuckie-stanes,* one half the size of the other. Maureen, my wife, was on duty at the bottom to eagle-eye that last fraction of a second when the projectiles would crash to the paving slabs. Before this earth-shaking experiment could be sprung, two near-neighbours came out of their houses in high dudgeon, remonstrating with me for being so daft and with Maureen for encouraging me in my games. "Get him down at once," was the vociferous clamour. To Maureen's credit she did not flinch, but kept her eyes on the estimated point of impact just as I released my objects. 'Hooray!' The objects landed together at precisely the same moment. Falling bodies travel at the same speed irrespective of their size or weight. True!

CHAPTER 4

THE FIRST THOUSAND MILES

When I left Kimberley I had intended to make for Kuruman, some 300 miles to the north-west and very much out into the sticks, on the edge of the Kalahari Desert. I didn't expect to get many, if any, lifts and I fancied it might be quite a long haul. My reason for wanting to go there was because Kuruman was the first white settlement in what was, in the early nineteenth century, far north, wild, outlandish, territory. But why should any white people who were neither hunters nor prospectors want to spend their lives there, hundreds of miles away from their kinfolk, build the walls of their houses with the earth they dug from the ground, make their roofs with thatch, shape their furniture from the wood they cut from trees, and on-and-on? All with their own hands, because the local natives were too raw and unskilled to make any semblance of a European type house and trappings. They had to be very special, resourceful and dedicated, these people. And they were. They were missionaries.

The first two to come were Johan Kok and William Edwards in 1801. They were the first missionaries to come to the Bechuana people, the tribe with whom I would soon spend some time. They came from the London Missionary Society (LMS), but Edwards was recalled a year later and Kok was murdered. Robert Hamilton, an artisan-missionary, restarted the mission in 1812 and later was joined by Robert Moffat from Scotland, who had given up gardening to be a missionary. He and his wife Mary were later joined by David Livingstone who, later still, married their daughter, Mary Moffat (see *Tramp in Africa)*. I will be saying more about Kuruman and David Livingstone in the next chapter on slavery.

Having debated in my mind the idea of going to Kuruman, I came to the conclusion that there were too many factors against making that journey. On leaving South Africa my plan was to head for Bechuanaland (*Botswana)* and although Kuruman was in that direction, you were not allowed to enter that country at that place. Officially, anyone entering Bechuanaland from the south had to register for documentation, passport etc., at Mafeking. Since this meant I would have had to go as far to the north-west to Kuruman as I would eventually have to go north-east to Mafeking, I decided going to Kuruman was out of the question and I must head directly for Johannesburg.

Monday 13th April, Transvaal

Started off today heading for Jo'burg. Luckily I hadn't walked far when I got a lift in a truck going up to Krugersdorp. It was a grand lift but a cold one. Although the sun shone, the wind was biting when the truck moved. I was up the back and got the full benefit. I got on at about 8 a.m. and I was dropped off where he turned off the road at 7 p.m. It was a long, cold sit on the truck, but I was really glad of it.

Tuesday 14th April, 1953, Johannesburg

I slept by the side of the road where I was dropped off last night about 30 miles from Jo'burg. It was one of the coldest nights I have spent. The winter is truly biting here. I noticed it more of course coming up from the Cape to the High Veldt here. The wind just cut through my sleeping bag. I think the acute change of temperature brought on a little of the malaria I had exactly a year ago too, so my teeth were chattering in fine style.

However, I'm back in Jo'burg again. The first thousand miles of the journey home has been covered.

It felt good being back in Jo'burg. I put up at the YMCA and looked up some friends I knew from my time there eight months or so ago, during which I worked in the warehouse of 'OK Bazaars', one of the largest emporiums in the city. Like Richard Burton's _Viator_ in from a long journey, I revelled in the camaraderie, conversation and _bonhomie_. And out of all the natter and patter a gem fell out. Well, not so much a jewel or a nugget, perhaps more of a lump of old metal. But to me it was a treasure, a welcome, trusty companion that would buoy me up in times of great need and danger along the long trail ahead of me, until … but that is another story, a horror story that will be told in its own time.

I was talking to a couple of guys in the YM when one of them asked if I carried a gun. I said I did, two in fact. A tiny .25 Beretta pistol which was always in my khaki shirt front pocket, and a .38 Smith and Wesson Police revolver which I stuck in my belt when in places that might prove tricky. I explained that the pistol, which I had bought in Nairobi, would be useless against animals, but as a last resort I might shoot at the legs if attacked by wild humans. I then went on to say that, while I was pleased to have the .38

revolver and grateful though I was to the man who had given me it, I wished it had been a .45. One of the fellows asked why, so I explained.

The police .38 firearm is designed to shoot people. The bullets designed for its purpose are made of nickel, a hard metal that does not flatten on impact. In short, the gun is meant to stop someone in their tracks but not necessarily to kill. Contrary to this, guns that are designed for shooting animals, whether for hunting or stopping a charge, are made to kill. Even a badly wounded animal, a lion or an elephant for example, can kill the assailant and apart from the danger in that, no one ever wants to leave a wounded animal to die a painful death. Therefore, bullets for shooting animals are made from soft metal, lead mostly, which are designed to flatten on impact and create greater internal damage thus killing more quickly.

During the First World War it was fairly common for soldiers in the trenches to file a cut into the nose of their nickel rifle bullets so they would tear like shrapnel and make them more lethal. Such bullets were known as *'dum-dums'* and were deemed illegal by all Conventions.

In giving this little dissertation, I had a very poignant memory, which illustrated what I was talking about. During the last year of World War II when I was seventeen, my cousin, Peter Harrower who lived next door, came home on leave. He was about twenty months older than I and wore the red beret of the Airborne Troops. He had been in the thick of the fighting in the Ardennes, I think, and was keen to show me his special, illegal, trophy from the fighting … a German 8mm automatic pistol. He came out of his bedroom, pleased as Punch, with it in his hand, his arm raised in the shooting position, finger on the trigger. Luckily, I was standing by the table, sideways on to him as I raised my hand to take the weapon when there was a BANG… and involuntarily my arm dropped to my side.

Uncle Jim, the village grave-digger and church caretaker, not long in from his work, seated in the big wing-backed chair by the fire, smoking his pipe and reading the newspaper, flew to his feet, paper thrown in the air, a strangled exclamation half lost in his throat and Peter his face pillar-box red and a picture of disbelief, dropped the gun in horror.

And me? I hadn't felt a thing and was as surprised as the others with the noise. But my arm hung limply by my side, useless. There was no obvious blood and no apparent hole in the sleeve of the leather jerkin I wore. The bullet had entered through the seam of my jacket, gone straight through my forearm, clean between the two bones, the *radius* and the *ulna*, hardly touching the sides, and out the other side and then drilled its way through the family piano.

I was incredibly lucky, if you can call being shot 'lucky'. Had the table not been in the middle of the room so that I was standing sideways-on to Peter, I would have been meeting him straight on and the bullet would have almost certainly gone straight through my chest, and quite likely my heart. As it was, the wound healed fairly quickly and never bothered me throughout my life. I used to smile inwardly to myself that I, at seventeen, was one of the 'War Wounded'. I still carry the thin scar tissue marks of the entry and exit holes on my forearm that were made that day.

So much for hard-nosed, nickel-plated bullets, especially designed for use against humans. Now, if that gun my cousin carried had been loaded with soft-nosed bullets, the one that entered my arm would have flattened on impact, smashed the bones and almost certainly I would have lost my arm. Moreover, I would never have been in the army, never have gone to Africa and I would not be writing this book.

On the converse side of that tale; later, while in Uganda, an incident occurred when soft-nosed bullets certainly saved my life when I was charged by a herd of rogue elephants. Now, thereby hangs a tale! But it will have to bide its time until I get there, a year and more down the trail home.

The upshot of my conversation with these fellows came the following day when one of them looked me up, all excited, to say his father had a .45 revolver and he would be delighted to exchange it for a .38. I went along to meet his father and said I was very interested. I'm sure we both felt we would each have the best of the bargain. His gun was obviously of old First World War, vintage perhaps, but it looked in reasonable condition. Unlike some rifles, small-arms are seldom used and don't wear out unless after long, regular use on a target practice range. Despite my keenness to have the weapon, I said I'd like to test it first before clinching the deal.

With this proviso, I met the son a day or two later. He had his father's revolver and I had given some thought to where we could go to practise. In those days Johannesburg was nearly completely ringed with alluvium dust-mountains, the residue of the mines workings, and looked for all the world as if the city was situated in the middle of a desert. Indeed, at certain times of the year when the wind blew wildly in the wrong direction, sand-storms played havoc by blasting through the old rattling, loose-fitting window frames of the day and seeped into every crevice of rooms, making the lives of the city inhabitants a misery. There was no double-glazing in those days.

These mine heaps have all gone now and the city is now situated in green and fertile land. But back then, the almost lunarscape was the ideal place for our test. We walked around the great mounds for a bit and there, at last, was our butt. Sticking out of a dust-mountain wall, like the arm of a buried skeleton, was the blanched, bark-less branch of a buried tree. But I still needed a target to aim at. My friend came to the rescue. I didn't smoke, but he did and produced his box of matches. I wedged the box into a cleft between two fingers of the long dead skeleton and paced out my distance. I took the weapon, broke the chamber, loaded it with six rounds of ammunition, closed it and made sure the safety-catch was on. Now!

Like an old-fashioned protagonist in a duel I took slow, careful aim, squinting down the barrel and fired. Nothing. The matchbox was laughing at me and no doubt my friend, a few paces behind, too. Another shot and the stick quivered to the left. Better! Perhaps it's shooting slightly that way. I aimed a pinch to the right and a twig higher but more central jumped. After four bullets I was getting the drift.

Then I got to thinking: playing the game of duelling was all very well, but life was not like that nowadays. Those times of 'pistols for two and coffee for one at dawn' were long gone. If I ever had to use my revolver there would be no time for the niceties of posing and carefully cocking an eye along the barrel and using sights. That's all very well if you are the attacker with a rifle… you can choose your moment. But for me, side arms are purely for defence. The situation must be dire … Me or It or Him… You don't have time for the subtleties of aiming over sights when a charging lion is coming for you. You shoot by the seat of your pants … or without them if you're wearing a kilt!

So, I dropped the weapon to arm's length by my side, took a breath, then as fast as I could, brought the gun up, poised a second, then leashed off two rounds, rapid fire. The first hit snapped the finger twig, the second smacked the matchbox which exploded in a pyrotechnic extravagance, bits of matches everywhere.

"Jesus …!" my friend let off a machine-gun burst of expletives, which I never knew whether was meant as an accolade or a lament for his lost box of matches.

The upshot of all this, of course, was that we exchanged revolvers, and each was perfectly satisfied. He because he wanted the gun to shoot humans, if necessary, and I to have a weapon with the power to stop a charging lion. One last and happy thing about this bit of trading was that my 'new' gun came in a fine, shiny, leather holster with lanyard and belt. What was more, across the holster were sewn six leather loops to accommodate a full re-charge of bullets to save raking for them in my rucksack pocket, perhaps a lifesaver if a large animal was only wounded and I needed to dispatch it quickly. I felt no end of pleasure wearing the weapon and with the feeling of added security that it gave me.

In contrast to my splendid holster, my previous gun came in the old newspaper it had been wrapped in when it was given to me by a man in Durban, a native of my village and an old friend of my father, who had emigrated to South Africa in the 1920s. Mr William Nagle was 'high-up' in both the Natal government and the National Parliament in Cape Town. For valiant service, the great dam built in The Valley of a Thousand Hills was named after him and I was very proud when he and Mrs Nagle took me to see the magnificent Nagle Dam in its awesome setting in the land of the Zulu nation.

How he came to give me his revolver is a hilarious tale, even though something of a black comedy, involving a nocturnal burglar and William Nagle, MP, taking up arms to save his wife and property, not to mention his own life. Ironically, it was not the burglar who gave them the biggest fright, it was William Nagle himself. That episode is told in *A Tramp in Africa* and has no more place here

I enjoyed my sojourn in Jo'burg, visiting old friends and making some new while wallowing in the comforts of modern living. But I am not a city man – busy streets, concrete buildings and a plethora of traffic lights at every crossing telling me when to go and stop when it suits them. So I decided that while I was waiting for my passport to be renewed and before heading north, I would hitch my way down to Natal to visit old friends of the downward journey.

Mr and Mrs Milne lived at Spitzberg Farm in Escourt. The hitching was easy but, of course, I had to walk the sixteen miles from Escourt up to the farm. They gave me a terrific welcome. I felt almost at home with them and it was grand being back on the farm with the family. When I first met them I was walking along the road on my way to the Drakensberg Mountains when a car passed me and stopped. It was driven by Mr Milne who had just picked up his three daughters from the town. The girls were full of questions about where I was going, where I had been and why was I in Africa wearing a kilt. Their father hushed them and asked where I was heading and invited me to come and stay at the farm.

During my stay I worked with Mr Milne on the farm and lived as family. It was a lively house and I was invited to the homes of their friends and to events and dances – altogether a happy and relaxing time for me. One afternoon, one of the girls offered for sale some of her old clothes and shoes to the women working on the farm. I was amazed how the ultra modern slang had crept into the native vocabulary. One referred to a coat as an 'ama-Jeep'. After a time, everything had been sold except two pairs of shoes, a pair of high heeled silver dance shoes and a pair of low heeled walking shoes. I thought the high heeled ones were the last thing they would want, but I was wrong. In fact, two of them decided they wanted them. They argued for a while then they decided that one would take the 'ama Jive' and the other the 'ama Goluf' (golf).

I learned an interesting detail about the way farmers dealt with a certain kind of poisoning in cattle. On many farms a plant called wild tulip grows. It is a very dangerous, poisonous plant if eaten by the cattle. Funnily enough, any cows which are born and brought up where it grows will not touch them. But, if a strange cow comes from a place where it does not grow, it will eat this wild tulip. The cure for a cow in these circumstances is unique. If a cow has eaten a wild tulip or even if it is new on the farm and the farmer wants it to learn not to eat it, the remedy is to burn the petals and the ashes are fed to the animal. An animal who is suffering from poisoning will be cured and will not look at the tulip again.

Another episode which interested me was the way an old man's age was assessed. Mr Milne realised that his old cook was well over the age for old age pension. The old man in his ignorance had never claimed it; he also had no idea of his own age. Mr Milne asked him how old he was at the time of the Zulu War. The old man thought. Then he said he was 'Umfaan' – a boy, but he was past the age for leading cattle. Then he was asked his age at the time of the Boer War. The old boy knew that without thinking. He was an 'Nsiswa' – a young man in his prime. Lastly he was asked his age at the time of the great influenza epidemic. He rubbed his chin thoughtfully as he recalled the 'Flunza'. Then he remembered. By that time he was a 'Keshla' – an old man.

Mr Milne assessed his age between seventy and seventy-five, a very old age for a native, especially a working native. He was supposed to have stopped work long ago but on hearing that the cook had left Spitzberg and Mr Milne was without a cook, he had come back of his own accord to 'look after them' until they got another. This was the only case I ever heard of a native feeling duty towards an employer. Unfortunately, his type was dying out and in their place the youth were arrogant and had a chip on their shoulder.

I took my leave of the family after ten days and made my way back to Johannesburg. It had been a special time and I had made friends who I correspond with to this day.

But now wild Africa was calling, her sirens singing their soft, captivating songs and playing their enchanting, hedonic music, all carried on the soft, distant winds of adventure and I was not prepared to tie myself to the mast lest I succumb to her, Africa's, alluring temptations. Viator was ready to go.

***

Tuesday 19th May 1953, Rustenburg

Left Johannesburg today. Walked down the length of Commissioner Street and out past the mine dumps that look so much like huge sand dunes, a man-made desert that is slowly but very surely encircling Johannesburg. A few miles out I got a lift to Krugersdorp. The driver, a Jew, was very decent.

He had been in the Somaliland Camel Corps during the war and since I was the first person he had met since he left there who had been to Somaliland we had a lot in common. Naturally, all the conversation was on Somaliland, but he did take time to explain to me the differences, between the High, Low, Bush and Klip Veld, and although I knew most of them already I didn't stop him. I never stop anyone telling me things, even things I already know. That way I learn a lot from the people who give me lifts.

He invited me home for lunch. It was quite interesting because I learned something of the Jewish way of life. On the table there was no butter and he explained why. A Jew never mixes any milk or fat product with the other foods. In fact they keep special plates and cutlery for the two separate foods and never mix them up even when washing them. At least the devout Jew does this. Not everyone adheres to his religion so well as that, but he did.

The scenery changes around Rustenburg. It becomes more hilly, a change from the flat country around the Jo'burg area. The tarmacadam ends at Rustenburg. I cleared the town. The cars that passed left a trail of choking dust that got in my eyes and down my throat. I am just sleeping at the side of the road tonight. I won't bother putting up the tent since it doesn't look like rain.

It was dead of morning. The sun hadn't rubbed the sleep out of its eyes yet and some early birds were telling it to waken. But really, that part of the tale is written from memory, as I knew it would have been, from many, many nights sleeping on the open veldt. This time, when the incident occurred, I was deeply asleep. But let me catch up on this moment from the day's events.

It was some time after I had left Kimberley and I was making my way to Johannesburg. I had walked a long way that day and was thinking of packing it in and making camp when along came an Afrikaner farmer driving his inevitable, little *bakkie* pick-up and stopped, full of friendly wonder at meeting a white person walking alone with a pack on his back. He knew all about the kilt and Scotsmen and let it be known he wasn't really surprised at such eccentric behaviour. At least I took it as that. I didn't know the Afrikaans for *eccentric* (nor anything else for that matter).

We talked a bit as the miles slipped under the wheels and I could not but wonder at the miracle of motor vehicles as the scenery flew passed. So easy, so quick compared to my long hard day. I began to feel drowsy with the comfort and ease of the journey.

I was brought back to reality with my friend saying this was where he branched off the road to his farm quite a distance away. I said my thanks and we both wished our *'tot-sen's* (goodbyes). I was pleased to be more than a day's journey on from the time that I had been going to stop and make camp, but the trouble was, it was now dark. And cold. My, how cold it was.

The winter was truly here and it was one of the coldest nights I had spent. I had noticed it more, of course, coming up from the warm Cape to the *high veldt* here. I couldn't think of pitching my tent, far less making fire and cooking. I walked some distance from the road and made my camp by spreading my groundsheet on the open grassland, taking off my kilt and spreading it on the ground as a mattress, putting on my long trousers and jersey from my rucksack, covering my boots and revolver in its holster with my spare shirt as a pillow, and finally, completely burying myself in my sleeping bag with the tent – using it as an extra blanket – pulled over my face, a tip I learned long ago from the natives when sleeping out. It prevents mosquitoes and other insect bites, and also does not leave the face exposed to snake and hyena or baboon bites.

As it was, there was little danger from mosquitoes here on the high veldt. They don't like the cold and it was cold. There was a thin crescent moon in the velvet sky and the grass had a sprinkling of white hoarfrost that covered my bedding with a crisp layer that would crackle when I disturbed it in the morning.

It was early and I was still rolled into the bundle made of my tent when, still asleep, I was awakened by a large animal nudging my head with loud, hot sniffs. The steam came through the thin tent canvas. Instinctively, I quietly drew the revolver from its holster and slipped the safety catch.

To the best of my knowledge there were no wild animals here. Perhaps there were some lion and others up in the northern Transvaal by the Rhodesian border and in the Kruger National Park, of course, but here and in the rest of South Africa they had all been killed or dispersed long ago when the Bantu, Boers and British invaded these parts. Indeed, in modern times, when some South African farmers found tourism more profitable than working the land and decided to go into the safari business, they had to import wild animals from northern countries or zoos and fence their patches to keep their valuable animals in.

Be that as it may, when being wakened in the dead of night by the hot breath of a large animal in Africa, your hackles rise and your first thought is how best to handle the situation – to fight or flee. So saying, I threw back the tent cover and brought up the revolver, quickly, and stared within inches into two, big, startled, bovine eyes. For a moment we shared our sudden fright before the large cow shied away and trotted off, back to the rest of the herd, which was all around. I don't think they realised what I was and I was sure I was going to be trampled underfoot by them. Nevertheless, I put the cover over my head and tried to go back to sleep, but a great bull thundered past, only inches from me and at that, I gave them best, struck camp and got on the road. So I survived …but only just!

Later in time, further along the trail by some months, much the same thing happened to me again. I dozed on an afternoon, back against a tree with my hat pulled down over my eyes. When I wakened I found myself in the centre of a herd of buffalo. They were not there when I had sat down. Some were cropping grass less than twenty yards away. Many experienced hunters will tell you that they rate the buffalo as the most dangerous animal in Africa.

***

Thursday 21st May 1953, Mafeking
Last town in the Union of South Africa

Mafeking (now Mafikeng) was quite small and quiet, but it had an aura about it like a charismatic person who appears bigger, stronger than their measured size. Perhaps the image was only in my mind, for as I walked its streets, I felt I was walking through history and a place of great achievements. This, after all, was the place that withstood and won the great siege in the Boer War. Men, women and children played their part, the men to man the ramparts in constant watch, the women, as women do, to provide and feed from so little as starvation bit cruelly, and yet keep the cohesion of the citizens as a family together. And the children? Well, there lies a tale!

The army officer in charge was one Colonel Baden-Powell. He organised the boys as runners to carry messages between posts or stations where the men lay in wait, constantly ready to counter-attack should that be necessary. Eventually the siege was broken and later the war ended. But Baden-Powell never forgot the character-building value that developed with the boys as messenger runners and their value to the defence of the town. From all this, the Boy Scout movement was formed. It proved to be an enormous success in Britain and throughout the world. And of all the thousands of Troops that were formed, that of Mafeking was registered as 'No.1'.

I enjoyed my short time in Mafeking. I thrilled when passing Dixon's Hotel which was Baden-Powell's headquarters at the time of the siege. An interesting and historical town, Mafeking, but at that time it held an even more important role for me, for though on South African soil, Mafeking was the Capital of Bechuanaland (Botswana).

Every frontier crossing was always a time of great tension for me. A border officer could refuse me permission to enter if he thought I was a vagrant or a person of insufficient means, which might render me a burden to that country. It had happened before ...twice. But I need not have worried for the officer made some friendly comments, stamped my passport and said nothing about the revolver I carried.

Within the day I was out of South Africa and into the wild Africa that had captured my heart years ago.

CHAPTER 5

THE CURSE OF SLAVERY
'The Mark of Ham'

On the threshold of another new country, Bechuanaland (*Botswana)*, I mentally pause before leaving South Africa. There is a matter I must explain before I leave that land that was my ultimate goal when I left my home so long ago to travel the African continent, and my haven of friendship and succour through these past months while I recouped from the years of hard travel.

The matter in question is 'slavery' – slavery in South Africa. I can hear readers saying, 'You must be wrong. There was no slavery in South Africa!' But I am not wrong. Indeed, I will go so far as to say that South Africa grew out of slavery and the British demand for its cessation. That remark too may surprise many. After all, 'Was it not the British who took the slaves from Africa and waxed fat on the proceeds of their sale?' To that I must agree, but that is only half the story.

To put Britain's involvement in African slavery, for bad and good (yes, I do mean 'good', for a very strong reason that will unfold) we need to go back to near the beginning of mankind. Slaving may not have been the oldest profession, but it can't have been far behind. From Babylonian days, when the Hebrews were taken into slavery in about 600 BC, and even before then, the stronger nations had been pillaging and enslaving the weaker ones. The Romans depended on slaves to power their galleys and what pathetic lives those poor wretches must have led, chained to the great, long oars. Long before the West African slave route to America was conceived there were, and still are, roads or paths throughout the African bush and desert along which one can follow the routes through history, led by the bones littered along the way. There were two well-known slave roads running from Ethiopia and the Upper Nile to Egypt and at least two more crossing the Sahara and Libyan deserts to Northern Africa. Rumour has it that there is still slave traffic on these routes even today.

The first European to bring African slaves to the West and later the Americas was Antao Goncalves. Out of a pale blue sky and sparkling sea, the tiny ship, minuscule as a virus, on the distant horizon, grew in size and sailed into its home port in Portugal carrying the first cargo of black slaves. The year was 1441. From that date onward, the Western world would never be the same again.

It was the Portuguese mariners, of course, who were the first to have rounded the Cape of southern Africa and founded the passage to the fabulous wonders and treasures of India and the Far East. As early as that time, Henry the Navigator tried, but failed, to have the Slave Trade stopped. The commercial potential of the trade was already too good to lose.

Portugal held the monopoly on the slave trade for the best part of a century, by which time other countries were fast developing the trade for their own benefit. Spain had acquired her colonies in southern America and a great number of slaves were taken to Brazil and elsewhere.

But it was the Dutch who finally broke the Portuguese hold on the industry. And here we come to the kernel of what was to become the making of South Africa. Before dealing with that though, I'd like to clear the pitch of Britain's entry and breaking of African slavery.

Following the Portuguese and the Dutch involvement in the African slave trade, other European countries edged their way in for a share of the spoils. After Holland came France, Sweden, Denmark and others. Last but not least, King Charles II took England into the slave trade. In 1663 he chartered the 'Company of Royal Adventurers of England Trading in Africa'. To commemorate the start of the Company's trading he ordered the Royal Mint to strike a new coin made of the purest gold, worth the odd figure of 21 shillings, which he called a 'guinea', named from that part of Africa from whence the precious metal came.

Although the last of the European nations to join the West Africa slave trade, the British soon became the most proficient. They devised the 'Triangular Route' whereby the slave-ships took off from their home ports, Liverpool, Bristol and others, and sailed for the Atlantic coast of Africa. They carried liquor, firearms, some cotton goods, and a great amount of bric-a-brac trinkets that were exchanged for slaves to the militant African tribes who captured the unfortunate, milder people, and brought them in from the hinterland. Those wild kidnappers had no use for money but loved the gaudy trash. In exchange for these pennyworth baubles, a male slave who had survived the passage could sell from £15 to £35 … an extremely handsome profit for those times. These mind-boggling, scalp-creeping, commercial values are beyond belief. Unbelievable it may be, but it was all true.

The next leg of the triangle was known as 'The Middle Passage', an unmitigated, hellish horror that will forever be a curse on our history.

Once on board, the slaves were made to lie down in rows along and round the deck, feet inwards, thus forming a huge oval shape. This done they were then shackled by their ankles until they arrived in the West Indies or American continent two months or more later. This was done to stop any mutinous uprising, which would be short and bloody considering the relatively small crew each ship carried. Food and water were minimal and sanitation was appalling. The odours of slave-ships could be overpowering to other merchant ships a mile or more away. Each ship lost much of its cargo as many, many slaves died and their bodies thrown overboard before the ship arrived at its destination.

The third and last side of the triangular journey was the homeward one to England, and once again the ships carried very saleable merchandise, particularly molasses, the thick, brown, bitter syrup obtained from sugar from which rum is distilled.

The 'Black Ivory' trade must always be a stigma that every nation involved must carry with shame. I use the word 'stigma' advisedly; no other word could be more accurate, more precisely appropriate to the subject. The Oxford Dictionary gives this: 'stigma' – *Mark branded on a slave*. But from the beginning of Biblical times it had always been known as '*The Curse of Ham*', of which I will have more to say later.

It would be wrong to try to minimise Britain's guilt in the crime of slavery, but it can be said that it was here in this country that the first rumblings of a national conscience against the evil practice were to be heard. Not one of the other European nations made any response or effort to end the evil trade. In the British Parliament, however, the rumblings grew in volume to end the slave trade, orchestrated by a great number of people such as William Wilberforce, who entered Parliament in 1780 at the age of twenty-one. Finally, in 1807, an Act of Parliament was passed in London prohibiting slavery and making all dealings with it unlawful.

That Act of Parliament marked the beginning of the end of the West African slave trade. Gradually, other European trading nations followed suit or were forced to do so, and it was as well for the African people that Britain had the will and the clout in having the greatest navy in the world to do her bidding. Nevertheless, it took another half-century and the American Civil War, which was fought by the southern Confederates who wanted to retain slavery and Abraham Lincoln's Northern Party who wanted slavery abolished. The Northerners won and so ended the West African slave trade.

But that was not the end of slavery in Africa. Not by a long chalk!

On the Eastern side where the Indian Ocean laps the shores, slavery was still in full operation. And however bad it had been in the West, it was much worse in the East.

In East Africa slavery had been endemic since the thirteenth century when the Bantu people arrived from West Africa and Persians (Iranians) and others, realised the Black Gold that Allah had given them for the taking. Later the Omani Arabs from the Gulf took over the business and they were indescribably ruthless and cruel. Few people in Britain and Europe ever knew that East African slavery even existed. Yet in its day the trade there was far more prolific than that in the West and the slaughter of captured natives was unimaginable.

It was reckoned that of the thousands of slaves taken from their homes in the area around Nyasaland (*Malawi*) by the Arabs and their Swahili henchmen, only one tenth ever arrived at the great Slave Market in Zanzibar. To get there the captives may have had to walk more than 600 miles, shackled by forked branches back and front of the neck and carrying elephant tusks and other merchandise weighing seventy pounds or more. These shackles were never removed, from the beginning to the end of the journey. Women were not shackled, but they carried loads not much less than the men, with no reduction made for those who carried babies. If any such women could not keep up, their babies were taken from them and slaughtered. Any travellers following a slave route knew when they were approaching a slave train by the clouds of vultures circling in the sky and the dead bodies they passed.

This was the scene David Livingstone conveyed to his university audiences during his two visits to Britain. He was most likely the first white person to witness the terrible Arab slaughter. It is likely that some mulatto/ Portuguese may have witnessed this carnage, for they had been around the interior for a couple of hundred years before the British came. But they would not have been interested in taking slaves from East Africa since the journey round the Cape to the west and over the Atlantic Ocean would not have been profitable.

Whether first or not to witness the Arab atrocities, Livingstone was the first to bring the awful Africa holocaust to the notice of the British people and the western world. It is for this reason he made his plea for people to go and live in the country which would be called Nyasaland (Malawi). Many British people did, mostly Scots, and when the community was large enough to take on the Arabs they declared war and fought and won but not without casualties.

This is just a very short summary of the East African slave trade which I described in much greater detail in my book *A Tramp in Africa* the account of my downward journey through Africa.

So, after centuries of horror for the African people, the curse of slavery was finally erased from both West and East Africa, mainly by the sympathy and humanity and, dare I say it, bravery of the British people.

Although Britain had eradicated slavery in East and West Africa, the vile trade was not gone from the continent that had drawn me to it forever. There was still the problem of slavery in South Africa.

I doubt if there are many people who are aware that slavery existed there. But it did and I should like to put into perspective the part Britain played in the development of South Africa, and the way the British ended the evil practice that had existed there from the very first days of the Boers' arrival in the Cape hundreds of years before.

Nevertheless, let me say that the slavery in South Africa was in no way the same as that which had prevailed in other parts of Africa. However, if slavery can be defined as people who are forced to work against their will for nothing, then there was indeed slavery in South Africa, for hundreds of years before the British came to that land.

To get the gist of this, we have to go back to the beginnings of South Africa as a country. As mentioned elsewhere, the Portuguese navigators, Bartolomeu Dias in 1488 and Vasco da Gama in 1498 rounded the Cape at the most southerly point of Africa and thereby opened up the passage to the fabulous treasures of India and the Far East. Dias found the seas round the Cape so stormy he named the place 'The Cape of Storms' and, although Portugal held sway over the Far East route for well over a century, their mariners never made use of the land there, other than to put-in to take on fresh water.

All this changed when the Dutch, rising in stature these past years, realised that whoever controlled the Cape controlled the passage to India and all the treasures of the East. They set about creating their land base, which would later be called South Africa. Theirs was the first white, European colony to settle in Southern Africa. The Dutch named their new colony the 'Tavern of the Seas', rather more appealing than the Portuguese epithet to the wild Cape they encountered.

The Boers were overjoyed with their new home country. Indeed, they saw it as their own God-given land which they accepted with alacrity. And here we come to the kernel of what was to become the making of South Africa and the reason why the Boers hated the British. Few of the new people could read, as was common in that time of history, but those who could read did so to the others and the one book they read was the Bible. Now we come to the few words that shaped and made, for better or worse, the world of South Africa, a world of bitter hate and misery and untold deaths of blacks and whites.

How all this came about lies with Noah, he of the Ark fame. All Afrikaners know the story and I certainly had it told to me many times by those who vehemently asserted that Noah gave them the right to make black people their slaves. The proof was in a phrase that Boers loved to quote, more than any other, as proof that it was their God-given right that they should have black people to do their work and bidding. This was the curse, as they knew it, which God, through Noah, had laid over all black Africans, the clincher that condemned them to be forever 'hewers of wood and drawers of water'. On that ethos the Boers built their country.

Intrigued, I spent some considerable time searching the Bible for that tale which had been the root of all evil, untold misery and death during those centuries in the fair land of Southern Africa, but I could not find any reference to 'hewers of wood, etc' within the story of Noah's curse on black people.

Biblical records show us Noah was born of Lemech in 3400 BC, some 5000 years before the Boers went to Africa. The great Flood was reckoned to be about 2800 BC Nevertheless, according to the early Dutch settlers, it was Noah who played a decisive role in their relationship with the black people from the moment they set foot on the shore under Table Mountain.

It is written in the Bible that Noah had three sons, Shem, Ham and Japheth. One day Ham ... But wait... let me give the actual words as they were written 'In the beginning'. Mind you, the words as they appear in the Bible had been carried by word-of-mouth for three thousand years before they were committed to writing. All that time the Hebrew history had been compiled and retained by special people, who kept it alive by rote before the words were finally committed to papyrus scrolls when the Hebrews learned to write after they were taken into captive slavery by the Babylonians, around 400 BC, and were then able to compile the Old Testament.

Read now as it appears in Genesis 9. 20-29.

And Noah began to be a husbandman, and he planted a vineyard; And he drank of the wine, and he was drunken; and he was uncovered within his tent. And Ham, the father of Canaan, saw the nakedness of his father, and told his two brethren without. And Shem and Japheth took a garment, and laid it on both their shoulders, and covered the nakedness of their father; and their faces were backward, and they saw not their father's nakedness.

And Noah awoke from his wine, and he knew that his younger son had done unto him. And he said, Cursed be Canaan; a servant of servants shall he be unto his brethren.

And he said, Blessed be the Lord God of Shem; and Canaan shall be his servant.

God shall enlarge Japheth, and he shall dwell in the tents of Shem; and Canaan shall be his servant.

And Noah lived after the flood three hundred and fifty years.
And all the days of Noah were nine hundred and fifty years: and he died.

So there we have the few words that the early Boers in South Africa took to their hearts and passionately believed that because Canaan was of black skin they, the Boers, had every right to take, forcibly if necessary, the black Africans as their slaves to work their farms and do their bidding for all their days. From this little Biblical story hundreds of thousands, perhaps millions, of black Africans over centuries, led accursed, miserable, painful lives and deaths.

The whole of the story is difficult to take in. Why, for instance, did Noah punish Canaan and all his progeny so badly until Doomsday, when the culprit was really Canaan's father, Ham, and on whom was laid the Curse? And why could – should – Noah have such power when surely only God, and only He, had that kind of power? And did people really live to nearly a thousand years in those days? Truly, beyond all understanding!

All that is interesting, but the real enigma of it all is that there is not one word, not a hint of any 'hewers of wood and drawers of water' in this particular Bible story.

That then may be the end of the Noah story, but after further research I did find a Bible reference to 'hewers of wood ...' but it had nothing to do with Noah nor the black people. Let me give a few more words from the Bible which will show that the Boers of South Africa got it all wrong.

In the lands of Lebanon and Jordan great wars were being fought by the people of Israel led by Joshua. Some Hittite, Amorite and Canaanite people came in stealth, saying they wanted to join Joshua. They were accepted and given the full rites of the people but were discovered as enemies, people of the towns that Israel was about to destroy.

Joshua 9:17-21
And the children of Israel journeyed and came into their cities on the third day. Now their cities were Gibeon, and Chephirah and Beeroth, and Kirjath-jearim.
And the children of Israel smote them not, because the princes of the congregation had sworn unto them by the Lord God of Israel. And all the congregation murmured against the princes.
But all the princes said to all the congregation. We have sworn unto them by the Lord God of Israel: now therefore we may not touch them.
This we will do to them; we will let them live, lest wrath be upon us, because of the oath which we sware unto them.

**And the princes said unto them. Let them live; but let them be <u>hewers</u>
<u>of wood and drawers of water</u>** [my emphasis] **unto all the congregation;
as the princes had promised them.'**

So here we have the cusp of all the tragedy and oppression that the Boers
laid on the Africans when they arrived at the Cape. It is obvious from
this story that the curse laid by Israel had nothing to do with the black
people of South Africa. Whether it was by malevolent design, ignorance
or by plain mistake the Boers devised the holocaust that was laid over the
black Africans for centuries, we will never know. Whatever, it condemned
generations upon generations of black Africans to slavery and awful deaths.
The Boers *really* believed that black Africans were there for their sole use,
to do their bidding, for no reward.

And they could be cruel to their slaves. Not everyone. The majority
would be good, homely people. But there were some who had hard, rough,
tough ways. I met many people like that, back-veldters and their like, who
wished to educate me, a stranger in their land, in how to handle 'the Blecks.'
'Treat your dog better than you would do those *kaffirs*', the last word heavy
with insult.

In his book *Missionary Travels*, David Livingstone describes an incident,
an affray, near his Mission station at Kuruman, when he saw over seventy
native women being herded away for a day's work on Voortrekkers' farms,
carrying their own food and tools, and how they, the Boers, smashed his
house and everything that he had made with his own hands, and tore up all
his precious books, because he had remonstrated with them. From that day,
he said, he never owned anything more than he could carry on his travels.

A few words on page 28 of his book sum up what he thought of the
Boers:

*The Bakwains of Kolobeng... [and some more tribes] ... were all groaning
under the oppression of unrequited labour. This would not have been felt
as so great an evil but that the young men of these tribes, anxious to
obtain cattle, the only means of rising to respectability and importance
among their own people, were in the habit of sallying forth ...... to
procure work in the Cape Colony. After labouring there for three or
four years, in building stone dykes and dams for the Dutch farmers they
were well content if they could return with as many cows. On presenting
one to their chief they ranked as respectable men in the tribe for ever
afterwards. These volunteers were highly esteemed among the Dutch,
under the name of Manatees. They were paid at one shilling a day, and
a large loaf of bread between six of them. .... I do not believe that there
is one Boer .... who would deny that a law was made in consequence*

of this labour passing to the colony, to deprive these labourers of their hard-earned cattle, for the very cogent reason, that, "if they want to work, let them work for us their masters," though boasting that in their case it would not be paid for. I can never cease to be most unfeignedly thankful that I was not born in a land of slaves. No one can understand the effect of the unutterable meanness of the slave-system ...'

***

The beginning of the end of South African slavery came when five of the Royal Navy's Men o'War sailed into Table Bay in 1795. It is said that the British Government sent the navy to thwart the French intention to take over the vital port where all ships heading East turned the Cape, before making the long haul to India, Sumatra and elsewhere. If that had happened, Britain's rising commercial power there could have suffered a heavy blow. If it is true that the British wrong-footed the French, it was the best thing that ever happened to the black Africans there for the French had no intention of stopping slavery.

As the Dutch had knocked the Portuguese off the world sea-trading pedestal, now it was the turn of the British to rule the roost on the world's seas and also to end the last bastion of slavery in Africa. It took another hundred years and the Boer War before the evil practice was finally eradicated, but this was the beginning of the end.

No two peoples, the British and the Boers, could be more diverse. The Boers with their simple, Utopian lifestyle with no wish to – could not even contemplate – change, and the British, full of get-up-and-go, constantly wanting to change things, improve everything, full of new ideas, and inventing new things that would improve their world. The two were incompatible.

At first the British took over the running of the colony and then handed it back, only to retake the administration and hold it until after the Boer War. The Boers did not like the way the British ran things, hated it in fact. So much so, many grouped together under an accepted leader, hitched up their great 16-span oxen-wagons, put what they could take along with themselves in them and lit out into the great unknown to find a new Heaven, far away from the accursed British laws. Some of the families would have been in the Cape for over 200 years, so the situation had to be extreme for them to give up their homes and all that they knew and accept the dangers and travail out in the great unknown. So why, like their American Wild-West counterparts in their covered wagons, who lit out over the endless prairies into the wild, blue yonder in the hope of finding a land of promise, did the Boers find that they too had to load up their great covered wagons and light out to fresh sunsets and pastures new to start all over again.

There was a difference though. While the Americans went in the hope of finding a land of promise, the Boers firmly believed that they were heading for the Promised Land, for many Boers firmly believed that, like the Jews, they were a chosen race.

To find the reason – and there is a very good reason why the British and the Boers could not abide each other– we must, once again, go back to the beginning, to the time when the Dutch first landed at Table Bay and started their colony in South Africa. The people who came were farmers who led simple lives and expected others to do the same, so what was it that made the British so hated by the Boers? Why did we make such terrible laws that the Dutch farmers had to leave the farms their forebears had created and worked for centuries, and go into the wild unknown and start all over again? I'm sure there are many, many people outside Africa who believed that Britain was the oppressor.

The real reason for all the terrible British laws was that at the time the Royal Navy ships sailed into Cape Town Bay in the late eighteenth century, Britain was at the helm of her anti-slavery campaign that she, and only she, had brought about. One of the first laws laid down by the new British administration decreed that Africans must be paid for their labour by their employers and the workers must not be abused. This was a bombshell to the Boers. Who had ever heard of such a thing! Pay the *Blecks*? Never! Never!

Now we have the reason why so many Boers, Trek-Boers or Voortrekkers, as they were known, gave up the farms that had been in their families for generations, loaded up their great wagons and left the Cape forever and lit out into the unknown territory across rivers and mountains. They were brave, resourceful people who lived tough lives to find their dream. When they had gone as far as they thought they needed to be free of the accursed British and their laws, they settled where they found their Utopia, essentially where there was a peaceful or subservient tribe whose people could be yoked or coerced into doing their bidding.

Not all the tribes were such people. The Zulus and their derivatives were not given to slavery and had to be fought when the Voortrekkers entered their territory. To their great credit the Trekkers were excellent, brave fighters. When faced with an impending battle they laagered their wagons in a circle in open land, with all people and animals inside. When charged by the warriors, the men lay by the wheels shooting between the wagon wheels, while the women reloaded the guns. When needed, the women would use the guns too, with great accuracy. I do not think there is any record where natives broke a Voortrekkers' laager.

Eventually, the Trekkers would choose a place, set their boundaries, name their new country, such as *Transvaal* and *Orange Free State*, etc. and put down roots, then claim the local people as their serfs. But not for long. Eventually the Brits would come into their country and before long would be running it and installing their hateful laws that enforced 'employers' to pay their workers proper wages. And the whole rolling stock would start up again. This was the way a great deal of the land that is known as South Africa came about.

So who were the goodies and who were baddies in the game that made South Africa? It cannot be said that the British motives were altruistic, that they followed the Boers wherever they went in order to stop the slavery that the Boers perpetrated. The real reason lay in the natural way of history that never stays still. Dormant people who wish to remain forever in their past lay themselves open to go-ahead people who have no time for those who are not. It is the way of the world and has been forever.

And if ever there was a go-ahead people back in the eighteenth and nineteenth centuries, it was the British. In all the world there had been little or no advancements made since Roman times, 2,000 years before. Horse transport was still the vogue, and building methods and materials had hardly changed. Then two Brits, James Watt, born in Greenock in 1736 and who is said to have recognised the power of steam by watching his kettle boil and observing it lift the heavy iron lid, and George Stephenson, born in Wylam, near Newcastle, in 1781, son of a colliery fireman, gave us steam engines for railways and powerhouse factories that created the Industrial Revolution, and the world was changed forever. Britain was the hub of the world, to where the best brains in Europe came to learn of the new inventions, the latest techniques and developments that were changing the world. Britain was at the very zenith of technology as it was at that time.

It was not entirely right to say that Watt discovered steam power for in Alexandra, 130 BC Hero wrote a thesis on this power and others along the way did so too, but none had mastered the complex medium. But Watt and Stephenson did. Now there was steam power for great factory workshops where huge metal beams could be cast for bridges, railways, trains, engines, ships ... power, power, power, the likes of which the world had never known. The world and its ways had changed forever!

***

I pause for a moment to give a little aside which may be of interest. George Stephenson's son, Robert, born 1803, following in his father's footsteps, was educated at Edinburgh University, went briefly to South America but returned to manage his father's engine works. Now Robert had a son, born 1850, who was called Robert Lewis Balfour Stephenson, but he, for his own reasons when only eighteen, changed the spelling of his name from Stephenson to Stevenson and Lewis to Louis and dropped 'Balfour' altogether. He was, of course, the great writer, Robert Louis Stevenson who gave us *Treasure Island, Kidnapped, Doctor Jekyll and Mister Hyde* and many others. Interestingly, he called one of his main characters 'David Balfour'.

Of lesser import, but not to me, was the fact that R.L.S was brought up in Edinburgh and as a child and boy he had a nanny called Alison Cunningham. As a boy and throughout his life Robert called his nanny 'Cummy' and in later life he always said that it was to Cummy that he owed his gift of being an author. It was she who read stories to him and saw how quickly and cleverly he adapted his own and from these beginnings she coaxed him to be a writer.

Now, there is a little interesting point to this bit of history which is very close to me. You see, Alison Cunningham was not only born and brought up in my village, Torryburn but actually lived in the upstairs rooms directly across the street from our home. Our house was knocked down to make room for modern development, but 'Cummy's' still exists, and is lived in to this day. As a boy writing my masterpieces of cowboy tales, sea yarns and those of the frozen north and the like, I would look out our window as I wrote and see Cummy's room directly across the street. I would be pushing ten or eleven, but even now I would like to think that Cummy's aura from a century before wafted across the street and inspired me to write this book.

A bit of nonsense, but I thought you would like to know that!

***

So, with the arrival of the British, the Boers had a rude awakening from their Rip van Winkle lives. The time had come for change. If it had not been the British it would almost certainly have been the French or some other nation. The industrial nations were waking up and of all those in Europe, Britain was the most benign and caring. I say that with knowledge, having been to and lived in almost every British and other colonial country in Africa. It grieves me so much when I hear those vociferous firebrands who preach ill-informed cant to the affect that we British must apologise for our sins to black Africans and carp on about Britain's 'terrible' colonial past. If they only knew …!

Some of the inhumanities to Africans exacted by many European colonists were truly terrible. The Germans were cruel and murderous beyond belief, the Belgians, in the Congo, unspeakable for their mutilations to force the natives to work harder. The Portuguese were also cruel, especially their mulattos who were a cross with the black and white races. The British never indulged in any of these practices. I will be describing some of the evil practices used in other European colonies as I go to these countries later in the book. Meantime, I will reiterate that the British administrators and overseers of natives never indulged in those evil ways, even during the Mau Mau campaign in Kenya, of which I had considerable experience.

Although great Bible readers, particularly of the Noah saga, the Boers seemed to have a completely blank spot for another Biblical edict which inferred that *'The labourer is worthy of his hire' Luke*. But as the *'labourer'* appears in the New Testament it is obvious the Boers never read beyond the Old one.

Having made a case for the fact that the Boers were ultimately responsible for the break-up of their old way of life and their continued harassment by the British was because of the slavery they practised, I have to say that it wasn't all quite like that. The real reason for the British following, hounding, the Boers was more mercenary. When diamonds were discovered in The Orange Free State and gold in the Transvaal and other precious metals elsewhere, the Boers old way of life and the countries they had created were in serious trouble. The Boer farmers had little interest for the baubles of stone and metal dug up from the ground and only wanted to continue as they had always done. But the moving finger does not allow stagnation.

As soon as the strikes were announced, men came from all over the world to find their fortune and most of those were British. Before long they would be running the new country and again making the Boers pay their workers. In the end, there was no part of the country where the Boers could carry on with their slavery. Friction was always there and several small wars were fought until in 1899 the Second Boer War erupted.

Most British people assumed that this war would be a short, sharp lesson to the Boers and our soldiers would be back for Christmas. The soldiers in their fine red coats were marched off to the railway stations led by the pomp and pageantry of brass bands and later to loud cheers from rapturous crowds when they embarked on waiting ships. Alas, it did not turn out as expected.

Far from the quick knockout, the Boers proved a tough nut to crack and the war went on for three years. Indeed, in the beginning, it was the British army that was on the defensive and suffered the heaviest losses.

From the beginning too, the Boer did not play fair. Up till this time in history the British army had always fought its battles like men, as battles should be fought, as they had been fought for untold centuries, army to army in a field, man-to-man, with civilians well away from danger. What other way should a war be fought? But the Boers were devilish to fight. They didn't follow the rules of the 'game'. They rarely exposed themselves, using all the hunting skills they had learned from childhood. This way they held the initiative in the first year or so.

Another way the devilish Boers fought was, far from not fighting where there were civilians, when the British army was least expecting it they would surround a whole town, women and children included, and besiege the whole place for months with civilians frightened and hungry.

The sieges of Mafeking and Ladysmith were the most sensational, but there were others. After months and months, when the news of the relief of each town was brought to Britain there were parties and celebrations. On a humorous note it is believed some cad read the announcement with hesitation, as in 'Lady Smith, has been relieved'.

But no whimsical connotation could be used when describing much else of the Boer War. Despite anything that I have said of the Boers in relation to their slavery practice, no one could but praise their fighting qualities. They fought hard and bravely and the war went on into the early twentieth century, dragging on for a second year and a third. More and more troops had to be brought from Britain, their embarkation now marked with less pageantry.

Queen Victoria never lived to see the end of the war. She died in 1901, soon after her Diamond Jubilee. Her death heralded her ageing son, Edward VII, to the throne and with him 'The Edwardian Era', a time noted for its elegance and grace in lifestyle, art and design, in sharp contrast to the bold, heavy, ornate Victorian designs and structures as befitted the greatest, strongest nation in the world. The Edwardian' era was short, a mere ten years before the King died in 1911, but their influence lasted well into the twentieth century. Even now, in the twenty-first century there is an eager renaissance of the Edwardian style and design in many circles.

Despite the change of monarchs the Boer War dragged on. With the increase of British soldiers the Boers changed their tactics… with devastating effect.

They developed bands of courageous horsemen who would go behind the British lines to perform lightening attacks where and when least expected, to kill and create mayhem, and leave quickly into the night before the enemy had time to muster retaliation. These highly mobile and lethal groups of soldiers were called '*Commandos*'. During the Second World War Britain 'borrowed' this type of shock warfare and with it the name for the units, 'Commandos'. Those Special Forces of the British Army worked behind the lines to great effect against the Germans and other enemies.

But, back to the original shock troops of the Boer War, also commonly referred to as the South African War: when a secret message would come from the Boer Command, some local farmers would leave their farms and gather at a clandestine rendezvous to form a Commando. They would carry the minimum of weight, their guns and ammunition, a water bottle and some pieces of biltong, (dried meat, tough as leather but very nutritious). They could travel great distances on horseback through the night, hit the enemy and be back in their homes before morning, even in bed or working their fields, should any British trooper come to see who might be missing.

The way the British High Command broke the Commandos' stranglehold and eventually ended the war was to bring about one of the most infamous episodes in British history in Africa. Knowing that the Commandos depended on returning to their farms to work the land and appear non-militant, the British High Command had the army build huge internment camps, then go round the Boer farms and take all the women and children into custody. These prisons were called 'concentration camps', another name that was taken up from the Boer War and used in the Second World War, this time by the Nazis. But while the German meaning of the word came to mean 'extermination camps' the British intention was not to kill the women, but to separate them from their men folk so that they, the Commandos, had nowhere to hide and obtain food and succour after their forays.

This plan, however, went horribly, tragically wrong. In these quick-built camps sanitation was very poor and, in the heat, deadly virus epidemics broke out for which, in those days, there was no known cure. Thousands of the women and children died. Although the ruse virtually ended the war, this episode was one of the most infamous in British Military history and took British/Boer and world relationships to an absolute nadir.

With the war over, South Africa went through many changes. The old country was gone forever. The British set up a democratic government, comprised of two leading parties, one being the mainly Boer 'National Party' and the other mainly British influenced 'United Party'. From the start The United Party was in power and for nearly fifty years maintained that power position. black and coloured Africans were not allowed the vote.

Two significant changes came about with the new post-war era. The word 'Boer' was declared undesirable and was replaced by 'Afrikaner' who spoke Afrikaans, not Dutch as before. The second major decree issued by the new Parliament was that English would be the new first language, in which the people wishing to hold any post or position of authority had to be fluent.

In the new South Africa the two main political parties were not necessarily peopled by those born to each language. Anything but! Some English-born speakers joined the 'Nationals', while many of those whose first language was Afrikaans joined and became leaders of the United Party. Field Marshall Jan Smuts was a notable one. He had fought the British long and hard, but after the war became a great ally and later one of the very highest ranking and able soldiers on Britain's side in Europe during the First Great War.

This then was the South Africa that lasted through the first half of the twentieth century. It was not Utopia, but for those fifty years there was relative peace. Dutch and British settlers lived in comparative harmony and native Africans were assured of getting working wages and no torturing or bullying by their employers. Indeed, since the end of the Boer War, when British type laws were introduced, the African natives' lives had changed beyond all recognition. So much so, white farmers often thought that they were the victimised party rather than the Africans, a fact that few people outside South Africa would have believed.

The beginning of the end of that relatively benign period came in 1948, when for the first time in the short history of a unified South Africa, the Nationalist Party, which was based on the principles of the old Boer days, won the election and gained power. South Africa would never be the same again.

Three years or so later when I arrived in the country, the English speaking South Africans were in a state of foreboding, as well they might be. One of the first changes the new government decreed was to make Afrikaans the first language of the land. This brought about an immediate reversal of roles in industry and commerce, which stood the country on its head in more ways than one.

Although I did not realise it at the time, I now know how fortunate I was to be there at that moment in history. Today, looking back down the long trail of the past, I realise I was there in the very place to witness the first cracks to appear in the cobble-stones of white power in South Africa. During the fifty years of British-type rule, the Africans and Coloureds rubbed along with the whites fairly happily. The political situation was not right, but authority was quite benign and generally most classes got along together in reasonable harmony and prosperity. But with the new regime, based on the old, Boer philosophy of blacks being totally subservient to the whites, fifty years of peace was completely turned on its head.

It did not take black Africans long to abhor the Nationalists' Boer-type, way of running their country. Even at that, they may have gone along with the new government for some time, but they could not abide the draconian measures brought in by the new government, by way of the introduction of *Apartheid.* Coined in Afrikaans, the word in English means 'Racial segregation'.

Here we have the heart of the matter that brought the downfall, the end of white supremacy in South Africa. With the introduction of Apartheid great areas of land were cleared and designated for black Africans only. Families, tribes even, were uprooted from places and lands where they had lived for untold generations and forcibly relocated to designated regions where they were allowed a certain amount of autonomy in the running of their areas. This legislation took the country back fifty years to the Boer administration, such as it was. Black Africans, from now on, would only be allowed in 'white' areas to work but not to live. It was an impossible, inhuman, degrading manner of government that was bound to flounder in the modern world. In the half-century of British-type rule the Africans had found a new world and a self-confidence that they never had before. In addition, all Africa was shedding the yolk of European imperialism. Gradually, 'incidents' happened, laws were flouted, and eventually there developed an out-and-out breakdown of law-and-order, with murder and mayhem rife. Foreign agents and countries, Russia for one, were blamed for the insurgencies, but in the end it was the rising of the black population that ended white domination in South Africa. Nelson Mandela was released from his long incarceration in Robben Island Prison in 1990. Four years later, when the ANC won the first multiracial elections with an overwhelming majority, he was to form a government, so ending four hundred years of white rule.

***

In this brief history of the slave trade in Africa and particularly that of Southern Africa, it is evident that I have played up Britain and the British as the 'Goodies' and the Dutch and Afrikaners as the 'Baddies'. Like most facets of history, events and ways of people are rarely as clear-cut as portrayed. That said, I would like to emphasise that in South Africa and elsewhere, I met and shared the company of very many Afrikaner people, most of whom I liked very much and was proud to call them my friends and pleased that they reciprocated in kind. Nevertheless, I stand by the facts I quote, particularly in relation to slavery, the main theme of this tract. I have tried hard to explain that no Briton should ever feel the need to grovel for our part in that awful industry. Better to learn the real history and so be able stand tall and proud for the good that Britain did in ending slavery in all its roles.

The ethics of today are so different from those of the past. Everything we know now had to evolve, every piece of empiric knowledge had to be worked out by people who thought ahead of their time and each of those gems of wisdom later became so common place that future generations take the developments for granted and assume that our forebears were always as wise and informed as we are today.

As an illustration of this, let us look back that long, long road of the past and think of this ... As mentioned before, in 1663 King Charles II took England into the slave trade. Today we might think what a tyrant he must have been. What an unmitigated fiend to trade in human beings. How cruel a monster ... etc., etc. Now consider this...

One of the last witches to be put to death in Scotland was Lilias Aidie, a resident of Torryburn, my village, about the time Britain was dealing in African slaves. Before Lily's time, it was common for declared witches to be burned at the stake on the Ness, a green, grassy area by the shore. After a lengthy trial at the Session Court at Culross, Lily admitted that she had *'on a night convened with the Devil in the Glebe* (the Minister's field) *at Torryburn'*, less than fifty yards from the house I was born and grew up in. She was condemned to death for such a heinous crime.

For centuries the punishment for this terrible crime had been *'TO BE BURNED'*. "In Dunfermline, for instance, as many as six women were burned at the Witches' Knowe in 1643 and from Lilias Adie's confessions, many more had been burned at Torryburn." I quote from the excellent book *That Portion of Scotland*, referring to Fife, by John Westwood, our local historian who lived just down the street from our house and with whom, as a young man fifty years his junior, I struck up a close relationship through my interest in everything he wrote and did, such as studying the stars through his telescope in his little garden on an evening.

Lilias Adie was not burned, however. By 1703 when she was condemned, a new, enlightened, modern age had developed. Burning was now regarded as inhuman. In place of this now barbaric practice, she would be, *'Chained to the Leigh Craig* (Low Crag, where we as children used to play and swim) *until drowned'*. So Lily would be chained to this large rock that is washed over deeply twice a day as the tide in the Firth of Forth comes in, no doubt watched by most of the local villagers including, almost certainly, my ancestors, for our old house went back before the date of Lily's death. Local history says her bones were buried in the shore by the big rock, but her skull, which was said to be very small, was preserved in St. Andrews University, and no doubt is still there.

The point I make here is that, in the time of Lily's death, the people really thought they were being kind to her by drowning rather than burning, in the same way that slavery was so common that most people involved in it did not know or realise how wrong it was. Looking back down the centuries, we do not see these people who burned 'witches' as being wicked or inhuman or uncivilised. They were people of their time living the ethics of their time. As a final point, think of it this way; if Britons had been as wise, humane and informed as we are today, we would not have gone into the slave-trade: and if the Britons of the day had not risen above all other nations of that time and realised the inhumanity and evilness of slavery, we would never have gone to such lengths and danger to have stopped it.

I cannot emphasise too much that it was Britain and <u>only</u> the British who wiped out slavery, that awful canker that bedevilled the African people for centuries. Make no mistake, there are thousands and thousands of

Africans, millions even, who are alive today who would not have been born had the British not taken up the crusade and saved their forebears from terrible deaths.

CHAPTER 6

BECHUANALAND: A LION HUNT
The Making of Botswana

I am in Africa. The 'real' Africa that drew me to its heart from the day I first landed on its shore. Leaving South Africa and entering Bechuanaland (Botswana) was like stepping through Alice's looking glass – the sudden complete metamorphosis of atmosphere and general ambiance of the land and its people, their way of life, and the thrill of my journey lying ahead with what wonders anew?

I lie by the camp fire in my sleeping bag with the zip half down, arms behind my neck and gaze up at the wispy clouds that drift across the three-quarter moon and realise how lucky I am. Less than a dozen feet from me are two lion, a female in the sleeping mode and a huge male, with a great, shaggy mane, in the sphinx pose. They are both dead, of course.

I can hardly believe that this will be only my second night in Bechuanaland, so much has happened. If I had not written up my diary I doubt if in a few years I would have believed what a difference a day can make.

Saturday 23rd May 1953, Mahalapye

Another country to add to the list! This morning I left Mafeking with Mr Globber, who had offered me my first lift into that territory. We crossed the border 14 miles out.

At Lobatsi, the first town, I reported to the police to have my passport stamped. There are simply no restrictions here to anybody with a British Passport. Quite a change from some of the others on the way down. We had lunch in the hotel there, then came on through Gaberone to Mahalapye.

These places in the British Protectorate are only very small and very far apart. Quite a change from the Union. Mr Globber introduced me to the proprietor of the hotel here. He, Mr Sharp, invited me to spend the night free of charge at the hotel. It is right on the railway line. I met most of the men of the town here. This country is teeming with game and as luck would *have it I met two men who are going lion hunting tomorrow, Monday and Tuesday being holidays.*

My diary gives the facts of the story but it does not, in this case, breathe the life, the excitement, the sheer adventure in the atmosphere I thrilled to that night. More than half a century later, I recall the moment so vividly as I write, I feel the vibes – no, I will not use that slang word and give the moment the proper word –'vibrations' for that is what shivers my spine as I remember the living moment as clear as if I am standing in the throng of that moment. The reason for my elation at that moment was that Mr Jack Chase, the leader of the lion hunt scheduled for the next day, had invited me and John Seaman, a local fellow of my own age whom I had met only an hour or two before and with whom I was already firm friends, to join the hunt.

That evening in Mahalapye was memorable. The place came under the term 'town', but it really comprised only a few houses, a number of official offices and residences and the hotel, the hub of the white community. Mahalapye lay at the side of the railway track that ran all the way up from South Africa to Southern and Northern Rhodesia (Zimbabwe and Zaire) and it seemed the town waited the day through for the arrival of the evening train. When it came with billowing steam, great puffing and huffing and clanging of the bell, everyone in the town was there to meet it, black and white, and it seemed everybody knew each other. People carried lanterns and held them up for all to see. The hotel was emptied and most people carried glasses of beer for themselves and to hand to the passengers. The atmosphere was happy and convivial for a short time, then the great engine blew its horn to tell visitors and passengers to sort themselves out and the doors clattered loudly and the engine blasted out great puffs of smoke and steam and soon disappeared loudly into the night. And a great silence fell over the community. But the hiatus gradually died away and people returned to the hotel and elsewhere and the evening returned to normality

Next morning I thanked my host gratefully and went to see John Seaman, the fellow I met at the hotel the previous night. He had to go out to his father's store at Ramakonami first before we made for the camp where we were to meet the two men who were lion hunting. The store was about 40 miles from Mahalapye and way out into the wild bush. It was the proper 'Prester John' type of store, strictly for African natives, which I loved to go into wherever I was in 'Darkest Africa'. As manager, John's father bought hides and skins and cattle and traded generally with the natives. I would have liked very much to stay there longer, but the sky was already on the turn and we had a long way to go to meet up with the hunters.

The roads in Bechuanaland were really bad. One hundred miles in a day was a marathon run in a car. The main road was bad enough but when you went onto any side roads – whew! They were only tracks and twisted round bush and trees whichever was in the way when they were made. Long stretches of loose sand made the truck chug along in second gear for miles on end. You couldn't measure a journey in miles in Bechuanaland; you counted it by the hours it took. By the time we reached the camp it was 9 p.m. and quite dark.

The previous evening when we struck up our mutual, easy friendship I just liked the guy, but by the time we arrived here I was full of great admiration for John's navigation and driving skill. How he got us to the camp in the bush with no road or tracks to follow at that time of night was beyond me.

Jack Chase made us very welcome and got the cook to prepare a hearty supper for us while we lounged by the blazing fire and heard the wild goings-on in the day's hunt. The two dead lion lay in the place and position at which I watched them later when I turned-in and lay in excited anticipation before going to sleep. The other man there, a Mr Botha, (pronounced *Bo'ta*) was rather quiet and, I had the feeling, uncomfortable. I wasn't sure whether he was a friend or client of Jack's.

Jack, the lion hunter, who had fifty lions to his name, had shot both of them. He remarked casually that the male had been a bit 'cheeky' and had only been shot when it charged them at close range. I gathered later when Mr Botha was not around that he was supposed to have done the killing, but he missed badly on both, and other occasions, so when they were charged Jack had had to go in for the kill. It was evident that had Mr Botha been on his own, he and possibly the Africans too, would have been lion meat.

Early next morning, after a hasty breakfast, we all piled into Jack's old jalopy. It was a miracle on wheels. An old 1929 model Ford, it went like a bomb, but rather slowly and steadily as became its elder years. There were three native trackers and the four of us. A bit out from the camp they picked up a spoor and Big Nose, the head tracker, trotted along in front of the car. Jack left the road and headed cross-country, *bundu bashing*. The other trackers followed behind Big Nose and soon there was cry. A lion had been seen! The jalopy picked up her skirts and like an old dame in second childhood bucketed across the veldt, bouncing into potholes and beating down bushes while we bounced about inside like dice being rattled before a throw.

Anyone not acquainted with Africa could be excused if they thought the trackers had been wrong when they shouted 'Lion' for there were three, two lions and a lioness, standing about two hundred yards away. A magnificent sight. As to the grammar in counting animals, it is common practice to refer to a group or herd in the singular, i.e. 'a pride of lion' or 'a herd of elephant'.

This was to be Mr Botha's day. Alas, alack … the lions were quite safe with him on the end of a rifle. He had three shots and three times he missed. I think he was over excited. The lions split up and were off like the wind. At first they thought the lioness had been hit so we chased. After a time though, when the spoor had been examined thoroughly, they were pretty sure it hadn't been touched, nevertheless we continued the chase.

We left the *'chorri'*, Jack's jalopy, and went on foot now. Big Nose was a wonderful tracker, How he picked out the spoor and followed it across *klip veld* (grassy, stony plain) was amazing. Mile after mile we went on with Big Nose reading the ground like a book, remarking in Tswana (the native language) which was translated to me.

"Here she stopped and rested"

"Here she lay down"

"Here she turned round to look at us"

"Here she got a fright"

"Here she started running"

All the time Big Nose pointed to the spoor with his thumb or all fingers extended, never with his index finger. A native will never point with that finger at a lion spoor. He considered it an insult to point his finger and he respected the lion too much to insult it. In the afternoon we saw the lioness again, but it was too far off for a shot. We never saw it again even though we roamed for a while before making our way back to camp. It had been a long day, but I enjoyed every minute of it.

That night the lion got something of their own back at us. There was a cattle post nearby where we camped into which the animals were put at night. Through most of the night a group of lion roared almost continuously in an attempt to stampede the cattle into breaking out of the stockade. Had that happened there would have been some slaughter. The night was pandemonium. The lion seemed to have the place surrounded. One roar would be answered by another from the opposite direction. The cattle bawled with fright and the natives howled and shouted as they tried to keep the matter in hand. As for me, lying alfresco in my sleeping bag, listening to the pandemonium and looking up at the stars, I hoped that all the lion were too busy to be interested in a small bite like me. Nevertheless, I was very pleased to have my .45 revolver with a fully chamber of soft-nosed bullets in it very close to my hand all through the night.

In the morning there was excitement in the air. This was the last day of lion hunting and with so many of them obviously about, there were great expectations ahead. There was a happy fever in the atmosphere as rifles were 'pulled through', bullets checked, water cans and bottles filled, the 'chorri' filled with petrol and oil and a hundred and one things done in preparation. Before the hunt the native trackers put a piece of bark from the *Moretta* bush round their wrist. This is to give immunity from attack.

But again our luck was out. After last night they were obviously enjoying a long lie in somewhere in deep, cool, safe foliage country. We did get on to the spoor of one huge lion and followed it until afternoon. It led us into impossible country of low, thick, thorny bush. We searched in there for about two hours after which we were scratched and bleeding and our clothes ripped. Horrible country. John Seaman got a glimpse of the lion, but it was impossible to give chase in those conditions. Moreover, in that dense foliage the lion had all the odds in his favour for he could have been on us before we spotted him. So we gave it up.

Although we were not lucky enough to get a lion while I was there, I enjoyed the hunt. There is something about lion hunting that is like no other. You walk all day and it's much more tiring walking slowly, casting about for signs of the spoor all the time, than just plain walking. Hours drag past and you think it's hopeless. You are even bored. Then the trail leads into a thicket, a natural place for the lion to lie up. Immediately the tiredness, the parched throat, the boredom, the feeling of the uselessness of all your efforts is forgotten. In its place is a glow that comes with impending danger. This is the 'kick' you get out of hunting big game. The group circles the thicket and the dogs go in, little fox terriers, barking. The group closes in, then you walk through the bush with your senses at hair-trigger tension. Then there is the anticlimax – the lion has gone. Back comes all the old lethargy and nonchalance returns and you go off again. There is a few hundred yards of open veldt in front and you know you will not see the lion for some time. There is the long search to catch the spoor. Then you see the tracker running. Again the excitement, the exhilaration. Even the dogs know when a tracker runs it means business. You run up and there is the lion, standing majestically in the sunlight. An unforgettable memory even though the moment is so brief it is gone in a flash and, for me at least, so pleased it has gone to live another day. Just the sight of it is more than compensation for the long hours of drudgery and fatigue.

After that it was time to pack up and go back to Mahalapye where we arrived in time to enjoy the bonhomie and camaraderie of the evening railway train stop once more. As the train went off into the night with great hooting and puffing Jack Chase asked where I was staying and when I said I'd find a place to pitch my tent, he was aghast. He said he took it that I was going back to the hotel where I had stayed the other night. I said that that was a generous one-night gift from the hotelier and that I could not afford to stay there. I explained that I was very used to camping and would find a place on the veldt and be perfectly all right, but he would have none of it and insisted that I come home with him.

On entering Jack's house it was obvious that this was a hunter's home. There was a mounted lion's head on the wall – Jack's first – lion skins on the floor for rugs, 'karosses' (blankets made from pelts) on the beds and a rack of heavy calibre rifles in the living room – a man's home. Mrs Chase welcomed me with homely friendship and I thoroughly enjoyed my time with them and learned quite a lot about the country and the people.

Jack had a pack of fox terriers he used for lion hunting, some of whom I had met on the hunt. The eldest was Peter, a wily veteran of many campaigns. He carried many scratches from close shaves with lions. In fact, he got some new ones from the one Jack shot on Sunday. Peter was eight years old. While the other dogs run about needlessly all day expending their energy, Peter remained quiet, almost sleepy, until the tracker started running. He knew then that the lion had been sighted. Then he woke up, as I saw on the day's hunt. It was he who led the pack into the bushes. Mrs Chase said Jack should 'pension' Peter off and not take him hunting anymore since he was getting old. But Jack said if Peter could speak, he was sure that the dog would say that since he had lived a hunter's life he would want to die a hunter's death. He'd go on until he was killed by a lion.

With Jack's invitation to his home, I didn't realise how lucky I was. In later times when I mentioned to people that I had hunted with Jack Chase and been a guest in his house for some time, and hearing their awed and envious remarks, I realised that the man was a legend throughout Bechuanaland. In later years I have seen his name in several books written of the country at that time. From the time I had been with him, his world seemed to have changed. He now had a great position as Acting Chief Game Ranger for the Bechuanaland Government. From photos, I saw he now had a grand new, big safari vehicle and I wondered if he had retired his old jalopy or embalmed it for posterity. How I should bump into him and hit it off with him so well within minutes of arriving in Mahalapye was quite incredible. There were many people of the day who would have given their eye-teeth to have had Jack as their guide and mentor if they had paid handsomely for a hunting licence to shoot some big game and knew nothing about how to go about it. Mr Botha must have been a case in point. I have no idea if their association was commercial, but there is no doubt that Hollywood actors and authors such as Ernest Hemingway and the like, paid a King's ransom to the best professional hunter/guides of the day when following their sport in East Africa.

After my short stay with Jack and his wife, I said my thanks and goodbyes and got on the road for the 60-mile tramp to Serowe, the capital town of the Bangamwatu people, the largest tribe in Bechuanaland.

The road was fairly straight and level so I hunched my shoulders, thumbs through the straps, and set a good pace. It was a good day, for after two or three hours a large P.W.D diesel truck came along and took me on board. Hal Barker, the driver, a cheery, comfortable man was glad of my company as I certainly was of his. His conversation was not just easy patter but real interesting stuff. Bechuanaland was in ferment, the likes of never before. I had caught an inkling of something in South Africa, but it was obviously of little import there and lost in the daily goings-on. But now Hal was filling me in with the gist of the national political turmoil that could burst into war of a kind and tear the country apart. Hal admitted he was not really sure what it was all about, but his reason for going to Serowe was to take up a load of petrol, equipment and provisions to the British police camped beside the tribal capital.

British police in Africa! To my knowledge this had never happened before. British soldiers, yes. But police, surely not? But it was true, as I was to find out rather quickly.

The 60 miles to Serowe took four hours, and that was on the main road. On arrival, Hal headed for the 'Security Camp', the police barracks, on the edge of the town and in no time I was given quarters there and made welcome for the time I wanted to stay. A folding camp bed was laid down for me and all meals provided. I was one of the boys. Just like old times!

***

Since my entry into Bechuanaland I had not realised I had entered a country so deep in racist furore and massive, political intrigue. The racism was vibrantly on the surface, while the political skulduggery and machinations, massive in its international power, did not surface until many years later. Even today, I doubt if more than a handful of the public know anything about it. Yet in my time there, the game was being played at the highest international level and the stakes for Bechuanaland, or today's Botswana, was the prize for which the dice was being thrown.

On the racist question, the matter could be said to be bizarre, insomuch that in the colonies and protectorates administered by Britain, marriages or unions with whites and blacks were frowned upon, even abhorred, particularly in South Africa. In almost every case of this kind it would involve a white man and a black woman, but in Bechuanaland this matter of racism was reversed and the boot was on the other foot!

The furore was all to do with a black man marrying a white woman. But this was no ordinary man. The husband was no less than Seretse Khama, the Heir Apparent to the Chieftainship of the Bamangwatu tribe, the largest and most advanced tribe in a wide area. The lady he had married without consulting with the tribe or consent from the Chief was Ruth Williams, whom he had met while studying Law in England.

To understand something of the matter we must go back a long way to the early 1800s, when the Bangamwatu tribe was not as coherent a group as it became in later times, as were many tribes of the large area who were known collectively as Bechuanas – hence *'Bechuanaland'*. David Livingstone says this about them at that time:

The Bechuanas are divided into numerous tribes named after certain animals, which probably indicates that in former times they were addicted to animal-worship like the ancient Egyptians. The term Bakatla means "they of the monkey"; Bakuena, "they of the alligator; Batlapi, "They of the fish". When you wish to ascertain what tribe they belong to, you say, "What do you dance?" from which it may be inferred that dancing was also part of their ancient rites. Each tribe has a superstitious dread of the animal after which it is called, and never eats its namesake. They use the "ila," – hate or dread – in reference to killing it.

This little bit of information from Livingstone's time showed how far the Bang-am-watu (watu means 'man' or 'people') in particular had progressed beyond other tribes of Bechuanaland and elsewhere in Africa. This sudden development was, undoubtedly, due to the tribe giving up their pagan ways and their acceptance of Christianity.

But this assertion is jumping the gun at this stage, because the metamorphosis did not happen by chance nor did it come easily. It had to be fought over at a cost of lives.

It was David Livingstone who introduced Christianity and the Bible to the Bangamwatu tribe. To do that he had to perform the near miracle of crossing the Kalahari Desert and discovering Lake Ngami. Livingstone is often written into history books as the first white man to cross that near waterless wilderness, but this is most unlikely since there were certainly white hunters gathering ivory there before the missionary's time. Indeed, I was surprised to learn from his own book, *First Expedition to Africa*, on his famous journey he was accompanied by two Englishmen, Messrs Oswell and Murray, and that they travelled by ox-wagon and horse. Nevertheless, that journey across the Kalahari Desert was the stuff that makes history. The natives said it couldn't be done except perhaps in special times or years. They, the natives, had never gone there and knew nothing of what lay 'over the rainbow'. Finding enough water for their animals and themselves in the heat of the day was a remarkable achievement, but they did it. And now we come to the moment in time that makes countries, or at least Botswana, as it is today.

As previously mentioned, the Bangamwatu tribe, as with most of the Bechuanas, was not as coherent as it latterly became. The change that was coming about was due to the Chief of the day, Sekgomi 1 who welcomed David Livingstone after his journey. During his stay Livingstone talked a great deal about Christ and Christianity and Sekgomi was impressed. No doubt the fact that the missionary spoke fluent Bechuana must have impressed the Chief. Interested and impressed Sekgomi may have been, but he would not accept Christianity.

But his eldest son, Khama, did. An erudite young man who saw the wisdom and knowledge of the white mans' ways from which his tribe could benefit. Khama embraced Christianity, much to the chagrin of his father. The tribe was divided and they fought a war over it. Khama won and took over the Chieftainship and his father was banished. So well did Khama govern he became known in history as Khama the Great.

Before going further into the conversion of the Bangamwatu tribe to Christianity I must put the record straight regarding the parts played by David Livingstone and his father-in-law, Robert Moffat. While it must be said that it was Livingstone who first introduced the Bangamwatu to Christianity and therefore could have claimed the first conversion if he had been that kind of man, in fairness to Robert Moffat it was he who was the backbone of the transition, the stalwart who saw his place, his life's work, as being with that tribe. Livingstone was a different kind of man. An irascible doer of things, not an easy person to get along with; a man driven by an iron will to take Christianity into the very depths of the Dark Continent where no white man had gone before. A man who looks beyond horizons, not a teacher who gladly spends his life in one classroom and thrills at the man who stands before him, while remembering the little boy with wondering, eager eyes he made into this adult, Christian person.

I have no wish to deprecate David Livingstone in any way, nor laud Robert Moffat's pastoral role. They were just two different people at the very opposite ends of their spectrum, both in their own way doing remarkable good for emerging Africa. In the end they parted company, with Livingstone, after sending his wife and children back to Scotland, disappearing for years into the depths of uncharted territory and Moffat to his Mission School.

Like Livingstone, Robert Moffat was a Scot, (1795-1883) born in Ormiston, East Lothian. Owing to his early Christian beliefs, he gave up his job as a gardener and with little training, he was sent by the London Missionary Society to South Africa (1813-73). After some seven years in southern places he went north into the hinterland that was Bechuanaland, where few white people had gone before, and settled in the tiny Missionary

Station of Kuruman (modern spelling, *Kudumane*) where he lived for forty-nine years with his wife, Mary. Some years after, he was joined by David Livingstone who stayed in association with him for nine years and, as noted, married their daughter, Mary.

Robert's young life as a gardener proved a great asset to all for by his own hands he built a paradise. More and better houses, gardens of flowers and vegetables and, best of all, running streams and shady trees and grass meadow. But above all that, his missionary work was sublime. He became fluent in Tswana and other dialects and most important of all, he translated and printed both The Old and New Testaments of the Bible. As an aside, one wonders however did he get a printing machine up as far as the Kalahari Desert and did he first have to teach the raw natives to read their own language before tackling the Bible?

Between the two, Moffat and Livingstone, the Bangamwatu tribe owe, to a great extent, who and what they are, indeed, what the whole of Botswana, the country, is today. Without those missionaries' Christian endeavours, Bechuanaland would have been gobbled up long ago by South Africa and the most trouble-free, advanced and least corrupt country in Africa would never have developed.

***

To go back to those early, embryonic years, not only did Khama take the Bangamgwatu into Christianity, he banished all the tribe's folklore and fetishes, animal-worshiping, child circumcision and initiation ceremonies, these latter practices in the tribe's rituals, being particularly brutal. He even banished all beer and spirits. Perhaps most contentious of all for native African tribes, Khama declared polygamy illegal. Since the beginning of time, if a man could afford it, he could take as many wives as he wanted. No doubt, one would assume that as his wife grew older a man might look to a younger one and so on. But it was not always like that. Very often a man could be very happy with his lot and have no wish to give away some head of cattle to procure another young wife, but his No.1 wife might say she was feeling rather tired now, having had all these children to bear and bring up, prepare and cook all the meals, look after the house, dig and plant the garden – men do none of these 'women's chores' – so he had better think of getting himself a younger wife to help her, apart from anything else.

So what *did* African tribal men do in running the home? Well, when he was not actually fighting for his Chief, he had to be prepared at all times to defend his home and family, always to have his spear handy in case of attack, even if it was casually stabbed into the earth while he, the man of the house, was down on his hunkers, contemplating serious matters of great import behind half-closed eyes. And if they were travelling, the woman would carry all necessaries in a bundle on her head, latest baby in a sling by her breasts, which left her arms free to look after children big enough to walk beside her, and if necessary one hand given exclusively to the last toddler. Her husband, naturally, would be striding out in front, spear in hand, guarding his troop manfully, full of daring-do!

So one can see that many of his tribe were not very pleased at some of their Chief's big, new ideas. But they just had to put up with it all, for Khama the Great was not for turning. It was as well for the Bangamwatu that Khama 1 came along at the time he did. Dark, satanic clouds were already building up over Bechuanaland and without help, the indigenous people would soon become serfs.

The immediate trouble was the insurgents, the renegade Zulu army led by the great Mzilikazi. They had fled their own lands by the Swartberg Mountains, gone north and now claimed most of the land that would later be called the Transvaal. Already the Matabele had come as far west as Bechuanaland, but the Bangamwatu bested them, more by subterfuge, it may be said, than hand-to-hand fighting. It was the first time a Zulu-type *impi* (a group of Bantu warriors) had ever been destroyed by a non-Zulu army. On another occasion Mzilikazi pushed further west, where he met Robert Moffat. Though completely opposed to each other's beliefs and ways of life, they each formed a great respect and liking for each other that lasted all their days.

With Mzilikazi on his doorstep, Khama knew that the days of the Bangamwatu's freedom was merely a question of time. In addition, there was another serious matter, every bit as dangerous, and moreso, than the Matabele threat.

The Trek-Boers had arrived from the south! Their way with natives had long preceded them and Khama concluded the only hope for his tribe was with the British. He went to Robert Moffat who took aboard the Chief's fears and passed them on to the British Commissioner, no doubt emphasising that the Bangamwatu was the only Christian tribe in all Africa, but nothing much was heard of that matter for some time.

Khama then took the bull by the horns and with two of his senior leaders asked permission to go and see the Great White Queen in London. Miraculously, his wish was granted. One can only wonder what it must have been like for the Africans to have witnessed the clash of the two cultures, the great city of London and the Palace, contrasted against their mud and grass huts, together with Queen Victoria's Royal charm and the Africans' sense of wonder and awe. More to the point, Khama won the day and went home with Britain's assurance that from that day forward, Bechuanaland would come under the umbrella of British security and be known as the 'Bechuanaland Protectorate'. No more Matabeles or other tribes, no Trek-Boers or others to enter the land without permission or they would reckon on the might of the greatest nation on earth. The future looked good, but as is so often the case, there are rarely any 'Happily Ever After' fairy-tale endings.

The trouble came not from the Matabeles or the Afrikaners but from internal strife within the Bangamwatu themselves. And that was why I was living in comparative, Army-style tented luxury in the Bangamwatu grass-hut Capital of Serowe.

***

Little did I know, on the day I entered the Bechuanaland Protectorate, that I had happened into a country in deep crisis, even potential civil war. The trouble all started back in 1950, about the same time as I set out on my journey through Africa. This was, of course, the Seretse Khama business, in which, as heir-apparent to the Chieftainship of the Bangamwatu tribe, he had married Ruth Williams, an English woman.

This seemingly innocent love story nevertheless set off a chain of events that could have ripped the tribe apart and sparked a whole range of trouble with South Africa. This then, being an internal affair, was the reason why Britain had sent in a battalion of police rather than army in order to stabilise the situation. Even after five years the tribal atmosphere was still a tinder box.

Police they may have been, but they looked for all the world like soldiers. They dressed in khaki uniforms, wore solar topees (helmets) like soldiers of the time, drilled like solders, carried rifles like soldiers and swore like troopers. They were a great bunch of chaps and we fell in together like old comrades. I felt at home with them.

On my first morning in Serowe, I wandered downtown to the centre of the great African town. I liked the atmosphere, the feel of the place, the smells, the women with and without sarongs, carrying huge bundles or water pots on their heads, walking in bare feet, so upright, so graceful, so poised, so African. I had not seen or smelled the like since crossing the Limpopo on the way south.

Near the centre of the town there was a wide-open space in front of the Tribal offices. Here there were shady trees and a semi-circular wall a couple of feet thick, made of stakes driven into the ground; a protection against the prevailing wind. In this area quite a number of men squatted on the hard-beaten, earthen floor, while in the centre sat a man reclining on a folding deckchair. While most of the natives were dressed in African wrap-round cloth, the man in the chair wore a pair of well-worn trousers, a rather frayed Harris tweed jacket and was crowned with a battered brown, felt hat. The man was Rasebolai Kgamane, the incumbent stand-in Chief of the Bangamwatu people. Only a fortnight before my arrival he had been appointed 'Native Authority', a term used to cover the time until the Chieftainship business was settled. Whatever the euphemism of the day, Rasebolai *was* Chief in every way. He may not have looked like a King, but he had the reputation of a strong character. I was told he was a non-drinker and non-smoker and that he had been a Regimental Sergeant-Major during the war.

This special area where the proceedings were taking place was known as the *'Kgotla'* or the High Court of Justice, the Assizes, and Rasebolai was Judge and Jury. I learned that there were other Kgotlas of lesser standing in some smaller villages, but this one in Serowe was the highest in the land. Yet there was little pomp or ceremony; Rasebolai, laid back easily in his creaky chair, listened quietly to the plaintiff or accused, and with little ado summed up his justice, which was quietly accepted.

Interested, I stood and watched the proceedings. I realised that this was a very special meeting. I had listened for some time to his words of wisdom without understanding a word, when, between cases, he looked over and said in perfect English for me to join him. Someone was sent running to fetch a chair, an ordinary, straight-back table-chair, not as grand as his throne but, nevertheless, gratefully received. Obviously he had heard of my coming and knew I was with the police, but no doubt assumed I was some kind of official. Little did he know I was a mere tramp, a 'bum' as our American cousins would say. Not only did he welcome me into his Court, but he sent someone to run post-haste to fetch a very special man. Peter Sebina, Headman of the Bakalaka, came in measured gait and haughty bearing, clothed in a dazzling, white towel thrown round his neck and down his back, looking for all the world like a Roman Senator. He addressed me in very posh English, 'I, Peter Sebina, welcome you and am pleased to be at your service and assistance.' Standing in high, elegant pose, I almost expected him to doff a huge Cavalier hat with swept-up side and ostrich plume and bow to the knee with a swirl.

I was seated a couple or so paces behind Rasebolai so as not to be part of the court proceedings. At Sebina's grand eloquence Rasebolai swung his head to the side and said in Tswana, something that seemed to have an edge to it, such as – to use another Americanism – 'cut the cackle and just tell the man what he wants to know'. Whatever, it cut Sebina down to size and it was a more humble man who translated some of the proceedings and explained why they were happening.

The following is a straight lift from my diary of the day, showing the Royal line of the Bangamwatu tribe.

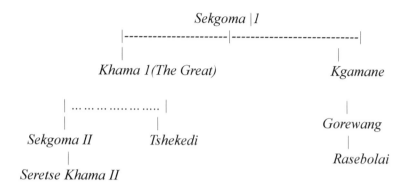

Information from Peter Sebina, Headman of the Bakalaka

Khama died 1923. Sekgoma II died 1925. Seretse Khama was then four and a half years old. Tshekedi was recalled from college to take over the Regency. Seretse went to Oxford to study Law. There he married Ruth Williams, without first consulting the tribe. When he came back to the tribe the marriage was frowned on. Then he was allowed to return to finish his studies in England. While there rumours started in Serowe that Tshekedi was trying to stop Seretse from coming back so that he would become Chief. The rumours got so much of a hold that the tribe swung to the Seretse side and said they wanted him back.

To his credit, Sebina was no ordinary man and in many ways had the right to hold his head up high. He was the tribe's historian. It was he who was responsible for keeping written, detailed records of the daily running and events of the Bangamwatu people. The main events of the time, going back nearly five years, was Seretse Khama's marriage to Ruth Williams, a white woman, which had split the tribe asunder and was destined to go on for quite a few more years.

It was all the problem of the 'colour bar', the division of blacks and whites in Africa, but particularly in South Africa, where the majority of Afrikaners were vehemently opposed to the union of the two races.

And so dark thunderclouds began to build up over all South Africa and Britain – all because two young people had decided to marry. The furore this caused went far beyond the frontiers of Bechuanaland and nearly brought Britain to her knees. Unbelievable as this may sound, it is true.

The trouble lay with the Nationalist Afrikaners, the extremist right-wing group of the South African Government who advocated 'apartheid', i.e.

segregation of people by skin colour. For nearly fifty years the British-type United Party had won every election and its *laissez-faire* style Government allowed people of all colours to rub-along fairly well. Sure, whites had certain privileges, such as having their own queue in the post offices and the like, but on the whole there was little trouble.

All this changed when, in the last election, the Nationalists won and stood the country on its head. From day one they wanted to turn the clock back fifty years and put 'the blacks back where they belonged', well away from the white domain, except when coming in to work.

And it was said, the 'Nats' were going to manipulate the constituencies so that United Party would never get in office again.

Within days a plethora of new laws were driven through Parliament. The Mixed Marriage Act made marriages between races illegal and the Immorality Amendment Act made sexual intercourse between different races an indictable offence, and so on. In this atmosphere one can imagine how incandescent the South African government must have been when the Seretse/Ruth story broke in Bechuanaland, literally on the South African doorstep.

Although they had no rights in the matter, the Cape Town Parliament immediately demanded that Britain have the marriage annulled. Britain refused, naturally, but there were unseen political currents of diabolical intensity that put Britain in very dire straits and made South Africa cock-a-hoop that they would get their way in the end.

To understand the whip-hand that South Africa's National Party believed they had over Britain, we must go back to days of World War II and after it. The greatest secret that the USA shared with Britain at that time was the Atom Bomb. Through all of its development Britain shared in the making of it and for her assistance the USA promised they would do likewise towards the making of a similar one for Britain.

As I go on, I can feel the reader cringing with exasperation ... what has all this to do with Seretse Khama and his young, English wife? But *bide-a-wee* and you will find it does tie up ... and I'm nearly there!

After the war, dramatically ended by the USA dropping two atom bombs on Japanese cities, the Americans kept their promise to Britain... nearly. The essential ingredient to make that bomb is uranium of which the USA had a supply and Russia has oodles. But with the change of presidents, America reneged on Britain and she was left high-and-dry, two steps down the world pyramid of power, with the USA and Russia vying for the top position. Without uranium and with her Empire dwindling, Britain could be shouldered out of world politics in very short time.

Uranium, the silver-white, radioactive element is not easy stuff to come by. There was one source that Britain had assumed she could rely on during the complex build-up of the bomb, and that was South Africa. When the United Party and Jan Smuts were in power it was taken for granted that Britain would have all the uranium she wanted. But with the flip of the political coin landing on the wrong side, Britain was out in the cold and a jubilant Nationalist Party Government said they would do no business with Britain unless she went along the road of apartheid and forced the break-up of the Khama marriage.

Had Britain gone along that road, her status in Africa would have been nil and South Africa would have taken over Bechuanaland, which the Boers had long coveted, especially since precious minerals had been found there. The Afrikaners would have poured in, taken over the land and forced the natives into segregated areas in the most useless places.

Britain did dally for a time while assessing the situation, and more than one travel book I read assumed that she had lost the will to be bothered with Africa. But far from that assumption, things were at fever pitch in London in efforts to sort out the Bechuanaland/South African affair, the doing of which was one of Britain's most closely guarded secrets. Less than half-a-dozen members of the innermost Cabinet in London were privy to the goings-on that were, to my knowledge, never exposed. In the end, however, Britain fulfilled her obligation to Botswana and the Seretse/Ruth affair was eventually settled after some years. Seretse never was made Chief of the tribe, but great modern developments evolved in the tribe's constitution and Khama was made President and proved a most enlightened leader of the country. He died in July 1980 and was survived by his wife Ruth and their two sons

As for Britain, following her successful machinations to thwart the South African National Party's effort to take over Botswana, she got her bomb!

And the South African Nationalist Party Government? It destroyed itself by its draconian measures toward the black Africans who rose up against the tyranny they perpetrated and in the end destroyed 400 years of white rule.

CHAPTER 7

NO SIRENS IN GHANZI

Tuesday, 2nd June, 1953, as recorded in my diary, was a very special day in Serowe and throughout the world in all the British Empire, Colonies, Protectorates, Dominions and Home, 'over which the sun never sets'… for this was Coronation Day when Queen Elizabeth II would be crowned in London.

For weeks the Police and African troops had been 'bulling' their uniforms and boots and practising their drill. Now, at last, the great day had arrived with due pomp and ceremony.

Assistant Superintendent Wittsitt with Sub-Inspector Bob Martin as his henchman to back him up led the parade down on the football field and the District Commissioner took the salute. It all went off very well, even though one of the Africans dropped his rifle and the bugler had so much stage fright he blew more wind than sound when blowing the Retreat.

In the afternoon there was a picnic and gala on the grass, with children's races and even a few for older people too. After the races Coronation mugs were presented to all the children. Looking back down the years it seemed no time since I, a ten-year-old schoolboy of the day, also got a Coronation mug at the previous Coronation in 1937 when Queen Elizabeth's father, George VI was crowned. I noted in my diary of the day, *'I was just the same age as those children here today'*. Time flies!

A couple of days after the Coronation I said my goodbyes to my police friends and set off once more. It felt good to be on my own again, the only person in the world and feel the miles thump under my feet. My route actually lay back on my tracks from Serowe to the railway from where I intended to head north. This was all elephant country, but I had little fear of them, knowing that, unlike carnivorous animals, they would not bother me if I didn't bother them. I had not the faintest expectations of a lift in this empty part of the world and expected to take three days to arrive. However, about midday a lorry came along and the surprised, white driver stopped and asked if I did this for a living or did I want a lift. "Both," I said loquaciously and gratefully gave him my company. He burned me up with questions on how I came to be there and the miles rolled by until, after some hours, we arrived at Palapye. It had been a very bumpy ride, but who was I to complain? In my short time in the country I had come to know that the B.P. roads were the worst in the world.

Palapye, like Mahalapye, was only a railway station and a hotel and some houses scattered about. I picked a spot under a tree to sleep, pitched my tent and had a big fire going ready to cook something when someone came from the hotel with an invitation from the manageress to spend the night there instead of sleeping out. '*Hospitality is definitely better where the European communities are the smallest!*' I wrote in my diary.

At the time of writing Bechuanaland was a most unusual country, two-thirds Kalahari semi-desert and a third the beautiful Okavango lake and river delta. The strange thing about this land is that the river and lakes never ran into the sea. Somewhere on the edge of the Kalahari all that water ran underground and was lost. Winston Churchill, and no doubt many others, said when he went there at the time of the Boer War, "Why can't all that water be harnessed and diverted into the desert to make it fertile?" That seemed an obvious conclusion, but at what cost and so few people lived there? As it is, from what I have heard from modern tourists, a great deal of the lakes have gone, dried-up. Can it be that global warming is to blame? Or is it just the way of the world? Once, even the Kalahari was wet and fertile.

I had heard from people I met of the strange, contrasting wild and beautiful ecology of Bechuanaland and I determined to view it all.

I headed north and with a couple of small hitches and a lot of walking I arrived at Francistown, a sizeable town for Bechuanaland in that era. I had a yen to head up the old hunters' white chalk road, but that would have taken me north too quickly, for I still had a lot to see in this country. I intended to take the long road westwards that would take me well into the interior to Maun and, by an incredible coincidence, I met the man in charge of the Wanela business here and we chatted. 'Wanela', or to give its full name, Witwatersrand Native Labour Association was the organisation that recruited men for the gold, diamond and copper mines in South Africa. They scoured all countries east, west and north, gathering in the new labour force and returning the veterans of a year or two. The worker can stay longer if he wants to and if he is wanted by his employers. Some natives walked hundreds of miles to one of these centres to get employment. I had met the Wanela organisation in Mozambique and was familiar with their ways but had never travelled with them. This time things were different.

In Francistown, by remarkable chance, I met Mr Warren the representative and the man in charge of this area. He was friendly and intrigued by my journey. To help me along my way, as he said, he gave me a free ticket to Maun and Mohembo, worth £10, a lot of money in those days and a fortune to me.

By luck, a truckful of expats from South Africa was expected to arrive that evening and would go on their way towards Maun early in the morning. I was up and raring to go before sunrise. But we were late in starting because some of the natives had got drunk and caused some trouble with the police the previous night and were being held over for questioning. We got under way just after noon.

The huge, diesel truck was an open vehicle with wheels as big as tractors and heavy tyres like great balloons. They had to be for the 'roads' were mere tracks that had been carved out of the open terrain by these vehicles. The road between Francistown and Maun was the main road through the Protectorate going west and it was merely two tracks, like rails of loose sand and grass growing in between. The great vehicle was loaded up with drums of aviation spirit, bales of tobacco for some trader and spare springs etc. On top of the load sat about twenty returning natives.

For endless miles the truck just chugged along in low gear through the sand. Occasionally, a herd of springbok would suddenly appear and go bouncing away at high speed. Ostriches, two and three at a time would try to pace the truck. There were wildebeest too, as well as giraffe and zebra. I wrote in my diary, '*I am going right through the Kalahari Desert. This has been misnamed. It is not a desert in the strict sense of the word. It is really a land of low bush and sparse grassland, good cattle country. But you can go a couple of hundred miles between water holes. I find it very similar to the Ogaden desert in Somaliland*'.

It was dark when we arrived at Nata. This was only a Wanela camp with shelter for the Africans and a little hut meant for Europeans. There was no furniture in it so I slept on the cement floor. Anyway, it was shelter from the icy wind outside. In the early morning there was not much to see of the place, except a little trader's store with a hand-worked petrol pump outside. There appeared little else of the place, but at 5 a.m. on a bitter cold morning, who goes sightseeing?

Six a.m. brought the dawn and it was lovely to watch. Gradually the sky paled from black to purple then to mauve, afterwards to pink. The truck headlights faded away until they were hardly visible before being switched off. The land was beginning to come to life. A single wildebeest, startled from slumber by the truck lumbered off. A pair of kudu lifted their spiral horns and looked at us before dashing away. A herd of springbok scattered as we drew near. In the gloom of a tree shadow stood a lone bushman, naked except for a cloth round his middle. He crouched down as the truck passed. I was freezing inside the cab of the diesel.

The dawn seemed to thaw out the natives riding up the back of the truck. Above the roar of the diesel engine came the melancholy strain of a mouth organ and a few discordant notes as someone strummed on a guitar. With the sun, about 7 a.m., came the singing, the catcalls, the whooping and whistling that always accompanies a band of happy Africans. They were going home! Home to their wives and families. To the young men, for whom just a year ago a wife would have been a luxury too high above his means, even to dream of the idea, now had enough money for the 'labola', the thoughts of going home must have had added potency.

Suddenly the bush gave way to an endless sweeping grass plain with great patches of white – we had entered the great Makarikari salt-pans. Here there is game in profusion; springbok, hartebeest, wildebeest, gemsbok, zebra and giraffe.

We stop for breakfast at Odiakoe. The boys crowded round a huge three-legged pot on the fire and soon we are off again, on to Kanyu and beyond. All these names looked big on the map. Yet, in reality, they are only Wanela camps, merely a well and some huts, on average about seventy miles apart. This road was made by Wanela. In all the 300 miles from Francistown to Maun there is nothing save these camps, not a store or native village – desolation!

The miles seem endless. The truck grinds away the hours in the loose sand at a painfully slow rate. You get buffeted about in the cab and you are bruised and sore until you imagine you are in a tank careering across shell-pitted country. But then, suddenly, the scenery changes. From dry and semi-desert country we drove down a tree-shaded track. In front swept the gleaming, silver line of a river and the countryside was green and fresh. We had arrived at Maun.

At the depot I met Mr Boast, a big, broad man, the Wanela representative. He had been telephoned to expect me and immediately invited me to spend a few days with him and his wife.

Around the door of the office was a bunch of raw, native recruits who must have walked many, many miles to get there. What clothes they wore were in tatters. How they contrasted to the 'repats'. In a year they too will be returning as city slickers. Somehow I feel sorry. For the change is not necessarily for the better. The repats realise the awe with which their countrymen admire their fine clothes, their new, felt hats, their sunglasses with the wide, white-horned-rims, and how about those loud two-tone shoes and that one who is sporting a cane. They look an odd lot these repats. Some look like city dandies, some like circus clowns with big, gaily-coloured, bright yellows, greens and red patches on their clothes. Some have the seat of their trousers taken up with a nice, bright yellow cloth and the fronts of their legs with red. They are dusty and dirty after their long ride. Some have tied clothes round their new hats to keep them from getting dusty. Some wear balaclava helmets. All have gaily coloured tin trunks decorated with various decorations of spots and diamonds and there are the few who clutch fancy, flashy guitars.

The raw native in his blanket looks with big eyes at the people who were like them only a year ago. Is it possible that they too will become as wealthy? Everyone will be the envy of the village when he gets home. Oh! How the finger of the European moves across the face of Africa and changes all that it touches. I found myself feeling sorry for those who had been changed out of their natural mould and environs. 'Spoiled', one might say and wondered how it could be stopped. Then I mentally paused and mused: why should it be stopped, even if it was assumed that that were possible? Why should natives anywhere not change their ways in any way they please, even if there are those who would have them fossilised? If some Roman soldiers had been able to return to Britain three or four hundred years after they had left, they might have been appalled by the way the Brits had changed, for better or worse. Nothing can stop the world going round!

> *The moving finger writes and having writ*
> *Moves on: nor all thy piety nor wit*
> *Shall lure it back to cancel half a line*
> *Nor all thy tears wash out a word of it.*
> Omar Khayyam (Died AD 1123)

The five days I spent with Mr and Mrs Boast were most enjoyable. They made me feel so much at home and we made easy conversation. We went boating on the river, cleaving paths through the tangle of water lilies and journeyed on mini-safaris to places I had not seen on the truck.

On Thursday there was the annual race meeting here at Maun. Mostly native horses were run. What was more interesting and amusing though were the donkey races. A jeep drove at the back of them to make them run. Some of the jockeys sat right back on the donkey's hindquarters.

The Boasts wanted me to stay longer but though I would fain have done so, I wanted to go to a place called Ghanzi in the Kalahari, about 200 miles away to the south. Although I still had the part of my Wanela ticket to Mohembo in the northern Okavango, I had decided that I would rather head south to the deep Kalahari and, from what I had gleaned, Ghanzi was the deepest of the deep.

By all accounts it was an extremely isolated spot and very little traffic went there, at least not from the north where I was at the present time. Ghanzi was, I gathered, more accessible and connected to South-West Africa than Bechuanaland. Mr Boast warned me it would be a most difficult place to get to without one's own transport. Still, my mind was made up and Ghanzi it would be. What intrigued me most about the place was that it was the last place in Africa where some Bushmen, or San as they are referred to nowadays, still existed. Once these little people had had the whole of Africa, from the southern cape to the top of what is now Kenya, and perhaps even further north, before they had been all but slaughtered from existence by the coming of the Bantu Africans from the West and the white settlers from Europe.

When he saw that my mind was made up, Mr Boast said that there were two trucks going down as far as Cookie, over 100 miles towards Ghanzi, and he would see that I got on one. I liked my time with him and his wife and we all said our sorrows for my going.

For this part of my journey to Ghanzi I will take a straight lift from my diary of the day and hope it gives something of the feeling that rises in me as I read it.

Saturday, 13th June, 1953

Set out about 2.30 p.m. today with these two trucks taking poles for fencing down to Cookie. These poles are imported from the Union (South Africa) so the fencing must be an expensive operation. In one place a veldt fire was sweeping across the road and we had to beat out a path through it before driving on.

It was unfortunate that it was dark by the time we crossed Lake Ngami, that dried-up lake bed which was a great expanse of water when Livingstone passed through this area last century.

It was about 11 p.m. when we made camp in the bush. There is a big fire going. The two fellows I have come with have brought mattresses and loads of blankets and karosses, even sheets and pyjamas. This is the way the local people 'rough' it in Africa! I notice that is the practice wherever I go.

Sunday, 14th June, 1953

Rather a special day considering it is my birthday – my 26th: getting old now, well into my second quarter century!

This morning I went with the truck to the point where they dumped the poles. I learned that Cookie was only a position on a map and nothing else. I bade goodbye to the truck owners then realised I was in a bit of a fix – I was out in the blue and well off the main road. Luckily, the fencing contractors came along and said they would take me down to the main road to a man who was building a store there. There were two of them, both Afrikaners. They had a tractor and trailer, so I got on the trailer. It was nine miles to Mr Taljard's place.

[The 'main road' I mentioned earlier was just open, grass veldt plain, miles and miles of it, with only the tractor marks over it to mark the position we were going. How any white man could think of building a 'shop' there seemed ludicrous.]

I was surprised at Mr Taljard's camp. He has only a shelter of two walls against the prevailing wind made from the corrugated iron sheets that will form the roof of the store when it is built. He has beds and a chest of drawers with a big mirror. His wife and two other women live with him. One is old and looks like either his or his wife's mother, and the other is deformed. These Afrikaner women certainly follow their men folk wherever they go. It is characteristic of them that when a strange man is introduced they never say a word.

Later, I was invited to eat. The wife fanned the flies off us with an ostrich feather as we ate. We men sat at the table. The women ate later. The fare was the same as you will get at any South African Dutchman's home – meat and rice. They don't vary their diet much be they rich or poor.

But apart from being invited to eat and the many cups of coffee that were brought round at intervals I was almost completely ignored. The three other men sat together and spoke in Afrikaans all the time, the women were sullen and quiet and went about their business. I felt awkward as if my presence was resented. I was experiencing what I had heard about so often. The fact that the Dutchman reckons that Afrikaans is the only language and that it is up to a foreigner to learn to speak it. A few like these people refuse to speak English although they are fluent in it. It's the old Boer war feeling that is still alive. However, in the afternoon Mr Taljard said he was going on 16 miles by donkey cart to the next farm and he would take me with him.

It was about 3 p.m. when we started out. Once on the road together he was quite amiable and spoke away in his broken English. The cart was loaded up with the engine of an old car and part of the car body which Mr Taljard was taking to his neighbour, Mr Berger. But also, I think, he was going over to show off his new cart that he had made. For this was no ordinary cart. Although there was a team of six donkeys to pull it, there was also a steering wheel device. He had broken away from the orthodox cart. His idea was that if the donkeys galloped through bushes and stumps, instead of bumping into everything he could steer the cart round them.

Two boys ran at either side of the donkeys whipping them up. Everything would go fine until the donkeys took it into their heads to leave the road and dash off into the bush and no amount of whipping would stop them. The cart would career about like a mad thing, bumping over holes and bushes. Mr Taljard would be in a frenzy at the steering wheel trying to zigzag the cart round the obstacles while the donkeys crashed over them. Eventually they would stop and allow themselves to be led back to the road. Then we would go off again.

It was dark when we arrived at Mr Berger's farm. As we drew near lanterns began to swing and people walked towards us. After the exchange of greetings the others began to take notice of the new cart. Lanterns were held close to inspect the innovations.

"Alle Magtig," exclaimed one.

"Wragtig jong!" added the other. "Ware is die dusselboom?"

[In my time in South Africa I had lived with and met many Afrikaners and, naturally, gathered some of their language, but I'm not sure if my spelling is correct.]

But after a longer inspection Mr Berger shook his head and stroked his chin. He was sceptical about this newfangled idea. It was plain he preferred the old type.

The house is just a tin shack. A temporary abode until a house is built. The night is cold so they had a brazier inside the hut. We were given a meal of biltong, eggs and bread. Although I have seen and eaten plenty of biltong, this is the first time I have had it put to me as an actual meal.

Monday, 15th June, 1953. The Kalahari Desert on the way to Ghanzi.

Today I added yet a new mode of transport to my collection. Yesterday it was donkey cart, today it was horseback. Mr Berger said he would like to help me on my way. We were well off the road so there was no chance of getting a lift even if there was any transport there. However, he said he would lend me a horse to ride to the next farm, 15 miles away. He asked if I could ride a horse. I lied when I said "yes". I have never been on a horse in my life.

A horse was saddled and a donkey loaded with my kit. I was a bit apprehensive about finding my way across the veldt to the next farm, but I didn't want to show it. I was given instructions "Follow the track down about five miles. Strike west when you come to the 'Waggebiejie' (Wait-a-bit) bushes. You can't miss them, there are lots of pot holes with white stones round them that the 'Morama' roots have pushed up during the rains. Head for the tall trees over on the horizon then you will come to the path you must follow to get to Meneer Cotzer's farm."

I tried to look confident, but it was with a funny feeling in my stomach that I set out. The veldt was like a sea, every tree looked identical. A mistake on my part may mean disaster for you could wander for a month in this veldt without coming across any place of habitation. I had in mind the tale told of the Police Officer at Ghanzi a few years ago who wandered some way away from his truck and never found his way back. By a million to

76

one chance he was saved a few days later when he happened into some Bushmen. He was more dead than alive.

However, I managed to find my way all right. But as the time wore on I began to feel sore with the riding. I just sat and walked the horse the rest of the way – I didn't try any trotting or galloping! Towards afternoon I felt as if my body would fall apart. I feel horrible now as I write. Maybe a good sleep will put me right. Mr Cotzer received me with surprise but gave me a good welcome and a good meal.

His house is the usual humble abode of these Afrikaner farmers. Mud walls and thatched roof. There is the solid table, the hard chairs, the big trunks or chests, three or four rifles in the corner and 'karosses' on the beds. Even in the bedrooms biltong is hung up to dry.

Apparently I have landed rather lucky again. Mr Cotzer is travelling by donkey cart to another farm 22 miles away tomorrow to dig a well. He gets paid £2 per foot. He expects to go down 40 ft. So I will go with him. The farm he is going to is well off the beaten track but it is in the Ghanzi direction.

Tuesday, 16th June, 1953

After a breakfast of 'mabela' (kaffir corn – millet) porridge, coffee and rusks we were on our way. Four donkeys were harnessed to the cart. It was the orthodox kind with the single tram or 'dusselboom'. Now I agree that Taljard's cart with the steering wheel was no good. It is much better to have reins to guide the donkeys. We kept at a steady trot all the time whereas with Taljard's we could only go to the speed of the boys who ran at the side.

Mr Cotzer couldn't speak English very well. Nevertheless he tried to make conversation.

"This my motor car," he would say with pride and a laugh. Then, pointing to the donkeys, he would say "Engine". Holding up his whip he would add "Petrol". When the donkeys galloped he would say "Top gear" and "Low gear" when they walked. Everything would go fine until I started whistling, then the donkeys would stop. I couldn't understand it until Mr Cotzer said with a laugh "Brake".

The donkeys had been trained to stop at a whistle and they were only too ready to comply when I unwittingly gave the signal. Three times I halted them like this. It was a day for whistling. The sun was bright: the track we were following was almost overgrown so it seemed as if we were driving through virgin country, a slight breeze fanned my cheeks and there was melody in the jingle-jangle of the harness. Before I could realise it unconsciously I broke into whistling a tune. Then it would happen. The donkeys would stop.

I dropped off the cart when Mr Cotzer headed away south. I watched the cart drive into the haze then realised I was in for a night in the veldt. The next farmer was 12 miles from where I left the cart. I reckon I've covered about seven of them. Although it is moonlight I don't think it would be wise to attempt the last five miles. Lions roam at night and it's hard to follow the path I'm on even in daylight. I'll get there tomorrow. I've fed off biltong and bread and my fire is burning brightly.

I wonder what they are doing at home now. Sometimes it seems a long, long time since I left. How I would like to see them all again!

Wednesday 17th June, 1953, Kalahari

I came to Mr Crail's farm this forenoon. I went in to get my water bottle filled. Mr Crail was away but his manager, Mr Fisher, was there. He regarded me suspiciously through the gauze mosquito door. I suppose it is queer to have someone in a kilt carrying a pack and sporting a revolver at his belt, appear out of the bush on foot in a country where walking between two places is unknown. At first impression they generally regard me as an Army deserter on the run, and perhaps desperate.

Mr Fisher finally decided to risk a meeting. After he had decided I was neither a robber nor desperado he welcomed me and invited me to lunch. It was an early lunch and I set out straight away to try and reach the next farm 12 miles away before dark.

Walking in loose sand is the most trying thing I have done. It's like walking in deep snow. That's 17 miles I've done today and it seems like seventy. Before I reached Barton's farm my pack felt like a ton instead of the normal 80 or so lbs. However, I made it. When I arrived I found Mr Barton had gone and the house empty. I camped nearby because I needed the water. It had been a very welcome sight when I saw his windmill.

[Later I learned that Mr Barton was the richest man in Ghanzi.]

Thursday, 18th June, 1953, Ghanzi

Walked the last 13 miles into Ghanzi camp today. All loose sand too. Ghanzi is not even a village. It is a district. The names on the maps are merely farms. Where I was heading and am now is the 'camp' – D.C. office, police depot and other administrative offices – the nucleus of the district.

I met Mr Midgley the D.C. He welcomed me to the district and offered me accommodation in the Government rest hut. So I am O.K. It has been some journey from Maun – truck, donkey-cart, horseback and walking – variety!

So began my time in Ghanzi. I soon realised how fortunate I was in meeting and hitting it off so well with Mr Ernest Midgley, the District Commissioner, for so many interesting things and fond memories emanated from our new and easy friendship. Mrs Midgley too was so friendly and warm and knowledgeable on the ways and history of the Bushman and other African people. We corresponded frequently after I left Ghanzi and I kept her notes for future reference.

The Midgleys had two children, a boy and a girl, whom I did not meet since they were at boarding school in Cape Town. At that time white children did not begin school until they were seven years old. Since most families were scattered throughout the Union it meant that the majority of children boarded and it was thought that seven was the earliest age suitable for children to be separated from their parents and family. And if it was thought that the many children in distant, remote places in the wild and woolly South African *bundu* had a hard time to make it to school, then Ghanzi was an even more lonely, empty and forbidding place for young, unchaperoned children to make the journey to the Cape. First they had to go 200 miles in a great, thunderous truck driven by a local Afrikaner man who swigged whisky from a bottle he carried in his hand as he drove, through Bechuanaland's Kalahari Desert and on into South-West Africa (*Namibia*) to Windhoek and thence by train nearly 1,000 miles to Cape Town.

There is an interesting little addendum to my 'long-time-ago' friendship with the Midgleys which is rather interesting and up to date. My wife and I had a telephone call from a very close friend, Harvey Griffiths, a retired naval padre and vicar, who lives quite near. Harvey went on to say that he and his wife, Jean,, were entertaining a long-time naval colleague and his wife and, knowing she had grown up in Bechuanaland, he had brought out his copy of my book, *A Tramp in Africa*, whereupon she had knocked the wind out of his sails by saying, 'Oh, that's David Lessels, my dad used to tell us about him.' She was, of course, Fay, the daughter of Mr and Mrs Midgley whom we now meet frequently.

Part of my reason for including this incident is that Fay and her husband, George, lived only a couple of hundred yards from Portsmouth College of Art where I had taught for over twenty years and during a number of those years Mr Midgely had lived with them. Unfortunately he had died before the dinner party meeting. What a shame, so near for so long! It would have been wonderful if we had been able to meet and remember old times. All my fault ... I should have written my book years ago. *C'est la vie!*

So, such was Ghanzi then. I dare say that it will have come up in today's modern tourist world, but half a century ago Ghanzi was the loneliest moon-world, forbidding and foreboding to any British Government Officer unlucky enough to be posted there. All officials given this post were strongly advised, ordered, in fact, to have all their teeth taken out and have false ones made. As at Ghanzi, where dentists and doctors were 200 or 300 hundred miles away at least and primitive roads impassable at times, an officer debilitated by toothache with no hope of solace, was not a working asset. So it was, in the interest of the Empire, for all Government officers in remote places to have their teeth removed. I believe Mrs Midgley refused, but Ernest had his removed.

From this it may be gathered that Ghanzi was not the ultimate posting one might hope for when one's number came up for change in the rolling drum at the Whitehall Tombola Club. In fact, Mrs Midgley told me that Ernest was not popular in the Colonial Service because, being a staunch Quaker, he neither smoked nor drank alcohol, nor kept the wherewithal for either of these abominations in the house for visitors.

Strangely enough, they got very few visitors! Mrs Midgley was quite sure that that was why Ernest had been banished to the nether land of Ghanzi where no one ever wanted to go, nor even visit. A little tale that Mr Midgley told me summed up Ghanzi.

A year or two before I was there, a magazine journalist came to do a piece on Ghanzi. At that time all telephone calls had to be made from the D.C.'s office by wireless to Mafeking, from where any message could then be routed by wire to its destination. This meant that on the Bechuanaland side the 'World and his Mistress' could listen in to any conversation. This said, the journalist made his call to his wife in Jo'berg. During their conversation she said to him, "I hope you're not playing fast and loose with any of the Sirens there," whereupon he replied, "Believe me, there are no Sirens in Ghanzi".

The simile relating to the ancient Greek tales of beautiful mermaids, half-woman and half-fish, luring sailors to their death is so ridiculous because in the Ghanzi environs there is no water of note where sea-nymphs could live and cavort and have their evil way with lovelorn men.

Looking back on my time in Ghanzi it occurred to me later that the reason why Ernest Midgley and I got on so well together was that neither of us smoked nor touched alcohol. This was not from any religious or other pressure on my part. I just never liked either and never felt the need to develop or acquire the habits. I must confess that in latter years I have acquired a taste for a 'sundowner' of an evening, but that did not start until my late middle-age, when there were no more mountains to climb.

I liked my time in Ghanzi. I liked the sheer remoteness of the place, the primitiveness of the land and its people, the excitement of just being there. If this was the nadir of Britain's imperialistic responsibilities in Africa then Ghanzi and its environs was, to me, still a wonderful and interesting place to be.

Most interesting of all Ghanzi's charms and wonders were, of course, the Bushmen. Here in the Kalahari Desert, their last sanctuary on Earth, the last remnants of the people who once owned all of the African continent from the distant South where the Indian and Atlantic Oceans meet and North as far as today's Kenya and perhaps even further. Over all this great landmass of Africa and for untold centuries, the Bushmen were the only human inhabitants, the only people on Earth as they knew it.

But in a comparatively modern time of Bushman history they were all but slaughtered by the Bantu Africans who came from the west of Africa and the white Europeans who came and colonised the southern part of Africa. To be fair to the early Bantu people and Europeans, they had reason to believe that the Bushmen were more animal than human. Both lots of 'big people' saw the Bushmen as vermin who killed their cattle and other animals and therefore had to be 'put down'. Now the last remnants of these interesting, artistic and unusual people are to be found only in the Kalahari Desert, in the environs of Ghanzi.

The Bushmen are quite different to other black Africans. What makes them so unique is their bodies, which have developed to best suit their environment, and so can exist where other humans would die. Unlike no other humans, the Bushmen's bodies follow the pattern of some animals and plants by not excreting their body-waste and urine. This way, their metabolism turns the waste into fat so that when they have eaten well their food and water, now metamorphosed, can last a long time. This phenomenon, I learned, is known as *steatopygia*. They, like other people, would have to take some form of water after three to five days, which is for them supplemented by their ability to find water-rich foods like tubers, melons, etc. It follows that when the Bushmen's body larders are full their stomachs and buttocks are greatly distended and when hungry, their skin hangs like empty bags on them. Thus, unlike other people, their development allows the Bushmen to exist for longer periods without surface water in the desert.

My interest in the Bushmen goes a long way back, ten years or so before I went to Africa. Always an avid reader, I laid hands on any paper or book I thought might be interesting, especially if I thought I could learn from it. To this I have a memory, as a thirteen-year-old or so, of a bright sunny day lying on the grass of the railway banking, where the trains passed near our house. I was reading one of my dad's encyclopaedias and it was in there, not in Ghanzi, that I learned of the Bushmen's unusual body functions.

The phenomenon of the Bushmen's metabolism raises the interesting question of how did animals, birds and humans develop and why should the Bushmen be like no other humans? The two specialists on this subject were, of course, Lamarck and Darwin, each of whose conclusions widely differed.

The Frenchman, Jean-Baptiste Lamarck (1744-1829) concluded that acquired traits are hereditary, that changes acquired by organisms during their lifetime could be transmitted to their offspring. He put forward the developments in a giraffe, seeking to browse ever higher on the top foliage of trees on which it feeds, continually stretches its neck and the continuation of the habit results in a gradual lengthening of the limbs and neck. He also mentions the development of the camel that can store great quantities of food and water for long passages across a desert, and here we come again to the Bushmen. Followers of Lamarckism say there can be no doubt that individual organisms adapt themselves in various ways to their surroundings and environment.

In contrast to Lamarck's theory, Charles Darwin's (1809 – 1882) theory of life was based on the concept that nature will sort itself out and the strongest, those best suited to the environment, will win. He named his principle 'Natural Selection'.

The two theories of Lamarckism and Darwinism fought their way through the late 1800s and early 1900s, but in the end Darwinism won and is now the accepted principle taught in schools of learning today. Nevertheless, there are still those that hanker after Lamarck's opinions. Perhaps both factions are just barking up the opposite sides of the same tree and will meet at the top.

Think of this –it is now well accepted that the human race started in eastern Africa, the area in which we know the San Bushmen existed, long before they were slaughtered there by the Bantu tribes from the west, and the Nilotics and other big people from the north. If then, the Bushmen were the first people on Earth and had learned the power of speech and the ability to invent weapons such as spears and bows and arrows and learned to discover and develop poisons that killed animals but to which humans were immune when eating the meat, then many of those first humans must have dreamed they were in paradise where there was no pressing need to develop further. Those who did go on to further horizons and populate the rest of the world developed in so many ways by necessity, ecology, environment and whatever else that is needed or desired, as with (dare I say it?) Lamarck's giraffe.

So were the San Bushmen the first beings to cross from animal to humans? After all, they are the only humans who have the stomach for it!

***

My days with Mr and Mrs Midgley were interesting and friendly beyond the norm. Mrs Midgley told and showed me a great deal of the local African life that I would never have known by myself and Ernest took me to see caves and hanging rocks where Bushmen had painted wonderful pictures and etchings from aeons ago. Nearly all the pictures depicted the hunt, but there were others that captured the people dancing, perhaps in celebration of the food they had won and to the bravery of the hunters. I had seen similar paintings in the Drakensberg Mountains in Natal and the skills and media all were remarkably similar.

An interesting point: before fast cameras were invented, many people, experts no doubt, carped and lampooned the Bushmen artists because they never appeared to have got the feet, the hooves of running antelope etc., quite right. However, with the introduction of such cameras it was discovered that it was, in fact, the Bushmen who had got it right; the animal legs and hoof movements were as the San artists had painted them.

The rock paintings, therefore, were of particular interest to me, paint being in my blood. As apprentice, journeyman and paint specialist with ICI Paints Division and latterly a college lecturer on the subject, I feel I can write with some authority on the matter of paints and painting. I was approached by the City and Guilds of London Institute to write the examination papers at the Advanced Level for the UK and overseas countries, which I did for 20 years until my retirement. While still teaching, some years ago I had published in a technical journal a lengthy treatise on 'Paints and Painting in Ancient Egypt'. My research had been long and encompassed many interesting tomes and places, notably the British Museum. There I asked some questions of the staff, as a result of which I was invited to go upstairs into an inner sanctum where I was permitted to handle objects out of their glass cases and elsewhere.

From what I saw it was evident that the early Egyptians were skilled paint makers and craftsmen. To make paint, you must have pigments and a binder. The majority of paints were water soluble, but even in pre-dynastic times – about 5000 BC – the Egyptians already knew how to bind the pigment so that it did not rub off; something the ancient Greeks and early Romans could never do. At the height of their civilization – around the eighteenth dynasty – they were using a very clear resin varnish, a remarkable invention for that time and something that was only reinvented in Europe in 1300 AD Sometimes pigments were mixed with it, but mostly it was used as a protective coating over wooden coffins, wooden canopic boxes, painted pottery and on murals. Sometimes it was used over the whole mural and on others only the less fast colours, such as red, were coated. In places where it had been applied over white paint, even today the white is hardly discoloured.

Their skill in brush-making was not so marked. The brushes usually consisted of bundles of fibres of varying degrees of fineness, bound together with thin twine, or pieces of fibrous wood bruised or chewed at one end until the fibres were exposed in bristle form. Crude though they were, there is ample evidence of the excellent work of fine detail which was done with them.

In writing that particular paragraph I feel a spine-chilling shiver run up my back, a repeat of that which ran through me when, in the inner recess of the British Museum, I was allowed to take out of the glass cabinet the actual 'brush' pieces and handle them. When I held in my hand the little cutting-in brush and realised that the last man to use it had been alive 6000 years ago, I could almost feel the thrill, the bond, between him and me. Daft it may be, but I still shiver as I write.

My reason for including this piece on the paint technology and the application of it by the Ancient Egyptians may show a direct line to the Bushmen. After all, somebody had to start the ball rolling and, since the Bushmen with their rock paintings almost certainly pre-empted the early Egyptians and ancient Babylonians by thousands of years, we can surely assume that they, the Egyptians and all others, drew their early skills from those first humans on Earth, the Bushmen, who practised their empiric skills on cave roofs and the like, the last of whom exist only in the confines of the Kalahari Desert. It is interesting to note that all other paint-makers and artists throughout the world, since humans first arrived, owe their artistic beginnings to those little men.

***

'This is one of the biggest days in the history of Ghanzi and I reckon I was fortunate to be here.' So ran a day in my diary. After having written elsewhere that no self-respecting, high ranking British dignitary had ever deigned to set foot in this outlandish place, here was the 'daddy-of-them-all', barring Royalty, coming to see me. At least I assumed so, naturally! ... and that was exactly what happened. On this day the High Commissioner of the Territories visited Ghanzi.

For weeks there has been preparation. The new school, which was not quite finished, was hurriedly made to look presentable, for the dining hall was the only place big enough to accommodate all the people.

A few days before, Mr Midgley had said that I would have to move out of the Government rest house because it would be needed for the people coming with the High Commissioner. I said I would camp, and anyway, it was high time for me to move on. He wouldn't hear of that and said he would sort it out. A day or so later I was asked by a Mr Kinnear, a farmer, if I would like to come and stay with his family. I was delighted. What better place can there be to learn about people and their ways than living with them?

So I moved over to Mr and Mrs Kinnear's place. He had just started up his farm and all the family were living in tents. They were Afrikaner people whose first language was Afrikaans, but like most Afrikaners they also spoke English to varying degrees. The Kinnears had five children ranging from eighteen years to eighteen months, so it was a lively home.

I moved in on a Saturday and next day being Sunday was 'visiting day', just a drop-in on their nearest neighbours, 18 miles away. These farms in the Kalahari are vast, none less than 2,300 morgen *(a morgen is 2 1/8 acres, or a 100 yds square)* and some of them are 20,000 and 50,000 morgen. All are cattle ranches. Most of them run thousands of head of cattle.

Life on the farm was interesting and fun. I wrote in my diary, *'I'm learning to ride a horse. It's good fun, but sore'*. It sure was! My teacher, mentor and giggler was fourteen-year-old Sorrel, who, like all ranch farmers, was born in the saddle. Mind you, I don't know how they do it, but they do.

Next day, *'More riding. I'm sore but I'm determined to learn as soon as possible'*.

Next day, *'Rode a donkey bare-back today (the donkey had the bare-back, not me). A donkey has a sharp back-bone and I fell off more times than I care to count. When I jumped up on its back I landed back on its hindquarters. Immediately it started bucking. I did a marvellous somersault before touching down. Everybody was laughing including me. Mr Goyer, the police officer, said I must get back on to its hindquarters and stay there till it stopped bucking. Determined to see the thing through, I got on but didn't stay there. More laughter peeled out as I went down and a crowd of natives gathered. They must have thought it was rodeo day. But it was grand fun and I think the donkey enjoyed it too'*.

Next day, *'Came off the horse today. It stumbled and I went over its head. I didn't hurt myself, although I got tangled up in its legs when it went over me'*.

Next day, *'Fell off the horse again today. No damage done. Paying for my learning. The horse was galloping along at full tilt when it suddenly swerved to the left. I kept on going forwards'*.

As time went by I met quite a number of Afrikaner people. Most were friendly and interesting, but others I found rather, and even very, *dour*, as one might say in old Scots. One man I found most friendly, Mr Christian Lewis *(Levis)*, and he took me hunting for the pot on a couple of days. But we didn't even see a springbok. The veldt was empty, but I at least enjoyed the company and the stories he told of his life in Bechuanaland. Most absorbing were his tales of the annual cattle-run from the Ghanzi area to Mafeking *(Mafikeng)*, some 400 miles as the crow flies, but many more for cows who don't fly.

This was a fantastic story, one that, to the best of my knowledge, has never been fully told. There are mentions in books of cattle-drives going north, east and west out of Bechuanaland, but these are mere references from which readers get no idea of what the drives really meant. Bechuanaland, or *Botswana* as it is today, is a land-locked piece of country. When the early Afrikaner settlers came to this land they realised that this was ideal cattle country, so they bred them, thousands and thousands of them. But cattle have no commercial value until they go to an abattoir and that would be in South Africa. So once a year the round-up would take place and the great cattle-run, herded by the men on horseback, would be made across the country to the railway at Mafeking.

The going was tough and dangerous for the men as well as the animals. The danger came at night as that was the time lion came to make their kill. To do this they would roar to panic the herds into making easy meat for the killers. There was no way the men could put up temporary fences to guard their livelihood and it was all very dangerous for both man and beast. Christian Lewis said he had shot 157 lion and 15 to 20 leopard over the years he had done the cattle-run.

I also met his brother, an interesting man, in that he had killed a leopard with his bare hands, and had the scars and disfigurement to prove it. Shorter and stockier, with shoulders as wide as a barn door, one of them twisted out of shape through his encounter, he was the epitome of the tough Afrikaner character. On a dark night when guarding the cattle during the long trail, a leopard leapt on his back, as leopard are wont to do, and was already going for his jugular vein, its claws sunk deep into his flesh to get purchase. The brother, (I don't think I ever knew his name) with great strength and presence of mind, reached round and took the leopard by the throat and swung it round to his front, then with one arm round its back and the other pushing at its neck he bent it back until he broke the animal's back. Such are the stuff of which Afrikaners are made! No wonder they were hard to beat in the Boer War.

It is interesting to note how little was known of the Ghanzi and other cattle-drives in Bechuanaland, while the whole world knew all about the 'cowboy' era in the USA. So much was made of the American story in books, songs and later, films, and yet their cowboy tales pale in significance when compared with those of the Kalahari. The American cowboy story started with the end of their Civil War in the 1860s. The North needed beef and had very little and the South had plenty and wanted to sell it. So cattle-drives were developed; great herds of bovine beasts rounded up and driven on-the-hoof by horsemen over great distances from Texas and elsewhere in the South, all the way to the great stockyards at Chicago in the North.

It was a wild, historic time in America and the cowboys played their quixotic roles to the letter, all sitting easy on their saddles, all with lariats on the saddle-horns and all wearing wide cowboy hats and 'chaps' with thongs down their legs and six-shooter revolvers at their waist. All this according to the films. How well I remember those Saturday matinees!

While I have no wish to deprecate the American cowboys – they were all great guys and we loved them – but in the real world they had it easy compared to the cowboys of Bechuanaland. To the best of my knowledge, they did not have to drive their herds, horses and men, through hundreds of miles of waterless deserts and hope that the next well had not dried up. They did not have to contend with raging lions and leopards and other savage, predatory killers of man and beast, particularly in the depths of night: they did not …I could go on, but I'll stop it there, apart from to mention that while the American cowboys were sung about and lauded to the highest, the mainly Afrikaner cowboys of Bechuanaland lived their lives much more dangerously, more stressful and unsung than their US of A counterparts, and the Bechuanaland cowboy era also lasted much longer. The American cattle-drives history lasted a mere twenty years, from the end of their Civil War in 1865 until the late 1880s when the railways developed and took over the trade. The Bechuanaland cowboys had been at it for nearly a century, from the late 1890s to the 1980s, at which time, I am informed, a new tarmac road was made, allowing the cattle to be trucked to the railway at Mafeking. So ended a most exciting period in Africa's history.

***

And now we come to the great day, the most important, the biggest in the history of Ghanzi and I reckon I was fortunate to be there to witness the ceremony.

The morning was hectic in the Kinnears' household. Everybody had to put on their best clothes and children's faces were thoroughly cleaned. I wore my kilt, bush shirt and hat – my travelling companions of many campaigns, all showing their signs of wear and tear and obvious repairs with my deft make-do-and-mend stitching and patching, of which I was secretly very proud. Since day one of my journey through Africa I had carried my old army 'housewife', with which every soldier was issued in those days. It contained needles, thread, wool for darning socks and the like, and even buttons. A veritable treasure trove for a tramp like me!

I waited outside for the family to tumble out of the house when Mr Kinnear, breathless with all the effort, turned to me and looked askance. I couldn't possibly go like that, he said, half in Afrikaans in his dilemma. Did I not have proper clothes for this very special occasion? Quick, come with me and he gave me some of his own clothes to put on. I thanked him for his kindness, but I was adamant and said I was who I was and preferred to keep on my own clothes. So off we went, but, oh dear, worse was to come.

There was a good turnout and looking round at the crowd they looked almost 100% Afrikaners. All appeared what they were – farmers – and it was difficult to imagine that most of them were rich. Some looked as if they had just left the fields with rough, creased clothes, dusty shoes and unkempt hair. Others looked uncomfortable in collars and ties. Looking round, though, they all appeared good, homely people.

The ceremony got underway. There was music and drums and the High Commissioner of the Territories was introduced to the populace and speeches were made. After the pomp and ceremony, in good British tradition, tea was served. In the middle of this I was thunderstruck when Mr Midgley brought the High Commissioner over and introduced me to him. He was quite friendly and we had a cup of tea together. He asked about my journey and we spoke for quite a time. During our meeting, I could not help inwardly smiling at Mr Kinnear and his wife and friends whose faces were absolutely dumbstruck.

***

A day or two after the High Commissioner's visit I took my leave of Ghanzi. I said goodbye to Mr and Mrs Midgley and the Kinnears. Ernest was not happy about my going on foot and his wife even more so. She and I had struck up an instant rapport on African history and the local people and each enjoyed our conversations and later, by correspondence, even when I was well up through Africa. But I was resolute. I said that mine was a wandering life by desire and I knew within myself when it was time for me to move on.

My farewells to Walter Kinnear and family were different and very moving. They were such typical Afrikaner people that I regarded myself extremely lucky to have been a guest in their house. Maybe their ways were a bit different to ours: what if the children were not trained and created bedlam, and the boys ran barefoot all day and climbed into bed at night without washing them: what if the hens had a clear run of the place and squawked horribly and ran across the beds and left their droppings, and the youngest baby always had a dirty face: maybe their food was monotonously plain – rice and lumps of meat – yet I liked them. They were good people, good in heart I mean.

Walter Kinnear, the father, almost made me ashamed when I witnessed his faith. The way he said grace before meals and his sincere belief in the good of God and his fellow men made me feel so humble. Walter was big and slow and good as no other man I had met. They were poor people – he only managed the farm – yet the way they wanted to share and give the little they had touched me more than I could say. When Walter pressed one of his handkerchiefs on me as a present and keepsake and asked me "Please to remember your friends in Ghanzi", I appreciated it more than if he had presented me with a handful of notes. I kept that handkerchief for a long time as a talisman, but in the end it was lost… and thereby hangs a tale! But later…

When Walter wished me God's guidance and protection on my travels, his words felt so sincere I found it hard to answer. Funny how you can't find words when you want them most. There was only a constriction in my throat and I tried to make my eyes convey the thanks I felt. I found it more difficult to say goodbye to that man and his family than I did to most people I met along the road, and my life of that time was made up of continually saying "goodbye" to people as I passed in and out of their lives.

***

Once on the road, I had only been gone a couple of days when a large truck drew up beside me. The two fellows in the cab appeared thunderstruck to find me walking blasé on my own in the wilds and promptly offered me a lift when I said I was heading for Maun. I wonder if anyone who has not been in such a wilderness for days can appreciate what it is like to suddenly be offered a passage out of it. I know what it is like, but I doubt if I could put my intense feeling of relief into words.

There was room in the cab for the three of us and my rucksack went up the back. Also in the back was a little Bushman, small as a boy and wizened as a prune and all alone. The fellows said they were taking him to prison at Maun. They didn't know why, or what default he had committed. I thought how unusual: prisoner with no escort who could be relied on not to run away. Obviously Bushmen must be law-abiding to the extent they would accept their punishment and make no attempt to abscond.

Like all the roads in Bechuanaland the one we were on was, putting it mildly, terrible. The truck ground away in low gear for miles and miles on end, but I wasn't complaining. For the second time in my journey through the British Protectorate I crossed Ngamiland, the part known as the Native Reserve. This must have been one of the first terms or notices to be erased when the local people gained full control of their land.

Crossing this land I passed over Lake Ngami for the second time, but this time it was in daylight. This was the great lake that early historians had given David Livingstone the accolade of being the first white person to view. That, however, was almost certainly a misnomer for early elephant hunters and the like had brought back ivory and other trophies from this area before the great missionary had arrived there.

What was interesting was to find that Lake Ngami was a water mass by name only. Now there was not a drop of water in it. Where once sunbeams danced on the beguiling waves, the dried-up bed was home to withering and dying trees that stood like old men with withered, outstretched arms. Dead trees outnumbered the live ones. It was a pitiful and depressing land and now when we arrived, many of the trees were actually on fire.

It was hard to think how fires could happen in such a lonely area, but they do. A glass bottle stupidly thrown out of a car window can act as a magnifying glass and ignite a fire.

With the fire ahead, the two fellows stopped their vehicle and considered their and my options. The fire was over both sides of the 'road' and the smoke was heavy. What to do? How far into the forest did the fire go? Was this the start, so we would blast through quickly, or was it worse further in? Some of the trees were already burned out and just smoking, their barks crisp and done. We each had our say and decided to go through. Were we blasting into a holocaust or freedom? The fact that I am writing this gives the game away.

That night we made camp by a cluster of some low trees and bushes that sheltered us from the cold wind. Once a good fire was going and a meal eaten – I shared what I had – we chatted a while before curling up in our bags, alfresco, and going to sleep.

I mention this with some purpose regarding the little Bushman who had sat on his hunkers by the fire since it was lit, accepting the food given him, and now settling in to go to sleep in the same position and posture he had posed from the moment he had climbed down from the vehicle. He had no blanket and was completely bare except for the tiniest loincloth.

When I awoke in the morning he hadn't moved an inch. How he didn't get cramp poised all night like that I don't know. The night had been bitterly cold, with an icy wind, and being naked that must have been a great test of endurance. Like other Bushmen I had seen, our little man had large, pink blotches on the dark skin on his stomach and shins. When I remarked at this to the fellows, one said that these were the result of heat blisters due to them crouching so close to a fire and falling in. When I looked in horror he said, "Oh they don't bother", then added as a throw-away, "They don't have the same feelings as us, you know".

I pondered this deeply along the way and oft times later. Were Bushmen really so different from us and other Africans? I had learned that the Bushmen had a different anatomy to all other people, but could they have evolved a propensity to endure pain and extremes of cold and heat?

This mind-twisting personal debate, nevertheless, had its advantage too through the day, for it anaesthetised, to some extent, the excruciating discomfort of travelling in the cab of the vehicle we were in. These old Albions were built for strength and not comfort. In the morning you got frozen. During the day it was stifling. Always in your nostrils was the nauseating stench of diesel oil. And all the time you were butted and jerked and buffeted about until you imagined you had been caught up in a cement mixer. But I was not complaining and only too pleased to be carried away to the place I wanted to go. By the end of the day, we had travelled the last 110 miles stretch to Maun.

I thanked my friends and extended my goodbyes and was making my way down near the hotel to camp when luckily I met Malcolm James of Wanela, whom I had met the last time I was there, and he insisted I come back to the camp with him. *'So here I am.'* I wrote in my diary. Looking back down the years I could really believe that there was a guardian hand over my shoulder!

***

Bechuanaland was a most unusual country in my days there. Unusual because half the country was arid desert and the other half was almost swamped with an over-abundance of water. I had experienced the waterless Kalahari Desert and now I was heading for the Okavango Delta in the north, where there was more water than land. I say 'in my day…' because from what I have heard from modern-day tourists, the water-table of the Okavango appears to have dropped considerably since I was there. If this is so, could Botswana be moving towards the edge of a new climate of perhaps considerable proportions? It had all happened before, long before there was 'global warming', assumed to be due to the use of fossil fuels or the like. In the long and distant past the Kalahari was said to have been fertile and verdant. If so, that might have been before the water of the Okavango Delta changed its course and ran underground as it does to this day and never visibly reaches the sea. Could the same change in the water movement that caused the Kalahari to dry up be happening again in the Okavango Delta? Be this as it may, I can only write of the vast water expanses that I saw when I was there.

After a few days with my Wanela friends, during which time I was partied in various houses and taken on afternoon river jaunts, while awaiting the arrival of a company truck which was going to Mohembo and on which I had been given a free passage.

The journey took two days of the usual rough, tough, low-gear, milk-churn thumping, heaving and twisting, for all of which I was eternally grateful – on my own mode of travel it would have taken me a little longer! On the entire journey I never saw another vehicle. This was, of course, Wanela's own made road, ground out by the great wheels of their trucks.

Halfway to Mohembo Wanela had a camp, typical of many others throughout the territories. These havens of mercy for the native *pats* and *repats* going and coming to the South African mines, would not be greatly received by today's tourists. The buildings were made of wood or mud bricks with thatch roofs and some, but not all, had cement floors. And that was that! No beds, no comforts. I slept, rolled up in my sleeping bag on a cement floor…and grateful I was to have the comfort and safety provided. The land was teeming with animals of every type, from elephants to snakes and rodents.

Some distance from the camp was a trader's store where the truck driver had to unload some stuff. It was rather like John Seaman's father's shop at Ramakonami but much bigger, and the trader and his wife and their young teenage daughter stayed there.

It was interesting watching while I waited. The place was the usual type of traders' store: a sprawling, corrugated-iron roofed shack. Inside, the walls were lined with shelves packed with blankets and other merchandise, mostly clothes. From the roof, hanging on the end of a string dangled pairs of boots, fancy scarves, and gaudy coloured shirts hung on coat hangers so that they caught the eye. The native has an eye for bright colours. There are fancy hats too, from loud checked soft caps to big blue sombreros with white bands and trim trilbies. In a corner stood a group of rifles ranging from old rusty muzzle loaders to gleaming magnums, all in for repair. The trader must be a handy man. There is a hammer broken on one, a sight loose on another, and some barrels have come loose from the stock. He must see to all or if the job is too big, he'll send it to Bulawayo or Johannesburg, but he can fix most.

In an area where the trader is the only white man, he must be doctor as well. The trader dished out medicines guaranteed to cure them of anything from headaches to unwanted babies. Forebye, being a jack of all trades he must be a psychologist as well, for the act of selling to African natives is not just a case of pushing stuff across the counter. He must know what they want to buy and he must have patience and a good knowledge of their ways. An African will walk ten miles and pass three shops if he takes a fancy to one trader.

It is interesting to watch as these natives come to buy. Always there is a crowd at the door. Maybe they'll stand for hours before they go in and buy what they want. They'll stand and gossip and giggle. Some will saunter in and look around. A young buck would take his wife or girlfriend in and buy her a new headscarf. Among the crowd are the Damara women. They were interesting because they still wear Victorian-style attire, long dresses and innumerable underskirts. This custom comes from the Victorian women missionaries. The tribe copied the fashion and have never changed it.

The women of the Damara tribe are extremely tall, light skinned and fine featured. The shopkeeper's wife explained what they wore. Their clothing consists of: top dress – 10 yds cloth and 3 yds lining; at least four underskirts – 4 yds each; headgear or 'Dock' – 1 yd square and it is packed high with other cloth; shawl – 5 ft. by 4 ½ ft.

The Damara are interesting people. When they get married, the bridegroom must buy his bride a complete new rig-out of white. This will cost him anything from £10 to £15, a lot of money in those days. Before the wedding, he has the bride 'on approval' for an indefinite period. They live as husband and wife, nothing barred. On the man's satisfaction that she is the one for him he pays 'labola' – 'marriage price' – to the girl's father, of one ox, two heifers, and three sheep. The standard price! On the day of the wedding a feast is prepared at the house of the bride's father. A number of cattle, according to the wealth of the father, are killed. The bride and bridegroom must not eat any of this meat. They must not eat for 48 hours after the wedding. There is no actual marriage ceremony, only the feast. The heads of the animals are the last to be cooked.

One strange custom is that, on the wedding night, the bride sleeps with the groom's father, and the groom sleeps with the bride's mother. I hardly believed this until the trader's wife asked an old Damara woman who works for him if it were true and she said yes, it was. Like most tribes, a man can have as many wives as he can afford to buy and keep.

Mohembo is a beautiful spot. Nestling by the cool banks of the Okavango river, lost in the tangle of these vast swamps it appears almost like a mirage. Big green trees spread delightful shadows and slender palms lean over and nod their feathery plumes at their reflections in the water. Occasionally, a Mbukushu native (the river people) stands in his '*mokoro*' (dugout canoe) and ripples his reflection in the mirror surface of the water with his long paddle as he passes to and fro.

In the afternoon I got a couple of boys to paddle me up the river in a *mokoro*. I saw about a dozen crocodiles. On the way back I stopped at the village and wandered around the huts. I was interested in the way the Mbukushu women weave strips of the bark from the Mokosumo tree into their hair with fat, so that it looks as if they have long hair. Many of them wear wonderful beaded skirts and many bangles and leg rings.

The Mbukushu men wear home-made knives at their belts. The sheath is made of a single piece of wood, the slot being burnt into it. They are fancily decorated. The handle and sheath bear a queer fish-like shape.

When I returned to the Wanela office they had a surprise for me. They had been told that a plane was coming next morning bringing repats back and taking others away to Francistown. I was elated but also disappointed not to have more time by the Okavango, but this was too good an opportunity to miss. I thrilled at the opportunity given to me. The plane arrived in the morning and naturally I was up and ready to go and we got on our way.

CHAPTER 8

ZAMBESI ODYSSEY

Today has been something of a record. I have travelled further than in any other day in my life. Also, I flew for the first time.

The plane, a big Dakota, arrived about 8.30 this morning. The recruits had their inoculations and boarded. A feeling of elation gripped me as I climbed on board. This was something new. Although I was in the pilot's cabin, I hardly noticed the take off until I saw the tops of the trees level with the windows. The truck we had come up with and the group of native sightseers swung underneath the wing, then Mohembo was gone.

Recently, a Wanela barge was lost and presumed sunk by sabotage by natives who had lost the ferry trade when the barge had taken over. Mr Mathias, the rep at Mohembo, returned last night after a fortnight's fruitless search in a *mokoro*. He asked the pilot of the plane to have a look. So we swung down low, banking and following the curves of the river. How clear the water seemed. I could see where it shelved in from the sides and the blackness in the middle. There was no sign of the barge. Then we climbed and the swamp land was like a map below. Miles and miles of tangled swamps with huge pools and the great Okavango river that split up and ran hither and thither before joining up again. It seems impossible that all this water never reaches the sea. It drains into the Kalahari at the great Makarikari salt pan and there is nothing to show for it, not even green vegetation.

It was good to see the country from the air, but all too soon it was finished. The journey that takes days for a weekly truck was done in two and a half hours. Francistown appeared below; it looked so small, a few houses clustered together in such a vast ocean of wasteland. Then we were swinging down out of the clouds. The plane bounced once, then settled down.

It was about 1 p.m. when I got down to Francistown. I wandered down the street at a loss what to do. Then I met the manager of Barclays Bank whom I had met at Maun; no-one passes a man in a kilt! He said he knew of a fellow leaving for Bulawayo right away and the man agreed to take me. It hardly seemed real to be here in a city tonight when I was away at the back of beyond this morning.

I had no trouble in getting into Southern Rhodesia; I came up via Plumtree. It was night when I arrived and the streets were empty. There is something dismal and depressing arriving in a strange city at night with no place to go, especially when you can't go to any hotel. I was planning to lose myself behind some building and sleep till morning as I had done before. I wandered up to a hotdog stand for some coffee. There were two fellows there and we got talking. They work for the railway and invited me up to their room so I'm sleeping on the floor. Something always turns up.

On Saturday, Bulawayo had exhibition fever and justly deserved it. It was lucky that I arrived there at the time of the Rhodes Centenary Exhibition and I went along and visited it and it was a wonderful show. Each country had a pavilion and the standard was high.

I couldn't stay in the railway place and had to change my billet. Luck was with me again when I met a man and got chatting with him. He offered me his room in the boarding house hotel as he was going away for a week or so. The manager didn't know and I hoped he wouldn't find out! It's so good to be in a city again after a couple of months in the 'bundu'. Good to see the big shop windows, the warm friendly neon signs, feel the companionship of the people, the gaiety in the air. Nice to drop into a café for some coffee. Fine to be able to buy the daily paper and maybe watch a soccer game or go to the cinema. All these things are fine, but I knew I would tire of it soon.

The streets were the widest I had seen. On account of Rhodes' foresight, they were made wide enough to turn around an ox wagon and a full span of sixteen oxen. I was so pleased to be there for the two public holidays – Rhodes and Founders days. The city was crowded as visitors had poured in from all over Rhodesia. I went to the exhibition again; one could spend days there and not see everything. It was a perfect fair day, the crowds of sightseers viewing the wonders of a whole continent condensed into one area.

The next day I went to Matopos to see Rhodes' grave. It is about 20 miles from town. I got a lift. Matopos is a smooth topped hill of granite. On the top is a ring of huge round boulders. In here Rhodes is buried. The native name for it is *Malindidzumu* – The Abode of the Spirits. This apt name was given long before Rhodes made his personal request to be buried there.

The original tribe of this area was the Makalanga and they gave the name 'Amatombo' – the Bald Topped Hills – to the Matopos Hills. The Matabele corrupted it to 'Amatopo' from which the modern name comes. The Matabele took refuge here in the rebellion of 1896 and Baden-Powell learned a great deal about scouting here during operations which broke the Matabele power.

The history of the Matabele is yet another instance of how the Zulu nation has influenced the history of the whole of southern Africa. Mzilikasi was the founder of the Matabele nation. He was one of Chaka's generals. Chaka was at the height of his brutal reign. Any beaten 'impi' which returned was marched to their death at what is now known as Chaka's rock. Chaka ruled his land with an iron, bloody hand. He had murdered his mother because she had borne him illegitimately. He had killed all his sons lest they should overthrow him as he grew old.

For some reason, Mzilikazi thought it unhealthy to remain after a quarrel with Chaka. He marched his 'impis' north in approximately 1820. After a few years sojourn in the Transvaal, from which he was expelled by the Voortrekkers, he settled in this country about 1837, making a number of Royal Kraals in the Bulawayo area. He died in 1868 aged 70 years at one of these Kraals – *Mhlahlandhla* – the only Zulu Chief to die in the fullness of his years for many generations.

***

I moved off the next day. I had to wait to get my rucksack fixed up as it's getting well-worn and tears at the slightest provocation. I hope it lasts out. I was not sorry to get on my way. Ten days have been plenty. It was fine at first, but the crowds, the cars, the hooters, flags, bunting, queues for everything, side-shows, big wheels, rockets, ice-cream and candy floss all in one mad whirligig – a city. It was too much of a whirlpool after wandering about in the bush. I enjoyed it though. But it was good to be off to the Victoria Falls. I have been promised a lift there tomorrow.

We arrived at the Wankie Game Reserve around 4.30 p.m. The warden refused permission to drive through because it was too late and my lift decided to take the road around the reserve, to carry on to the Falls. I was in a dilemma as to whether to go on with him or stay to explore Wankie. I chose the latter and I am glad I did. Before allowing me to enter, the warden asked me if I carried a gun, which I did, a revolver. I had to give it to him and collect it before leaving, not that I was intending to shoot any of the animals! The reserve is teeming with animals – two big herds of buffalo, various types of buck including eland and sable, giraffe, zebra and elephant. One big bull stood in the road about twenty yards away and trumpeted while I fumed and cursed because it had caught me while I was changing the film in my camera. The following day I was invited to join a busload of tourists; very kind of them, but driving in a bus isn't my idea of seeing the country.

Instead, I set off on foot to Victoria Falls.

The Falls are terrific! I would not have believed a natural view could be so impressive. I am dug in at the camping ground and it's a good place. The Falls seem to cast some hypnotic spell as you gaze into them. From miles away you can see the spray, as if it were smoke issuing from a great hole in the ground, and there is the constant rumble of the water like an endless train passing over a bridge. It's almost impossible to obtain photos of the Falls except at low water. The spray is so heavy like fog and though it can be seen naturally I don't think the camera would take it in. In the spray there is a perpetual rainbow. What a sensation it is to stand on the bridge that spans the gorge when a train is passing over it and feel the whole structure vibrate and swing and see the mad, broiling cauldron of water 350 feet below – as if waiting for you. I wandered through the rainforest today and saw the Devil's Cataract and Livingstone's Memorial. It made me feel proud to see him standing there.

There is a tall tree nearby where Livingstone carved his initials. When I was there the letters must have been a metre high and now must be twice that. I have spoken to people who believe it had to be someone else who did it because Livingstone would never have done such a thing, but it is true. It gave me quite a thrill to know we shared the same initials

The Falls had a small airstrip and I met the pilot of the little four-seater plane used to fetch and carry people and goods. He was good enough to offer to take me up. It was a great little plane, much better than the big Dakota I flew in from Mohembo and it was wonderful to see the Falls from the air. The pilot dropped the plane down into a lumber camp in Chobe where he was to pick up someone. I was welcomed by the men there and taken back to the camp from the airstrip and invited to stay the night. The men were housed in wooden huts made from rough, sawn planks. In the hut I was in, whole sides of meat were hanging up to dry to make biltong, so widely used, particularly in South Africa.

In conversation around the fire that night the men were very interested in my journey and anxious to help me on my way. I learned that twenty miles from the lumber camp was a Wanela camp in Kazungula, from where barges are run further up the river, so I thought I would have a go at that. Unfortunately, the next barge was not due to leave for a few days, but next morning, I said my farewells to my new friends and got on the road to Kazungula.

Walking along the road I felt I was deep into the back of beyond. It was wild country. An elephant crossed the road ahead of me but moved off and watched me go by. However, I reached the camp without incident. I was told that elephants come right into the camp, sometimes into the peoples' gardens. I was housed in a little rondavel, completely bare, with a cement floor and only my sleeping bag for comfort, but compared with some nights outside it was very comfortable!

Wednesday 29th July 1953 Kazungula

I am finding it very interesting here. Mr Thompson, the doctor here, is an anthropologist and scientist and dear knows what else. He knows more about the inside life of the African and their customs than any man I have met. I enjoy listening to him. He blethers a lot of boring stuff, but it's worth listening to an hour's gruelling boring stuff if I get five minutes of good interesting material, for he can tell me things about the African that no other man can. He leaves here in a fortnight for Bulawayo where the Museum has requested him to write up his notes for them. They have given him a grant of £1,000 to last two years.

I went out to see the hot springs near here. There are big holes in the ground full of fine hot water. The elephants seem to like them for the mud round them is pitted with their great foot prints. In the afternoon I collected a boy and set off for Old Kazungula, which is on the border of Bechuanaland and Southern Rhodesia. I photographed the big tree there where Livingstone carved his name and under which he camped. That photograph will be particularly interesting because it takes in four countries, South-West Africa, Bechuanaland, Southern Rhodesia and Northern Rhodesia.

On the way back we almost walked into an elephant. In the grey dark of sunset it's hard to see them in the bushes. It was just standing watching us coming towards it. It was very, very close. It was a race then, but I think I beat the boy by a short head in the race to safety. There is something exciting about seeing an elephant at close range without the feeling of security a coach or motorcar round about you gives. Next morning I walked several miles along the road but didn't meet another elephant. A car came along and gave me a lift along the eight miles to Kasane, which is the place where the barge leaves from.

It's a lovely spot, this Kasane. Like Mohembo it has the palm trees, smooth water reflections and natives standing in *mokoros* paddling up and downstream. I was entrenched in a little guest hut that they have and safe from the roaming animals. There was elephant spoor right in close to the buildings. The elephants must stand and watch the people moving around as they eat. In fact, that night one came right into the camp and broke down a branch from a tree. Nobody saw it, but the broken branch and the footprints were there. Later, I watched the natives bringing in the fish. Enormous tiger fish with big spiked teeth – not a river to swim in!

The sunsets here are among the loveliest I've seen. Perhaps the colours in a desert sunset are more varied and vivid, but there is an irresistible charm in these sunsets which are deep red shading to browns and blues, with the palms silhouetted against it and all reproduced in a topsy-turvy replica on the wide smooth mirror surface of the Zambesi.

There is an air which a red sunset casts, an air of calm that stops all physical activity and lulls the mind into reverie. When I sat down to write my diary the sunset was in full bloom. The sky captured my eye and I had to write down what I saw. But then that spell settled over me, that peaceful calm, and I forgot my writing. My mind began to drift, tumbling back down the years: school days, army days, climbing in the Cairngorms and Glencoe, painting houses, swinging and hoisting a three-part ladder 50 feet up, books, faces, places and home. Aye, always there when I reminisce. I heaved a sigh and came back to reality. The barge goes on Tuesday.

***

The first day's journey on the River Zambesi is over. This morning at dawn the mine repats were shepherded on board. There are three barges lashed together, only the centre one is power driven.

Ken Manson, the barge master is a short, chubby fellow. The hours go by as we chug upstream. Crocodiles lie among the tangled reeds on the banks. They are hard to spot and usually slip into the river as we draw near. But one big fellow basks openly on a sandbank and doesn't even wake up as we chug past him. Occasionally, a hippo surfaces and shows itself. A profusion of colour is lent to the scene by the Zambesi parakeets that flit about. The laurie birds protest angrily with their squawky "Go away" "Go away" as we disturb the scene.

Occasionally, a native standing in a dugout canoe, slides passed us holding long fish spears. Sometimes there is hardly an inch of free board on these canoes and it seems as if the man is standing on the water. There is a young fellow on board, Burton by name, who is crocodile hunting. We drop him at his camp then go on.

We pass native villages. Grass huts grouped on sandy patches with canoes drawn up out of the water. Fish nets hang up to dry. Darkness falls and we are still going steady. Then in the distance there is a light. As we draw nearer I see it is a boy swinging a lantern and behind him are fires that were hidden from view by trees. This is the Wanela camp, the end of today's journey.

We were up while it was still dark this morning. In the pale light of dawn, with lanterns swinging here and there, the barges were loaded. It was cold. The repats were all muffled up with blankets and all around there were their gaily coloured boxes and souvenirs from Jo'burg: umbrellas, sticks, gaudy cloth, fancy hats and one even had a Rexine-covered chair. At times their simplicity, their childish delight for these worthless trinkets almost brings a lump to my throat.

Soon we were off. All wrapped up against the cold, I used my sleeping bag as a shawl. Ken was buried in an Army greatcoat. The repats were huddled together. Nobody feels like talking. There is only the phut-phut-phut of the engine and the swish of the spray at the bows. Gradually the darkness clears and the sky is ribbed with gold-flecked clouds. Over the water a low morning fog hovers. It's only a few feet high and it gives the impression of sailing on clouds. The tangled undergrowth on the banks is still misty grey yet. But, gradually, the sun that had previously high-lighted the clouds lowered its beams onto the grateful land. The mist dispersed till only little will-o-wisps drift about. Then even these disappear. The trees on the banks lose that neutral grey colour and become green with distinct, black shadows. The cook boy gets the primus going and we were soon sipping hot coffee. The natives come to life and one starts an infectious song. Soon all the barges are joined in quick, syncopated native community singing that is laced with the twanging of a guitar.

The day goes by just like yesterday. There is the occasional crocodile and hippo to see; the parakeets; the natives in canoes; the wide water vista between the tree-lined banks and the tang of adventure in the air, as if it were a hundred years before and you, like Livingstone, are penetrating deeper into an unknown Africa.

We arrived at Katima Mulilo at about 4 p.m. Trucks were waiting to transport the repats to the camp. A human chain formed and the boxes were taken from the barges up the hill to the waiting trucks. At the camp I got quite a welcome from the staff. They had heard about me coming and John Fysson, one of the clerks, has invited me to stay in his place. It is a big house, built as a shooting lodge by a wealthy man called Blake about fifty years ago.

Here at Katima Mulilo there are rapids in the river. The house overlooked them. There is always the thunder of them in the air.

John asked me if I would like to shoot the rapids in a canoe with him. I jumped at the chance, although I was a wee bit apprehensive. This afternoon, after John finished work, he collected another fellow, Jack Bellbounds, I think his name is, and we set off up the river. John had the canoe there. The canoe rocked a bit unsteadily. I, the novice, sat in the middle, with John in the front and Jack at the back, each of them with paddles. The river was smooth and slow. The roar of the rapids seemed detached from the tranquil look of the water. I joked about this and tried to make my voice casual, to hide the taut knots that tied my stomach and threatened to rise and envelope my throat. John whistled nonchalantly and answered my jests with some of his own. Jack sat silent at the back. When I looked round his face was drawn and serious. Perhaps the fact that the last time he had done this, the canoe had struck a boulder and split in two and he had to swim for dear life with crocodiles in the vicinity, made him realise the danger more than us. Also the fact that he was married and had the responsibility of a wife and family made him more sensible.

The river extends treacherous fingers and grips the dugout and stealthily coaxes it further into the web. Gradually, so gradual that it is barely noticeable, the canoe gathers speed, faster, faster until there is a white crest at its head where it cleaves the water. The paddles, as a means of propulsion, are useless now and can only be used to steer. The first wave of the backwash from the rapids bites the canoe and its nose goes up and we slide into the first trough, up and over the next and the next. They are coming quicker. There is no turning back now. The first rocks are just ahead and the only way out lies between them. The waves come quicker and are more savage now and the rocks are racing towards us.

I remember the time in Tanganyika when I went over the rapids. That time the canoe overturned and I have a horrible sensation that it is going to happen again. Maybe this time I won't be so lucky. The water is all whipped up and furrowed like corduroy. We are heading for a rock. No, we've missed it and the canoe nosed between them. Half of it goes out into space, then it drops and we're into the rapid proper. Things happen too quickly to think. The canoe banks up sideways onto a solid wall of water then pitches down to the bottom of the furrow. Then up, up almost vertical and it doesn't quite make the top as the wave bends over backwards. The canoe crashed through the wave and we're soaked and it's nearly swamped. Then it's all a mad, mixed-up progression. We slide down a steep runway between two ridges of rock. The canoe is heading for a great, rounded smooth boulder with an inch or so of water running over it. Jack roars to John to keep his paddle out. We've had it. Can't miss it. Wait, wait for the crash. Jack delves his paddle in at the back. Precision timing. The nose lifts. The glistening rock passes right underneath and the canoe slaps right into the water at its side, then we're through. Oh that dizzy sense of relief! We look at each other and laugh, pull into the side and we are on good, firm ground again.

***

I am 110 miles further on. I got a lift in a Wanela convoy coming up to Nangweshi. The journey was uneventful except to observe that the roads are all sand and are banked up and covered with cut grass. It's a good idea.

It was late afternoon when we arrived. Next to the Wanela camp is the S.R.G. camp, the rival organisation that provides natives with facilities to go to Southern Rhodesia to work. The man in charge is Jimmy Warren. I had heard he was quite a good hunter so I went across to see if he was planning anything for the weekend and if so, could I join him. As luck would have it he was planning to go out and agreed to take me. Nangweshi is the place for lions. Sometimes they walk through the camp at night.

Yesterday, Jimmy, Mrs Warren and I set out in the truck with some boys in the back. We went about 40 miles across the plain, straight cross- country with the truck in gear all the time. The radiator continually boiled so we had to collect water at every pan (depression where the water has collected – like a small lake).

The place was alive with game. Great herds of zebra, oribis, tsessebi and wildebeest. Jimmy carried quite an armoury: a .450 double-barrelled rifle and P.14. .303 rifle, a short Lee Enfield .303 rifle and a double-barrelled shotgun. He shot an oribi at long range. A good shot. Then, later, when we came on a herd of them, he said he wanted a zebra as bait for the lion. He started shooting into the herd with the P.14 to my surprise and disgust. A good hunter doesn't fire into a herd for there is no telling how many you wound that way. I was sickened by the random shooting and wished so much that I hadn't asked to come along. Maybe he was showing off, but he went down in my estimation and was certainly not the good hunter he made out to be. Certainly, it was permissible to shoot for meat for the natives but not in this manner.

In the morning a boy who lives nearby came to Jimmy and said a lion had killed and eaten one of his cattle. We went out in the truck and saw the horns and the bones, all that remained after the lion and hyenas had finished. The boys said that the spoor indicated a lioness and two cubs and I was thankful they had left the area. I was glad Jimmy had given me no opportunity to use one of his guns and glad also to leave the next day.

CHAPTER 9

DEJA VU

I left Nangweshi with the veterinary officer, John Tremlett, who arrived from Mungu. He was staying overnight at Senanga where he intended calling on a Mr Harrington. He was a very interesting character, a pioneer of the country and a missionary. John liked to call on these elderly characters in his district to have a chat and I admired him for it.

The drive to Mungu was pleasant. We came along the forest road which, as usual, was very sandy. Mungu is the administrative headquarters of Barotseland, this province of Northern Rhodesia I am in now. It is a scattered community with about one hundred Europeans, traders, missionaries and government officers. John chatted to me about his interest in Scottish dancing. He took his degree at Edinburgh Veterinary College, and while he was there he became interested in the dancing and although an Englishman, he became quite an expert. He influenced the start of the Scottish dancing in Mungu and was one of the organisers of the club which was now so popular, although out of all who attend only three or four are Scots.

Naturally, John invited me to the dance and, of course, being a Scot, I could hardly refuse. I felt quite ashamed that I, a Scot, among so many Sassenachs who were proficient in Scottish country dancing, couldn't join in because I didn't know how. I can do all the ordinary stuff, reels, etc, the fun stuff, but this was advanced stuff, done with great precision.

I was introduced all round and it was then that I met Colonel Studdard, an ex-Indian Army officer. When he was told I was travelling round Africa on foot his only reply was "Why?" I was taken slightly off balance. I have grown used to people asking all the usual questions when I've met them. I've heard and answered them so often it took me slightly by surprise when asked this unorthodox question. Inwardly, I thanked the old man. I was reminded of my meeting with Grasso Stellario, the little Italian, who asked the same question as I set out on my journey on board the ship "Esperia", three days out of Genoa bound for Alexandria.

"Why?" It was hard to put into words without making it sound ridiculously boyish.

"Oh, you know, wanderlust, to see the world, adventure," I answered, groping, trying to analyse my own thoughts.

"Are you going to write a book?" he asked.

"I hope to do so," I said.

"I thought so. You'll write a book and you will make all who read it, especially the young ones, unsettled. They'll want to wander like you. My God! As if we haven't had enough wanderers, people with itchy feet, in the last two generations. Oh the wars were the reason, but we don't want the young people to follow suit. We want people in the Colonies and Dominians, young steady, people who will build up the Empire and Commonwealth. We don't want them to be just 'passing ships' like you. As you are, you are no asset to any country."

I winced at that. The truth often hurts. I liked this old Colonel. He was a man, a soldier: no shilly-shallying, say-what-you-mean and, right or wrong, you know where you stand. In my defence I answered, "Is there no place in the world of today for travellers? Will there be no place in the Britain of tomorrow for travel books? Was it not travellers with a spirit of adventure who won the Empire in the first place?"

"Ah, there you have me, young man," he answered, melting a little, "Yes, I must admit we must have books and certainly travel books and before we have them, we must have travellers. As for the Empire, the world is closed nowadays and the days of Empire building are over. But we must consolidate what we've got, or My God, we'll lose them. We are losing them and will lose all unless we get the right people from the home country to come and settle: young people with the spirit of adventure in them. Oh yes, make no mistake, young man, I admire you for yours, but we don't want rolling stones, not that kind of adventurer. We want people to settle and make their homes here and build up the country for themselves and for Britain. There is a lot of foreign influence creeping in here and the only way to stop it and keep the country British is to bring more and more Britons to live here.

"Roam the world if you must and go home and write your book, good luck to you, but when you do, tell them, tell the people, these young married couples, these young men who are looking for a new adventurous life, tell them there is a welcome for them in the colonies; no, more than that, tell them we need them, Britain needs them here.

"Write your book and tell the people how wonderful it is to lead the life of a vagabond, carefree, no responsibilities. Yes, tell them about it but – most important this – tell them not to do the same."

There was an air of finality in these last words. He was leaning forward in his chair and his grey, bushy eyebrows were bunched as his old, wise eyes bored into mine to thump home the meaning of his words. I had the feeling that both of us were still in khaki and that I was 'on the mat'. I seemed to hear him dismissing the case with a brief, "severe reprimand". In my mind I heard the R.S.M. start his sharp commands 'Prisoner and escort ...'

"Thank you for your advice, sir," I said, extending my hand, "I'll do just that." His grip was the firm, steady one of a man. Such is the type that has made Britain Great. I hoped there were many more like him.

***

Yesterday I met a little fellow, Jeff Richards, commonly known as 'Geordie', because he comes from the Newcastle area, and he invited me duck shooting for the weekend. He borrowed a single-barrelled shotgun from a native for me and about 1 p.m. we set out for a pan away across the Barotsi plain, with us was a boy, Derek Gray, son of the District Administrator here. The plain is the area about ten miles width on either side of the Zambesi which gets flooded with water when the river rises each year. The floods had receded, but there were still deep pools here and there and parts of the road were still underwater. We got stuck many times on the way out and only by digging and hard shovelling did we manage, but a spring of the truck was broken in the process. However, we got to the pan or lake and made camp. The sun was low and darkness not far off when we went to take up our position to shoot. I had never even fired a shotgun before – rifles aplenty but never a shot gun.

Derek went to one side and Geordie and I the other. We crouched in the long reeds to make ourselves as inconspicuous as possible. How still the evening is. The sky is copper coloured. The lake is smooth. Occasionally a fish breaks the surface with a plop to catch a fly and leaves round, widening ripples. A boy stands motionless in a canoe ready to retrieve any birds that fall in the water. There is a hush over the land as if the whole world is waiting.

"Here they come," whispered Geordie. His eyes are better than mine. Then I see them. A flock comes from the east, huddled together, calling plaintively and flying swift and smooth, as if they were suspended on wires and needed no movement of the wings to give propulsion. They are coming over us.

"Now," whispers Geordie, "mind and fire in front of them."

They seem to have spotted us for the flock suddenly scatters and veers off the wither side of us. I single one out and follow it with the bead sight. With the explosion the bird crumples up and drops out of the sky. It hits the water with a plop. My elation at getting my first duck mingled with the surprise I felt.

"Mokorro" I shout. But already the canoe boy is pushing his way out to retrieve.

How quiet it is. The world is deep mauve, the sky, the lake and there is only the 'phlut, phlut' of the paddle as the boy canoes out to the bird. The canoe is so low it looks as if he is standing on the water. This place has plenty of crocodiles. On a previous occasion, when Derek came with his father, a crocodile pulled a fallen bird under right in front of their eyes.

Another flock of duck come in. Geordie gets one and I hit another. Mine is only wounded and it goes in a long steep dive and lands in the water, swims a bit and tried to take off again, but fails. The canoe boy gets it. Some more come in, but I miss this time.

This morning again we were up before dawn and waiting for them, but the ones I got yesterday must have been flukes for I had five shots this morning and missed every time. We left the truck with an African and after that we had to walk the 17 miles back to Mungu. Geordie did well but confessed it was the longest walk he had done in all his life!

CHAPTER 10

LUNCH WITH A KING

The Paramount Chief of the Mlozi has two camps, one in the forest at Lumalunga and the other on the plain at Lialui. Each year when the plain floods, he moves by barge to the forest. When the floods go down he returns to Lialui and on both occasions there is quite a ceremony attached. The one in April, when he moves from Lialui to Lumalunga, is the bigger of the two, but the one I witnessed when he left the forest to return to Lialui was quite spectacular. I consider myself lucky that I arrived in Mungu just in time to see it. Lumalunga is about 17 miles from Mungu. The District Commissioner loaned me his Land Rover and driver for the day – extremely good of him.

I set out in the Land Rover, armed with my camera. Where the road wasn't bumpy it was feet thick in fine, loose sand and it taxed even the Land Rover's front-wheel drive. Villages are dotted along the whole route. I was travelling in borrowed plumes and the village life ceased momentarily to look when they saw the D.C.'s Land Rover coming. Mlozi women with bundles balanced on their heads would turn to look. Men thatching roofs stopped their work. Children at play looked up. Hens with their elbows tucked in, necks stretched out and heels kicking high tried to beat the truck on the race across the road and at the last moment, when death seemed inevitable, they would throw up their wings in despair and screech and somehow always managed to make the other side.

At Lumalunga I was received by an *Induna* (Headman), Katena, one of the senior *Indunas*. Everything was ready for the move and it only needed the Paramount Chief, King Mwanawena III, to appear to start. I was shown to the Kota, where the King holds council with the tribal elders. It is a large building without sides, with only a thatched roof supported on long poles and a floor which is made of beaten clay mixed with cow dung. There are a few steps to a raised platform where the Chief sits.

While we waited, *Induna* Katema told me some of the history of his people. In typical fashion he kept meticulously to the pattern of events, being particular to quote times, places and names, for this was the way history lived when passed on by word of mouth. If one were slipshod in their quotation, then those details would soon be forgotten.

"Barotse is the collective name given to the various tribes in this land, the largest of which is the *Lozi*. The people who belong to this tribe are *'Malozi'*, which in your language means 'people of the river plain'. The Malozi originated from Nyambe, eleven generations and nineteen Kings ago. [Nyambe is the Lozi god.]

"In the reign of Malambwa we were conquered by the Makololo, a warlike nation which had begun as a Matabele *impi* under the command of Ngabi. On their march through Bechuanaland they were joined by people of many conquered tribes and the mixed people were known as the Makololo, which means 'the people who scraped the country clean'. It was a Kololo Chief, Sebituane, who was in power when David Livingstone visited the country in 1851. The Makololo occupied our land until the reign of Sipopa, when we rebelled and killed them to a man. Their language, Sikololo, however, remained and is spoken today."

Katema went on to tell how the land had become a British Protectorate at the beginning of the twentieth century, when a Lozi chief had asked the British for protection in return for certain mineral concessions. At that time, he said there had been many fine canals in the land, which were maintained by free labour, every man in the country giving up twelve days a year to work for the State. Unfortunately, to Members of Parliament in far-away London, 'free labour' smacked too much of slavery and one of the conditions of the proffered protection was the cessation of this practice. So the canals dried up. "They were good canals," Katema added wistfully while taking a pinch of tobacco snuff from the *mokoma* nut shell he kept on a string round his neck and inserting it well up his nostrils with finger and thumb. "It is a pity your Members of Parliament did not understand our ways better."

When I had been announced I was taken to meet the King. He was dressed in European clothes. He welcomed me but asked to be excused since he was busy moving. I was then shown to the *'Kashandi'*, the King's eating house and where he hears the appeals from the *'Kota'* or court, to wait until the ceremony started. All the chief's possessions were laid out and divided among a host of royal porters to carry to the barge.

The ceremony started with the Mlozi band starting up. The band is a three -piece group consisting of native drums and a crude xylophone. The porters picked up their loads and, in line, they headed for the royal barges, which are built in the shape of dugout canoes, each with a sun canopy made of wicker. The King came, followed by the *Moyo* (Life) Queen, a rotund, matronly woman also dressed in European dress, followed by his two children, the children of two concubines, who do not appear in public. The crowds were excitedly waiting at the head of the canal where the barges were already loaded and the 'Nalikwanda', the barge that the King travels in, was loaded with the royal war drums. When the King came in sight all the people clapped their hands and started to 'Kandeleli' as he moved among them – the ovation was loud and enthusiastic.

The King and family climbed on board the Nalikwanda and a fire was lit in a bowl of damp mud and dung. The fire is a symbol of the King's presence – a sort of royal standard. When a new king is installed all fires in the land are supposed to be put out and runners are sent to bring back a lighted brand from this royal fire on the Nalikwanda.

The scene was colourful. The paddlers of the Nalikwanda wore leopard skins with red capes and lion mane plumes. The paddlers of the other royal barges called 'Notila', which carry the royal belongings, wear monkey skins and a head dress of feathers of the 'Lishewaj' bird.

What a sight it was! The barges, accompanied by a flotilla of canoes, moved down the canal that in places was so narrow that a barge would brush either side as it passed. Off they went, paddles flashing in the sun, head-dresses dipping in unison, with the crews chanting their beat while the crowds of people lining the banks prostrated themselves and women trilled in high falsetto voices. It takes about three and a half hours paddling to reach Lialui. When the King arrives they beat the big war drums to tell the land that the King has come back. The drums have a sound radius of 30 miles but are only used twice a year when the King moves.

Next day I borrowed a bicycle and cycled the 11 miles across the plain to Lialui which is a big native village or town. There are no streets like an ordinary town, just a jumble of native huts. In the centre is the King's kraal, or palace. The Paramount Chief was sitting in the Kota and a stool was laid beside the Chief for me, on the platform. Great festivities were in progress and the crowds were dancing to welcome the Chief home. The Chief explained each group to me. There was a group of men dancing the Bunyanga – the dance of the elephant hunters. Another group was dancing the Ngomalume – the dance of the Men. But all eyes were on a group of young women who caught the eye like a splash of red on a white door. They were dressed in all their finery, long dresses in colourful cloth. They were dancing the Lilombola Dance of the Maidens Reaching Womanhood. And there, most striking of all, were the Makeshi dancers with their hideous masks and weird costumes.

The Mlozi women's dress is extremely colourful. Like the Damara women down in the Kalahari, they wear old Victorian dress. But they wear even more than the Damara for the Mlozi make a bustle at the back. They wear from five to eight underskirts, each of eight yards length, the surplus being gathered up at the back to form a bustle. Over this they wear a top dress that is made from two and a half yards of cloth. So the whole dress measures from forty-two to sixty-six yards of cloth. This in strong summer heat.

The men are almost equally over-dressed. They are the only tribe I have seen wearing a dress very similar to the kilt. They call it a *'sisaba'*. There are from ten to thirty yards of cloth in them. Considering the cloth costs up to seven shillings and six pence a yard, both the women and men are expensively dressed. The *'sisaba'* is made in two parts, back and front. The cloth is puckered up into kinds of pleats. Apparently, I caused quite a sensation when I walked in wearing my kilt. It was the first time they had seen a European in a *'sisaba'*.

In Barotseland, there are a collection of tribes and among these overdressed Mlozi are the Balavale tribesmen who wear only a loin cloth and hunt with bow and arrow. The Mlozi are the main tribe. All the other tribes are known collectively to the Mlozi as Mawiko – the People from the West. As we sat watching the dancing, little groups of people arriving would come to the entrance of the Kota and give the royal salute. Standing and kneeling they would push their hands forward and shout 'Yosho-o-o-o'. These were the people from the outlying places paying their respects to their King. Then they would go and join in the dancing. I was thrilled when the Chief invited me to have lunch with him and, of course, I accepted.

"The trouble with the land," said the King, stirring his tea with a dessert spoon, "is bad communications. Most of the canals are dried up and the roads are poor."

Thus, King Mwanawena summed up his domain. I agreed with him. I had seen some of the shallow trenches, which had once been canals and my aching bones were personal reminders of the state of the tracks which served as roads in this the largest of Northern Rhodesia's six provinces. At the long table, the Chief sat at one end and the *Mojo* at the other. I sat in the middle. I could not be sure if they were used to eating European style and using knives and forks, for the cutlery was in all the wrong places, but it was a good meal of rice and meat and a good experience. Sitting at the table, I couldn't believe I was having lunch with the King! As background music to the meal, the wild, vibrant rhythm of dancing drums tumbled into the compound from the town outside and rolled on in waves that tingled the blood. From staccato down-beats up into frenzied crescendos, the drums carried with them the singing and shouting and stamping feet of a great crowd rejoicing.

The following Tuesday, the District Officer was going out inspecting the road and gave me a lift to see the big celebrations of the King coming to the Chieftainship. The road was pretty bad and the Land Rover got bogged down a couple of times and had to be lifted out bodily by a gang of natives.

It was interesting to learn that, by strange coincidence, the King's two elder brothers had died of poisoning.

At Lialui I wended my way between the huts towards the Royal Kraal. There was the atmosphere of a fair abroad. Since morning the people had been dancing and the drums playing to commemorate this fifth anniversary of the coming to power of the Paramount Chief, King Mwanawena III. At the palace, I was met by one of the *Indunas* who asked me to wait while he informed the Chief of my arrival.

Before he entered the palisade that surrounds the royal home, as was the custom, he made the royal salute, known as to '*Kushoelela*' as I had seen the previous evening. He stood and pushed his hands forward, palms turned towards the King, and shouted 'Yosh-o-o-o-o' twice, then he went on his knees and did the same, and repeated it standing once again. When his presence was acknowledged by someone inside, he knelt twice again and shouted the Yosh-o-o-o again, before entering. In a little while he came and asked if I would come in. As on my previous visit, I followed the *Induna* through the opening in the reed fence to the court, up the hard path made from beaten earth mixed with cow dung. There were the usual number of elders and servants squatting round the 'Kashandi', waiting in case the Chief should need them.

Mwanawena stood waiting for me in the door of his house. My guide began to '*kandeleli.*' I remembered my last visit when I wondered what was the proper thing I should do: was I expected to '*kandeleli*' like the rest? Was I supposed to remove my hat when I spoke to him, like the others? I walked up to him, shook his hand and only removed my hat when I entered his house. Inside, the house was spacious and high and other walls, also made of mud and dung, partitioned off the rooms.

A servant got on his knees to '*kandeleli*' before he brought in the tea. Even the Queen had to get down on her knees and clap her hands when she entered. I felt sorry for her for she is a big woman and to see her labouring to get on her knees and back up again touched me, but it is a tribal custom.

Presently, the Chief said we would go and watch the dancing. Walking behind him along the passage way towards the dancing, we passed the Queen, who graciously acknowledged me with a raised hand from her seat on what appeared to be an Elsan Can! No embarrassment at all, only mine!

An *Induna* was sent to get the band started and the Mlozi band started up to warn the country that the King was coming. Immediately, a hush fell over the dancers. We left the royal grounds and sat in an enclosure to watch the display. With their King watching their antics, the dancers put more zest into their movements. Again I saw the Dance of the Elephant Hunters – '*Bunyanga*', the Dance of the Men – *Ngomalame* ", and the exotic

112

Dance of the Maidens Reaching Womanhood – *'Lilombola'*. But perhaps best of all were the 'Makeshi' dancers. Dressed in their hideous masks and their fibre costumes they looked grotesque as they pranced about in front of the royal enclosure. How pleased and honoured I felt, as they had been specially sent for because I had admired and asked about them last week, particularly as their village lies three days' journey away.

I dined again that night with the Paramount Chief and his Mojo, thanked them for their hospitality and said my farewells.

The next day I was back at Lialiu, again travelling in the Land Rover with John who was going to judge the cattle and present the prizes! It was the third annual cattle show organised by the Government to try to stimulate a better idea of good cattle among the natives. They don't usually bother about quality as long as the quantity is enough. There were also prizes given for the best craft work. The inhabitants of Barotseland are extremely industrious and talented in many crafts. What was so remarkable was that each village seemed to specialise in one thing. For instance, in one village they carve wood, another will work in iron. A further village will go in for basket work and yet another will cure and prepare skins. In each line their standard is extremely high as far as native crafts go.

I went back again the next day with John to see the show. As a cattle show, it was a bit of a flop; the standard was very poor and only a few cattle were entered. The natives said the prizes were not big enough, although I think the first was £5.00. They don't seem to get the idea that the honour of obtaining a 'first' for your animals is worth much more than the monetary value. Still, that's Africans!

However, I found the village crafts very interesting. There were some really fine exhibits. The iron workers had entered axes and spears – various types ranging from big heavy ones for spearing crocodiles or lion, to long, slender ones with barbed heads for spearing fish. The basket work was first class. Many had quite intricate patterns woven through them. There were some very fine prepared skins too, but perhaps the woodcarving was the most interesting. The Mlozi are really fine craftsmen.

It had been a fascinating experience to witness the celebrations. How pleasantly simple and carefree these people were. How long can it last I wondered. What will happen to the partially cut-off land when the outside world floods in with its forgotten rules and misplaced values, its slick talk and pop music, its prejudices and hate, its bullets and fear? Will these people still retain their simple dignity or will they become like their chip-shouldered, politically demented cousins in the built-up, Europeanised parts?

That evening, over a cup of linden tea with missionaries at a nearby mission, I listened as they discussed the impact they had made on the

Barotse people. Their schools were doing well and they had reason to be pleased with the progress they had made, although they had no illusions as to the thinness of the veneer which was slowly being spread over the old pagan Africa. But, given time, they were sure great things could be done to emancipate the African from his primitive past. The administrative officers I had spoken to in Mungu were of the same opinion.

Given time! How much can they hope for in an Africa that seems to be caught up in a landslide that gives too much too soon? Perhaps, King Mwanawena, it is as well your land is so inaccessible. In the light of more recent events you would be well advised to open the door slowly so that the 'wind of change' blows in gently – throw it open and the sudden rush of wind might be disastrous. Perhaps those poor communications you lamented may not be the trouble with the land, but its salvation.

***

There is an interesting little sequel to the Mwanawena story. Many years after my sojourn in Africa when I was teaching in Hampshire, my wife, Maureen, and I were browsing in an antique shop. She for her part was interested in the antiques while I wandered to an area where there was bric-a-brac. Imagine my amazement when I saw a face that I recognised. I picked up the plaster head and looked more closely at it and turning it over there it was – Mwanawena III engraved on the back. The plaster model must have been made when Mwanawena came to England for the coronation of King George VI. Of course, I bought the head and he looks down at me from the shelf above my desk!

CHAPTER 11

TRUCKS AND TRAINS – LIFTS AND DETOURS

In the morning John Tremlett came to me saying there was a truck going to Mulobezi, 250 miles towards Victoria Falls. Although I was intending to go into the Congo from here and it is a pity to turn south again, I decided it was too good an opportunity to miss for retrieving my revolver that I'd had to leave behind and which is invaluable as I walk through wild country. I went to meet Tony Sarano who runs the Barotseland Transport Company and said I would like to accept his offer. I don't know when the truck will be going but I think Tuesday.

While I was in Sarano's office seeing about my lift, an African came in wondering when the plane was going to Balavale. The little plane comes once a week. He wanted to go somewhere halfway. The woman handling affairs tried to put him off.

"It's very expensive. You will have to pay special landing fees for that is not a normal stop"

With the casual air of the business man who doesn't bother with trifling money matters he said, "Oh, that doesn't matter. Just make out the charges, my business there is urgent." He owned some Kaffir stores ('Kaffir' is a derogatory Afrikaans word for a black person). Here was I bumming a lift and he was flying and not caring a button for paying special landing fees to go where he wanted.

Next day, to use the time, I borrowed a bike and cycled out to Kandi, five miles away, which is the village of the Balavale tribe and got them to give a demonstration of their archery. I was impressed how accurate it was. I also visited the local blacksmith and the iron workers who, with the most primitive tools and bellows made from hide, were turning out spears.

When I returned I learned the truck was leaving that night or, at least, in the early morning – 3 a.m. John drove me down to the truck. He's a grand chap, John, a steady, straight type and I really appreciated what he had done for me. The truck was already loaded up with hides, all stiff as boards, and we set off. The road was bad, but I dozed now and again. Dawn broke and the sun rose and the heat increased till it was like an oven in the cab and the African driver drove without saying a word. The road is only loose sand with some straw laid over it. At midday he called a halt at Luampa village. I made some porridge then spread out my ground sheet on the floor of a hut and slept. At three o'clock we were on our way again. The road was much worse now and we crawled along. The hours dragged on and I got stiff and cramped. At ten o'clock the driver stopped at a village and I lay down beside the truck and slept. Fourteen hours in a truck is a long time in one day – the driver must be tough.

We set out at five in the morning, and travelled all through the day without a halt, this time till just after midnight. How the driver kept going I don't know. It was the most gruelling ride I had ever had. Hours and hours on end of grinding away in the sand in the oven heat, with hardly any distance to show for it. The scenery was the same monotonous bush – bush – bush, dust and sand and all the time, the truck was bouncing about and vibrating like a pulsator separating diamonds. It was the first time I had ever had blisters rubbed on my back from a seat. But who was I to complain about that – I was grateful that I was lucky enough to be taken so far, though it was a killer day. After all, I was a tramp!

Yet, when one puts one's mind to it, it is even possible to forget these hardships. I thought of the places I would go. I dreamed of the places I had been to and sometimes I managed to lift myself out of the jarring hell. I imagined I was up on the Songwe river hunting crocodiles, or in the Hadhramaut among the Arabs. I thought of Nairobi and Spitzberg farm. I remembered Cairo and the treasures from the tomb of Tutankhamun and tried to imagine myself in the land when these things were new. Again, I lay on the smooth pebbly beach of the French Riviera and walked across the snow up in the Alps; I swam afresh in the warm, caressing waters of Flamingo Bay in the Sudan where we put in a couple of times when I was on the "Cory Freighter" in the Red Sea. Only little boats can go there and it's mostly used by dhows. After I swam there, I used to lie on the sand and watch the big combers come rolling in, all white on the blue sea, and listen to the breakers rumbling as they broke on the shelf and came rippling up the smooth sand. How picturesque the dhows were with their big white sails. Once we were there in moonlight and they seemed like phantoms, all misty white on the waves and I used to imagine them to be like the 'Marie Celeste', the ship that sailed the sea without a crew. Again, when the songs of the seamen came drifting in from the sea to prove that there was life on the dhows, I made them pirate men o' war. All this I remembered sitting in the truck. Maybe it was in that mad helter-skelter that I craved the opposite – someplace calm and serene with the music of the sea as a lullaby, and why I thought so much of this place.

I woke to the truck shuddering to a halt and spade work needed to dig it out of the sand. Later, at about 10 p.m., the load came loose and it took about half an hour to fix it. The boys lit a fire and I sat dozing beside it, glad of the respite. Over the whole journey, 5 miles per hour was the average speed. Sometimes in short stretches the driver managed to get it up to a spanking 15 miles per hour, but then it seemed as if the bottom was going to drop out. Midnight came and went and we pulled up at about one in the morning. I was thankful to unroll my sleeping bag and climb into it. How the driver managed to drive continually as he did for a couple of days over such a terrible road amazed me, but he got a bonus for the number of trips he did in a month so I expect that explained it.

***

On the map the name of Mulobezi looks big. Actually, it is not a village but only a big sawmill. From here the Zambezi Sawmills Railway runs to Livingstone and carries timber from the mills. The distance is near enough a 100 miles and I hoped to get a lift on it. I waited for it and it came in about three in the morning.

I had heard a lot about this railway. Apparently, it is a rather haphazard affair and it is not uncommon for it to come off the rails. The driver may stop the train and hunt if he sees something, and if he makes a kill, the train will wait till he cooks the liver, etc. and has a meal. I heard of one man travelling at the rear of the train who saw a kudu and wanted the train to stop while he went after it. The train was going round a sharp curve at the time so the fellow put a couple of shots over the engine to alert the driver, who waited while the hunter chased and shot the kudu. Such is the Zambezi Sawmills Railway. I waited beside one of the water tanks where the train must stop and according to what I'd heard there was no question of fares. I sat under a tree where the grass was long and listened to the wind, which seemed to talk as it passed by.

As sleep began to overtake me I rolled myself in my groundsheet. I didn't want to undo my kit and roll out my sleeping bag for I wanted to be ready to jump when the train came along. I dozed, half asleep, waiting for it. At about 3.30 in the morning I heard it a long way off, long before I saw its head beam piercing the darkness. It drew up heavily and seemed to be in an exhausted condition, belching steam and gasping for a drink. The glow from the fire stained the driver orange and painted the tender brick red. It looked cosy and friendly up in the loco, but I ran down the train into the darkness before heaving my kit up and clambering onto a wagon. I made myself as comfortable as possible and hoped I wouldn't fall off when I dozed. When it had quenched its thirst, the engine let out a loud hiss of satisfaction and started up with a jolt that had all the buffers clanging, as if it was eager to be on its way. As the hours went by I began to wonder if the local rumour that 'this train has square wheels' was true, for it seemed impossible for round ones to run with so much jolting and noise as these did. The tales I had heard of it jumping the rails seemed quite possible, if not imminent. It rattled and jerked and whistled with glee as it careered along the twisted, narrow gauge railway. It stopped many times, mostly beside the tall water tanks on stilts, to slake its thirst.

On these occasions after the dawn and the sun had come up, the train would be besieged by hordes of Africans, some clambering on as passengers, others selling little bits of cooked food and eggs and even tea in bottles. Each stop was like a fair ground with the crowd milling around. Then the engine would whistle a warning and end the melee when it jolted into movement. After these halts you could almost feel the new spirit in the loco and it hit new highs in reckless abandon.

On one of these stops after dawn I found a closed-in goods wagon. It was empty except for a few natives who had beaten me to it. I went back and got my kit, climbed in and slid the big door closed. After that, I was relatively comfortable lying on its floor, although the way the boards twisted and jolted as they went over the uneven line was not conducive to sleep. It arrived at Livingstone about one o'clock in the afternoon and I wasn't sorry. I walked out of the timber yard onto the road and headed for Victoria Falls. I soon got a lift along the five miles and I dug in again at the camping ground.

***

There was not nearly so much water in the Falls as there was six weeks ago when I was there before. So I have seen them in flood and when they are low. Though perhaps not so impressive as when full, they are better to photograph because the spray or mist is less. Today I went down the 'Boiling Pot', right down the chasm where the water tumbles in. To stand right at the bottom, a foot away from the column of water and look up creates the weirdest of feelings. It seems as if the water is going to crash over you. But the spray is heavy down there and wets you through.

I got a canoe over to Livingstone Island and stood on the very brink of the Falls and looked over. I think that is the most impressive view of all. I visited the big baobab tree, famous for its enormous size, and had a walk through the rainforest. I roamed around and walked over the knife-edge, a narrow ridge with a three hundred foot drop on either side into the broiling cauldron below. I was so glad I had had the opportunity of coming back and hadn't missed out on all this.

118

Next day, I picked up my .45 from the warden's safe and got on my way again. I had no trouble getting my money back for the filter and sun shade I returned to the camera people. It came in mighty handy for I was right down to rock bottom since I lost my purse up at Mungu.

Although I reported with the immigration authorities at Mungu, I was told I must report here also and I ran into trouble. Of all the bad luck, the Officer in Charge remembered me from a couple of years ago, when I was stopped from entering at Tanduma. He got a bit nasty again, but this time he had to admit me since I produced the £100 Letter of Credit, which was a requirement when travelling through the various countries. It had been sent from the bank in Dunfermline, Scotland, after the first debacle with him, although I never liked to carry it with me in case of theft or other problems. He only gave me a month in the country and made me cash the Letter of Credit, so I walked into town, waited till the bank opened and finally satisfied the immigration authorities. I didn't know what I was going to do though. I was near broke and was banking on working in the Copper Belt but with permission to stay for only a month in the country and no possibility of an extension, my chances of earning a bit of money were nil.

I walked out of Livingstone, somewhat depressed. The dust was terrible and I was bothered by a plague of small, persistent flies which were aggravating, all of which didn't lighten my mood. However, I was lucky to get a few lifts and arrived in Choma, about halfway between Livingstone and Lusaka.

***

I intended going up through the Congo to Kasenga then over the Luapula River into Northern Rhodesia again but was informed that the ferry was out of order, so I had to head back for Mokambo. I managed to get a lift to the outskirts of the town, then walked all day. I had done about 17 or 18 miles and it was getting to the time when I was looking for a likely place to camp in the next two or three miles, when I got a lift from a car that was going right through to Mokambo. Sounds a bit daft, I could have got the same car without all the walking if I had just waited. Yet I don't like doing that. I go on the idea that if I don't get a lift then I'll get there by walking. Anyway, here I am back on the road going north.

I got a lift to Fort Rosebery with a truck that runs manganese ore from a small mine to the railhead at Mufulira and crossed the Chombe ferry. It was almost dark when I was dropped off. I went down near the river, the Mansa River, and made camp. I didn't bother to pitch my tent but just put up my mosquito net. By the time I had cut and hauled enough firewood to my camp it was dark. I was just about starting to cook when two European police officers came along with a dog. Some natives had told them about me since it was unknown for a European to travel about without "boys", making his own camp and hauling wood. They therefore came to investigate, in case I was an escapee on the run from prison. However, they said they had read about my journey in the paper and half-expected it to be me. They warned me that there were lions in the district that sometimes roamed near the town and asked me if I wanted to sleep at the station. I was tempted but my gear was all over the place and food half cooked, so I said I would stay put. However, I loaded my .45 and kept it handy just in case. The policeman's parting words were, 'If you change your mind just come down to the station. Drop in any time'.

I was not disturbed in the night. No lion. Not even a roar. I wonder how many people know what it's like to sleep with a loaded revolver below their pillow and be tensed, even when asleep, in case of attack. When you wake up you don't come to sleepily but are instantly alert, listening, waiting, wondering what it is that has wakened you. I got on the road and walked a while, then got a lift on a road grader. It was the first one of its kind. I sat perched up there with the dust rising in clouds, while the thing tore along at about five mph. Presently, Paddy the driver, switched off the grader and we careered along all out, throwing safety to the winds at the breakneck speed of 12 mph, the vehicle's maximum effort. I travelled 15 miles in this. At his camp Paddy, an Irishman, introduced me to his coloured wife. I drank some tea with them then set off again.

It wasn't long before I got another lift from an agricultural officer in a little Morris Minor and returned to Kawambwa. It was dark when we arrived. I was dropped off at the Government Rest House, and was going to camp near it. However, a fellow who has a business running fish from Lake Mweru and selling it on the Copper Belt said I could use his room. He had booked and paid for it but had decided to drive on through the night. I might as well use it, he said. So I was lucky.

Also staying there was a young District Officer who had not been long in the country. He looked fresh and well turned out. His long shorts were nicely creased, his white topee on the chair was almost new. He talked about the Africans like black brothers and claimed they should have equal rights and equal pay as Europeans. I wonder how long he kept these ideas. Still he was no worse than anyone else who comes out from Britain at first. We all had these philanthropic ideas, but you learn – and quickly.

As far as equal wages with Europeans go, I asked him if he had ever been in charge of African workmen. Had he seen their standard of workmanship or how slowly they work in anything other than the crudest manual labour? Had he experienced some of the silly things they do like the time George Christie started a building gang on the foundations of a house then went

120

down sick for a few days. The boss boy came to him and said the bricks were finished. When he went to the job, they had built up the walls of the house 16 feet without a door or a window in the place. Or the time he left a boy to paint a little handrail on a staircase and the boy stayed on the job days and days, painting it over and over again until the paint was finished – two gallons of it!

No, he had had never seen anything like that, but his African clerk was wonderful. He was very prim and proper, this new District Officer. In these Government Guest Huts you provide your own food. He sat down to a three-course dinner, put up and served in 'Savoy' style. I sat at the other side of the table and surprised him by having a plate of porridge at night time (!), then chewed away at a piece of biltong and drank a mugful of strong coffee. I must have appeared rather boorish. I'm afraid I rather shocked him.

Kawambwa is a lovely little spot. I was struck by its freshness, its greenness, its big shady trees and the view from the escarpment across the wide expanse of hazy blue territory. After so much travel in flat, uninteresting country it was a pleasant relief.

The agricultural officer who brought me here said there was a car going to Mporokoso tomorrow morning, so I might just as well spend the day here as the road is very quiet with hardly any traffic on it. So I took the advantage of the day to get some washing, darning and mending done.

The rains were catching up with me. In fact, I thought they had had some showers already. In the afternoon big heavy clouds rolled across the sky and made it dark. There was a thunderstorm but no rain. Because of the minerals in the ground in Northern Rhodesia these storms are exceptionally severe. When it starts, the thunder never stops rumbling and lightning flashes all the time. Sometimes you can see it running along the ground.

I got that lift in the morning. It was a Government Labour Officer on tour. We made it to Mporokoso but had a lot of trouble with the car. I expected it to rain that night, the atmosphere was stifling and the sky heavy. I couldn't really afford to keep staying in the Rest Huts at 7/6d a night, providing my own food, so I planned to sleep on the verandah to get out of the rain instead of camping.

It was a good decision as it poured during the night, but I kept dry on the verandah. The boy in charge of the Guest House still wanted to charge me the 7/6d but he didn't get it. I wasn't going to pay the same for a cement bed as I would have for a room of my own and a spring mattress. I had been warned not to walk in this area as the lions are particularly dangerous around here. It was in the newspapers that 'all lions in the Mporokoso district are man-eaters'. One old male had 102 Africans to its name when it was shot by a young cadet administration officer.

That night I stayed with John Murran, the District Officer. I was getting a lift from someone going to Abercorn via Kasama the next day. I was awakened at 6 a.m. by Maxie Potter, a genial Afrikaans fellow. His wife was deaf and seemed to have no roof to her mouth and could only talk with great difficulty. Even then, it was very hard for strangers to understand her. We were in Kasama by 10 a.m. Maxie had some work there. Kasama is the Administration Headquarters of the Northern Province of Northern Rhodesia. It was 6 p.m before we left again, arriving in Abercorn about 9.30 p.m.

I stayed the night with them and next morning went down to Lake Tanganyika. Mpulungo is the little place there. There was only a fishing station there, but it was a lovely run down. It was very green and the mountains looked lovely and at the lake it looked like a Scottish loch with the hills. On the way back we went up the hills to a place where Maxie had some boys building weirs in a little mountain stream for irrigation purposes. Next day we went along the Tanduma road, as far as the Chozi River. It's good to get round about and learn the district. On the way out we went to a pan where Maxie knew a lone roan bull wandered about. As luck would have it, it was standing right in the middle of the *vleis*. A long shot, but Maxie missed.

We went out to a farm where Maxie sank three wells. This farm was literally being carved out of the forest. It was only started last year and they were still felling trees and digging out the stumps. The farmer, an old fellow in his seventies, had them on task work, 25 stumps per man per day. He was going to grow coffee. The farm was a thousand acres. I wondered how the farmers at home would do if they had to clear bush first before being able to produce anything.

I changed my abode from Maxie's home to camp by the side of Lake Chila, the little lake only half a mile from the town. Maxie went on tour again so I voluntarily left the house. I didn't feel comfortable staying in the house with his wife when he was not there. It was a lovely spot by the lake. There were no crocodiles, nor bilharzia, a parasite common in water in Africa. The water was clear as glass and the kind of palm trees that look like big ferns shaded the bank. I was swimming most of the day.

As I wrote by firelight, it was night and a full moon. Earlier on I went for a stroll along the lake. Walking through the palm glade when the moon was high, the shadows were solid and black. The places where the moonbeams filtered through the feathery stems of the palms were blue. A breeze rippled the water and spread the moon dust and the atmosphere the moon cast the sun could not compare with. The hills beyond the lake were black against the luminous sky, the water dark blue and the moon had painted a silver path down the middle of it which sparkled and glittered as the ripples broke it up. I walked along the beach and listened to the crunch of wet sand below my feet. There was only the sound of the little waves lapping the sand and the flutter of an occasional owl or some other nocturnal bird breaking the silence.

I went for a swim before I turned in and put a couple of big logs on the fire so that there would be a fine blaze when I came back. Have you ever seen the inviting blaze of a camp fire through the trees when you come from the beach fresh and cool from a moonlight swim? I didn't bother to erect my tent that night. I just lay my sleeping bag out beside the fire. I was finding my sleeping bag too warm but tonight should be fine. There's the fire and a cool, night breeze.

The following day I started out for Tanganyika. I wanted to go up into the Western Province although at the time, there was only an old German road hardly ever used by traffic. People advised me to go to Tunduma and get on the Great North Road where all the traffic passed. But I had been through that district. I knew it would be much easier to go that way, but I had made up my mind to go this other way.

CHAPTER 12

THE POWER OF PLEASE

I shook the Rhodesian dust from my clothes and re-entered Tanganyika. I got a lift in a truck belonging to the International Red Locust Control. The border between the countries was only a little stream and there was a ramshackle board telling you 'You are now entering Tanganyika', yet you didn't need that to tell you. The road suddenly deteriorated. What was amazing was the way the country changed suddenly whenever you crossed the border. You would think the boundary was natural instead of man-made. The landscape suddenly becomes mountainous and green. The road twists and climbs and the speed of the vehicles is cut by half. Although slower, it was much more interesting country to travel through than the monotonous, flat bush country that is Rhodesia and Bechuanaland. You feel it getting colder as you climb.

All over the place were little kilns made of anthill brick. High and conical shaped, they were the furnaces where the natives smelted the iron. However, although some were still being used, this was being discouraged by the government because of the wood being burnt in the process. We passed the 'Nave', the sacred mountain where any new chief must come to worship when he is installed. These were the 'Ufipa Mountains', with the people who lived here called the Wafipa.

It was dark when we arrived at Sumbawanga, which lay high up in the mountains. A wet mist hung over the town. I was dropped off at the Rest House, which definitely didn't compare with its Rhodesian counterparts. There were no beds, no lights and I slept on the cement floor, which was not very clean. The boy in charge couldn't cook. But, also, it was free.

I went along to the D.C. and got fixed up without any trouble with a three-month visitors pass and was told if I needed it extended to go to any District Commissioner. What a fine welcome into the country compared to Northern Rhodesia's nonsense. It was good to be back in East Africa again. I felt almost at home. Here I could speak the language and know the customs.

Sumbawanga was run by Arab traders. How the scene changed suddenly when I came to Tanganyika. Here was the breath of the East. It seemed as much separated from Rhodesia as if a great abyss cut them apart. You could see there was no European trade here. The shops were all mud hovels, none of them specialising in any commodity. Everyone was a general dealer and I wondered how they all prospered. The shops or *'dukas'* were arranged in a square, in the middle was the open market. In the streets there were picturesque Arabs with great turbans and flowing *'kanzus'*. I wandered round about the shops to see if they had any trucks going to Mpanda.

I had found that to get anything from these people you must become one of them. You don't barge in and just ask. Oh no! You'll get nowhere fast like that. I suppose that's how the European differs from these other races, Indian, Arab or African. Whereas we like a person to say straight out what he is about, they always lead up to say anything they want. I've learned to do the same when dealing with them. I walk into a shop. There is no counter. I greet them with some of the Arabic I remembered from my days in Aden. I'm really hazy about it now. I sit down and wait. As always, they brewed up some tea and coffee and served it in shallow little cups without handles. They squatted down on the split cane mats. The tea was flavoured with ginger, the coffee was black with neither sugar nor milk. They gave me the tea first and then the coffee. Both tasted vile. I drank it and tried to look as if I enjoyed it and went back for more, although it was tearing strips off my inside and I fancied, (professionally), that either would make an ideal paint remover. They filled up their cups and scoffed the contents in one or two gulps and refilled endlessly.

Then, casually, as if I couldn't care less in the world about it, I asked if they knew of any truck heading for Mpanda or any place going north. If they did they would tell you and, should it be their own, then you stood a better chance of getting a lift. Asking in the European way they would expect you to pay a fare. It's a much longer process this way, but much more effective and more interesting than the other. It took me nearly all forenoon going round the few shops. The self-inflicted punishment I sustained in drinking their coffee has hardened me, so that I'm sure I could swallow proof whisky laced with carbide, and still smile.

However, it paid dividends, for I got a lift to a little place called Namanyere, nearly halfway to Mpanda. It was leaving at about 6 p.m. In the meantime, I am sitting writing under a jacaranda tree.

I got the lift to Namanyere and slept the night in the house of an Arab who travelled on the truck. In the morning I started walking. Namanyere is on the edge of the tsetse fly area. They make life hell. Their bite is like a bee sting, although it is itchy rather than sore after it. As I walked I had to keep a leafy branch waving, but even that didn't keep them at bay. When I sat to

125

rest it was sheer torture. It nearly drives you mad. When you kill them you see they have thick red blood like an animal. I was all red blotches.

The area was pretty much alive with game. Elephant spoors were all over the place with the usual trail of broken branches and chewed twigs that they leave behind. The sand was fairly loose and made walking heavy. I hadn't come across any water to fill my bottle. As usual, I had rationed myself to a sip every few hours. Rather an ordeal to just wet the mouth when you feel you could finish the lot in one go, when you are sweating with the heat. And it was hot now, the kind of stinging, heavy heat that precedes the rains.

The next day was yet another of foot slogging. It was a heavy day and I struck very loose sand that was terrible to walk in. It saps the energy and makes you want to drink water by the gallon. But I had to do the opposite and I cut my water ration as it was nearly finished. My one thought was that I must get water tomorrow. I used to feel sorry for troops in the North African campaigns when they were issued with half a gallon of water per man per day to wash and drink. Now I envied them. Four great big pints in one day! But now I was teasing myself. Of course, I couldn't wash. I felt encrusted with dirt with the dust sticking to the sweat.

I saw some elephant, but they were quite a bit off the road. At least I heard them breaking branches and saw one standing, rear end view. I was exhausted and knew I must sleep.

I got walking next morning and was really worried about the water situation. I don't think anybody can appreciate what it's like. However, towards early afternoon, I came on a little African village. I could hardly believe my eyes. I walked in and felt like wringing the hand of the first native who came near just for being there. They were rather apprehensive at first. No doubt my appearance must have been repellent, with haggard face and a three-day beard caked in red dust. However, after they realised I was a 'bona fide' traveller and meant no harm, they couldn't do enough for me. One brought some eggs, another a small hen and another a bowl of hot water. Very thoughtful of them, especially the hot water! How good it was to have a wash and shave and eat a proper meal instead of a bit of biltong and dry porridge oats with sugar and a little salt – sugar to build up the expended energy and salt to replace that lost in sweating – and a couple of sips of water. That was my fare and how good it was to feel secure for a night. Even then, in the security of the village and with an abundance of water, I could hardly believe it was as bad as I thought at the time. A truck passed while I was here but didn't stop.

On the way again I saw some giraffe. They stood at a safe distance and looked on interestedly. I also saw some baboons while I was searching for wood. I needed plenty of wood to make two fires and I slept between them, hoping they would keep any lion at bay that might stray near. The road was very quiet, at least during the day. At night, the odd vehicle might pass but, of course, they don't stop when it's dark and only a fool would be on the road at night.

Another truck passed today but didn't stop. I saw some more elephant this morning again, luckily quite a bit off the road. Sometime afterwards I came on a village with an African 'hotel' run by natives and was pleased to have a break. I think they were surprised when I walked in and asked for tea. It tasted good. I filled the water bottle again and carried on; it was too early in the day to stop. The hotel was only a mud hut with a fire in the centre of the floor and a couple of tables and folding chairs black with smoke. It can't be far to Mpanda now. It was 100 miles from Namanyere.

Mpanda at last. A hundred miles since Sunday, five days walking. In the loose sand that was not too bad. Mpanda was just a little place that had grown because it suddenly became a railhead after lead was discovered and a mine built nearby. The usual little Tanganyikan village, Indian dukas grouped round the four sides of a square with the open market in the centre, but only one train per week runs.

But the street I walked into that afternoon could have been Princes Street, Edinburgh, or the Strand, for neither of these mighty boulevards compared with the importance of Mpanda at that moment. How good it was to see even the dirty hovels that pass as shops after the tension of walking in the bush, where the problems of water and wild animals are always on your mind.

I walked to the edge of the town to find a place to camp. I was sheltering under a tree when I was hailed by an old fellow who lived in a mud hut. Mr Tim Downie was his name and a grand old fellow he was – a real pioneer – an Australian who came here in 1903. An old prospector and alluvial gold miner, he spent 25 years in the Congo around these parts trading rubber and mining. He was also up on the Lupa for years.

He invited me into his home. Listening to him that night as we sat chatting, I got a glimpse of a life spent here in Africa. He was employed by the mine in charge of boys cutting trees for the furnace in the mill. At the time he was on long leave, spending the three months at the mill as he had nowhere else to go. He felt it was degrading that he, with all his experience of mining and prospecting, must finish his days on this paltry job. A lonely old man who liked to talk for the sake of company, but I had to get on my way heading for Tabora, 200 miles from the mine.

I had been told there was hardly ever any traffic on this road, but I saw plenty of elephant spoors and, that night, slept in an African village. The following forenoon I passed a Mission but didn't go in. It had been a hard day, all up hill and heavy going and, although there were signs of buffalo, I didn't see them. One of my boots burst away from the sole and I tied it up with a strip of bark, which didn't make the going any easier.

That night I was awakened by something walking close to where I slept. I shouted and it stopped. I shouted again and it went away. What it was I didn't know, lion, leopard or cheetah, but it was a soft-pawed animal. Walking on again and still no traffic, I couldn't help thinking that maybe I would have been better going by Mbeya, but I convinced myself that I would feel better for coming this way. It was fine to arrive at a village and better still that there were some Indian *dukas* where I was able to get water.

Next morning, on leaving the village I walked for a while then got a lift in a truck. I could hardly believe my ears when I heard it. I had long since given up hope of the possibility of getting a lift on this road. Indeed, I wondered if traffic ever used it at all. How pleased I was. The truck drew up suddenly with a jolt and an African jumped out but held on to the door.

"A Scotchman," he said in good English. "You are the man who is walking round the whole world like David Livingstone?"

He was drunk.

"Yes," I said. In his state it was no good to disillusion him.

"I heard about you a long time ago," he went on.

He was short and stout and well dressed in jacket and shorts and yellow stockings. A pair of the inevitable steel rimmed, plain glass spectacles completed the outfit. These spectacles the Indians sell for 7/6d. They are the epitome of dress to the city or educated boy. One just isn't properly dressed without them. They remind me of the old Chief who always kept a pair of spectacle rims – no glass – to wear to impress any visitors. He could put them on and be very proud and conscious of them. Occasionally he would take them off and clean the imaginary glass with a cloth, perhaps to draw attention to them. And, to really make sure they were clean, he would draw the cloth through the hole where the lens should be.

Anyway, this boy had a pair, and a pipe with a bent stem stuck down the leg of his stocking. He hung on to the door and swayed with it.

"I, Mr Jacobus Simanga, educated at Livingstone Mission, Nyasaland, welcome you Sir. My teacher was a Scotchman," he said. "In the Grace of the Father, the Son and the Holy Ghost we must assist Scotchmen."

As the door swung back he nearly fell. I bundled him in and climbed in myself. How good it was to see the road slide beneath me without feeling the grind of the gravel under my army boots and the weight of the load on my back. At my side, Jacobus drank deeply from a bottle and blessed me in the name of God. At times he worked himself up to the pitch of a soap-box, street corner bible thumper.

"To think that God Almighty should send his only begotten son to die on this Earth so that I, Jacobus Simanga, a poor sinner, should be brought from the Darkness," (an educated African's term for the illiterate state of his fellow countrymen), "so that I may assist you, a Scotchman." And, as the truck bumped into a deep rut – "Bloody fool!" That last exclamation to the driver.

He went on to preach the gospel to me in the manner a child recites poetry he has learned off by heart. He would take gulps at the bottle and the liquid ran from the corners of his mouth. Somehow the sermon, and the drunken, slurred words, the occasional 'Bloody Fool!" and the alcohol that was breathed into my face from a couple of inches distance, seemed incongruous.

The truck was going to Nyonga, about 40 miles from where I was picked up. Actually, it hadn't brought me any nearer to Tabora for Nyonga was 18 miles off the main Tabora road, but now I could sleep in a village and get water and still be no further away than where I would have been had I just continued walking.

It was dark when we arrived at the village. The usual type of Tanganyikan place with Indian *dukas*. The driver drove up to the store of the Indian who owned the truck, who gave me a meal of curry and rice. I decided to take a rest for the day as there was a Government Rest house which the D.C. and other admin officers used when on safari. I settled in there. There was only a table and a chair, but no beds, so I slept on the cement floor. No doubt they brought their own camp beds. In the morning a messenger came from the 'Baraza' – native court – to see who I was. He must have carried back a favourable report to the Chief, for in the afternoon Chief Shambwe II, Chief of the Ukononga tribe, came to visit me with a whole crowd of his council. He brought gifts of eggs and a fowl and some bread. They were gifts, but his chief elders remarked privately that if the Bwana had any 'rasasi', cartridges, he would be pleased to accept some for the chief. I had no cartridges, but even if I had I wouldn't have given them to him, chief or no chief.

However, we sat and talked for a while and I asked about the tribal customs, etc. But it was no use asking a chief these things. He always tried to make out his people were completely civilised and these little oddities were long since gone. Half the eggs were bad!

Before leaving the next day I was warned not to walk the stretch of road to Tabora because of elephant and lion, but I must get there and, fortunately, it was very quiet. I came to the area I had been warned about after crossing the Ugalla River and arrived at a village where they gave me a meal of dried fish. Here the lion are common. The tension as I walked was quite a strain as I had been warned of both elephant and lion. When a buck or a monkey moved, and there were plenty of them here, it made me whip round expecting to meet danger at my back. However, other than these buck and monkeys I hadn't seen any animals of danger, but at night I had to be really on the alert. I was woken by a lion grunting or coughing, but it was some distance off. However, it was quite a spine-chilling sound when sleeping in a tent and expecting trouble, but there was no disturbance.

The next day was the same and I was very tense. The forest was quite thick on either side and made me feel awfully closed in. I walked all day. I was getting worried about water as it had been two and a half days since leaving the Ugalla River. I had the biting, knowing thirst I had experienced before and it was terrible. My bottle was almost empty and even then it was even more than lukewarm. The little sips I took didn't relieve the thirst, but it kept me going.

Late in the afternoon I saw a woman. She ran away at the sight of me. I called after her in Kiswahili, *"Oh Mama Tafathali Njoo, nina kiu Mama, Ninataki masaada ninataki maji Mama, tafathali"* "Oh Mama, please come. I am thirsty. I need help. I need water Mama, please." Tafathali – the word that probably saved my life was the word almost never used between Europeans and Africans.

She stopped and I sat down. Gradually, she plucked up courage and came back. She must have seen I was in sore need of water for she told me to leave my pack but bring my *'panga'* and come with her. I did so and she took me to a *'mkondo'* – dry river bed. She took the *panga* and scraped a hole and the sand got wet. Deeper and the water started to run into the hole. I helped until we had quite a sizable hole, maybe 18 inches deep, and the water was clear as crystal and filled it in like a basin. Surely nectar could not have tasted better, even though there was a slight salty tang. Not much really, just a taste of it.

We went back to my pack. The woman put it on her head and walked with it with ease. It weighed between 70 and 80 lbs. The village was two or three miles away on a path from the road. I would not have seen it had I been on the road by myself. I couldn't understand why the woman was so far away from her village. She said there had been other women with her, but they had run away when they saw me and had not come back.

At the village the woman took me to her hut. I sat at the door. The people gathered round, shy at first, then as they became bolder, eager to know where I had come from and why I was in the bush on my own. It was when one youth addressed me as *'Mzee'* – the respectful term for 'old man' – that I wondered at my appearance. A glance at my steel mirror told me. My face was haggard and the dust, caked to mud on my four day beard with sweat, aged me considerably. No wonder the women took fright. My shirt was torn with the rucksack, and dirty. My boots were burst and looked odd with strips of bark round them. Perhaps my face also wore the anxiety that the lack of water had brought. How good a wash and shave felt! I was given the inevitable gift of eggs and a fowl which I baked in clay. It was very good and, after my meal, I slept.

Next day I got back on the road again and walked till midday. Then to my joy I heard the sound of a motor coming. It was a native bus going to Tabora. The Indian in charge willingly agreed to give me a lift. There was an Indian woman with children in the front compartment with the driver, so I got in the back.

The bus was an Albion diesel truck. The wooden seats were placed down the sides and the luggage stacked down the centre. What a pile there was – sacks of flour, bundles of clothes, wicker baskets with hens in them, lamps and tins of paraffin, a table and some chairs, some gaudy coloured tin trunks, suitcases and small children and all kinds of paraphernalia jumbled up in a disorderly pile. The passengers sat jammed tight. They were happy, laughing and joking, sweating and stinking. Still, it's not so bad when you get used to it and anyway, much better than walking. No doubt I smell awful to them too. The Africans say the European smells to them.

I sat between an old Arab and a fat *'bibi'*. The old man had a big, shapeless turban, a lined face and grey beard and wise, twinkling old eyes. He sat with his feet tucked under him on the seat. How he didn't get cramp I don't know. He told me of the old slave days in the territory, but I couldn't follow his Kiswahili very well. He spoke very quickly with a thick gutteral Arabic accent. The fat woman on my other side insisted on sharing her *'mohogo'* root and ground nuts with me (tapioca is made from *'mohogo'*.) I was glad of them.

You learn a lot travelling this way. I saw a wedding in Nyonga and didn't understand all the moves. The bride came from a hut covering her face with her hand and knelt down in the centre of the circle of people. The bridegroom stood at the back. The woman wore lots of fancy buttons and plastic butterflies in her hair, while the groom was immaculate in three-quarter length trousers, gaily coloured socks, a white jacket that was too small to button and white horn-rimmed, very dark sunglasses. Fine, except it was after 6 p.m. and the sun had gone down. Now I could ask the woman to explain the intricacies of the ceremony. She came from Nyonga.

"Mama, what was in the bowl that the old woman dipped into and touched the hand of the girl and the man?" I asked.

She thought it a huge joke that I should be interested in this. She laughed heartily and the seat shook as her huge bulk vibrated.

"*Mafuta tu, Bwana, Mafuta*"

"What kind of oil, Mama?"

"*Mafuta ya Karanga,*" she answered with another burst of hearty laughing. But that didn't tell me much for *'Karanga'* means 'fry' and also 'monkey nuts', so I don't know whether it was ground nut oil or just any frying oil.

"Mama, why did the old woman run round the bride singing?"

"*Shauri ya bahati, tu, Bwana.*" To bring her luck.

"Mama, why did the boy shoot an arrow into the door of the hut after the *bibi* went into it?"

At this she laughed so heartily, the baby slid off her lap and the tears rolled down her fat, black cheeks. She shook her head from side to side, "Oh Bwana, that was to tell her she was a '*bibi*' now and belonged to her bwana and that if she took another man to herself, she would be shot with this arrow."

So it went on. It was good fun and I think the old woman thought so too.

***

I was glad to reach Tabora. There was something good in the feel of the tarmacadam streets under my boots when the bus arrived. The sand and the thirst were behind me and I had done 250 miles in sixteen days! That night I made my camp in a grove of mangoes.

Tabora is known for mangoes, a legacy of the slave trading days. Here was the main centre for the slave collecting before they were marched to the coast. The seeds of the mangoes they ate have grown into big shady trees and there are groups of them everywhere. They line the streets and it is said there is a line of them along the old caravan route to the coast. Perhaps right there where I sat writing up my diary, a group of slaves rested.

In the night it rained and I got wet as I hadn't bothered putting up the tent. However, I was tired enough not to be bothered too much with the wet sleeping bag and, in the morning, I took my boots to a cobbler to be mended. They were on their last legs and the cobbler considered a while before he agreed to try to put them right.

A touch of fever hit me the next day and I laid up most of the day. I took a couple of Daraprim tablets and later I felt a bit better, but not right.

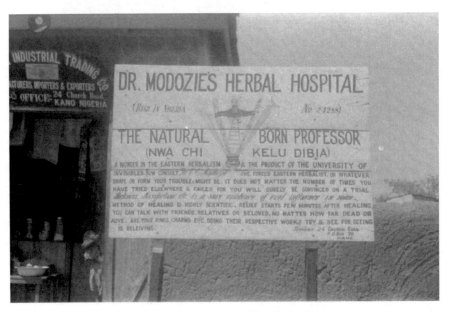

Dr. Modozie's Herbal Hospital, Kano

Groundnuts awaiting export. Kano was known for them but the project
failed

In the garden of the D.C., the Witch tree with D.C. Eric Lanning and his son John

D.C Eric Lanning, Peggy, John and Lindy taking David on his way

The pot in the ground. Now in the museum in Uganda.
Given the name "The Lessels/Lanning Pot"

Porter standing in smoking earth on the volcano

Men with drums and pipes for the
arrival of the Queen

Two splendid hunters

David and pygmies ready for the hunt

Mother with exotic hairstyle and baby
in the Belgian Congo

Crossing the river by canoe

The Queen arriving to open the Reserve

The Queen approaching the Kabaka and porch leading to the stand that
David was involved in building

Small working elephant with rider in the Uturi forest

David with the hubble bubble pipe

Paddlers on Mwanawena's barge

The talking drums

King Mwanawera's drummers

The royal barges of Mwanawena

Barotse natives spear fishing

Watutsi women

CHAPTER 13

WHICH WAY TO GO? TESTING FATE

I felt rough next morning so I had the day to rest and felt better after a good sleep. I wanted to know something about local history regarding slave days. Tabora was Tippou Tibbs' H.Q. I went to the *boma* and they put me onto Major Scarth, a retired army officer, who has lived in the district for years. However, he could tell me nothing, but best of all he did have some books, 'Livingstone's Last Journals'. He drove me back to my camp and was appalled to see me just camped under a tree with my kit open to thieves while I went around. He insisted on me going back to live in his house. He was a bachelor and had only one bedroom, but he fixed up his garage with bed, chair etc. and it was very comfortable. It was really good of him. He seemed to be the general factotum of Tabora as, although retired, the Government gave him all sorts of jobs to do. He was a member of the town council, inspector of vehicles, as well as the censor for films. He also ran the sports, was the local reporter for the Tanganyika Standard (Dar-es-Salaam) and was the cartoonist for two African papers, which were currently running two separate cartoon strips.

In the morning, before I met Major Scarth, I walked out to the place of Chief Fandikera II, Chief of the Wanyanwezi tribe. It was about three miles from Tabora. Chief Fandikera was a big man and with his robes and turban – put on so I could take a photo – he looked quite massive. He looked more like an Arab Sheik than an African Chief. The long domination of the Arabs in this area has left its mark and most of the natives are Muslims. He spoke good English and he showed me round his house and grounds and made me a present of a bow and arrows he had when he saw I was interested. Outside were the drums, four of them hanging on a pole, the biggest I had ever seen. It took about six men to lift one. His house was new and had a fine carved door. It stood on the ground where Fandikera I – who was Chief when Livingstone passed this way – had his. Round the courtyard were the ruins of the rooms where he kept his harem. After him there was a woman as Chief and she had her harem of men. Chief Fandikera II told me he had four wives.

In the afternoon Major Scarth drove me out to Kwihara to see the *tombe* or house where Livingstone and Stanley lived; the house was presented to Stanley by Sheik Sayid bin Salim and Stanley brought Livingstone back to live there after he found him at Ugigi. The house is a tumbledown ruin, the roof having fallen in and I had to heave with my shoulder to push the debris away when I opened the carved door. The original doors were 'stolen' by a past D.C. and are now in the Afrikaner museum in Jo'burg. The house is in danger of being demolished all together for lack of funds to reconstruct it. One officer said if he were to write to *The Times* in London, he would get the money, but he was not allowed to. (On my return to Scotland I wrote myself but never learned if the work had been done.)

I wanted to see Williamson's diamond mine near here. I was lucky with lifts and only walked a few miles, arriving in Shinyanga late in the afternoon. The mine lies 18 miles from the town and I had walked about six miles along it when I came on a native hut. I approached and asked if they would take me in for the night. The *bibi* was surprised but after thinking for a moment, she welcomed me in with pleasure and, when the meal was prepared, I was asked to join them. The *posho* was in one big pot with a dish of meat beside it. Everybody dug in with their fingers and it was a case of 'may the best man win'. There were four of us and I was at a disadvantage. The food was so hot I could hardly touch it far less scoop up some and keep it in my hand, yet all the natives took great handfuls and rolled them into balls before eating them. Still, I was satisfied and given a place to sleep on the floor that night. I appreciated their hospitality.

Of all the luck! After walking the last dozen miles up to the mine I was not allowed to enter by the security people. The officer said I must have direct permission from Dr Williamson and he was in Nairobi meantime. Rather disappointing after walking all this way and walking out to the mine too, then being turned back. However, I got a lift back with a young prospector for the mine, Bill Deane, and he brought me 20 miles on my way to Singida, not the main way, just a bush track, but it cuts off the long way back to Nzega. The country was dry and bare.

I came to a real 'bush' village. The houses and shops were terribly dilapidated and it had the air of complete isolation. It gave you the feeling you would have on a desert island. It seemed completely cut off from the outside world. They were all Arab traders here – no Europeans. The streets were wide and dusty; the huts were square, squat, mud *tembes* with no windows and thatched roofs that were almost flat.

The village idiot crawled about in the dust completely naked. The children teased him and threw water over him and everybody laughed. Then he got up and threw stones at them and one of the men went over and beat him with a stick. No life for a lunatic in an African village.

I was invited into an Arab house. I like the old Arabs. They are fine people. It's good to eat all the different foods and learn their customs. Here the diet is curried meat. They give you a plate of chapatti with it. No knives or forks. The idea is to tear off a piece of chapatti and use it like paper, scooping up a piece of meat and eating the lot. Before and after the meal they pass a bowl of water round to rinse your hands. After the meal you rinse your mouth, draw up some phlegm from the soles of your feet, spit, belch, blow your nose and lean back and sigh 'Humdillilah' as if you have gorged yourself. Then they are pleased.

In the morning there was a truck going to Igunga along the old resin road. It belonged to an old Arab, Halmis Rashid, who claimed the road as his since he cut it himself way back in 1929 to open up his trade in resin. Now more people have come into the resin business and villages have sprung up along it. The natives collect the *manyewe* resin from the Marura tree, a small tree covered with vicious, long white thorns with hideous black knots at their base.

The truck was old. There were no doors on it, nor cover for the engine but I was glad of it and considered myself extremely lucky since traffic never uses this way. Igunga is 50 miles from Kenengi and then only 26 miles to the main Nzega-Singida road. But my luck didn't hold out like that. We started out. An Arab/African drove with me in the centre and old Halmis Rashid on the outside. The land was a desert – a complete desert – flat and hard as a dried lake bed and the wheels barely made a track on the cement-like surface. The road was merely a mark on the sand. Tracks led off this way and that. How the driver kept to the one he wanted I don't know. We went off the straight route and presently came on a native hut. A first-class piece of navigation.

There was something pathetic about that hut there: a spot in the vast wasteland without even a tree to shelter it from the great, burning, inverted basin of a sky. In a nearby piece of black cotton soil were the traces of a '*shamba*' (cultivated piece of land), but even that soil was as hard and barren as the sand. They would have to wait for the rains to come to grow anything. The hut was made of grass thatch and I wondered where it had come from. Yet they say that the land becomes a prairie of waving grass when the rains come and the soil is so soft that a truck would bog down to the axles if it attempted to pass over it.

A couple of skulls and a set of gazelle horns lay in the sand. A few spears were in a pile beside the door. A woman pounded some meal, another sat doing nothing in particular. A native with greying hair came from the hut wiping the sleep from his eyes as we drove up. Some goods in a bag were dropped off the lorry and the native brought out a bag of resin. Where he had picked it was a mystery for there wasn't a tree in sight. Perhaps over the horizon was a wood. I looked inside the sack. The resin was like little chunks of solidified varnish. Halmis Rashid said a man can pick two kilos a day among the trees. We drove off and left that little lonely homestead. The children came running and stood waving goodbye till we passed out of sight. Soon the ground ceased to be flat and even. The surface was cut up with little drifts. The truck nosed its way down into them and squirmed through the loose sand and up the other side. During the rains these will be raging, mad rivers that will run for a few hours or days, then dry up again.

A wind blew up carrying sand with it. It came across our path and increased in volume till it was a fair-to-middling sandstorm. Old Rashid unwound part of his turban and wrapped it round his face and I pulled my hat down on the side of my head to shield that side of my face. They should have stopped, of course, with the engine open as it was. Soon the inevitable end came. The engine seized up and the rubber tube connecting the radiator blew out.

The storm soon rolled passed us. All attempts to improvise a connection for the radiator failed and even if they had been successful, I don't know if they would have got it started since it was all clogged up with sand. I waited till they gave up and sent a boy running across the desert back to Kenengi for help from someone they knew who also had a truck. They fancied Kenengi was about 12 miles away in a straight line, and that Igurubi was about ten. I decided to walk on to Igurubi although it was rather late to start. It was nearly one o'clock in the afternoon, but I set out hoping I could find my way. My water bottle was full.

When the truck had passed out of sight the land seemed terribly vast and there were no trees or hills to bring the horizon closer. I felt very small and puny and didn't like the feeling. This land seemed too big to try and walk across. How I wished I was in Scotland. There, there is a friendliness about the country, even when it works itself into a temper when you stand on Ben Nevis and watch the black thunder clouds roll down the Glen, or when you see it in a happy mood when the sun dances on the blue waters of Loch Katrine. Aye, there the land has character – it has moods and feelings. This wilderness I was in was as expressionless and unfeeling as the eyes of a disillusioned street woman. It was worse; it was as merciless as a ruthless killer. When I came to a place where the track forked, I could almost sense that great sheet of white hot metal it had for a sky twist itself into a sadistic grin as it saw me stop and wonder. A wrong decision could be fatal.

There was a feeling like panic in me when I saw the fork. Which road led to Igurubi? The other one might go anywhere. Even just to miss Igurubi and have to spend a night out there could be lethal, as there were man-eating lions around Igurubi. Only a week before a woman was eaten. And there wasn't even wood to light a fire. The panic gave way to a fatalistic feeling where I felt resigned to the future. 'Well, if this is it – it's it!' I took the right-hand fork. It's rather a queer feeling when you are walking and don't know if you are going to or away from your destination.

Presently I came into some trees and felt thankful for them. In them I couldn't see the track I had been following, stretching for endless miles ahead of me. They were Marura trees. All over them were lumps of resin which had hardened after oozing out of a crack in the bark. They seemed wicked and vicious with their long needle spikes. In places they were so close together and matted that a breath of wind couldn't have passed through them without getting torn to ribbons.

I cannot explain my relief when I saw the outline of Igurubi come into view. It was like the snapping of a bow string, the lifting of a great weight from my shoulders, the jury's verdict of 'Not guilty' when you are expecting the death sentence. It was evident, even by its appearance, that Igurubi was in lion country. The little mud shops were built in four unbroken lines to form a square. There were only two openings and these were for the road that passes through it. At night these loopholes were sealed with thorn branches and Igurubi became a little walled town. The sun was gone, with night not far off and already the hyenas had begun to 'Hou-o-o-p' when I entered the village.

I slept the night on the verandah of an Arab shop. In the morning I started out again. It's 28 miles to Igunga from Igurubi and hardly possible to do it in one day, with the heat and my pack for the sand is loose in some places. I walked around 15 miles to where there were trees and I could make a fire.

There were no lion in the night, but plenty of hyenas howling quite near. I arrived at Igunga the following afternoon. The lull of the siesta hung over the place. I dumped my pack down and shook an old Arab who was sleeping on the verandah of his shop. The doors were wide open and anyone could have gone in. He woke with a start and was very surprised at seeing me. When I told him I was walking and thirsty and wanted some tea, he tottered on shaky legs trying to hurry through his shop to bring his wife. I wanted to pay for it, but he wouldn't hear of it.

There was something wrong with the old man's eyes. His upper and lower eye lids seemed to be rolled back leaving red, open flesh round bulging eyeballs. He wasn't able to close them right and they were continually watering. The poor old guy was in serious trouble and looked quite hideous.

Here in Africa these Muscat Arabs do not adhere rigidly to their customs and the women do not veil themselves or hide away. His wife was big and fat and her face was covered with '*wourse*', the yellow powder mixed with oil the Arab women put on their face to keep the skin soft and her eyes were dark with kohl. They both made a great fuss of me. I took off my boots and sat on the mat. The old man came back breathless with a dish of dates that were just turning from yellow to a ripe black. Then his wife brought tea and 'Halwa', an Arabic sweetmeat that is something like Turkish delight. They made me very welcome. Later, they brought me a dish of curried meat and chapatti.

***

<u>Monday 16th November, 1953</u>

'Now it is late afternoon, almost sundown. The best time of the day. I am sitting on the mat on the verandah, writing. Two Arabs are sitting outside playing a game like chess with stones in holes in the ground. An African has passed strumming on an instrument like a bow with an empty gourd attached to it that gives it a deeper bass note than the twang of an ordinary bow string. Little dust devils rise and swirl across the square. They are like miniature tornadoes.

A bright-eyed little Arab girl curls herself shyly round a verandah pole. I give her some biscuits I have left from what Bill Deane gave me, just to see her eyes light up.'

Little did I know that, one day, I would have four little girls of my own.

CHAPTER 14

THE LION MEN

Thursday 19th November, 1953, Singida

On the way again I passed the village of Makomera, seven miles from Igunga. The trees here are widely scattered, just one here and there in the sand. I had to go quite a radius to get firewood. I hope to get to the main road tomorrow.

Yesterday I came on the main Singida road and I camped right by the road. It was dark when an Indian truck came along. It said a lot for him stopping when it was dark, but he took me on. We arrived at Singida at 3.30 in the morning. I slept in the back of the truck till about 8 a.m. It's quite cold up here. Tanganyika's climate varies so much if you are travelling. One night you may be down on low ground and sweating, the next night you will be on a high plateau and cold.

Singida has an interesting past. Here is the home of the Lion Men. People who dress up in lion skins and kill people by tearing them with the claws as lions would do. They are ritual killings and there was a great spate of them around 1949, when over 200 deaths were reported. Since then only an occasional one. Just last week they thought they had one, but it proved to be just an ordinary murder. Some Lion Men were caught and hanged, but they were never able to get to the bottom of the mystery. They don't know why they killed in this way, but they thought the women were at the back of it.

The tribe involved in this is the Wanyaturu tribe. I wanted to get some information about it all. I went up to the *boma* but they didn't know much about it. (*Boma* has several meanings – a livestock enclosure; a stockade or kind of fort; a district government office. The term is widely used in many parts of eastern, central and southern Africa.) I found that many Government officers were very ignorant of the country they governed. They seemed to take no interest in things other than those with which they were directly concerned. Besides, they were continually changing around so you rarely found a person who had been in the district for any length of time. It was the same in Tabora. I'll have to write to Dar-es-Salaam to get to know any information I want. Also the police officer who was here at the time is up at Moshi now. So maybe I can go and see him. Stewart is his name.

Later I went to see Stewart and he told me that between 1946 and 1948 there were over a hundred reported cases, but there may have been scores more and reports went back as far as 1923. He certainly knew a lot about Lion Men (Lycanthropy – the dictionary gives "the supposed magical transformation of a human being into a wolf" (in this case a lion) and I quote Superintendent Stewart:

If you believe in Lycanthropy then these things can be explained. I don't! Policemen are paid to believe facts, yet I have seen things that make you think.

A man came to a police station and confessed he had killed a woman. When I went to investigate, the man showed me the spot where he said he had killed her. He had dragged her to another place where there was blood and some beads. It could have been a real lion. In a damp patch there was one lion paw mark, I had seen it on four previous occasions. Now, lying on the ground was the woman's armlets standing one on top of the other. He said he cut off her hand and slid them off. A woman's bangles cannot come off unless the hand is removed. When asked what he did with the body he said he cut it into bits and threw it into a bush.

When I asked him what he was wearing he said his loin cloth, yet there was no blood on it. Nor were there signs of the body. Even if little pieces had been dropped there would be ants about. The witchdoctor said the man had done the murder and the man himself would firmly believe that he had.

You must understand the native's mind. They believe so much in the 'mchawi' (witchdoctor) that if he says they did something they will confess to it, even if they have done nothing. Our police work is hampered by people who confess and, when the confession is broken down, we find the people couldn't possibly have committed the crime.

I was very interested in what actually happened, but personally I couldn't accept that such a thing as lycanthropy could take place in real life and if you asked me if I believed in it, I would have to echo Superintendent Stewart and say firmly "I don't".

***

Singida lies high on a plateau formed by a fork in the Great Rift Valley and it was very windy there. Perhaps it was because of the wind currents that the clouds there were wonderful. I remember Singida for its cloud effects –

apart from the Lion Men. I walked across the dried up Lake Singida in the forenoon. It was fine, with the wind blowing and the big clouds and blue sky. Down in that lake bed and all over the Singida area are huge rocks standing on end as big as double-storey houses.

Towards evening I walked down the opposite way to Lake Kindai. This little lake was fast drying up too. There was about 18 inches depth at the most. There were strong salt deposits in the soil and, as the water diminishes, the fish were dying. The natives are reaping the harvest, wading out and catching a load of them with ease.

It was almost sunset. The big red tinted clouds drifted slowly by. A solitary bird wheeled and winged its lonely flight towards the distant horizon with a melancholy call as it went. Over on the far side of the lake the flamingos covered the water like a pink island. I wanted to see them closer. I circled the lake, my boots sinking in the soft clay where once the water had been. The alkaline odour hung in my nostrils. An exact replica of the purple sky and red flushed clouds was painted on the water. As I drew near some of the nearest birds became restless. Some rose and flew further out. Then, as I came close, the whole flock began to take flight. There were thousands of them. The flapping of their wings was like a rush of air, faintly as the first took off, then rising to a crescendo as the main body rose. It was like a blizzard of pink blossom against the darkening sky. This was beauty; this was beauty that surpassed words. High overhead they spread out, circling slowly, and covered the sky, then coming together they formed long lines like gigantic squadrons of planes, calling hoarsely to each other. Like a cloud of insects they swept out of view.

I stood for a time watching them go. The evening was balmy, the clouds, the sky, the red sunset behind the lake. Nearby, a native herded his cattle into the kraal amid a cloud of drifting dust. The wind sighed. It was all so peaceful. It was hard to imagine behind all this, right here, lay the ugly, primitive ritual killing of the Lion Men. On evenings like this, people have been ripped open to satisfy some secret religion.

I turned and made my way back to camp. As I thought and wondered over the setting, I realised there was something I couldn't put my finger on, something sinister. It was *too* peaceful.

***

I left Singida next day, walked for a while then got a lift to Katesh, about 50 miles from Singida. Here is the home of the Chief of the Wamangati tribe. This tribe is infamous for the murders it commits annually and I want to spend some time here and learn about this. Katesh is only three mud shops in a row.

These Wamangati are like the Masai. They drink blood and milk and must blood their spear before they are declared brave and they continue to kill people of other tribes. An average of 8–10 murders a year are on the police records. They also resemble the Masai in that they build low dung huts. I went inside one where the man had three wives. There were four compartments and each wife had her own fire and cooked her own food for herself and her children. Inside it was dark and I had to crawl about. It was like a rabbit warren. As my eyes became accustomed to the darkness I made out rows of skins hanging up. The bed was of hard hide.

Once outside I was aware that there must be many hyenas about here. They 'hoop' all night.

It's some business trying to get information from the natives about their tribe. However, there is a school teacher from the Chagga tribe here and he is very helpful.

The women of the tribe wear skins and plenty of decorations. When their lover has killed a lion or a man they can wear extra bangles and leg bands. I wanted to photograph a woman whose lover had killed a lion and who wore the extra bangles and they sent a man out to bring one in. He went yesterday, and I hoped he would come the next day. The women came, but unfortunately none of them wore the extra decorations that denote their man has killed a lion. The skins they wear are the softest I have seen on any native. They soften the hide with their own urine.

I had been making notes, separate from my diary. I had to keep asking, asking, asking to check on everything. But eventually I got some valuable material that few people know about this tribe. In my search for information I spoke with Augustin Thomas, District Commissioner of Mbulu, Tanganyika Territory. It was not a pleasant story and certainly not for the squeamish. I quote:

The Barabaig Murders –

From the earliest each boy has a mistress, but it is seldom that the boy marries a girl he has had as a mistress. The relationship may go for a while before the girl wants her lover to prove himself brave. When she desires this a meeting of young unmarried lovers is called – this meeting is known as a Sayu. At this meeting, the girl publicly declares she wants her lover to bring to her the hide of a lion, or an elephant tusk or either the breast of a woman or finger and ear of a man. The human victim must not be of the Wamangati tribe.

If the boy refuses to take the risk, she takes the boy's blanket – he cannot refuse, (this is the tribal custom) – and spreads it on the ground in front of him. She then calls another man, who has already killed, to have sexual intercourse with her on the blanket in order to shame her lover into doing the deed.

If the boy agrees to bring to her what she requests, two or more young men who attend the Sayu will go with him as witnesses, to see he collects the trophy by the proper tribal rules. If it is a person who is to be killed, it is usually one of the Wanyaturu tribe they go for. If it is a lion, the rest of the party – there may be a whole crowd of them – will assist in killing it after the man in question has thrown the first spear. He is credited with the lion if he inflicts the first wound.

Should it be a human being they go for, they will wait by a path or a well and kill whoever comes along. Mostly it is women and children who are killed. In this respect their method of killing is not very courageous. It is not as if they killed a man in armed combat, although a couple of months back (September 1953) three Wamangati met two Masai near Oldeani. A quarrel arose over cattle that led to a fight. The odd Wamangati stayed out to make the battle even. The Wamangati won and both Masai were speared to death. The method of killing in these murders is to strike first with a stick which still has parts of branches left on it which have been sharpened into spikes, then finish off with a spear thrust to the throat.

The parts of the body the girl has asked for are cut off and taken back. When the boy returns and gives his trophy to his mistress, she will ask the other girls to assist her in making the Sabogjig – string made from the roots of the Getamohog or Maleshi trees. This is part of his prize for his daring. When these are ready, another Sayu is called. At the meeting this string is wound round the waist of the boy and covered with 'ghee' (boiled butter). He will wear this for a month. [The amount of string involved is hard to estimate, but when I asked I was told '*enough so that a spear thrust will not go through it'*.]

Over and above the prize of his Sabogjig, and perhaps the most important, the boy receives cattle from all his relations. He may win between forty and sixty head of cattle for a lion and over one hundred for a human, although that is hard to say.

Although most of the murders are instigated by the will of the mistress, sometimes it is the boy, of his own accord, who wants to kill to receive his Sabogjig and cattle. In that case he will call a Sayu and get his mistress to declare what she will have him bring back to her.

The women of the Wamangati all wear many beads and bangles and many ornaments and rub 'ghee' on their skins. They mix this with Getigang'adid, – the dried leaves of the Guboyand tree – to take away the smell of oil. But when a young woman's lover has killed, she may then wear longer leg and arm rings and a bigger collar of brass wire round her neck. This extra decoration is known as Ghajirochanda. Perhaps it will be only for the chance to swank this Ghajirochanda in front of the other girls of the tribe that she will make her lover kill. Even if her lover kills a man, if she is unscrupulous, she will probably at a later date want him to kill a lion or a man if he killed a lion first. After he has killed, the man may also wear a Ghajirochanda, extra leg rings, etc., and he will freshen up his blanket by redyeing it with red ochre and 'ghee'.

At the time of marriage the dowry is one cow and two or three gallons of honey. The name of the special vessel for measuring honey is 'Maghast'.

When a girl is married, she receives as many cattle as her father can afford, plus three cows from the first wife and one cow each from each additional wife. So, if a girl of a man with three wives marries she will receive five cows from the wives and as many cattle as her father can afford. She may refuse to marry if she feels her father can afford more cattle than he offers her. If she is the daughter of the second or third wife, the first wife will not give her own cattle. She will take three of her husband's and give them.

The first cow is a reward for allowing the belt which is put round her neck to lead her to her husband when she marries.

The second cow is a reward for putting on shoes (sandals made from cowhide).

The third is a reward for leaving her parents to go to her husband.

But all these cattle belong to her husband until she produces a son.

When the son's first teeth appear, he is given one cow from his father and one from his mother, plus one cow from each wife.

So, in simple terms, the boy receives his cattle when he is born and the girl when she is married and bears a son. The boy has the advantage that his cattle are increasing each year so by the time he reaches manhood he has a good-sized herd.

In all cases, if the wives are poor and have no cattle, (perhaps have never borne a son), she will give a donkey or a goat as her part of the marriage arrangements to the children.

At death, the father's cattle go to the eldest son. If the boy dies before he is married or before the wife bears a boy, his cattle will go to his eldest brother.

CHAPTER 15

AT HOME WITH THE MASAI

<u>Wednesday 25th November, 1953, Endelsak 953</u>

There were no lifts on the way to Endelsak, which is only three or four shops in a row by the side of the road. I slept in the store of a Somali. In the morning I walked for some time, then got a lift in a truck going to Mbula and visited the Catholic Ndareda Mission. The missions are certainly an education and prove what can be done. All the building is done with local materials – bricks, tiles, woodwork, even furniture. They have a fine hospital. The bricks and tiles were moulded and fired, lime was burned, timber was cut and shaped in the workshop, not only for the rafters and rough building work but for doors, including a big four-panelled one, window frames and fine polished furniture.

It was interesting to visit the different missions – Roman Catholic and Protestant – but quite often I didn't go into the Protestant ones as I felt I was under pressure and, although I was a Protestant myself, I couldn't just discuss religion with them, whereas the Catholics in the same situation made no effort to convert me.

Some distance from the mission the road climbs the escarpment in great loops. The mountain side is covered with thick bush and is the haunt of many rhino. Halfway up you get a wonderful view of the plain below and there is a large dried salt lake glistening white in the sun.

The truck ground its way up round the curves, hesitating at the corners, to draw on its last reserves to get round each one like a rheumatic man, and you could almost fancy it sitting with its head between its knees. At a little stream it stopped to draw breath and the driver gave it a drink of water. Onwards again at walking pace, up, up, up. Women crossed the road carrying huge bundles of firewood on their backs and, high up over the mountain stream, two boys mended a little bridge with bolts and brace and bit.

Up on top of the plateau is rolling country, greener than down below. I liked it up there. There was a certain peacefulness in the sighing wind, and loneliness. On past Dongo Besh and you drop down into Mbulu. What a lovely spot it is. At first sight I thought it was one of the finest spots I had seen in Tanganyika. There is an old German fort used, of course, as the *boma*. It was one of the best castle-type *boma* I had seen. I wish I could have stayed longer in Mbulu, but I was lucky enough to meet a man who was going to Oldeani and I decided to accept his offer of a lift since it may have been days before any other opportunity came along.

It is interesting to see the two different types of huts the Wambulu build. One is the type they used to build long ago, the ordinary rondavel type. However, inside they make it into a two storey with a wooden platform. Up on the top storey they keep their grain and sleep. In neither place can they stand upright.

But this type of house was too dangerous with the lawless Masai nearby. When they, the Masai, used to come stealing cattle, they used to set fire to the houses just as an encore to the show. So the Wambulu got to building low, flat huts right into the side of the mountain. There are no sides in these huts, just a low, sloping roof that rises from the ground to about four feet and slopes down again. This they cover with earth and the door is only a 2½-foot slit. They look like upturned saucers and are almost invisible from a distance. Only the black slit of a doorway shows and it looks like a mouth of a small cave. Also, this type has the advantage of not being flammable. When I asked if the rain came through the almost flat roof I was told that it did, but they just threw more earth over it.

There was a Government Guest House at Oldeani, but I found it full up with people from Mbulu who had come for an anniversary dance at the club. There was quite a large white population around, since there were about thirty-five European farms, mostly coffee, in the vicinity. So I went down to some native huts and cooked my food there and slept in one of the huts.

There was a drizzle of rain and a sweeping wind blowing when I left Oldeani in the morning to come to Ngorongoro. Ngorongoro is a mountain with a huge 12-mile wide crater. It is teeming with game and I wanted to see if I could get some elephant photos. I hadn't gone far when I got a lift for the first six miles to the turn off. From there the road started to climb steeply. It was heavy work with my big pack and by twelve o'clock I felt pretty fagged. About then I came upon a P.W.D. camp. I drummed up some coffee and was about to move off when some of the labourers came in and said there was a herd of buffalo blocking the road a little way up. Not wishing to come to grips with them I decided to call it a day and sleep there. They gave me one of the huts to sleep in.

156

Next day, I came up the rest of the way. I saw some buffalo and a lone bull elephant, but they were all off the road. I was given (free of charge) one of the little log cabins that sit on the rim of the crater. How comfortable they are! They are the real log cabins, with the logs notched and fitted into each other at the corners. It's really cold up here at night, but there is a big fireplace and plenty of logs provided and with the fire bright and the door closed how snug it was. A real cosy little home.

The following day I had arranged for the game scout to come with me. We left at the crack of dawn and it was bitterly cold. We walked for about four miles but had to give up. The mist was blowing in clouds and, when it settled, visibility was reduced to just a few yards. Of course, photography was impossible and we were in danger of stumbling too close to elephant or buffalo. The hut, cosy with the fire, welcomed me back and breakfast tasted good.

Later that morning we went out again, this time to visit a Masai *manyatta*. The Masai live in huts made of tree branches, mud, grass and cow dung. They live in families in a *manyatta* (a form of enclosed homestead). A fence made of thorny bushes surrounds the *manyatta*. We saw the old Chief and watched the women sewing skins. In the afternoon we went out again, on the warpath after animals to photograph but still no luck. But what a country this is! Off the road lies a dark, hideous world of damp, green, lichen-covered trees that look like huge hairy spiders waiting ready to strike as you pass under them. I almost walked into a patch of "washa-washa" nettles or buffalo nettles, the terrible nettles that can drive a man mad if stung badly by them.

I left Ngongoro next morning and got a lift down the mountain. I stopped at Mto-wa-Mbu, River of Mosquitoes, which I had heard is great elephant country and I was still after photographs of them. I went to see the Game Warden and he invited me to stay the night and said I could have a game scout next day, but it was another fruitless day. The game scout was armed with a .404 rifle. It was real jungle with great trees and dangling creepers and although I walked him off his feet, we didn't see a thing, although we surprised a herd of buffalo which ran off. One was in a bush hardly six feet away before it started to move. I got quite a fright when the whole jungle suddenly came to life and for an instant I thought they were charging us.

I walked a long way after I left Mto-wa-Mbu in the morning, then got a lift in a car going to Moshi. I decided to come right through because I wanted to see the Senior Police Superintendent Stewart who was the man in charge of Singida during the time of the lion murders, hoping he would be able to tell me something of them.

Last night I wondered where to sleep. I walked round the town, had some tea in a café and then walked some more. Coming across a partly built building I went in there, scouted round about, then got down to sleep. At midnight I was awakened by some police who had been told I was sleeping there. It wasn't the thing for a European to be sleeping out and they said I had better come with them to the station. I told them I was fine and used to sleeping out and they went, but later a Police Officer came and said I must come to the station. I had no choice but to go with them and slept on a table in the office.

Next day I looked up Senior Police Superintendent Stewart, but he was getting ready to leave on a patrol and he hadn't time to talk but said he would make some notes and send it on when he had more time. (Sure enough, when I arrived in Nairobi, at the Poste Restante, his letter was waiting for me.) Meanwhile, he gave me a lift along to Arusha and wandering around there wondering where to go, I went for a haircut. The barber, a Pole, got talking and invited me along to stay with him. Later he had to go out and asked if I had a gun. When I said I had, he said to keep it handy and not to be afraid to shoot if anybody tried to break in. This was the first inkling I had had of getting near the Mau Mau country. Here in Arusha we were on the fringe. Perhaps the future could be exciting.

Thirty miles on I arrived in Monduli, the headquarters of all Tanganyika Masai land. I heard there was a big *Baraza* (get together/ meeting) with dancing so went along to see it. I was staying with the District Officer and had been questioning the *Wazee* (old men) from the *Baraza* all day about the Masai history and customs.

The Masai must be the most interesting tribe in Africa. This *Baraza* was one of the biggest of the year, with the main item on the agenda being to see what could be done to curb the *Morani* (warriors) activity because cattle stealing had been so rife at the time. Before going on a raid, the *Morani* gorge themselves on meat so that they are able to go two or three days without food if they are chased after stealing cattle.

I learned quite a lot about the tribe chatting to people at the *Baraza,* and was keen to follow up the information that high up in the mountains behind Monduli, which are known as Monduli Ju, lived the chief Liabon (medicine man) of all the Tanganyikan Masai. He rarely comes down and I wanted to meet him so I hired a guide and headed into the hills. After a few hours climbing we came to his *manyatta* (kraal).

I stood outside and waited till he came. Presently he did. He didn't look too impressive and certainly didn't seem like a real magic maker. He wore a blanket and his head was shaved like any other elder but, unlike the others, he wore a necklace of lion claws, teeth and other magical odds and ends. Yet, as I spoke to him, I was aware there was a strange air about him. Perhaps it was his eyes that created this. They had a penetrating quality and perhaps the fact of his eyebrows being shaved gave them a more stark prominence.

158

He would not allow me to go into his *manyatta*, but after much talk and cajoling on my part he consented to show me the horn in which he kept his tools of trade and the black stick decorated and inlaid with beads, which was his insignia of office. However, no amount of coaxing would induce him to show me the contents of his horn. I had heard he possessed some stones which were brought from the Nile when the tribe drifted down from Egypt hundreds of years ago. No white man has ever seen these stones.

When I started to ask questions, he became taciturn and then almost offensive. I waited for a while because I didn't want him to think I was going away because of this, or that he had intimidated me in any way. When I thought a suitable time had elapsed I left and came down the hills back to Monduli. Perhaps he had put a curse on me!

There was a big *Ngoma* to commemorate the *Baraza* next day. (Ngoma drums are instruments used by certain Bantu-speaking peoples of East Africa; 'ngoma' is simply the Swahili word for drum.)Yesterday evening and this morning companies of '*moran*' came in dressed as for war, spears gleaming but with the points sheathed by a mall made from ostrich feathers. Their shields had been newly painted, their heraldic designs looking like ultra-modernistic paintings. Their blankets had been newly dyed, their hair newly plastered with red ochre and their faces, some painted, surrounded by huge ostrich feather headdresses. The girls wore their best finery.

During the forenoon the *morani* were given two cows to eat. I asked them to show me how they drew the blood from the neck to drink. They put a cord round the cow's neck and drew it tight so that the vein stood out. Then they shot a special arrow that is tipped by a knife edge inside the point into the vein. The blood spouts out and is caught in a 'kibuya'. When enough is drawn they sealed up the hole with some dung and released the cow.

Later they killed the cows. All other tribes cut the throat of any cattle they kill, while the Masai stab the animal in the back of the head with the spike end of their spear. They then cut a slit in the skin at the neck to form a bag. The jugular vein is then cut and the blood gushes out and fills this bag. Each *moran* and the small boy attendants went in turn and drank the blood. The animal was then skinned and the meat cut up.

The dancing started in the afternoon. The warriors and the girls stood in two groups facing each other. They sang and chanted and hopped forward in rhythm till they met then turned and went back. Sometimes, between the dances, a warrior would go into the centre of the ring of people and start jumping with his legs straight and his body erect. As soon as he was finished another would take his place. Occasionally, one would go into a frenzy and his companions would hold him down on the ground till the fit was over.

So it went on into the night. I found it fascinating and was keen to learn more about the tribe. Maybe their customs change in different countries. These were the same tribe but of a different country – Kenya and Tanganyika. What I had learned so far gave me plenty to think about as I walked on the road through Arusha to Namanga, which was where I had been charged by a rhino on my downward journey. However, while I had to be alert for animals there was no trouble this time and I got a lift into Nairobi. It felt good to be back and I settled into a room in the British Legion club again and stayed there for a few weeks.

I phoned Pam, with whose family I spent a lot of time on my downward journey, when I arrived and visited them several times. (Pam and I had become close when I had visited them previously.) In fact, I spent Christmas with them. Together on Christmas day Pam and I drove round the National Park and sat watching four lion at about ten or twelve yards distance, and much closer than that on one occasion. The lion stared back with cold, haughty eyes as if they treated us with contempt. But Pam and I were two different people now and what had gone before was dead.

While I stayed at the club I looked up my friends Jim and Ella Ramage, friends from Dunfermline whom I had met on my downward journey when Jim and I had worked together on the Kenya Railway in the workshops. They were thrilled to see me and invited me to stay with them until I was ready to move on again on my journey. It was a happy time.

CHAPTER 16

THE MAU MAU

It was the Kikuyu tribe that developed what came to be known as the Mau Mau and its presence in the country was evident everywhere, with violence in town and country rife. Trouble with the Kikuyu went back a long way, as far as the early twenties, and they were very antagonistic to the European, mainly British, in their country. One of the main reasons was that the Church of Scotland was adamant that Kikuyu rituals, which had been in place for hundreds of years, had to be stopped: rituals such as the circumcision of girls and women.

Nairobi was not the same place I had known in the Army, nor in the previous year when I arrived there on my journey down to the Cape. The balmy days of peace and pleasure were gone and the days of a pleasant smile on an African face were no more. I knew that the European was no longer welcome. When you saw the big buildings going up all over the city you could hardly imagine there was a revolution in full swing yet, after a time, you did realise that things were not normal.

The Mau Mau was right there in Nairobi. You knew by the reports you read of the oath-taking ceremony that was broken up in the grounds of one of the main European hotels. You knew it when there were no vegetables in the market because the gangs had held up the trucks coming into the city. There was talk of forming the trucks into convoys and bringing them in under escort. You realised how close the Mau Mau was when you heard the news or read the *East African Standard*. You saw it in the way everybody wore holsters and pistols, even women. It looked like a Wild West town. When you see a man in evening dress with the end of the holster sticking out below his jacket and you could bet his elegant lady had a pistol in her handbag. It looked very odd to see stout, middle-aged women wearing a pistol in a holster at their side.

Just a few days before I arrived, General N-Six, a Mau Mau leader, was arrested after being found in possession of a revolver. He had brought ninety-five of his men from the forest into the city with him. I met up with two Kenyan Police Officers going down into Pangwani native location one night. When I asked if I could go with them it appeared that they were very pleased to have me, especially seeing my revolver. Down among the close-packed hovels the Mau Mau was rampant. It was nerve-wracking. You had to walk in the shadows and run across the street when you came to crossroads. Two days previously, four policemen – three African and an Asian – were shot dead in this location. The three Africans were walking together and were shot by a terrorist with a .25 pistol. (Good shooting for that type of gun.) The murderer escaped. Less than an hour later the Asian policeman was shot dead. The place was dimly lit and the stench in places atrocious. An African stood naked washing himself at a street well.

The police stood listening at a door, revolvers in hand and could hear whispering voices inside. They kicked open the door and walked in. In the smoky interior we could see faces glistening in the lantern light. Two women talking in one place and in another were six men and a host of *'totos'* (children) in one room. There was no way of knowing what they were talking about and the police couldn't do much except check their papers. Everyone could be a Mau Mau, but how could you tell? What could you do? We carried on down the street – careful at the corners of the houses and the narrow alleys that divides them, knowing that you must not be afraid to shoot.

I wrote an article for the local *Sunday Post* which was accepted and another for the *East African Standard*. I also made a broadcast on Radio Nairobi, for which they paid me two guineas. When I arrived in Nairobi quite a bit of money was waiting for me from articles, four guineas from the Cape Times and seventeen guineas, Australian currency, (£14. 0s.4d. sterling) – the highest yet – from "Man". I wanted to go up country to the Mount Kenya area where the actual fighting was going on, to see if I could see some action.

The Battle of Kaguma
Wednesday 6th January, 1954, Nyeri

It had been quite a day to put it mildly! I wanted to see some action but never expected it to come so quickly. I got a lift in an Army truck to Nyeri (90 miles). Kenya looked what it was – a country at war. There were military camps and troops and barbed wire everywhere.

At Nyeri I walked down the street while deciding what should be my first move, when I was hailed by a short, stocky man with a beard and a low-slung revolver at his side.

162

"Hallo Jock! I saw you in Nairobi once and had been going to speak to you." I had also seen him and wanted to speak to him but the moment passed.

It was only when he introduced himself I realised I was talking to the most famous man in Kenya at the time. A lot of men had found prominence in this Mau Mau battle, but out of the mass one man had emerged head and shoulders above the others. His name was Davidson, but from generals down to the man in the street he was known as Davo.

He was a gunman. The type you read about, fast on the draw – he carried his .455 revolver in a spring holster – and combined it with sharp shooting. He was reckoned to be one of the finest small-arms shots in the world. His name was legendary. When I mentioned to people I wanted to see what it was like fighting the Mau Mau, they usually said "You should try and meet Davo". I never expected that I would.

Davo's role in the battle was hard to discern. He was a Special Police Officer. He wore no uniform. He had no base. He went where he liked and was welcome at any unit. Apparently, he was self-appointed to track down and kill the Mau Mau General, especially Marshal Dedan Kimathi, Commander in Chief of the Mau Mau.

His past life was hard to follow. Although an Australian, born in Queensland, he was a regular soldier in the British army and held the rank of Sergeant Major. Before that he was in the United States, where he was everything from government officials' bodyguard to a hired gunman looking after the interests of gambling dens. He had recently been wounded by the Mau Mau. He got three bullets in his stomach and one in his side and was out of action for five months. In fact, he had just come back when I met him. Altogether he had been wounded seven times, yet never while in the army. He also carried the scars of several knife wounds.

All this I had learned when voicing my wish to find him and, needless to say, this was Davo I was speaking to. He asked me if I would like to join him. He was going down to Fort Hall and said he might be ambushed. Did I still want to come? I was only too pleased to have the opportunity of going with him. However, we didn't get far before we came upon a crowd of Kikuyu Home Guards (loyal natives), armed with spears and wearing blue bands round their hats to signify their status. One man wore a yellow piece of cloth on his. He was Chief Williams. When Davo asked what was on, the Chief told him a big gang under General Gitambomb (Atombomb) had been encountered near Kaguma. Davo's plans for Fort Hall were forgotten when he decided to join in the battle.

Davo was a marked man with £500 on his head. He always drove with a Mills hand grenade in his hand in case of an ambush. Now he handed one to me and off we went to do battle. He scanned the landscape with his binoculars. He had eyes like a hawk. He said he thought he saw someone looking out from behind a hut across the valley. We went across and, sure enough, a young man was there, sitting in the *boma*. He had papers in order but could not explain why he was there. He was clean and well dressed, but on searching, we found old, dirty clothes wet with sweat. Apparently he had made a rapid change. In another hut we found another man in the grain store, well dressed but with a wet blanket, a sure sign they had been out all night. They were taken into custody and later proved to be Mau Mau.

This was all a new experience for me. I had hunted lions, but never pointed a gun at a man, not even in the Army. Yet, here I was covering the men – aye, and ready to shoot – while they were being searched. But more, a lot more, was to come.

A lot of shooting was coming from beyond and the opposite side of the glen. We crossed and moved up towards the trouble, searching the huts as we went. Quite a tense atmosphere as you close in, expecting a burst of fire any minute to greet you. But there was none, at least not yet.

Davo asked me to go back and bring up the Land Rover. I retraced our tracks and drove up as near to the firing as I dared and then ran across to where Davo and the Home Guard were advancing. Some of them had rifles, most of them carried spears. Suddenly, about thirty yards away, a Mau Mau terrorist who had been lying doggo, fired off his home-made rifle then got up to run. A Home Guard shot him before he had gone a couple of steps. So I saw my first dead Mau Mau within three hours of arriving in Nyeri.

There were some huts nearby with some women in them. They must have seen the gang pass, but they wouldn't speak. Suddenly, firing broke out again and bullets sprayed all around. We went to ground behind a hedge with the Home Guard lying along in a row, but we couldn't see anything to shoot at. We could not advance any further than the clearing where the huts were without exposing ourselves. We waited for some time then crawled forward, but they had gone.

At the road we came on a Police Officer and a District Officer who said the gang had broken out across the road and the Army, the Buffs Regiment, was chasing them. Altogether eleven Mau Mau were shot dead and two captured wounded. Since there didn't seem to be any good hanging around as the gang had broken out and were on the run and it might take hours to make contact with them again – we went back to Nyeri.

***

Davo came to a farmer friend of his, Mr Maxwell, to spend the night. The name of the farm was Maxwelton. We were invited to stay around and, living there, I got an insight of what a settler's life was like these days in the

Kikuyu land. Of course, everybody wears their gun and at night all doors are locked. When dinner was ready the boy knocks on the door, the farmer unlocks it and covers the scene with his revolver as the boy brings in the food. The boy goes out and the door was locked before we sat down to eat. It is not that the boys are bad, but they may be intimidated into committing murder by a gang hovering around. Recently two men were murdered when the servant threw the plate of boiling soup in their faces and grabbed the guns which were lying handy on the table. The Mau Mau waiting rushed in and slashed them to death with *'simis'* (large knife).

To be suddenly transported into this world of nervous tension took me some time to get used to. Had I read of this, I would have thought it rather exaggerated, too melodramatic. Yet, it was true. For these settlers this was what their life had become. Phrases that marked the mode of life such as: "Come away from that lighted doorway. Stand in the shadow" and "I used to like listening to 'Take it from Here' until I found it was claiming too much of my attention concentrating on the jokes." And "Turn down the radio."

I would have laughed at all this as typical Hollywood gangster film stuff. Yet it was all too real here. The families had to be constantly on the alert, even with their own house staff.

I had the greatest admiration for the settlers who had stuck it out – especially their wives – and refused to be intimidated into leaving their land. Two years of this must have played havoc with their nerves – always on the alert, never able to relax, not even behind locked doors, not being able to trust their own servants, even those who had been with them for years. Nearly every attack on Europeans had centred on the servants, either wilfully murdering their employers or acting under the threat of their own death from the Mau Mau. It took guts to live on day after day like this.

Little did I think when I left Nairobi that morning that I would be told at night, "If they come we'll shoot our way down the stairs (an outside stair) on to the verandah", and it didn't seem melodramatic.

***

I quote from my diary:

Thursday 7th January, 1954

What a night last night! The guest house here at Maxwelton Farm is about fifty yards from the main house and between the two are a lot of trees and bushes. We had just walked across and entered the guest house when a burst of machine gun fire suddenly exploded and the bullets zipped over the roof of the hut. Another burst followed over on the right and a few single shots were fired almost next to the house. We dowsed the light and lay low. It looked as if they had got us bottled up. Mr Maxwell was very anxious about his wife who is expecting a baby in a few weeks and said he must get up to her. It looked like suicide to try and cross that 50 yards yet he was determined, so crouching low we ran up the path that wound between the trees, our guns ready, expecting any second to be met with a hail of bullets.

We reached the verandah. Mr Maxwell went to his wife who was in their bedroom leaning over the little boy's crib and told her to ring the bell they have to sound the alarm. Nyeri is only a mile as the crow flies. The verandah is enclosed with wire netting, except for the gate.

There was something grim about crouching in the dark with revolvers and grenades ready, with the bell ringing out, appealing for help. The time dragged by, the minutes were heavy, each one impregnated with suspense. I wished something would happen to release the tautness in my stomach.

Suddenly, the bell stopped ringing. The metallic silence that followed was louder than the previous clanging. The cord attached to the bell had broken. Mrs Maxwell's hands were blistered with the friction.

Mr Maxwell said he would go out and ring the bell again. Davo went with him to cover him and I was left to cover the verandah. I crawled round and round expecting every minute a volley of bullets. By now three quarters of an hour had elapsed since the shooting and still there was no sign of help coming. Eventually Mr Maxwell and Davo came back and Mr Maxwell said he would go to Nyeri himself for help. We reasoned with him that it was too dangerous to try, but his mind was made up. Davo went with him and they dashed down the path into his car. As the car burst into life and swung down the drive and through the coffee bushes, we waited to hear the agonising Sten gun fire open up. But there was none.

We could do nothing but wait now, me crawling round the verandah on hands and knees, revolver in hand covering the garden approach to the house and, upstairs in the nursery, Mrs Maxwell, eight months into her pregnancy, kneeling over little Gavin's crib – he was little more than a year old – ringing the bell with a loaded pistol in her other hand. That picture alone perhaps conveys the life of the Kenyan settler then.

Presently, Mr Maxwell returned, the news he gave brought the evening's excitement to rather an anticlimax. The house had not been attacked. At the Operations Room at Nyeri they told him there was a police ambush at the bottom of the farm. They had not had any reports in as to what they were shooting at. But they must have been shooting at something. So we went to bed in rather a dubious frame of mind. The guns were loaded and the grenades primed and ready.

166

We learned next day that the police in the ambush fired at four people they saw coming down past the house. The fire was returned and the guest house where we were, was caught somewhere in the crossfire. Also we learned that the Buffs regiment heard the bell ringing, but since it was out of their area they ignored it. Such is this war!

It was a war, or revolution, no matter if the government refused to call it anything else but "The Emergency", and this was really worse than war for the security forces, for there was no such thing as being taken prisoner by the Mau Mau.

Next day we went down to Nairobi. Davo wanted to collect his Beretta sub-machine gun which had been repaired with a new stock. There was quite a tale behind the breaking of that stock. Last July Davo was some way ahead of a patrol of troops on Mount Kenya when he came on a large force of Mau Mau headed by Dedan Kamathi, self-styled Marshal of the Mau Mau army, coming in the opposite direction. Davo killed eight and wounded countless more including Dedan Kamathi. But he himself was seriously wounded. He was shot at ten yards by a .303 rifle. Luckily, he was wearing his bullet-proof waistcoat which, although not being strong enough to withstand a bullet of such heavy calibre at such short range, was enough to take most of the force. The bullet splintered and the parts entered his body.

Immediately afterwards a terrorist, whom Davo took for dead lying at his feet, fired three .38 revolver bullets at point blank range which from that angle went under the jacket and wounded him in the stomach. Another bullet hit him in the hand. Although severely wounded, he continued to fire into the enemy until his ammunition was exhausted. At this point a terrorist lunged at him with a *'simi'* – a long sword-like knife. Davo smashed his gun over the man's head, killing him, but also breaking the stock of the gun.

He was carried down to base on a stretcher and was not expected to live, but after a spell in hospital and a long convalescence lasting about five months, he was back and as fit as ever.

The ironic point of this was that his stretcher bearers were Kikuyu. I think that was what people at home didn't realise. It seemed the people in Britain had a contorted view of the state of affairs that pertained then and thought the Mau Mau were the heroes of this 'play', fighting for their country, with the government forces the terrible villains who shot defenceless people only to protect the white man's property. How wrong they were! What they didn't realise was that the vast majority of the Kikuyu tribe hated the Mau Mau more than we did and hoped to see the end of them. When the Members of Parliament at home denounced the British in Kenya for the war and gave the Mau Mau moral support, they didn't realise they were letting down the biggest part of the Kikuyu tribe and the other Kenyan tribes, who realised the Mau Mau was only a band of gangsters out to gain control of the country.

***

It was late when we left Nairobi and darkness had fallen by the time we got to Thika. All the way, we had to be prepared for a sudden ambush. As we came nearer we saw something was burning right at Nyeri itself. We drove up to the scene with guns ready expecting to find another Lari massacre.

The terrorists had attacked a native village – also Kikuyu, their own people – right at the edge of the township and set half a dozen huts on fire. They hadn't had time to tie up the doors to prevent the people inside escaping, which was their usual habit. No one had been injured, the gang had dispersed on the sudden arrival of police. We went to a Home Guard post nearby and there we saw a terrible scene. A long line of refugees trudging into the camp in search of security behind the barbed wire. There was something terribly touching in that pathetic line of humanity, some almost naked and shivering in the bitter night wind, some clutching a few meagre belongings they had managed to grab before leaving their blazing grass huts, the old people bent and shaken by the shock of this sudden unprovoked attack, the little children crying with the cold and fear, the mothers with their babies on their backs, some without even a blanket to wrap round them.

I wondered what the people at home who believed this was only a war between African and European would think if they could have seen that sight.

In the forenoon we went to have a look at the burnt out village to see if we could find out anything. A couple of huts still stood intact. Outside one three women sat. One was grinding maize between stones, but habit seemed to govern her movements more than necessity. The other two sat mute, as if still dazed from the last night's attack. Over the rest of the *boma* the sight was appalling. All that remained of the other huts were the blackened remains, burnt earth and some broken, blackened earthen jars. Some goats wandered aimlessly about looking for scraps, a cow standing amid the charred embers of a hut bellowed for someone to come and milk it, but nobody heeded its call. It was heart-rending.

We were sitting talking. Everything seemed peaceful. Suddenly there came the staccato rattle of sub-machine gunfire from the top of the rise and some bullets splashed in the hut near where we were. The women ran screaming while we went to the Land Rover. Davo handed me the Beretta to cover him as he backed and manoeuvred back to the truck. We drove up to where the shooting came from. As we topped the rise we saw a crowd of natives running across some *shambas*, pursued by others of the Home Guard with blue cloth round their hats. They all disappeared in a dip. We left the car and joined in the chase. We came on a crowd of Home Guard with two sorry looking terrorists sitting in their midst, one with blood streaming from a wound in his head. A home-made gun had been captured. Some huts were nearby and the Home Guard were searching them.

The rest of the gang had dispersed and were being hunted by more of the Home Guard and the police. We went with them, going slowly for the grass was high and the bush thick and a terrorist could be any place. Away over to the right there was spasmodic rifle and machine gunfire. We swept the area right down to the show ground, but the birds had flown. I went back for the Land Rover. Where the two Mau Mau had been captured, two huts were burning. I learned that partly made rifles had been found in them. The inhabitants had left so hurriedly that washing was still hanging on a line between the huts. The Home Guard had torched the huts.

In the morning the boy from Stanley Mathengi's gang told Davo where there was a Mau Mau 'arms' factory. It was right on the edge of Mr Maxwell's farm where we were living. At about 2.p.m. we collected some police *askaris* with a European officer. We drove up as near to the place as we could, but we still had half a mile to walk. Near the hut which the boy told us was the one, we split into two lines, the askaris with their officer went along the back and Davo and I approached from the front. There was a thick Maurisius thorn *boma* round the hut. Inside the *boma* were two men and three women. When they saw us the two men ran towards the hut. Davo fired a warning burst from his Beretta and shouted for them to halt. One did, but the other went into the hut. Davo shouted again and threatened to riddle the place with bullets and the other came out.

We closed in and entered the *boma*. The men stood with their hands above their heads. The women sat on the ground where they had been when we arrived, as placid as if nothing had happened. With Davo covering the men I searched them. One had no trousers on. I found them later in the hut. There were ten rounds of .303 ammunition in the hip pocket. On the other I found a pair of blue, police puttees and a K.A.R. shoulder title. He admitted he was a Sergeant under 'General' Stanley Mathengi.

Inside the hut we found a home-made rifle and a partially made one and plenty evidence to show the place was a 'factory'. Their production, so they said, was one per day. The *'fundi'* (artisan) was a son of Chief Nderi, the Chief who was strongly anti-Mau Mau and was killed and slashed to bits by them. It was queer to find one of his own sons on the side of the people who had done this to his father. Still, Chief Nderi had twenty-two wives and countless sons, so I suppose there was no direct patriarchal control or loyalty.

Outside, in the hedge, we discovered lengths of half-inch piping ranging from 12 feet to about 18 inches, the length of the barrels of the guns. There were also bundles of flat, banding wire, elastic and all the equipment needed for the arms production. Also, right under the almost solid hedge were spaces where it was evident men had lain-up, perhaps for days at a time. Bottles and tins with the remains of sugar and other foodstuffs were found. The *'fundi'*, until recently, had worked for Mr Maxwell as a carpenter.

While we were there we saw a woman watching us from the other side of the valley. When it rained and she didn't seek shelter, it was evident it was more than curiosity which held her there. Davo decided to have a sweep along the other ridge and dispatched the European police officer to take the prisoners back to Nyeri and bring some police reinforcements. While we waited and watched the other side of the valley about half a mile away, on Kahawa Ridge, we saw through the glasses at least six people in the thicket and evidence that there were many more. I mentioned to Davo it would be worth having army reinforcements and making a full-scale sweep, preferably if they went behind and swept towards us. Davo agreed and I went off at the double carrying my revolver in my hand. There were plenty of huts around and as I passed each one, I expected to hear a shot, thinking that as I was on my own they may have considered attacking. I was thankful to reach the jeep.

In the Ops Rooms, the brain of the districts, I got an inkling of the terrible set-up of things in this war, realising they didn't even know the scheme was on. When I asked for army reinforcements I was told to go to the Buffs regiment. I didn't know then that they were in direct contact with them by phone and being several miles out of town and because I didn't know the way, I wasted valuable time in getting there.

By now it was about 5.30 p.m. When I saw the Orderly Officer he said it was useless his Company going out because it would be dark before they got into position and they couldn't sweep at night. So it was called off.

I went back to Davo. He said the police had gone over the other side but hadn't contacted anything.

There was a scare the very next night. Davo had three boys, all Kikuyu and apparently Mr Maxwell's servants, also Kikuyu, had not taken to them. It showed how much the Kikuyu tribe was torn, each one suspecting the other. One of Davo's boys came and said that Mau Mau people had arrived and were in Mr Maxwell's servants' quarters. The boy was very much afraid.

We held a council of war and decided our plan of campaign when they attacked. The time passed slowly and the waiting, the expectations weighed heavily on our nerves. I felt sorry for Mrs Maxwell. She is a very brave woman. In her condition she stood up to the strain like a veteran soldier.

Eventually we decided that if they were going to attack, they would have attacked before this and decided to go to bed. However, I had an uneasy sleep. Several times we were awakened by machine gunfire. This morning we cleared up the mystery. The 'Mau Mau gang' were really Mr Maxwell's servants' wives coming in from the reserve. The servants had not said anything about them. In the dark, Davo's boys, already highly strung through their dangerous work of collaborating with Davo, imagined the worst. It was really nothing, but it shows again the state of nervous tension these farmers live in.

***

Near Nyeri is 'Treetops' a hotel in a tree overlooking a salt lick. We were talking about it last night and Mr Maxwell has kindly offered to treat me to a visit, in recognition, as he puts it, of my hand in all the action round his farm lately. I told him, as I believe, that I am being grossly overpaid for the part I played, but I was extremely pleased at the invitation. It will cost about £3 or £4 pounds, so it is very generous of him. The next party goes up tomorrow.

Davo left Nyeri next day. His present mission was to hunt down General Kimbo – which means chameleon. He got a tip that he was moving over to Thomson's Falls, so Davo had gone there. I had an invitation to join him again whenever I wanted to, but in the meantime he had asked me to stay over at Maxwelton until a big operation to clean up the district had come off. Apparently, things had been stoking up around here lately and I seemed to have turned up when it had just got to white heat. Davo feared that with the cleaning up of the arms factory so near to the farm, they may be attacked, so until this scheme comes off I was obliged to stay to help out in case of trouble. Mr Maxwell knew nothing about this move as it was all hush-hush. He invited me to be his guest and to all intents and purposes I have accepted, but I was keen to get on my way again as soon as I got back from Treetops, although his hospitality was wonderful and I enjoyed being there.

Tues 12th January, 1954, Treetops

There were fifteen in the party when I visited Treetops. We left the Outspan Hotel at about 2 p.m. in a large safari wagon. From the place where the track stopped we still had half a mile to walk. Here we were joined by two men from the Buffs regiment armed with Sten guns, who were the party's escort.

The most modern attraction to the variety of wild game likely to be seen around Treetops when I was there were Mau Mau. A few nights before we arrived, a party of Americans were there and an action ensued nearby. Mortar bombs exploded and I believe some bullets actually passed through the hotel.

In charge of the party was the game scout who was armed with a .500 Holland and Holland rifle. He gave a short lecture on the procedure the party was to follow should a rhino, buffalo, etc; block the path or charge on our way up. Every ten yards or so bars were nailed to trees to act as ladders. The idea was for the party to disperse as soon as an animal was sighted and shin up the trees. The party comprised people of all ages. Young girls in jeans giggled at the impending excitement, elderly ladies took a firm grip on their hand bags and a young boy took a business-like hold on his air gun. We didn't look like a jungle party! I couldn't help smiling when I conjured up the scene of these elderly and rather stout ladies climbing trees with a snorting rhino behind them. However, we reached the place without mishap.

Treetops then was a large, two-storey hut built 30 feet above the ground in a huge tree. After my time there it was extended and had overflowed the branches of the tree and was then supported by poles. It overlooked a small pool and salt lick.

On arrival, we were greeted by a huge baboon who sat quite unafraid a few feet away from the ladder. His family sat back at a safer distance and also acknowledged our arrival by giving us their wholehearted attention. We ascended the ladder, the luggage was pulled up and the ladder hoisted. We were high and dry now.

I was accommodated in the upper storey. The place was divided into several rooms with a long verandah along the side facing the pool. All openings were sealed with wire netting to stop the monkeys from getting in. The whole horde of them had followed us up, and pranced about the roof as mischievous as a band of schoolboys. They soon found any hole in the netting big enough to get their arms through and grabbed at anything within reach. One mischievous fellow stole a bar of chocolate belonging to a little girl. He was obviously an 'old hand' at the game and it seemed evident that his loot was of his favourite brand for he peeled the paper off as he ran and even had the audacity to turn and look – with almost the semblance of a triumphant leer on his face – when the girl burst into tears.

We had some tea and settled on cushions along the verandah. This was the tourists Africa I was living in for one brief day! Incidentally, all furnishing for Treetops – blankets, sheets, cushions, crockery, etc. – had to be brought up and returned to the Outspan Hotel before and after each of the party visits. They used to leave everything until a Mau Mau gang broke in and stripped the place of everything except the kitchen sink.

172

We sat for a while and the only sound was the rustle of caramel paper or the clicking of a lady's knitting pins. Occasionally someone spoke but always in a whisper.

The first arrival on the scene was an impala doe. She came into the glade and trotted towards the water. Suddenly she stopped, poised, listening. Her alarm was infectious. High up in our eyrie we automatically tensed ourselves too. She sniffed the air, then tip-toed cautiously forward a few steps, only to stop again to listen and smell. She repeated this performance over and over again, edging her way towards the water. Each time she stopped the atmosphere in our nest was electrified. No pan drops clinked against teeth, no papers rustled, the clashing of knitting pins momentarily ceased. We scarcely breathed lest that sacrilege of the silence would deaden any warning sound and bring destruction to the heroine.

Near the pool, with the sparkling water so tantalisingly near at hand, the doe stopped again and sniffed the air. Suddenly, she pirouetted with the grace of a ballerina and bounded off with long, beautiful leaps into the forest. The big whites of her eyes showed the fear that was in her heart. We never knew the cause of her panic. Perhaps a lion or leopard or some other beast lay waiting in the bush, hidden from our view.

We waited a long time before the next act and gazed as the sun's reflection in the pool died and long, swinging monkey creepers dangling in almost solid shadows like gnarled, hideous fingers of a Walt Disney witch, fell into place.

A family of warthogs took the stage. The old man ran bald-headed for the water. He was followed by his wife and kids, the latter squealing when their mother got too far in front of them They were soon followed by an assorted bag of jungle life – water buck, bush buck, impala and zebra. They arrived in ones and twos, drank their fill, licked some salt, then dispersed quietly into the bush.

When darkness fell the 'artificial moon' was lit. In the old days, visits to Treetops were only possible on moonlit nights. But in 1952 when the Queen, then Princess Elizabeth and the Duke of Edinburgh visited the 'house in the tree', even nature had to alter her calendar to suit. It was a moonless period and the visit seemed useless until someone thought up the idea of a lamp to act as a moon. It worked. The animals took no more notice of it than they would the real moon.

Incidentally, it was at Treetops that the Princess received the news of her father's death. A note in the visitors book tells how she entered as a Princess and departed as a Queen.

Dinner was served behind curtains beneath a shaded lamp. It was difficult to imagine we were sitting up a tree. Still, there were the branches growing up through the floor and out of the ceiling to prove that we were.

As we sat over coffee, we were visited by a herd of buffalo. They splashed in the water, then wandered over to the salt lick right under the lamp. We could hear their tongues rasping on the earth. From the forest an orchestra of crickets and frogs provided incessant background music. Occasionally, the howl of a hyena, or the bark of a buck could be heard and away over to the left, the staccato rattle of machine gunfire lent a modern air to this age-old symphony.

At about 10 p.m. a lone bull rhino trotted onto an empty stage. He made his bow by doing a turn in the pool. He danced into the water and, after a sumptuous drink, proceeded with his aquatics, rolling in the shallow water, getting up and rolling over the other way. Each time he rose he quenched his thirst from his bath water. His bath finished, he dressed for dinner by rolling in the dust. Newly clad, he sauntered over to the dining room. The *table d'hôte* must have been to his liking; his loud grunts of satisfaction as he found the salt were like the exclamations of a French connoisseur who is served his favourite dish.

After the first course he returned to the bath for a drink. He followed this routine for some time, trotting between the salt lick and the water. It was unfortunate that he was unable to carry a glassful to the table with him, instead of dashing to the bathroom every time he wanted a drink. However, he seemed quite contented with the set-up and presently adjourned to the forest. Later, three more rhinos provided the last act of the evening. Theirs was the highlight of a grand performance. They came in together – two bulls and a cow – and followed the antics of their predecessor in the water, before going on to the salt lick. I don't know how the trouble started. One moment they were a happy group, the next the two bulls were going hell-bent for each other amid terrible squeals and grunts. They charged each other and the very ground shook with their impact. It amazed me how they came head to head, or head to side on, yet their horn never seemed to make contact and pierce the other. At the side stood the luscious female. Whether it was the result of the eternal triangle or any other reason, no one could tell. The cow remained apart; sometimes she took it into her head to join in and would go for the one who was nearest her. The sound of the impact when they met could be heard above the scuffle. After each charge they would go on as if nothing had happened. Occasionally, one would go down on his knees, but always came up again to go for the other with increased venom.

The battle lasted over an hour then stopped as suddenly as it began. As if in one accord they dispersed into the bush. Soon after that I turned in. We were not lucky in seeing any more game in the morning.

***

The truck brought us back to the 'Outspan' where Mr Maxwell was waiting to run me back to his farm. Before he did though he took me and introduced me to Col. Jim Corbett, who wrote *Man-eaters of Kuruman, Man-eating Leopards of Rudraprayag*, etc., etc., and now *My India* his latest book. We had tea with him and his sister, Miss Corbett. They are an extremely fine old pair, but both miss India very much. They are living in what used to be Baden-Powell's suite in the 'Outspan'. I found them extremely interesting.

***

I didn't know how lucky I was to get on that trip. This was the second last party to visit Treetops. The place was then closed. Three days after this a trap was laid for the driver of the safari wagon after he had delivered the party to Treetops. He was suspected of being in contact with the Mau Mau. Sure enough he was joined by four gangsters and delivered food to them. He was caught. It was felt that Treetops might come in for some activity now that the food-running game was broken up and, shortly after this, the hotel was burned down.

***

Back at Maxwelton farm I wandered round inspecting the crop, which was mostly coffee. This was one of the oldest farms in the district; in fact it was the third one to start. Mr Maxwell Senior came here in 1907. It was the only farm south of the Chania River. At one time about two thirds of the original farm was handed back to the Kikuyu without compensation to Mr Maxwell and the farm is very small now.

There was rifle and Bren fire last night again. It was the start of the operation Davo had spoken of to me and it was every night now. Police ambushes were out every night and there was a lot of movement of the gangs. Apparently, they were being driven from the forest by the bombing and forced into the more open country of the reserves.

Today I went to see Capt. Perry of the Special Branch. He knew why I was staying on. Extra ambushes have been laid tonight and the sweep will be going on tomorrow leaving the 'stops' (ambushes) in place. They stay there tomorrow night too. The sweep is going right up the Chania valley and beyond. I was instructed by Capt. Perry not even to tell Mr and Mrs Maxwell about the operation until after dark, in case they might drop a wrong word. However, Mr Maxwell was leaving to attend a Caledonian Society meeting and didn't intend to return till after 7 p.m. I had to tell him enough in the afternoon to make him realise he had to be back before darkness fell. Anything moving on that road that night was likely to get caught up.

That evening on the news we heard that General China had been captured. Great news. He was in Nyeri hospital, less than a mile from this farm.

In the morning I went to the Special Branch, but no information as to the score had been received although there had been a lot of Bren gunfire. However, eight hats of assorted types had been brought in. There was a steel helmet, a blue and yellow forage cap, a K.A.R. hat, etc. etc. Some of them had blue and yellow tassels hanging from them.

There was almost continuous machine gunfire for nearly two hours the next morning, about two miles from the house. It must have been quite a 'do'. Mr Maxwell and I went to the native hospital to see if we could see General China, but I think he was only dressed here last night and moved immediately by air to Nairobi.

The sweep finished next morning. I didn't hear how many were captured. All I knew was that I can get on my way tomorrow. However, I did have to go back to Nyeri some time or other. The C.I.D. had been at the farm nearly every day getting a statement from me regarding the do at the arms factory. The trial of the two captured terrorists took three weeks or so to come up and since I was one of the chief witnesses, I had to be there.

Mr and Mrs Maxwell asked me to stay on. In fact they said they would like me to stay or at least go back in a month when the baby was due to look after things until after that crucial time. I would really have liked to stay and help them. I'm very fond of them both and there could never be better hosts, but I felt I must get on my way, there was still a lot I wanted to do and see, so I had made up my mind to leave. I wondered if I was letting them down in going, but I felt that they had a month, surely ample time to try and find someone to come during the time the baby would be born. And yet, they said they didn't want to get just anybody. They wanted someone they could trust. I was very proud of that compliment, and it made me feel rather ashamed at leaving them. But I had a long journey in front of me and leaving was never going to be easy. Go, I must.

***

Monday 18th January, 1954, Nanyuki

I left Nyeri, having got a lift in an army truck and was dropped off a few miles from Nanyuki. I had walked a couple of miles or so when a car stopped. It was driven by a middle-aged woman. She remarked her surprise at finding someone walking alone. "Kenya isn't a place to be walking on your own," she said and, when I got in and she drove off she asked, "Aren't you afraid of the Mau Mau?" I spoke the truth when I said that I was, but I said that I wanted to get around Kenya. I told her I thought it was admitting defeat if you wanted to go somewhere and didn't go because of the possibility of meeting a gang.

Her answer was rather surprising. She said, "Do you want a job as manager on a farm?" She hastened to explain that she had a cattle ranch. Since the 'Emergency' she had had two managers. The first had sold a lot of her cattle, pocketed the money and cleared off to South Africa. The next one left without notice when an Italian family had been killed and butchered nearby. Since then, nine months ago, she had run it and lived by herself. A very plucky effort for a woman I thought. However, she was feeling the strain and wished to get someone to take over. Now she was offering the job to me. She didn't know, nor did she enquire, if I had any farming experience. As far as she knew, I may not know the difference between a bull and a cow! It showed the state of things in the Colony when the only qualification one needs is that you don't mind being on your own. I thanked her for her offer but refused. I explained what I was doing and that I had no intention of settling.

I stayed that night in a police post and headed up to the Northern Frontier District via Isiolo. I wanted to go up as far as the Abyssinian border.

Bad luck today. I left Nanyuki and pointed my nose towards the Northern Frontier District and soon got a lift to Timau. It was here the first of the cattle outrages was committed. They hamstrung the cattle and even chopped off their legs completely and let them hobble about on the stumps, or slashed great open cuts all over them and left them to bleed to death.

I walked on beyond Timau and the country began to get more desolate. It was still very early in the morning. The sky was clear and the sun warm but had hardly dried the dew and no dust dimmed the far distance. Over the scene stood Mount Kenya, so regal and splendid. Up there on its rugged peak lives "Ngai", the Kikuyu and Masai god. Surely few gods can have a more majestic palace. This morning it looked misty blue and almost transparent. Variegated patches of snow clung to its gullies and clothed it like an ermine mantle; it is small wonder that the natives in its vicinity regard it with reverence. It seemed impossible that such a bloody and ruthless war was being fought on its very shoulders.

Later, in the forenoon, I got another lift, this time to Isiolo. As we descended from the highlands into the sun-scorched lands of the Northern Frontier District, the wind became hot and stifling as if it had fanned live embers.

Isiolo, the gateway to the Northern Frontier District is two rows of low, native shops down the widest 'street' I have seen. Standing even in the centre of the village the place seems empty and desolate. I reported to the District Commissioner as I had to get a permit to proceed into the area. He referred me to the Provincial Commissioner, surely a high honour for a tramp such as I. I never imagined my wants would be important enough to warrant the decision of one in a position at such dizzy heights.

The Provincial Commissioner said it was impossible to grant a permit to me. Regulations state that only cars in pairs, at least, are allowed through. Also a 44-gallon drum of water must be carried. Since I considered the latter would be rather heavy to carry and perhaps curtail my daily walking distance, I was inclined to agree with him. Still, I was very disappointed. I am staying at Isiolo tonight. I'll unroll my sleeping bag round the back of the shops when it gets dark.

It's good to see the natives as they are here, so very different to the sophisticated Kikuyu.

I got on the road today and walked for a long time. I was keen to get to Meru by the afternoon. I wanted to have a look at the east side of the mountain. In the afternoon I got a lift here.

I met Bill Williamson, the Assistant Agricultural Officer whom I had been told to contact. By queer coincidence he had just received a letter from a mutual friend about a couple of hours previously, informing him to expect me. I am staying with Bill tonight.

The D.C. saw me this morning thinking I was a Black Watch deserter – due no doubt to me wearing the Black Watch kilt. He ordered that I must report to him immediately. Even after he was convinced that I was no deserter, he still refused to allow me to stay. Apparently he didn't want to alter the attitude he had struck when he first saw me. He said the Meru district was a prohibited area and I should not have come there. I pleaded ignorance to this. I asked for a permit but he refused and said I must be out of his district before sundown or he would take action against me.

I had intended going right down to Embu, thus completing the circuit of the mountain. A truck from the Agricultural Department was going to Nanyuki and they said they would take me out. The road from Meru to Nanyuki climbs up over the shoulder of the mountain. At first you wind through the forest. The road is the border of the prohibited mountain area. Anyone found in the forest on the mountain side of it is liable to be shot on sight. Higher up you leave the forest and the way is open. On one side lies the rugged summit of Mount Kenya, on the other away below you, extends a desolate wilderness.

I didn't wait any time at Nanyuki but got on the road to Thomson's Falls. I had made up my mind to try and contact Davo Davidson again. At about sundown I came on a farm. I decided to seek hospitality since it would be nonsense to sleep out with the gangs roaming around at night. The farm was owned by an old man, Mr Batard, who lived by himself and was very deaf. He welcomed me warmly. I came on him just as he was about to leave for

178

his *boma* to count the cattle as they came for the evening, so I went with him and had a look round. He has nearly all Turkana and Masai boys.

As we came back to the farm house Mr Batard pointed to his mealies which were all dead and withering.

"Sixteen miles from the Equator and the frost killed them," he remarked. It did seem queer when you imagine the Equator as centre of the tropics.

At the farm I met Mr Maurice Randall, next door neighbour to Mr Batard. Last night a gang came to his farm and butchered a Turkana family. Mr Randall was still feeling bitter about it. He said he had gone today to fetch two of the six Members of Parliament who were touring the country, to show them the bodies, especially the little child slashed to bits, in the hope it would drive home the full meaning of this Mau Mau battle and perhaps impress the need for urgency in ending it.

Mr Randall exclaimed bitterly, "I hope they realise now what these people are like. I hope there won't be any more of this damned silly nonsense they get up and speak about at home, making the terrorists out to be just little bad boys. They are butchers and don't deserve an ounce of mercy."

I heartily agreed with him.

Mr Batard ran me as far as the river this morning. After that I walked 15 or 16 miles to Mr George Agett's farm where Davo was heading. It was a long 15 miles for I was tensed all the time in case I should meet a gang. When I passed some broken ground I carried my revolver in my hand in case I needed it in a hurry.

I arrived at Agett's farm to find the place empty. The servant said his 'bwana' had gone to Nairobi and Davo left last Monday. It was a disappointment for I felt tired and didn't feel like going on. Still, the longer I waited the less chance I had of catching up with Davo for he moves around plenty. I walked back to the road and continued on my way to Thomson's Falls, hoping to get some information at the Police Station.

Sometime later an Army truck with some 'askari' on board came along and drew up suddenly. The troops baled out as if they had been ambushed, and came running towards me.

"Shauri gani, Bwana?" the NCO said excitedly.

I said there was nothing wrong and that I was only walking to Thomson's Falls. He gave me a look as if I was mad. I was happy to have a lift in the truck which dropped me at Thomson's Falls and I stayed in the police station. They said Davo was here but had gone to Rumuruti.

I met Davo again next day and after walking some way from Thomson's Falls, got a lift to Rumuruti. I went along to the Police post and found that Davo was here, but was down in the swamp. Near the Police post there was a police striking force under canvas. I waited there. A few days ago a gang came to a farm, just outside the town, and killed six Samburu tribesmen who worked there Apparently, they came and demanded food, were given it and took their time in eating it. They then took the six people out one at a time and killed them.

Up at Maralal, another 75 miles north and the home of the Samburu, the tribe declared war and asked for a chance to come and avenge this outrage. The District Commissioner, with a few more of the Europeans from that area, brought down two hundred and fifty warriors. They were quartered in a camp near the Striking Force lines. Maralal was where *Mogambo*, the film with Clark Gable and Ava Gardner was made. The Samburu were the warriors who appeared in the film. But this time there was a difference. This was no play-acting – they really were thirsting for blood.

I wasn't there long before a truck came swinging through the lines of tents and drew up with a skid. A driver got out, ran towards the District Commissioner's place and minutes later the Samburu camp burst into activity. A forest of spears bristled in the sunlight, an air of urgency was abroad. It was evident that something had been seen and a battle was looming.

I checked my revolver, put some extra ammunition in my pocket and went over to the camp. Since these last few days when everything I tried to do was stopped by red tape, (my permits being refused at Isiolo and Meru), I was a bit sceptical of my chances of being allowed to go along. I went up to a European who seemed to be in charge and asked if this was a private war or could anybody join in. He replied, "The more the merrier!"

A gang had been sighted in the valley between Maralal and Thomson's Falls. The natives were loaded into a convoy of trucks and we dashed off to the place where they had last been sighted. Once there, the warriors piled out, excited and eager for battle. They placed themselves in their own battle order, strung out in a long line. I had always wondered what it would be like to go into battle in real native style. Some rubbed their spears smooth with a handful of gravel, some gathered up their '*shukas*' (the cloth that they wear), and wrapped it round their waist to keep it out of the way, regardless of modesty.

The order was given and they advanced into the bush. Looking up the line it seemed to be like a pin cushion with spears. I felt I should hate to be any of the Mau Mau in front. Although such a big force, they moved silently. The bush was thick and the line broke its straight formation. It was difficult to know what was going on other than in my own small area. I heard some excitement some distance away and went over. They had come on the remains of a cow. It was clear it had been left recently and in a hurry. There were still half eaten pieces left. Further on they found a water bottle which showed whoever was in front was jettisoning everything in a bid to escape. The warriors increased their speed. You could feel the tension in them.

Sometime afterwards, wild cries of excitement came faintly over from the far end of the line. I didn't go over because I felt we would make contact with the main gang at any time but, as far as I was concerned, nothing happened. We went right up the valley but didn't contact anything; however, over the other way they had met and killed three Mau Mau – that was when I heard them shouting.

Back at Rumuruti I ran Davo to earth in the club. He was with Mr Ken Cunningham, the District Commandant of the Kenya Police Reserve. They had had a good day in the swamp. The Kenya Regiment had mortared it a few days ago and Davo and Ken had gone in and found quite a few dead and wounded. Up at the hospital I saw some of the wounded. What a crew they looked these men from the bush – tattered, filthy clothes, long hair, one with his hair plaited into screws making it stick out like a golliwog – all with the nervous eyes of a caged animal.

Davo was staying with Mr Cunningham and he also invited me to stay at his farm.

***

Sun 24th January, 1954 – Sun 21st March, 1954

It is nearly two months since I made my last entry. It will be hard to put into words all that has happened. It has been hectic and it's given me more than a glimpse of this war.

We spent about a week at Ken Cunningham's farm. He was one of the finest men I had met. A quiet leader: a man you felt you could go anywhere with. I respected and admired him. During that week we went on a few schemes. A prisoner from the swamp had said he would show us where a hideout was. Ken collected a few of the local farmers and off we went.

The informer led us into a bush-choked gully. He said the hideout was a cave up on the left hand side. It was really more of a glen than a gully and once into that jungle, you were on your own. There could have been hundreds with you but as far as seeing them went, they could give you no support.

I struck a course up the side of the glen and through time I came to a solid buttress that seemed to run right up the glen. I followed a path that ran along the bottom of this wall and drew my revolver. The path ran in and out curves of the rock and, at times, it was a mere ledge where I had to squeeze into the rock wall to get along. On the outside the ground sloped away steeply, almost precipitous in places. I came round a sharp corner and almost cried out in surprise. I was at the edge of a huge cave. Looking in I could see the remains of a fire and food but couldn't see the whole place, as I daren't poke my head round in case someone was waiting inside.

I thought I had better go back and get the others for if a gang was inside I would be useless by myself armed only with a pistol. I retraced my steps along the path till I came to the end of the buttress, then climbed up over on top, making my way to the top of the glen where I thought the others would be. Only a few feet separated us now. Still I could see nothing. I heard the "snick" of a safety catch being released and I cocked my revolver. The click was like a peel of thunder. I immediately shifted my position and crouched down behind a tree. I heard the form coming. Each moment was an eternity. I saw someone and raised my gun, my finger tight round the trigger.

"Don't shoot, for God's sake don't shoot", I mentally shouted at myself.

Into my vision came Davo, his Beretta levelled menacingly at me. We moved forward and slapped each other on the back in silent pleasure that we had spotted each other in time. We had been stalking each other.

That's how it was in jungle warfare. Perhaps something that Davo had said some time previously had much to do with the healthy outcome of it. When we had heard of two Europeans of the police shooting at each other and remembering that more Europeans had been shot in this way than by the Mau Mau, Davo had said, "To shoot merely at a sound and not wait to see your target is a form of cowardice".

We went on and found the others at the top of the glen and I went back with them to show them where the cave was. But it was empty. Nearby was a smaller cave with the entrance nearly closed with logs that had been piled up. Inside there was a food horde. A large gang had used this place.

That was just one of many incidents. We were still on the trail of General Kimbo. Davo had picked up a woman who said she was his wife, so he was in the area. The next few weeks took us all over the western side of the Aberdares, from Thomson Falls down to South Kinin gap. We stayed at numerous farms and we were always made welcome. Davo was well known everywhere.

Although General Kimbo was our immediate object, Davo also looked for information regarding Dedan Kamathi. In a broadcast after he recovered from his wounds, Davo had said, "Even if you go to hell I will follow you", but, since he had wounded him, no definite proof had been received that he was still alive. Many conflicting reports had been received and a few days after the incident an important gangster died in the forest and his funeral had been attended by over a thousand Mau Mau. Was that Dedan? Again, all notes after the event sent by him to the police were only signed with the initials D.K. instead of his full signature, which was the norm previously. Some opinions said he was dead, others that he was well and healthy. Some said he was crippled with wounds and yet others said he was well but had fallen from command and no longer meant anything in the hierarchy of the Mau Mau.

The weeks went by. There were no Sundays or holidays. Davo's jeep was a will-o'-the-wisp that turned up wherever there was trouble or if there was no trouble, it didn't take long to start. Trouble had a way of following us. Invariably we would turn up in an area and perhaps the labour lines of that farm or the next would be burned down, or a gang pass through, or some of the African labour be killed or cattle stolen. It was as if our movements were watched. We were a team. We got to know each other's movements and, in trouble, we knew what each would do. The jeep was a little combustible unit, primed for action which became highly inflamed wherever we bumped into trouble. As previously mentioned, Davo always drove with a grenade in his hand. I sat with the Beretta cocked and ready. Ambush was a constant threat.

The work was a combination of secret service, bush tracking and plain fighting. Davo had two boys, Kikuyu, whose purpose it was to mingle with the house boys of any farm where we stayed to find out any information. Not a very honourable way to return hospitality, but it was really the best way, for more often than not it was the person's own houseboys who were his worst enemy. For instance, on an Italian farm in Kipipiri, the boys reported that the house boys had told them that a gang was coming regularly for food. The gang told them they wouldn't worry them but that one day, they would come for the *Mzungu* (Europeans), and they would be called upon to help.

Always it was the same, in every conversation, one had to be on the alert to catch any information. On the farms, in the police posts, in the forest among captured gangsters, always the same questions being asked, "Where is Kimbo? When did you last see Dedan Kimathi?" Interrogation seemed to be never ending. A word gleaned here, a name there and gradually a piece of information that made sense would form. Then off we'd go into the forest for perhaps a week at a time or lie in ambush where we thought the gang would pass.

Seventy per cent of the information was fruitless and endless days in the forest would only be rewarded with failure and a feeling of hopelessness. But we could not afford to neglect the slightest thing for fear that it might be what we were waiting for. Of course, there were the successes, and even the most moderate ones made all the past failures and wasted time and energy seem worthwhile. When I say that, it means a lot. I will never forget the crippling disappointment I felt after lying for three nights and two days in ambush at a place where we had heard General Kimbo was due to come. We fed off chocolate and biscuits for we could not make a fire. We couldn't even stand up for fear of being seen and giving the show away. By the morning of the third day we were stiff and cramped. All the while we took turns between the two of us to sleep. The days were endless, the nights interminable with suspense. Imagine the bitter blow when we found he had come to another hut only a half a mile away.

In the forest you develop a sixth sense, a kind of animal instinct. Many times we packed our sleeping bags with twigs and grass and then went to sleep in the bush some distance away. Through time you learned to read the signs left in the tracks from one gang to another – a broken stem of grass, two twigs placed together and many other ingenious signs that look so natural they are quite invisible to the uninitiated. The Mau Mau were master woodsmen. Living continually in the forest as they did, they became as animals. A great trick of theirs was to walk backwards along their tracks before branching off into the bush to foil anybody who might be trailing them.

But it was not only the Mau Mau we had to look out for. There were elephant, rhino and buffalo, all caught up in the battlefield. At one farm up on Kipipiri, the farmer said he often got a rhino in amongst his wheat, or even a herd of buffalo that trampled it down. That coupled with the atmosphere of fear that a gang might attack was a farmer's life then. Still, he said he didn't mind the animals; in fact, he would be sorry if they were shot out or driven off.

***

The Aberdare Mountains consist of three main mountains – Satima, Kipipiri and Kinangop. How the country varies! Driving through the rolling downs of the plateau with its hedgerows and small holding plots and neat fields, one could imagine one was in England. Yet, above and beyond on the slopes of the mountains, the deadly, treacherous jungle, a hell to all who enter it, there are places where no man has ever trod.

To me its personality varied with circumstances. When we were the hunted, when we knew they were coming for us, the tangled walls would come in and bring on a kind of claustrophobia and as if in preparation for the immediate future, the leafy boughs would envelope me like a green shroud. But there were other times when we were the hunters, when I lay in ambush with death harnessed in my hand waiting for the opportunity to release it – then the jungle shadows were friendly.

There were still other times when no immediate action was pending, when we sat in the one spot for a long time and had time to admire the place in which we lived. When you settled down and became part of the scenery, when birds accepted you as harmless and settled on twigs near you and chirped merrily as they moved in the breeze like a child in a swing, and the colobus monkeys with their long, bushy, black and white tails stopped to look at you, when you had time to take in these things, it hardly seemed possible that there was a war going on.

There is something wonderful, sublime about the forest. Sometimes I have lain on my back and gazed at branches high overhead bending over to form a ceiling like the tracery of a lofty cathedral. Beautiful trees! I remember going into an area immediately after a gang had been bombed. The mangled bodies of the Mau Mau terrorists didn't touch me so much as the great, blasted trees, split like matches. Some had been set on fire. I watched with awe as one giant tottered and crashed down with a roar like an express train, sending up a cloud of smoke and sparks. It didn't deserve to die. We wandered through the desecrated area, through the smoke and dust from the charred bush, and looked with pity at the great giants that had been laid low, with fire still burning in their bowels.

Well, that was all past now. While we were at South Kinangop, word came over the police radio network for Davo and I to report back to Nyeri for the trial of the two terrorists we captured when we cleaned up the arms factory. Davo excused himself from the trial and I became the chief witness. I was given a warrant and travelled back to Nyeri to appear in court.

The trial lasted two days. After I gave my evidence the defence barrister, Mr de Sousa, a Goanese, said, "Mr Lessels. I put it to you that your evidence is a complete tissue of lies."

Before I had time to deny his challenge the Judge, a New Zealander, firmly stated, "Mr de Sousa, Mr Lessels is a Scotsman and Scotsmen never lie."

Both men were found guilty of making firearms and being in possession of ammunition and were sentenced to death.

With the trial over I realised it was time to move on. I wished I could have stayed longer as I was enjoying the excitement, but I had a long way to go and I had already delayed too long.

***

One little thing I will mention. The Mau Mau all had bush names and some of them were quite funny. Recently, I had sat with Davo in the back of an ambulance questioning a Mau Mau leader who had just been wounded and captured. He went under the name of General Hitler. He recognised Davo immediately he entered the ambulance and greeted him, "Jambo General Hodari". Hodari – brave, strong – is the name Davo was known by to the Mau Mau.

***

Looking back I realised how lucky I was to meet Davo when I did. It was such a chance meeting and led to me being involved with him in many a skirmish with the Mau Mau. He was a unique and interesting character, in many ways a showman, throwing electric light bulbs into the air and shooting them down without a miss, but in the same way giving the police more confidence in the revolver as a suitable weapon for their work. Davo showed them how good a weapon it was. We said our goodbyes and I am sure his feelings were like mine. I knew I had been extremely fortunate to have shared his company and been involved with him at such an extremely interesting, if dangerous, time.

A native village

Oxen pulling cart with logs

On the road yet again

This crocodile was on the bank of the Zambesi as David left Kasane after the barge incident

Home made rifle found on Mr Maxwell's farm

Davo and Harry Thuku, Chairman of the Kikuyu Provincial Society

Davo showing off shooting bottles out of the sky

Uganda

Tree Tops as it was when David stayed there, later it was burned down by the Mau Mau

A Makeshi dancer

Bornu horseman – Kano, Nigeria

Great pinnacle boulders perched precariously in queer balancing acts of nature

Women of the plains

CHAPTER 17

FAREWELL TO KENYA

I went back to Thomsons Falls with Davo and then made my way up to Maralal, the home of the Samburu. I had several invitations from the Government Officers who were down with the Samburu at Rumuruti when I was there. I was supposed to go on safari with the Forestry Officer, but when I arrived he was already on tour and wouldn't be back for some time. Great as that would have been, I felt I couldn't wait for his return.

I stayed with the District Commissioner. A film company were just starting to make a new film there, *No Rain at Timburu*. I think the District Commissioner was going to play the part of the D.C. in the film.

It's an interesting place, Maralal. In its dusty street mingle the picturesque tribes of the Northern Frontier Districts; the Samburu, akin to the Masai with their hair plaited and clayed with red ochre; and the Turkana, with their original head-gear. They make a pack of cow dung and mud, and plaster their hair with it in the shape of a skullcap. They colour it with blue dye and into this mud pack they insert the dried tips of a cows' teats to act as air vents into their head. They usually stick feathers in the holes in the teats.

From Maralal I made my way down through Ol Kalou, to Gilgil and Navasha and on to Narok in the Masai country. Just as I was leaving Maralal I saw the biggest dust devil I had ever seen. I was in a truck at the time. Five miles away, across the sun-baked semi desert, a pillar of dust stretched from the earth into the clouds like a cyclone. I watched fascinated as we drew near, as this great funnel of wind and dust twisted this way and that. When I came almost to it, it suddenly swerved away off our course with terrific speed and then dissolved like smoke.

At Narok I got the usual greeting from the D.C. as to why I had come into his district. It was a prohibited area. I said I walked in. That made him worse. He said I could stay if I promised not to walk about on my own, as if anything happened to me in his district it would be his responsibility. I was only there about an hour when a report came in that a gang of twenty Mau Mau was heading towards Narok. The Masai *morani* were going out after them. I volunteered to go. I wanted to see them, the finest fighting men in all Africa, in action. The officer in charge asked if I thought I could keep up with them. He didn't go out with them because he couldn't keep up the pace. I said I thought I could, but I never knew how near I was to biting off more than I could chew.

I got my sleeping bag and slept beside them and early in the morning we set out. I soon saw what the officer meant. The Masai have a long, effortless stride when they go on a long journey. It taxed me to the limit to keep up with them, but I did. They never rested, just kept going, eating up the miles. Unfortunately, we never made contact with the gang so I was denied my wish. Before we left, some *morani* limbered up by throwing their spears, proud to show off their prowess to me.

The power behind a Masai spear is perhaps best explained in an incident that happened a few years before near Narok. The D.C. at that time had ordered the Masai to de-stock one area by compulsorily selling some cattle as the land was overgrazed. A market was arranged, but because the Masai were not keen sellers they proceeded in a dilatory fashion. Towards the afternoon the D.C., perhaps angered by their procrastination and eager to see the unfortunate business over, commandeered the cattle he wanted sold and ordered that the business be put through immediately. However, one young *morani* Masai came and said he had picked a special bull of his and would he, the D.C. exchange it for another. The D.C. refused. The Masai pleaded, but the D.C. was adamant.

What the D.C. didn't know was how much that bull meant to the Masai. Apparently, when the Masai was a baby his mother died. At the same time, one of his father's cows had a calf. The boy was fed from the front two teats of the cow, the calf was fed from the back two. The boy and calf grew up together and the boy came to regard the bull as almost a blood brother. This was the bull the D.C. had taken.

His appeal dismissed, the *moran* went and greased his spear. He returned and threw it at the D.C. The spear, seven foot long, passed completely through the D.C.'s body and stuck in the ground beyond. The D.C. was killed and, later, the *moran* was hanged for the murder.

I stayed a few days at Narok then came back to Nairobi. A few days after returning, I went up to Kiambu to see Davo again. Sometime ago we had received a report that Dedan Kamathi was coming to Kiambu on a certain date. We waited, intending to give him a reception fit for one of his standing, but he didn't turn up.

While at Kiambu we visited Harry Thuku at his home. Harry Thuku is an African farmer. Anybody who imagined that the black man was held down in Kenya would have been wise to visit this man. He was just leaving in his blue Consul car when we arrived. He was due at a meeting of the Kikuyu Provincial Society of which he was the Chairman. He returned to welcome us. Over at the garage was another car, a shooting brake. His was a European style house of stone. There was a verandah with pillars – a house that any European would be proud of. In his carpeted lounge we were served with soft drinks brought in by an African servant. The books and magazines on the table showed a good taste in literature. It all showed what an African could do if he was willing to work.

***

Now I am preparing for my next lap to Uganda and beyond. I'm a wee bit apprehensive about the journey from now on, but I'm eager to be getting on with it. I'm worried about my equipment, it's terribly worn and my rucksack is in such a state that it might pack up on me at anytime. Then I would be in a stew.

Tomorrow I leave for Kampala. I'm glad to be on my way but sorry in a way I could not have stayed longer."

***

Today I left Nairobi, perhaps for the last time. I walked out of the city then got a lift with a farmer coming up to Eldoret. It was a good lift.

There is something spectacular about a journey through Kenya – this way especially. If you have never seen the Great Rift Valley, then you have never lived. You leave the city and pass through Kikuyu. The road begins to dip. You swing round a bend and suddenly you see it. It's as if you had come to the end of the world.

In front of you is a sheer drop as the land drops away. Away far below lies the floor of the Great Rift Valley, that great cleft in the Earth's surface that includes the Red Sea and extends over a sixth of the circumference of the world. When one beholds the Rift Valley for the first time, it is so amazing that you catch your breath – the magnificent panorama, the great expanse laid out before you. Away down in the valley in a haze of dreamy blue lies the range of volcanoes, Longonot, Suswa and the rest.

You swing down the escarpment in great, tarmacadam loops to the floor of the valley. From this you pass through Naivasha and Gilgil, you see the dried up soda bed that is supposed to be a lake, Lake Elmenteita, and to Nakuru.

Lake Nakuru is also dried up. From the white lake bed a pall of dust drifted with the wind. The Nakuru authorities have been going to endless expense in an effort to control the dust that threatens to make this town uninhabitable. From Nakuru we went on, up the other side of the Rift Valley into the highlands again and to Eldoret.

I'm staying the night with the farmer who gave me the lift. Seventy per cent of the farmers around Eldoret were South Africans, many of them sons and grandsons of the Voortrekkers who arrived there around 1906/7. This was the end of the Great Trek begun in 1835, the highest point north reached by them. Actually the real place was Moiben some miles north of Eldoret. Eldoret is quite a fine place with tree-shaded streets.

I left in the morning and got a lift after walking a few miles. This was in a truck driven by an African. I went about 20 miles with it, then walked some more and had another lift with a Caltex salesman. He was going up to the Ugandan border near Tororo. This was well out of the main traffic route, but I was glad of it.

Now, here I am on the edge of the Ugandan border – my last day in Kenya.

Looking back to my first days in the Army that took me to Africa as an eighteen-year-old rookie soldier, it will always have a special place in my heart.

CHAPTER 18

UGANDA – THE QUEEN AND I

There was nobody about to ask its name when I crossed the little stream that was the border into Uganda. I had left early in the morning to walk the 26 miles into a new country. Arriving in Tororo gave me quite a thrill.

Twenty-six miles makes a terribly long day. Twenty is a good day; after that, my pack becomes pretty heavy, but I made the extra effort to get into Tororo. How thankful I was when the peculiar, round-topped shape of Tororo hill came into view. It was good to walk down the street and at the hotel I had some tea – how refreshing it was. The proprietor gave me it on the house and even fixed up a lift for me with a man at the hotel who was going into Jinja. He was a fireman with the electric company that was bringing the cable from the hydroelectric plant at Jinja to Tororo.

He dropped me off at the Ripon Falls Hotel. I had heard that John Dorward was managing it. It was good to see him again and meet his new wife. He seems pleased to see me too and has given me a room.

I went down to town in the morning to get fixed up with the immigration authorities as there had been a bit of bother over my pistols. Officially I was not allowed to have them so it was impossible to licence them. However, the District Commissioner seemed a human type and turned a blind eye and gave me an export permit for them for the Congo. It was the first time I had had them officially unlicensed.

I had a stroll round town and met more fellows from Glasgow who were out with 'John Brown's' (the John Brown Industrial Construction Company) working on the hydroelectric dam, the big scheme to dam up the Nile. They were typical Glasgow chaps and they invited me along to meet the 'boys'. The 'boys' were in a pub and this was about 11 a.m. They were all in working togs. One of them said if I wanted a job I'd get one on the dot for they were desperate for men. They said they were working at fever pitch to get one turbine ready for the Queen to open next month on her visit. Then, as he ordered another pint, he turned to one of his pals and said, "Hope old Charlie won't miss me this morning". Every one of them was down town on French leave. Working at fever pitch!

I asked if it were possible to get round the dam for a look-see. They said it wasn't, but if I liked to go back with them after lunch they would get me in. In the afternoon I went with them and one of the men well known to the gateman gave me his workman's pass. I got in without any trouble and it was very interesting. On the job you do get caught up with the tempo of the work and I could tell they were going all out to get things ready for the royal visit. One turbine was already working. It was enough to supply all the present day demand for electricity in Uganda. When the dam is complete, there will be four turbines working and provision made for six more to be installed singly as the country's industry expands and the demand increases. When the whole place is finished, the ten turbines will supply power to all East Africa.

What struck me most of all was the sight of the Nile passing through one small opening. That spout of water I watched was the life line of all the land north as far as the Mediterranean. In the evening I had a stroll along the Nile by Ripon Falls. Since the dam had been in operation the water had risen and Owen Falls had completely disappeared.

It was an interesting stop-over, but next morning I got on the road to Kampala. It wasn't long before I got a lift. Pam's mother and family had moved up to Kampala from Nairobi and I stayed with them. Kampala is the Rome of Africa and, like Rome, is built on seven hills. We drove to the top of one of the hills and it was quite an impressive sight looking down on all the lights.

The past fortnight had been fine. I visited a family I had met in Nairobi, and to earn my keep I did a lot of painting in the house, which they rented from the Regent who was standing in for the *Kabaka* – their King – exiled for subversive activity. The landlord came round now and again to see if his tenants were all right. The house was African-built without European supervision and there was not a straight line in the place. The workmanship was terribly shoddy.

Kampala was a strange place after living in the other African countries. Down in the 'Crested Crane' tea rooms, Indians and Africans sat at the next table. There was simply no colour bar. Uganda was a natives' country – they owned the land and its property. The tribe, the Buganda, were arrogant and, at times, openly rude in the street to Europeans. They had their own *Lukiiko* – parliament – which I would like to have seen in session but, disappointingly, it was in recess. I went down to Entebbe a few times swimming and, by chance, was lucky to see the 'Comet' arriving.

I had never seen so many African-owned cars – there were hundreds of them. And bicycles – every African had at least one new one. There were

202

rich Africans around this part of the world, and when I say rich I mean rich; some were raking in £6,000 a year and maybe more, this from cotton. And they didn't pay income tax either.

I was keen to get on my way. I had been hanging on waiting for my immigration deposit to be forwarded to me, but the government people were slow and I couldn't wait any longer. I left Kampala in the morning.

***

The cars passed, but I got a lift from a truck a few miles out. It took me to Mityana, over 40 miles. There I met with some of the Europeans working on building the railroad through to Fort Portal and one gave me a lift. He took me within 30 miles along the road to Mubende before he branched off. From there I walked five or six miles before being picked up by a chauffeur-driven car carrying the wife and two children of the District Commissioner of Mubende. She seemed quite amazed to see me and invited me to stay the night with them. At Mubende I met Mr Lanning. We got talking and it soon became apparent that we had many interests in common and chief of these were history and archaeology. His wife, Peggy, had suggested I put up my tent in their garden, but Mr Lanning, soon to be known as Eric, pooh-poohed the idea with a shout, "Good God man, bring your stuff in here!", and settled me in the house. There followed one of the most interesting times of my journey and a friendship which has lasted to the present day. We got talking and he had me interested in some things in his district.

The first of these was the Munsa earthworks. Attention was first drawn to these by Sir Apolo Kagwa, an African, but Mr Lanning was the first European to see and study them. These trenches were locally known as *Ensa Za Katebowa* (the trenches of *Katebowa*), a semi-legendary figure. The trenches run round three sides of a group of rocks situated on top of a hill. The *Kyeja* rocks run along the fourth side. These rocks are known as *'Bikekette'*. They are a mound of great granite rocks piled haphazardly on each other by nature forming a maze of passages and caves.

The trenches had mostly fallen in and were overgrown with grass, but their line could be followed and it was evident that at one time they had been about ten feet deep and some 15 feet wide. There was an outer trench that swept in a great semi-circle for nearly one and three quarter miles from the *Kyeja* stream which flows into the *Katerere* on the east flank, back into the *Katerere* in the west. An inner trench seemed to form a second line of defence. Between the outer and inner trenches streams flow and there was enough rock-free land to allow for extensive cultivation.

I wondered what had been the purpose of these earthworks. Mugeny was in charge of the land Katonga. His name is linked with the Bigo earthworks, the largest of its type in the district. Was this perhaps the headquarters of the great General Katebowa who was the Captain in charge of the Kakumiro area and was held so high in local legend and mythology? Some say he was captain of the Bechwezi, others say he came to the area with his idea of fortified camps after the disappearance or absorption of these people. Did the inhabitants withdraw inside this outer perimeter in times of war? It was evident that the shelters and caves among the rocks of *Bikekette* had been the home of men for many generations. As to more recent history, enough evidence has been found to prove these rocks were occupied up to the beginning of the present century. This is to be expected in view of the Bunyoro–Buganda wars, which on reaching their climax, ended with the signing of treaties by both kingdoms with the British Government at the close of the nineteenth century.

What people made these defences? Was it the extinct Bechwezi of whom still so little is known? Reports said the Bechwezi were a light-skinned race who had lived long before and were first reported by Stanley, who was mistaken for one of them by a native who thought the Bechwezi had returned. Mr Lanning had a theory that they may have been half-caste Portuguese from Abyssinia.

It is related that Katebowa used *Bikekette* as his battle headquarters. Below the rocks and over the first trenches is a large, flat granite slab. In this is a large hole from which, legend says, Katebowa, drank his beer. Apparently the beer was not made in it but was poured in there, presumably to keep it cool.

***

On Mubende Hill stands a huge tree of the species Pterygota. It was known as 'the Witch Tree' and was estimated by the Forestry Department to be at least 400 years old, a statement on which a forestry officer of many years' experience said he would stake his reputation. This is exceptionally old for Africa where ants and other insects usually kill a tree long before that and few trees live more than two hundred years. Apart from its grotesque, almost hideous shape at the base, with great fins like buttresses giving the impression it was something out of the ordinary, it had achieved world fame with its association with the priestess of the spirit of smallpox who, local tradition relates, resided here for countless years, probably long before the advent of the tree itself.

I wondered how long Mubende had been the seat of the governing powers of the district. Local legend says that the Bechwezi people came from Lake Albert. They brought with them a civilisation, but they were hit by a smallpox epidemic. The weakened force went north again. There is a place near the southern end of Lake Albert which some old men will point to and say, "the Bechwezi were last seen going over there at sunset".

Ndaula, General of the legendary Bechwezi tribe, had made his headquarters at Mubende, with his wife, the priestess *Nakaima*. Here they lived for half a century. We only know the folklore and legends of the local people who are full of tales of this strange, light coloured people. Who were they – half-caste Portuguese from Abyssinia or perhaps the ancestors of the Crusaders in the Sudan?

The office of being '*Nakaima*', the priestess of the centre – guardian of the spirit – was always held by the Bahima clan and had been handed down from generation to generation. The last authentic *Nakaima* died in 1910. Was it that *Nakaima* cured someone of smallpox, as the Goddess of smallpox was believed to be in control of the disease? Of such importance was the centre that in the past pilgrims visited it from far afield. They included the lowest as well as the highest in the land, including the *Abakama* (King) of the Bunyoro and, it is said, even the *Makabaka* of the Buganda people.

Kabarega, a rebel Chief, was the last Munyoro to visit the Witch Tree. He had opposed the British in 1894 and was evading the new authority which had taken over Bunyoro. One of his last acts was to come to Mubende Hill to speak with the *Nakaima*. He was already on the run when he gave her a spear and a bundle and said the parcel had not to be opened until he returned. He never came back.

How the spear came to the museum is a tale in itself. When Eric Lanning came to this district as District Commissioner, he was interested in local history. He talked to many old men and finally found one who claimed to have been appointed personally by the last *Nakaima* as guardian of her property. When Mr Lanning asked if there was any of the property left, the old man said no, it had all rotted away. But, sometime later, the old man walked into the office and out of the blue said if the District Commissioner would come he would show him the possessions of the *Nakaima*, of which he was the keeper.

Eric was taken to a hut and the old man brought out a bundle wrapped up in old, tattered bark cloth. It looked like rubbish. Inside, in almost perfect condition, were the *Nakaima's* leopard skins and other attire. Together with this was the spear with the parcel attached. Later, Eric obtained permission from the Mukama to obtain these treasures for the Museum. The mystery of what the parcel contains has never been solved. It has been suggested that it should be x-rayed. Perhaps it will be one day.

Although the Bechwezi left to return whence they had come, before they went, *Nakaima* planted a tree to mark the place that had been their home for so long and a hundred yards away from where I sat was the Witch Tree. By some strange twist of fate, or was it the supernatural powers of *Nakaima*, the tree she planted with her own hands was granted a phenomenal span of life and became the biggest and most grotesque tree in all the land.

The local woman who had inherited *Nakaima's* knowledge of the treatment of smallpox made her home beside this tree. She also became known as *Nakaima*, the Guardian or Goddess of smallpox. Her knowledge and title were, in turn, handed down. A strange thing is that the *Nakaima* was always a Mahima, drawn from a certain clan of the Bahima tribe, strange because Mubende is not in Bahima country, although many Bahima lived in the area.

When the British came to Uganda they found this part of the country in a state of war between the Buganda and the Bunyoro tribes. The initiative of the war had been swinging from side to side, but when the white man came they found the Buganda were winning. To finish the battle the British supported the Buganda and when the battle was over, Mubende was given or included in the land of the Buganda.

The tribes of Uganda seemed to be in a much more advanced state than the other tribes of East Africa, and the British found the country already partly civilised. Indeed, some of the tribes had their own form of government. The tribes also had their own Kings and could trace back their dynasties. There is the Kabaka of the Buganda, the Mubaka of the Bunyoro and the Mabula of the Wa Toro. Each of these titles means King.

***

It was twilight as I sat on the verandah of the Lannings' home on the top of Mubende Hill and looked out over the hazy expanse of the plain below. In the twilight the copper-coloured clouds were banked up in great, fluffy tiers and a huge bird flew in 100 feet below me and disappeared down the valley. Here, on a clear morning, you could see the snow-tipped crest of the fabulous Mountains of the Moon, 100 miles away to the west.

***

Ten days had passed since I made my last entry in my diary. I had spent these days at Mubende, or at least with the Lannings. Eric was going on safari to Kakumiro, and asked if I would like to accompany him. He said he would be doing some digging, so I thought I'd try my hand at archaeology, a subject that had long interested me.

Eric, Peggy, little John, Lindy and I set out for Kakumiro. I spent an interesting few days there. Lindy was a lovely little five-year-old girl when I met her first. With her fair hair, fetching smile and a winning way, she was going to break some hearts in years to come. We had become good pals during those couple of weeks or so, searched caves together, talked hours away with walks along the ridge of Mubende Hill with the wind blowing our hair and bending the grass. We competed to see who could best shape the racing clouds into the most interesting pictures. She was an artist and was always much quicker than I in picking out the billowy forms of a man's face, a knight on horseback, an elephant, a fowl, and many other things in her imagination. Lindy, of course, was Eric and Peggy Lanning's daughter.

In Buganda they don't have District Commissioners. It smacks too much of the idea of being governed for the proud Buganda. So the District Commissioners there are known as Protectorate Agents and they are only supposed to advise.

Eric Lanning was one of the most interesting government men I had met. Eric divided his time between his work as Protectorate Agent and archaeology. It was hard to tell which one was his hobby, although, of course, his official work took up most of his time. I think the administration would benefit if more of its officers could escape periodically into another world as Eric Lanning did. Perhaps it was because of this that he had few of the impractical theories many of his colleagues tried to put into practice. A good administrator, he handled his people with a firm but diplomatic hand.

He was also an amateur archaeologist of no mean standing. A lot of the stuff he had unearthed was on show at the Kampala museum when it opened in June, 1954. Near Kikumiro are the Munsa earthworks. Eric had been the first white man to visit and explore them. Among the rocks, Eric found two bone bark cloth hammers of a pattern not in use today. All hammers are made of wood now. He had also found Stone-Age implements there.

All over the district are these outcrops of rock, huge boulders leaning haphazardly together. With Eric I visited and explored the Bwansa, Gamucole and the Bride and Bridegroom rock shelters. In most cases the only white people ever to be there before me were the Lannings and, in a few cases, I experienced the thrill of being the first white man ever to enter a particular cave or climb some crag.

The Bride and Bridegroom are two huge pinnacles of rock that, if the imagination can run free, can be likened to the characters the name implies. The story goes they were just coming from their wedding and, for some reason, they were on no account to look back. Of course, they did and were turned to stone.

But perhaps the most interesting of all the caves I visited were the Semwema caves, where at the bottom of the mountain you enter a huge cavern where, again legend says, Katabowa held council. At the back of the cavern a small hole, almost invisible, marks the start of a tunnel which takes you through the heart of the mountains and brings you out at the summit.

In places the tunnel is mere inches high and it is only with an effort you manage to squeeze through while lying flat on your face. It is wet and dank in there. The floor of the tunnel is covered with guano. When you enter a new section, the sudden flight of thousands of bats is like the rush of a hurricane.

At the back of the Katabowa cavern I found an old, blackened one cent piece of a type not in circulation. We did some digging and riddling in a big square sieve but didn't find anything else. In the caves we picked up some odd pieces of pottery obviously old but not of much value as relics.

However, the day before we left, an African came to us to say he thought he had found something. This African was a big landowner; the whole Semwema range of hills belonged to him. But he was one of the most unspoiled Africans I've met. He knew what Eric was looking for, although I am sure didn't realise why. He took us to a place near his hut. Right in the middle of the road was a circle of the rim of a huge pot. The constant grind of traffic had brought it to light.

It was fun digging down, carefully scooping away the earth from its side with a trowel. What would we find? Unearthed, the pot was huge, but the top neck and rim were missing. It measured 70 inches in circumference. Nearby, also in the road, we dug a whole collection of smaller pots which appeared to have been buried inside one big one, of which little was left. This could have been a burial ground for it was customary to bury the possessions with the deceased. Beside the pots was a crumbled bone. The pots were carefully packed and sent by lorry onto Mubende. There when we returned we emptied them of the earth in the hope of finding some beads, etc. But although we meticulously sieved the contents, we found nothing.

The last night we were at Kikumiro the local Chief laid on a meal for us. It was a real local delicacy – white ants and 'matoki', the local staple diet consisting of cooked green bananas. The ants were done whole and served in groundnut sauce and I really enjoyed it.

All along the road in this part of Uganda, the ant heaps were covered with a shelter of branches and grass. This was the season the ants fly. The idea of the shelter was to prevent them from rising. A hole is dug near the heap and inside the shelter. A banana leaf is placed from the heap to the hole. By some phenomenon the insects are attracted to the leaf and follow along it into the hole. The person collecting them then scoops them up.

I spent Easter weekend back at Mubende. It was fun on Easter morning with Lindy and John. There were Easter eggs and Easter fare, rhymes and searches for chocolates and sweets. On Easter Monday, some of the White Fathers from the Mission were there. They seemed quite human, different from most missionaries one encounters in Africa, and they joined in football games and a sing-song.

The next morning Eric, with Peggy and the children, drove me to the end of his district to set me on my way. On the way he made a detour to visit a Bahima camp. They are nomadic people and have strange features for Africans, being light-skinned with straight, sharp noses. They all smoke a queer-shaped pipe with a sharp, square point at the foot of the bowl. They are moon worshippers, and at the full moon they dance and give offerings. They rear cattle and keep the milk in oddly shaped gourds hollowed out of wood. They never wash these gourds out with water but instead fumigate them with smoke. Consequently, all the milk has a smoky flavour.

***

After I left Eric, Peggy and the children, I walked some miles then got a lift in a car going to Fort Portal. As I walked on, I looked back over the time I had spent with them; a loving family, generous with their time and anxious to show me all that was interesting about the area in which they lived. I was not to know that I would meet them again some years later in London, when they came back to this country when Uganda got its independence. Eric had my address in Scotland, got in touch and I met them in London. I was about to be married and they came to our wedding.

***

At Fort Portal I asked to camp near the Mountains of the Moon Hotel. They charged me 2/ (shillings) 6d for the camping site. I wasn't impressed! I was even less impressed the next day when they were annoyed because I hadn't had any meals. The meals were expensive in my estimation. I said I hoped I hadn't offended them with my independence, but I had paid for the camping site so they hadn't lost out on the deal. As it was I couldn't make a fire, so they had only provided me with the water I had used. Rather expensive water!

I walked down to the *boma* there to see the District Commissioner to find out if it was possible to join a climbing party going up the mountain. The District Commissioner, Mr R. Stone, said it was impossible to go up the mountains now during the rains, since the rivers would be impassable. He invited me to lunch and, during the meal, asked me about my journey. He then offered me a job down in the Game Park for a couple of weeks to help in the preparations for the Queen's visit. Pay 10/- per day. I accepted. The pay would hardly foot my food bill, but it was a chance to see the Queen, and besides, I couldn't move anyway until my immigration deposit arrived from Nairobi.

This was at 1.30 p.m. and I started work at 2 p.m. in the District Commissioner's office, drawing maps and diagrams of the routes the crowds and processions would take. It was the quickest thing I've known.

Half an hour before I started, I had no idea I'd be working that day and the District Commissioner invited me to stay at his home that night. I came down the 50 odd miles to Kasese with Jim Fleming, Assistant to the District Commissioner, and in charge of this district which the Queen will visit. I had a full morning drawing maps before we left.

I discussed the fact that I had had no word of the money from Kenya yet and the District Commissioner advised me to send a Police cable, which I did. It made me mad thinking how the civil servants expected me just to wait their time before they did anything. Even after I had left their country I must still hang about while they delayed. It was now over three weeks since I sent my receipt to them. If I had needed to pay a hotel bill while I waited I would be some amount in debt. I had written a letter to the Immigration Department a week before saying any further expense I incurred while waiting for the money would be charged to them. Idle threats I supposed, but the wait for the money had worried me.

There was quite a lot to get fixed in time for the Queen's visit on Friday. There was the pavilion and all the enclosures for each district at Kikaranga. Then there was the camp that must accommodate 1,200 people, the enclosures at the airstrip, and many other things.

A week had passed since I started on the work there. It had been ding-dong from dawn till dusk and sometimes, later, every day. All the work had been done by free labour (*Bulungi Bwansi*) for the good of the country, supplied by the *Gombolola* (Parish) Chief. As there had been no monetary incentive to work, it had been extremely difficult to motivate the men. There were the huts to be built, water, rations, firewood, a football pitch that had to be carved out of the bush with ant heaps to be levelled down and a whole host of other things to see to.

The construction was finished, or so I thought, when on Sunday we had a dress rehearsal with the Governor, Sir Andrew Cohen, just to check up on things. To my horror he was not happy with the area of the arena, which he said should be increased to a diameter of at least 50 feet to keep the Queen safe from any possible attack from the people coming to see her. So we went to it again, dismantling what had been done before, this time speeding up the work with the help of a financial incentive for the Chief, who then made sure that the work was carried out at an improved speed. We worked through the night, fencing in the enclosure, lighting fires round the area to keep marauding animals away.

When the people arrived, 850 of them, they were some crowd to control! At night I had been camping down at Mubuku beside the people, as it was my responsibility to see they got up to Kikaronga on time. Organising the camp had been quite a job. Now, I was looking forward to seeing the Queen the next day.

The day started before 6 a.m. It was still dark and cold when I shook the bugler to sound reveille. Already there were people out and about making tea. I asked the man with the loud speaker van to play a few jazzy records to get them to start the day in the right mood. By 8.30 a.m. they were on the trucks and off. There was rain in the wind and it looked as though it was going to dampen the celebrations. Heavy, leaden clouds hung low. A local made us roll up the windows as we were crossing the Equator in Ted Evans' car, (the camp was in the Southern Hemisphere; Kikaronga, where the Queen came was 20 miles away and a couple of miles into the northern half of the globe. A concrete circle marks the line).

The crowds had already gathered in the enclosure Thirty yards away (security regulations) the pavilion – an open, thatched, reed shelter decorated with strips of black banana plant wound round the yellow reeds – had taken on an air of dignity that had seemed impossible to achieve while we were building it. At about 10.45 a.m., a quarter of an hour before the Queen was due to arrive, the sun decided to attend the occasion.

Mixed feelings were abroad in the crowd. To the general public the waiting was only marked by boredom. To those 'in the know' it was marked with tension. It was common knowledge that the Mau Mau had sworn to assassinate the Queen during her tour of Uganda. Everyone knew that Kampala, the biggest and main town in the country, had been put out of bounds to the royal entourage at the last minute, although thousands of pounds had been spent in preparing the town for the visit.

What they didn't know was that five WaKikuyu, confirmed Mau Mau, including Muthiga, reputed to be number three in the Mau Mau hierarchy, had been picked up in the district and were now in Fort Portal jail. Three WaKamba had also been detained. The fact that a game scout had deserted with a .404 rifle in the same area as Muthiga and his colleagues were caught, made the chances of an attempt on the Queen's life more imminent. Had the attempt been foiled with the capture of the king-pin or were the rumours that more high-ranking Mau Mau agents were still at large in the area true? Anxiety was apparent among the select few who knew all the details.

At about eleven o'clock, a cloud of dust heralded the approach of Her Majesty. The musicians of the *Mukama* (King) of the Batoro, stood up, took off the bark cloth covers from their instruments and struck up an awful noise that resembled something like a hundred, rusty door hinges opening and shutting, accompanied by an orchestra of half-toned klaxon horns.

People took up their positions. The few who were to be presented made last-minute checks to their dress; the *Mukama* pulled his furry headgear into position. The *Katikiro* (Prime Minister), the *Omukama* (King – the 'O' in front means 'the'), the *Omukete* (Treasurer) and the *Omukwi W'emisango* (Chief Justice of Native Law) straightened their cloaks. The scene was one I will never forget. The crowds: Indian women in exotic, coloured silk saris, Africans in their best European clothes, Europeans in Khaki drill, the women in flowing summer dresses, the *Mukama*'s band in their long, white *kanzus* with their python-skin covered flutes and horns and great drums; the African dignitaries in their colourful robes; the Queen and the Duke emerging from the dust-covered, bottle-green Land Rover: the Duke looking suntanned and well, moving through the ceremony in his easy, nonchalant way, the Queen, charming and beautiful but looking thin after her long Far East tour.

And, there in the background, stood the blue Ruwenzori, the legendary Mountains of the Moon. They lived up to their name. Here everything was grotesque: heather 15 feet tall and weird vegetation, swathed in the perpetual mist, played the part of the mystic Mountains of the Moon to the full. Queer white clouds playing round their base and occasionally a peak here and there momentarily emerged from the mist and appeared to drift with the clouds like castles in the air.

The Queen entered the Pavilion and climbed onto the platform. The *Mukama* presented the gifts from the people of Toro, the two royal spears, a decorated stool and a bark cloth bedspread. The Queen made her short speech. The oldest couple, the oldest inhabitant, the planters' representative and a few others were presented to the Queen. The Scout contingent sang a song of praise, with one boy singing the verse and the rest coming in on the chorus. It sounded impressive, although few could understand the language.

Then, the Queen knocked all the security arrangements into a cocked hat when she expressed her wish to walk round near the public barricade. The Governor motioned for the *Mukama* to accompany her. I don't know whether that was on a matter of principle or whether it was an astute move on his part for the *Mukama* to act as cover for the Queen, since any gunman might be reluctant to shoot if there was a danger of hitting the African King.

As the Queen moved round within feet of the crowd, security people held their breath. This would be the time. Sighs, almost audible, were expressed as she reached her vehicle and entered it. Amid the cheers of the crowd and the dubious noises from the band, she stood in the car and waved farewell as the royal convoy moved off. It was hard to imagine it was all over. All the work of planning, organising, building, the worry of a possible Mau Mau attack – all finished. Yet, for me, there was still work – 850 Africans still to be handled and seen back to camp. Organising Africans is harder than herding sheep. They just won't follow instructions. Now it was night. A feast to celebrate was in operation. A ration of '*pombe*' – native beer – had been issued. Now the camp was the home of a drink-crazed mob. I had to send one man to hospital with a broken head when he was hit with a lamp in a fight. I lost count of how many more went before the night was out. We worked all night getting all the natives back to their homes and finished at eleven o'clock the next morning. But, happily, it was a successful occasion.

Back in the house Jim Fleming the Assistant District Commissioner and I celebrated with a bottle of champagne. We then got on the road to Fort Portal to attend a dance at the club. Over 50 miles for a dance! The road was bad with rain. At one place the truck went into an uncontrollable skid, waltzed about from side to side and finished up by going off the road and standing on its nose in a six-foot ditch, balanced and ready to topple over. We soon got help from the George Gascoine Co. who were contracting to tar the road, but it took a long time and the best efforts of a huge crocodile tractor to haul it out. The truck was undamaged and we continued on our way. The joys of motoring in Africa, but the dance was fine, I enjoyed it! We returned the next day without incident.

***

Uganda, like all other countries, was divided into provinces and districts. Mubende was included in Buganda. The tribe was Batoro, while a member of the tribe was Mutoro.

The area I was in was in the Toro district, which was divided into Sazas. The Saza was something like our county at home and had its own Chief. Each Saza was divided into Gombololas, equivalent to our parishes and they also had their own Chiefs. Below them you have the Mukungu, the village or hamlet Chief. Below him you have the Miruku, or subChief.

This true story was told by Leslie Graham who owned the lime works a few miles away. The story was told to Leslie by his African wife (or mistress).

They usually got their vegetables from the tribe who lived in the mountains, the Bakonjo, a people less touched by civilisation than the Batoro who lived on the plains. Kikarongo Hill, where the Queen visited, was the scene of an old Kukonjo battle between the Batoro and the Bakonjo, the Bakonjo being defeated and suffering heavy casualties.

'On Wednesday the Mukonjo who usually brought the vegetables to Leslie, said his tribe was not going to attend the Queen's visit for they were sure this was another attempt by the Batoro to lure them onto Kikarongo Hill to massacre them. What was more, he said there would be no more vegetables, since he would not come down from the hills again until all the armies in the camps at Mubuku and elsewhere had cleared out. They feared all the activity at Kikarongo was the Batoro preparing for another battle.

This Mukonjo said none of his people were going to leave the hills for fear of being put in a pot and eaten.'

[The 'armies' he referred to were the boy scouts' camp and the camp at Mubuku with the Saza delegates!]

Eric Lanning told me a good story, a true one, which shows the amazing integrity of colonial administrators.

'The Assistant District Commissioner was out shooting and shot a buck. After he shot he realised he was on the edge of the Game Reserve, and actually inside it. Appalled at his action he charged himself with the offence. Later, at his office he tried himself and found himself guilty, levied a fine of £5. Later in meditation he wondered if he had been wrong in his estimation of the boundaries of the Reserve. He returned and measured it out and found he had really been outside. He appealed against his sentence – the appeal had to go to the High Court Judge at Kampala. The High Court Judge must have seen the funny side of this. He wrote back that he saw the legitimacy of the appeal but, since he considered the magistrate who had tried the case to be competent and fair, he could not consider revoking the sentence.'

***

I got the labour started on taking all the huts apart and my services with the Uganda Administrative Department then terminated. Jim wanted me to stay on another week or so, but I wanted to be on my way. I'd seen the Queen, and ten shillings a day was hardly enough to induce me to stay on. I considered whether to apply for a pension or superannuation, as most people do when they retire from government service, but Jim said there might be a snag or two – something to do with some brass hat at Entebbe or Whitehall blundering when I started, signing me on as a sub-headman or 'gambolola' chief or some other non-pensionable government position.

So I left Kasese with Jim giving me a lift to Mubuko in the morning. After that I walked all day with no other lift. I came to a P.W.D. camp at about 4 p.m. and decided to call it a day and stay the night. The camp of the road-menders was just a clearing in the trees.

During the day the weaver birds made a terrible noise. The colony was made up of hundreds of their nests hanging on all the branches. Queer how they always congregate where there is any settlement. I think it is perhaps because they are safer from the hawks where man is. Their nests always hang from the tips of the branches where a hawk cannot perch.

I was very lucky to have a camp like this to sleep at, although its comfort could not be recommended to the tourist. The hut I'm in is round. Looking up the conical roof looks like a big parasol. Unfortunately, the thatched roof leaked and green water marks ran from the top down the faded, white-washed wall. Lines of brown mud formed a pattern where cracks had been filled in. It was raining and water dripped onto my sleeping bag. It was no use moving, the roof was like a pepper pot. I was lying watching the pool of water grow below the wood and reed bed frame I had when I decided to write, although an optician would hardly approve. The glass of the lantern was broken and the flame fluttered in the wind.

'I wonder what it's like at home. I've been on the move a long time now, coming up for four years. Everything will be changed when I get back. Queer how you expect things away from yourself just to remain as they were. Hard to realise that life goes on for the others as well as yourself. Life comes in phases; nothing is ever the same again. Bill, my brother, married now. A new sister to meet – I wonder what she's like. The village was changing when I left with old houses being knocked down, new ones in their places. I can't imagine it any way other than the way I've always known it to be. Jock and Jack gone to Canada – I wonder if I'll ever see them again. Andrew married and teaching in Nigeria. Television in at home. Too many changes to take in.'

In writing this, I realised I'd been away four years. It was quite a time. I wondered how I would fit in when I got back. Had I changed very much, if at all? Only when I got home would I know.

***

I walked a few hours today then got a lift from the P.W.D. man, Struthers, to Fort Portal. I was very grateful to him when he asked me if I'd like to stay the night. He and his wife are quite new out from England, so new that they haven't yet lost all the nonsense they thought of in England in respect to Africa. They'll soon learn. Everybody does.

I was heading for Bill Pridham's farm. As well as being a farmer he was also the Game Ranger for Toro. I met him when he came on safari to Kasese and stayed the night with Jim Fleming and he promised to take me on his next elephant shooting safari. His farm was about ten miles out of Fort Portal. He ran thirty acres of tea and coffee in between his safaris.

I got a lift out to the end of his road, then walked up the hill three miles to the house. He lives at the top of a hill. I was glad to get the pack off for a breather by the time I reached the house. Bill was pleased to see me and gave me the news that there were some reports of elephant doing damage to some *shambas* down on the river. We go off tomorrow.

We came down to the *shambas* where the complaints came from and made camp near the Dwimi River. The river was running high and fast with the rains. We went in for a dip, but the bites from the tsetse flies hurt like bee stings. They have the advantage when one is in one's birthday suit! In the morning, with the light still grey, the huts and trees hadn't taken on their three dimensions and looked flat and unreal; an old man came to the camp to tell us the elephant had been in his *shamba* during the night. About the same time a leopard had tried to scrape an opening into his hut to get at his goats (the goats and he were living in the same hut). It must have been some night for him and his family.

As he told us his tale he looked away in a forlorn manner and dropped his gesticulating hands in a gesture of defeat, saying, "So many elephants have come to my *shamba* lately, I have lost all my crops and they have fouled my water hole with the result all my teeth are going bad." It was evident the last point was his biggest worry.

We ate a hasty breakfast and then inspected the rifles. Bill took a double-barrelled .600 Holland & Holland, the largest calibre in hand guns. He gave me a .416 Rigby's Special. Dominic, the African Game Guard, gathered some powdered ash from the fire into a cloth. This was for testing the wind direction. During the rains there is never any dry dust available.

We set out for the old man's *shamba*. At his hut there was plenty of evidence to prove a leopard had been there. It was a beehive shaped affair made of thatch. The animal had almost succeeded in scraping a hole through. In the *shamba* there were plenty of big, new elephant spoors. We followed them into the jungle and along the trampled corridors in the 12 feet tall elephant grass. Don't imagine an elephant is a clumsy animal. A dozen had passed and the path was barely a foot wide. And a herd of elephant can melt into a landscape and be invisible within seconds. A lone elephant, despite its size, can be as elusive as any Pimpernel and it was a long day's slog before we met up with the herd.

Let me say something about Game Rangers before we move into the attack. They are by far the sanest and happiest of all British Colonial Servants. Their open air life is infinitely more agreeable than the constricted life of the normal civil servant. They are the sanest because their subjects, the animals which they administer and live with, are more intelligent and interesting beings than the humans the other Colonial Officers deal and live with.

They are the policemen of the bush; the go-between that controls both human and animal interests. In Africa, vast areas have been set aside as Game Reserves which are purely 'declared areas' – no fences surround them. Yet it is an amazing fact that the animals soon learn they are safe there and will seldom stray from the boundaries. But, when they do and destroy the property of man, they must be 'shot' back into their own land. This is the job of the Game Ranger. Likewise, it is his job to keep a look-out for poachers who encroach on the reserves. Unfortunately, he is not allowed to deal so drastically with them as with the animals, as most Rangers would like to do, for I have yet to find the Game Ranger who, in their close contact with the animals, has not inherited a deep love and respect for them. Sometimes it is hard to know whose side the Ranger is on – human or animal – but the animal always gets the benefit of the doubt.

And now the herd was in front of us with their trunks raised in the air, like periscopes, sniffing. They were suspicious, but not definite about our presence. Dominica shook the cloth with the ash for the wind direction. We worked our way round to go in against it. The grass was waist high; the elephants were in a thicket of trees.

Bill pointed out the one to shoot. It had been agreed that I was to shoot first. The elephant stood there tearing lumps of grass up with its trunk and stuffing it into its mouth like an automatic coal feeder to a blast furnace. As its huge ears flapped they looked fine and feathery like a bat wing. I was surprised to learn later that, even at their thinnest part, they were half an inch thick of tough hide.

I thought of all the instructions Bill had given me before:

If it's a side shot, hit it in the ear hole for a brain shot – this isn't exactly a brain shot but it's a sure stunner. Aim for the top of the fore leg for a heart shot. If it's facing you, hit it between the eyes, but a little lower than the eyes – the third wrinkle down to be exact if you are that close to see – for the brain but remember your bullet has to penetrate 18 inches of bone before it reaches there so don't expect to kill it outright that way, but it will give you time to get another shot in.

I remembered the time down in Tanganyika when I had first crept up to a herd of elephant to 'shoot' them with a camera. I remembered how I felt then. Now it was different. The fear I had felt then was missing. But it is easy to feel brave when one is behind a heavy calibre elephant gun, with another one at your side which is the next best thing to a howitzer.

That was before I fired. After that I learned the difference between shooting with a rifle and camera. With a camera, provided the animals don't see you or get your wind, you start no trouble. When you work the mechanics of a rifle, all hell is let loose. At that moment my only fear was that I might duff my shot and look silly in the eyes of my companions, especially the Africans. I almost felt impertinent that I should be shooting on the very ground 'Samaki' Salmon had walked on.

In the days when hunting was considered a sport,'Samaki' Salmon was the greatest elephant hunter of all time. No other man has ever come near his estimated 'bag' of between 3,000 and 3,500 elephants. He was the man who, adroitly using the wind and cover, would walk right into the centre of a herd of elephant and drop them here, there and everywhere at will. A man who, when charged by three elephant as Bill said he saw himself, calmly picked off an extra big one in the herd before turning his attention to his attackers and, just as calmly, picked them off.

Yet this man never claimed to be a good shot. "I couldn't hit anything over a hundred yards. It's quite simple hitting them where you want to at close range." But what he didn't say was that at fifty yards you wouldn't have a chance to hit the same elephant twice if you missed the mark, should three or four be coming for you.

What is more remarkable is that Samaki had a weak heart and, when in England on leave once, collapsed under the excitement while watching a horse race. He was the guide, guard and companion of Royalty who wished to shoot big game. The Duke of Windsor – then the Prince of Wales – Viscount Lascelles and others hunted under the protection of his rifle, and usually before the safari had gone far he would be addressing them in conversation by their Christian names without causing any resentment.

He retired from the Game Department in 1946 and was Bill Pridham's immediate predecessor. He died in South Africa in 1953. Curiously enough, his nickname had no relation to his surname – Samaki is Swahili for fish – but came from his ability as a swimmer. In an incident during the 1914-18 war in Tanganyika, he swam across a crocodile infested river at night and wiped out a German machine gun post that had been bothering them all day. Since then he was known as Samaki.

Yet here was I shooting in the company of the people who had hunted with the maestro himself. It all seemed so ridiculous. The standard was high in this part of the country.

The rifle exploded. I hardly felt the recoil in my surprise at the elephant slumping forward. I had found the earhole mark. It tried to rise again with great difficulty. I ran forward to finish it off. Bill said to hurry, not to let it get back on its feet. Once a wounded animal, especially an elephant and buffalo is on its feet again it becomes almost super-human – if that term can be used of animals. It's something to do with the fluid adrenaline, secreted in a duct near the heart and pumped into that organ when the animal is angry or wounded. The animal then becomes supercharged.

I hit it again and it rolled over. Then trouble started. The rest of the herd, alarmed by the first shot and guided by the second, charged. I can think of nothing more frightening and exciting than being charged by a herd of screaming, express elephants. Until this day I had never lived.

In retrospect I can see the magnificence of it. Yet, at the moment I could only think "What have I started?" I was struck by the awful power released. Here was energy personified. Small trees in their path were either pulled out by the roots and thrown away or simply pushed aside. Their squealing was frightening, like the screaming of the soldiers in a bayonet charge strikes terror in the enemy.

Bill hit the first one with his .600. Still they came on. It was hard to say how many there were. I picked a head in front and hit it. It went down and stayed there. I pushed another round into the breach and, choosing another, hit it. It went down on its knees, then began to rise again. Dominica killed it with one of his .404's. They still came on. It seemed as if the shooting was having no effect on the herd. Bill dropped a big one barely a dozen paces from us. Then, when it seemed as if we would have to try poking them in the eyes they broke off the attack and dispersed on all sides of us. It was the most exciting few seconds of my life.

The last one Bill shot was not dead. It was rolling about and its breath was coming like a tuneless wheeze from an old church organ. I went to finish it off. I have never felt so sorry for anything as that elephant. In the charge it was different. Now in cold blood it seemed almost cruel. Have you ever looked into the eyes of an elephant that knows you have come to kill it? There's a sad, sorrowful dullness in them, and the feeble lift of its trunk is like the last plea for mercy of a dumb man who can only speak with his hands.

Unfortunately, during the battle one of the elephants hit managed to rise and make a hasty retreat. We followed its trail but did not meet up with it. There was barely enough light left to reach camp again. We'll follow it up tomorrow.

Sunday is not a good day for killing, but ours was one of mercy. We found the trail of the wounded elephant again this morning. A blade of grass with a drop of blood here and there showed we were on the right track. The day wore on and we never seemed to get any nearer. The spoor meandered aimlessly at first then seemed to get one general direction. Others crossed and mingled with it and it was difficult to keep to the one we must follow.

It is strange how animals know when and where they are liable to be shot. On many occasions where a road marks the boundary of a Reserve, you will invariably see animals in the Reserve side but not on the other. We pushed through endless miles of elephant grass where the breeze couldn't reach us and the air was thick and humid. We waded through rivers that were so keen to show off the strength they possessed in the rainy season that they threatened to make us flotsam. We trekked through the forest belts which line the rivers, where the black and white colobus monkeys with the long bushy tails leap fantastic distances from tree to tree as we passed under them until, at last, we knew where we were going. The trail was leading back to the shambas where it had started yesterday morning.

It was nearing sundown when we met up with the injured elephant. He was a lone wolf. None of the rest of the herd was with him. He was standing alone among some trees on the fringe of the shambas waiting for darkness before going in like a rascally schoolboy waiting for the opportunity to plunder an orchard. It is amazing how cunning they become: they know they won't be attacked after dark. The wound on his head was quite visible but he seemed to have recovered from it. Bill dropped him with one shot in the ear with his .600. He was dead when we went up to him.

It was a pity so many of them had to be killed when one may have been enough to drive the herd back into the Reserve. But we were left with little alternative under the circumstances. It was better them than us – or was it, selfish reasons aside?

***

We came back to Bill's place and Bill was busy with some office work.

When he had got things straight we were going on another safari down to the Semliki Flats. One of the reasons for this safari was to do some sleuthing, to find out what happened to the missing game scout who disappeared down here with his rifle.

Many conflicting reports had been brought in, but one seemed feasible. The porters said he wounded a buffalo which then charged him and the porter accompanying him threw a spear intended for the buffalo but in mistake killed the scout. In fear they buried him and all his possessions, including the rifle.

If the story was true then the body had to be found and the rifle recovered. All along the way Bill asked and offered rewards for information, but all in vain. If anybody knew they weren't saying. It remained a mystery.

We came down to Kichwamba and down the valley on the Bwamba road. The view down the valley is one to be remembered. The vista is triangular, with the valley forming two sides and the sky the third. The rains had been good. The mountainsides were like draped, green baize cloths.

The road hugs the left side and curls its way in and out of the wrinkles, going out of sight into some hidden recess and reappearing again further on, always on the decline, going down, down, down till it is lost in the haze. The Bakonjo – the hill people – have cut *shambas* out of the almost vertical sides of the mountain. They varied in colours according to the type and progress of the crops, and against the green background they looked like patchwork quilts laid out to dry in the sun. Away on the horizon, a metallic sheen among the clouds marked the waters of Lake Albert.

Once down the valley we left the road and followed a track Bill had had his boys cut through the bush.

The P.W.D. had surveyed this part of the country when they wanted a road to Lake Albert and said it was impossible. They had started cutting another through the mountains higher up at the cost of thousands of pounds and then abandoned it as impracticable. When Bill had wanted to make a road to the Lake to facilitate better control of the area against poachers, he was given £100 to do it. He was about three-quarters of the way there and the cost so far was £30. True, it was only a track he had made, but it included bridges over drifts and the Wasa River. Yet it showed a road was possible and at a trifling cost compared to the money wasted on the other one that failed. Such is the P.W.D. Down on the flats you could see the scar on the mountain which was the ill-fated road. You could see where it ended abruptly.

Bill had a camp down by the Wasa River. A safari in Africa was so good. You moved into camp. The boys put up the tent and served up a three-course meal on a table laid with a cloth and coffee in cups with saucers. How different to scrounging for your own firewood, pitching the tent on your own and doing all the chores by yourself!

It was dark and the fire blazed. A pressure lamp hung from the tree. The table was laid for dinner. After we had eaten we had a game of chess then turned in. We were just about equal chess players and gave each other a fair game.

We moved on to Tamarine Camp on Semliki Flats. It was grand country, wide and flat with short grass. This is the kind I like: big, open spaces where your eye can roam and you're not hemmed in with high grass or trees. We went on to the end of the track to see how far they had gone. Bill wanted to survey a drift that had to be bridged.

Wherever you go on these flats you never lose sight of Uganda Kob. They are a type of buck peculiar to Uganda. They are something between a Thomson's gazelle and an impala. Their markings are something similar to the Tommy and they have the same 'windscreen wiper' tail, but they are bigger and have the same neck as the impala. When startled, they go off in long, high arched bounds, again just like the impala.

It's risky going cross country during the rains. Several times we got bogged down and had to jack up the truck and put boards beneath the wheels to get out. In the afternoon we saw two herds of elephant. The elephants down here are nicknamed 'Congo rats'. They are a particularly ferocious species. Their tusks are long and thin and don't weigh much.

Bill remarked as we went after one herd of Kob to see if any were injured or wounded, since rumours of poachers were rife, "These are the first wheels ever to roll over this part of the globe." We had a run round to see if any poachers were in the vicinity and scanned a few herd of Kob with the glasses to see if any were wounded. We got bogged down a few times and got close to another herd of elephant.

We had been on safari for three days when we headed back to Kingami, Bill's farm. Bill was going down as far as Mbarara during the week. I decided to go with him.

What a day! Two blow outs and a puncture. They always come in threes. We had left Fort Portal in the morning and came down by Kasese. We didn't get far because of the trouble with the tyres and put into Leslie Graham's place to stay the night. In the morning we changed tyres then got on the way. We left the main road and came over the mountain road which the Queen came over to Mweya Lodge, the camp in the Queen Elizabeth National Park. It's a lovely route. The land is all pock marked with huge grass-covered craters. What mighty upheaval caused them? We stood on the rim of one and watched half a dozen elephants round a water hole down in the floor of the crater. They looked like ants.

Mweya Lodge is a pleasant place. The main building and the huts are made in log cabin style of Makindu palms. As we ate lunch, a herd of elephants wandered by, down at the foot of a hill. Later we continued on our journey, left the main south road and came via Katwe to Bwera. While we were in Bwera we checked at the Belgian Customs Post to make sure that there would be no trouble for me crossing the border into the Congo. It seemed it would be O.K.

Bill had reports of elephants coming in from the Congo and destroying crops so next morning we were out at 5 a.m. We checked the *shambas*, but there were no marauding elephants. We packed up after that and came back to Mweya Lodge where we had lunch and then headed down to Lototo Rest camp. What a lovely setting it was beside the crater lake of that name. The lake, like all the crater lakes, looked like a huge bowl half-filled with water.

We arrived at Mbarara next day and camped on the lawn of the game ranger for this district. I left Bill next morning and, alone again, walked on the road heading for Kabale. I was sorry to leave him. He had been grand company and I had learned a lot about his life as a game ranger and enjoyed our games of chess. But along the way this has been the name of the game – meeting people, learning about their lives and then moving on.

I walked all day till about 5 p.m. Ankole district may be lovely with its rolling green hills, but it is hell to walk through with a pack. You just get over one hill and there is another in front of you. I came to a little village and decided to camp, but then a truck came along and stopped at one of the *dukas*. It was going to Kabale and the driver agreed to take me. It was 9 p.m. when we arrived. I went to the Police Station to stay the night. The O.C. police (three pips), Mr Goodchild, has invited me to stay with him a couple of days. His house is on the top of a hill with lovely views.

I went along and collected my mail, then climbed a hill and, with my back against a fir tree, I read my letters. I can think of few things better than that: a lonely hill, the breeze and the sun, the world going by below you and some long-awaited letters to read.

Kabale is the highest town in Uganda at over 6,000 feet, and, like all the others, it is only a row of Indian shops. I'd been trying my hand at golf while staying with Mr Goodchild and thinking that I could get quite keen on it! However, I left Kabale next day and hadn't gone far when I got a lift from the doctor to Kisoro, the last place in Uganda

The mountain road from Kabale to Kisoro was something never to be forgotten. It rises to over 8,000 feet with excellent views of Lake Bunyonyi on the way up. But it was at Kinaba Gap that the drive is indelibly stamped on your mind. You suddenly top a rise between two mountains and there your breath catches at the scene before you. The magnificent expanse before you, the row of volcanoes, conical shaped, rising sheer from the flat floor of the valley up to the sky with their pointed summits lost in the clouds, looking like something from a fairy-tale book.

I was in the rest house at Kisoro. It was a fine place, with a fireplace, table, chairs, but no beds. I had to sleep on the cement floor. Next morning, while it was clear, I saw five of the seven volcanoes. They seem too typical to be real. All round here all the other hills are cultivated right up to the top. I have never seen intensive cultivation among Africans. The entire surfaces of the mountains are patterned with *shambas*. Yet it is practically impossible to get vegetables.

Now that I am on the point of leaving this country, I realise without a doubt that Uganda, certainly western Uganda is the most beautiful land in all Africa, at least what I have seen of Africa. Toro with its mystic Ruwenzori mountains and craters; Ankole with its rolling green hills; Kigezi, with the volcanoes it shares with Rwanda, (they are the border) and its patterned cultivated hills. All beautiful!

It is evening, almost sundown, and with the twilight there is a stillness that makes itself felt. The sun goes down quickly but not as fast as recounted in most travellers' tales. Even on the Equator there is a twenty minute to half-hour break between day and night. It is the best time of the day, and one can't help being a bit visionary at this time: when the future seems more real than the past and the present does not exist, for you cease to be an entity and become something abstract, drifting back and forward through the years.

The clouds round Muhavura, the nearest and highest of the volcanoes are beginning to disperse and drift away as they do at this time, leaving the mountain naked and clear. For the past half hour I have watched them break up and get ready for their journey. Away over on the right they are banked up in big fluffy tiers like creamy meringues, and here and there on their lonesome, single clouds like pink galleons tilted downwind, sail across the blue void.

CHAPTER 19

THE BELGIAN CONGO
Rwanda Burundi: Ruwenzori – Dicing with Death

Tuesday 1st June, 1954

Crossed into the Congo today. Weighed my pack this morning on the Customs scales – 91lbs, which didn't include my revolver and the ammunition I carried on my belt.

I walked the seven miles to the Rwanda Burundi customs post. There I was met by a rather fat Belgian Immigration officer. He puffed and wheezed as he filled in papers, the task obviously very strenuous. I thought the British Civil Service used up a lot of paper, but the Belgian colonial authorities in the Congo seemed to have made a prodigious effort in this line, for their paper consumption is something to be marvelled at, leaving their British colleagues 'stone cold'.

When I declared my two firearms the portly officer sat and looked for a moment, then remarked in fairly good English, "Give them to me and I will sell them". I was taken aback at this. "But you can't take my revolver. I am walking through the country and may meet a lion or leopard," I pleaded. "Very well," he answered. "You may keep one with you, but give me the other and I will *sell* it."

It was only after a lot of conversation that I realised he meant to 'seal' the pistol so that I could not use it in the territory. The paperwork involved in this was something extraordinary to see. It took me one hour and twenty minutes to clear that office.

He was a friendly type, the portly officer. As he filled in paper after paper he remarked, "It ees the paper age we live in today". As he worked he told me he was leaving the administration and had acquired a piece of land up near the mountain and would settle down as a farmer. In the Congo a man rents a piece of land. After five years a Government Lands Inspector surveys the farm to see if the farmer is using the land properly. If passed, the farmer can then go ahead and buy the land outright. A very sound scheme, I think.

I walked out of Ruwenzori, glad to be in the Congo and clear of all the frontier formalities.

I walked a while and when it started to rain I found an empty hut and prepared to make camp. However, I was visited by a huge 6ft 7"African, a Watutsi who, after some conversation in Swahili, invited me to stay at his house just along the road a bit. He has a fine house, a good stone European style one. He works for a European as a clerk. It was well kept and clean, a very much better house than those I have seen of many white people living in Africa, especially the Afrikaner farmers down in South Africa and Bechuanaland.

Walking up the escarpment the next day was heavy going. A couple of cars passed loaded to the gunwales, but a truck going for sand gave me a lift of five miles. It was very welcome. The following day it was pouring with rain and wasn't very pleasant. In the late afternoon, heading for Kivu, I got a lift in a truck driven by a spiv-type African. The usual type – steel-rimmed spectacles, trilby hat, creased trousers and a speckled sports jacket. For a truck driver on duty it seemed odd. He had the look which these types generally have, thinking themselves no end of a fellow. The truck was fitted with an additional horn outside worked with a cord. It was the loudest, most ear-grating noise I have ever heard on a motor vehicle. It simply blasted a path through the groups of natives on the road. He blew it at every possible objective – and then some.

As we swung down the road I renewed my acquaintance with Kisengi which had begun in 1947 when I came here on leave. The old magic caught me again. Earlier I stated that western Uganda is the finest country in all Africa. It doesn't stop there. I should have included Rwanda, for it is all the same country from Ruwenzori to Lake Kivu, divided only by the unnatural political frontier. And, of it all, Kisengi was the pearl. The town was like one wealthy estate: a palm-shaded esplanade, gardens of flowers that follow the pavements and billiard table top grass verges set with beautiful rockeries that run down to the sparkling blue water that laps white sand.

The shops were big, spacious and well laid out. The houses were a treat to see. Here there were no Indian shopkeepers. The Belgians gave them a place where they could carry on in their usual way. This, like all the towns I was told, was divided up into something like first-class and second-class areas. There was nothing to stop Indians or Africans owning a shop in the first-class area but they must build and conform to plans laid down by the Government. The second-class area was out of sight of the main through road – the Belgians hid their dirty linen. They had to do something or lose their country to both the Africans and Indians as had already happened in

British East Africa where poor development smothers any beauty there might be in the towns.

In Goma there was one Indian-owned shop in the first-class area. The second-class area was typical of the towns seen all over East Africa – Indian-owned, pokey, hovel shops crammed with every knickknack. And, as usual, they were on a rapid increase. South Africa is condemned in the world press for its attempted policy of 'apartheid', yet here in Goma, quietly with no fuss, it seemed to be a successful arrangement. (Just an observation!)

But the prices in the Congo! The country is rich in minerals – its people wealthy. The cost of living was prohibitive for a visitor. I went to the hotel and ordered some tea (my total hotel strength). A pot of weak tea, which in East Africa would have cost 50 cents (6d.) and tasted better, cost 15 francs (2s1d.approximately). I decided to give hotels in the Congo a wide berth in future, even for tea.

I was walking out of town looking for a place to camp when a truck drew up and the Belgian Mr or Monsieur de Munck, asked if I would like a lift anywhere. I told him where I was going and he took me down to the town camping site, a beautiful place by the lakeside, right in the town. A well-built open kitchen was at the disposal of the campers. As I started to pitch my tent, Monsieur de Munck, having second thoughts, invited me in his perfect English to his home, a few kilometres outside Goma. Goma almost joins Kisenyi but between them is the border of the Congo and Rwanda Burundi. Kisenyi is in Rwanda.

Monsieur de Munck's house was a wonderful place: a long rambling place, added to as he prospered, lined with local wood and filled with everything for comfort and beauty. The room I was in had fluorescent lighting, run from his own plant, and a bed as soft and deep as the sea.

The next day Madame de Munck drove me to her parents' place. Everywhere, everybody you met here had the air of wealth and prosperity. The houses here in the Congo were marvellous.

We drove across the lava flow of 1948. What an area of desolation and destruction. Next day we went across the lake in Madame's boat. They had a farm and she was looking in to see how it was doing. It was lovely going across the lake – the water smooth and the mountains mixed up with the clouds.

Monsieur de Munck had his own private plane. I flew with him to Bukaro (Costermansville) this forenoon. We went there and back for lunch. The journey by road took five hours each way.

Kisenyi and Goma looked well from the air. The streets conformed to a good plan, as if the whole place was laid down on paper beforehand. Bukaro was quite a large place, well laid out too. It was fun flying in the little plane. We flew low so we could see everything. We went out across the lake and the large island and came back over the coast. Back at this side we came swinging in along the edge, following the edge of the lake into the little bays and creeks, passing the house with Madame and the children waving to us and on to the airstrip at Goma. I enjoyed it.

I planned to go up the volcano the next day. It had been erupting continually for the past two months and had only stopped six days previously. I could have kicked myself for not being there to see it erupting. The volcano is Nyamuragira, 3,056 metres. It erupted in 1938, 1948, 1951 and 1954. On the 21st February a crack split the side of Nyamuragira about 2,300 feet up and the crack erupted. After the first flow, the whole crack ceased to erupt except at one point. This one part erupted continually until 28th May, 1954. A new hill was formed and named Mihaga.

Wonderful people these! Madame de Munck was a fanatic on the volcano and was up it many times when it was erupting. She was due to go that week but had to cancel on account of yellow fever injections. She had given me the ticket (200 francs) to get into the Albert National Park and was providing the partners and the safari for me. She wouldn't hear of me paying. They were really very kind.

Monsieur de Munck was a prospector and miner, for years living a prospector's life until he hit the jackpot in wolfram (tungsten). Now he lived in luxury. But they never forgot what it was like before. They were good, generous people who had not let the money go to their heads.

***

Next morning I was driven to the entrance of the National Park by a friend of Monsieur de Munck. Madame gave me three porters and I picked up a guide from the Park (included in the 200 francs). I was late in starting as the people who brought me were held up a while in Goma and it was 11.30 a.m. when I was ready to start off from the entrance. From there it was a five-hour steady hike and climb to the hut near the top of the mountain. Most people took much longer.

We had only been going for half an hour when we ran into elephant. I came round a bend and there was a big fellow standing in the road tearing branches off a tree. I was some distance ahead of the porters so sat down a few yards from the elephant, interested in its antics, but the porters refused to advance further than the corner. After some time the old tusker moved off the road further into the bush and the porters and guide came on. The guide said it would be better to go back and start tomorrow morning, because then the elephants go to the water. Now they will be all along the road, he said. I preferred to go on. So we went. But soon another elephant was on the road. It looked at us, flapped its ears, raised its trunk and ran towards us. I don't think it was a full-blooded charge but one only meant to scare us off. We ran! One of the porters dropped his bundle, another dashed into the bush. The elephant stopped and we stood at a safe distance. We could hear other elephants in the bush all around.

The guide now flatly refused to go on. I asked the porters if they knew the way. They said they did, but they also were obviously reluctant to go on. Although it is against the rules of the National Park to go without a guide, I told the one who was with me he could go back if he liked, but I'd go on without him. It took some time to find the missing porter who had dashed into the bush and still longer to find his bundle.

I set off up the path hoping that, by showing an example, my porters would follow. The first one, a bit braver than the others, picked up his bundle and started coming slowly behind me. Then the other two followed suit and finally the guide decided it was better to go with the crowd than go back on his own.

The next half hour was rather nerve-wracking. The herd was all round us. We had to go slowly, walking quietly, almost tip-toeing, with senses strained always on the alert should one of the beasts decide to come our way. It wasn't very pleasant walking through the middle of a big herd of elephant when you were not armed. I know the porters and guide were waiting for the slightest chance to start running back and any move on my part in that direction would cast the die that way. I put on an air of indifference and tried to walk as if there was nothing to fear. But underneath, daytime nightmares were rippling through me. I kept seeing the herd of elephant charging down on us as they did in Uganda, but this time I had no rifle and my legs were tired and I couldn't run.

Presently, we reached the first lava flow and I felt relieved when we climbed on to it. This a few days ago had been a living, red hot river of molten stone; then it had stopped. The crust had hardened and, as the inside kept flowing, it crumpled up and broke into great jagged slabs and rubble that wrinkled up into waves – a petrified, angry ocean. The lava was still hot as we climbed over it. We traversed three recent lava flows altogether. Burnt trees lay here and there where the lava had flowed through the forest. The trees beside the flow were burnt and leafless, naked as those in the snow. In Africa, among the green lush forest, they looked grotesque.

Once into the forest again the strain of being on the alert for elephant descended on us once more. We heard some and saw some fresh, steaming dung, but didn't see any more.

It was getting on in the afternoon now. We had been late in starting and had lost a lot of time with the elephant. Now there was no time to lose if we were to reach the hut before dark. As we moved up, the forest developed into a mesh of short, wet trees bearded with lichen; a hairy, damp jungle that made your skin itch. It rained – heavy, steady, torrential rain. As the clouds came down it got dark. When I looked back the porters were grey shadows. They had ceased to sing and talk and now the only sound they made was their feet splashing ankle deep in the mud.

As on Kilimanjaro I marvelled at these porters. Their load was smaller here (15 kilos), but they climbed the mountain with the same ease. Apart from the time waiting for the elephant to clear off, they never once asked to stop for a rest in the five-hour slog up hill. We reached the hut about 5 p.m. I was surprised at such a big place. Half of it was used as a laboratory for the geologists who visited here on rare occasions. It was good when the fire was lit and I had a change of dry clothes on. Outside the rain poured and there was a howling wind, but in the hut we were warm and snug.

I set out with the guide at 6 a.m. It was still nearly an hour's climb from the hut up to the rim of the volcano. The forest soon gave out to heather and gorse. On the way up we passed the cone of Shamubembe, the creation of the 1951 eruption that broke out of the side of Nyamalagira. Like the new one it is a satellite or 'toto' (child), as the guide described it, of the parent volcano, Nyamalagira. It was still smoking. As we climbed higher we were able to look down into its funnel.

Nyamalagira has two craters. The outer one is over a mile and a half (diameter 2,300 metres) wide. From the rim you look across a cracked crumpled flow of lava with smoke belching from the cracks. You walk across that flow, avoiding the cracks and sulphur fumes, and you come to the inner crater, a funnel with sheer sides and crumbling edges that goes down 500 feet into the bowels of the earth. Smoke gushes from this crater and hangs in a pall, until a gust of wind catches it and blows it away.

I wanted to go round the other side of the crater to get some photographs. The guide warned me against going. Foolishly, I didn't take heed of his warning. He had been so windy with the elephant I didn't place much value on his terms of danger. Once I got going I began to think otherwise. The area to cross was a wrinkled, brittle crust that cracked as I walked on it. I moved fast as I would if crossing thin ice, but even then fissures radiated out from my footsteps and smoke oozed from the cracks I made. I had the fright of my life when the crust broke and I fell through up to my waist, enveloped in sulphur fumes. It was quite possible my grave could have been bottomless. I got round and took the photos I wanted, but was glad to get back to the more firm ground where the guide had waited.

Now I appreciate the pluck of Madame de Munck. I truly didn't realise what it meant when I saw her cine film taken of the erupting volcano. Now I have an idea what it was like when, admission to the area prohibited, she did a ten-hour scramble across miles of old lava bed (that must have been killing), keeping clear of the paths, to reach the new volcano. She described how, when they crossed the new lava with the crust barely hard and still terribly hot and the lava still molten underneath, the rain came and with the steam created it was impossible to see their feet and where they were putting them. Once she went so near, a lump of red hot lava hit her on the back. She said the lava was soft and didn't stick and, provided you didn't get hit with a bit big enough to cover you, you were reasonably safe from injury.

We got back to the hut about 10 a.m., had a hearty breakfast and started on the way down to the new volcano, arriving there about 4 p.m. We made camp some distance from it and I planned to climb it first thing in the morning. Sitting outside my tent with darkness falling fast, Muhaga was smoking like a factory chimney and behind it, half-shrouded in cloud, was Nyirabongo. A couple of months before, this had been fairly flat country, but now a new hill had appeared, like a leaking, open boil on the side of Nyamalagiri.

At dawn I drank some coffee then went to climb Muhaga. Big watery clouds were running around the sky, but occasionally the sun made an appearance. The route to Muhaga lay over a sea of hardened but hot lava which it had so recently spewed up. A wide, reasonably smooth path wound up through a ragged, torn land. This was the solidified river that flowed continually for a couple of months, although all around had hardened and cooled. It was fed slowly to the last and cooled gradually so its crust remained intact.

The volcano itself was a great loose pile of black scree like a mine slag heap. My boots sank up to the ankles as I climbed. Near the top the ash got hot and my boots became almost unbearable. Long white and yellow smoking streaks of sulphur were running here and there like healing sores. The whole ground around me was smoking and burning. It was necessary to prod with a stick before putting a foot down. Sometimes the stick broke a layer of cinders revealing a burning hollow and the stick poking in it caught fire – without the stick that was where my foot would have gone.

Up on the rim it was difficult to see into the crater for the smoke. When the wind came my way the sulphur fumes caught and tore at my throat. Outside the crater the ash and cinders were black; inside, the walls of the funnel were brick red; from below, smoke rose from the very depths of hell, lingering for a moment and I realised I was witnessing the world in the making. Looking up I could see the great crack in the side of Nyamalaguri where the eruption started. After the first flow the whole crack ceased to function and concentrated on one spot, from where the lava gushed and Muhaga built itself up. Looking down, as far as the eye can see was a naked, devastated land, gutted and burnt like the surface of the moon.

The local legend was that people imagine their spirits go into the volcano when they die, each tribe going to its own particular one. All eruptions are caused by a dead Chief, with cause to be angry with his people. Only the Chiefs of the tribes near the volcanoes could make an eruption.

The next day I was back in the camp, had breakfast and set off for the road by 9 a.m. We reached the park gates at 1 p.m. Madame de Munck had arranged to pick me up at 4 p.m. It was queer to see the comforts of a home now. I wonder how many people appreciate it.

Monsieur and Madame de Munck had a parrot which was most amusing. I wondered if these birds have a sense of humour. Living with this one I thought they had. Whenever it is put out in its cage in the morning it starts and keeps up a continuous chatter all day. It imitates the boys; it calls the dog in its master's voice and scolds it when it comes. It has the servants running from the kitchen by calling in Madame's voice. It cries like the child and has its mother running to see what the matter is. It soon has all strangers by their names and calls and coo-hoos to them in Madame's voice, sometimes when they are away down the drive, and makes them come back. When it succeeded in its practical jokes you can almost see it shaking with laughter as it danced back and forth on its perch.

***

The Watutsi are the local people. They are tall, thin and Nilotic. They are the undisputed aristocrats of Rwanda Burundi. The true Watutsi does no manual labour; he considers himself above that. They have people of other tribes working for them as servants. Usually they are not paid. When someone of a different tribe wants to buy something, usually cattle, from the Watutsi and cannot pay, they offer to work for the Watutsi to pay off the debt. A Watutsi will seldom walk from one place to another and is usually carried on a litter by his servants.

Like the Masai in Kenya and most of the other Nilotic tribes, they indulge in the practice of drinking blood from cattle after drawing it from the cow's neck, which they puncture with a blocked arrow. But here they go one better. Instead of drinking the blood, they cook it until it solidifies and then eat it. Today I saw them doing it. They tied the cow's neck with rope, in the usual way, till the jugular vein stood out, then shot an arrow into it. They drew off about five or six pints of blood, then sealed up the wound with some dung. All that I had seen before; then came the new part. They scooped a hollow out in the ground and lit a bundle of straw (thatch). When this was burnt, they placed a new, fresh, banana leaf over the hot ash, pushing it into the hollow to form a shallow cup. Into this leaf they poured the blood, covering it with another leaf. Over this they kindled a fire of more thatch and kept it going for about three quarters of an hour. When it was finished it was congealed and looked like raw liver. I cut a piece off and tried it. It had a nondescript, sickly taste – or perhaps it was only my imagination that made it that way.

It was supposed to be the dry season, but it poured with rain the next day. Even when it was not raining it had been grey and rather dismal for nearly all the time I had been here. Like Kivu, it seemed to be sulking about something.

For the past while, my sleeping bag has been showing every sign of senile decay. Nearly every time I've slept in it in the past, I've wakened with feathers all over me and I've had to patch a tear. I've been worried about it, wondering where I'd ever manage to replace it. When Madame de Munck saw what it was like she insisted I take her own. She was going home to Belgium in a few weeks and said she wouldn't need it again.

How kind these people were. Every day they did something that made me more and more indebted to them. But, all the same, I missed my old sleeping bag, it was like missing an old friend and over the last few years I had become attached to it.

I said my grateful goodbyes to the de Muncks and started out for the north and west. Monsieur de Munck gave me a lift as far as Rutshuru. After that I walked a while then got another lift to Rwanda camp. This was slap in the centre of the Albert National Park. It was rather unlucky that I finished the day at this camp. In the National Park you were not allowed to camp or make a fire. I was obliged to take a room which cost sixty francs (8/8 app.) The meal was another seventy francs. I couldn't afford that, so I went hungry. That day, 14th June, was my 27th birthday.

I was hungry when I set out this morning and I didn't feel very good walking through the Park. Some gazelle and water buck were quite close. After a while I rested. In the hot sun and not having eaten, I was feeling a bit tired. I dozed a few minutes. When I came to myself I was surprised and a bit scared to see about a dozen buffalo grazing not far away from me. I wondered what I should do. It was obvious, with me sleeping, they had not noticed me. I decided I was best to remain where I was as the movement of me getting up and going might attract their attention. While it would be most likely they would run if they saw me, there was always the possibility of one deciding to have a closer look. With buffalo you can't afford to take chances. So I sat and watched them but I wouldn't say 'at my ease', hoping they wouldn't come any closer. Gradually they grazed their way further away from me and I was able to get on my way again. I don't like walking through National Parks.

In the afternoon I got a lift in a truck going to Lubero. The road, once you leave the Rwanda plain, twists and turns like a great snake writhing in mortal agony, all the way to Lubero. The sun was low when I arrived. I walked down the wide dirt street. The Africans stared at the kilt and pack. A few Greeks came to the door of their shop to have a look. Passing the hotel a woman, the manageress ran out into the road and took me by the arm. She poured French over me. I didn't understand that, but I did understand her pulling at my arm towards the hotel. I went. She broke into some English and asked why and where and how. She asked what I'd like to drink – I said tea and it was served. I thought she was inviting me, but she made me pay for it. Still, I didn't know that as I was drinking it so I enjoyed it.

A tall Greek with tousled hair and roll-top jersey said he is running a truck to Stanleyville tomorrow and I can go. I'll go as far as Mambasa with it. I pitched my tent on some waste ground over from the hotel, so I will be handy for the truck tomorrow. But now I doubt if I'll be going on it. A lot of Africans gathered round as I made my camp. Two had an argument as to whether I was a man or woman. They had never seen a kilt before. I paid no heed that I understood what they were saying.

As darkness fell, the crowd swelled and hemmed me in so that I barely had room to cook. They just stood and looked. Suddenly, they scattered like charred paper that has caught a gust of wind. I was blowing up my fire at the time. A voice at my back spoke a torrent of French. I looked over my shoulder into the muzzle of a heavy automatic pistol, held by a European police officer. He spoke more French. I didn't like his manners, the way he introduced himself, so I ignored him and turned to tend to my fire again. That must have put him off balance for there was a long silence while he seemed to be wondering what to do next. My fire blazing fine now, I stood up. We looked at each other for what seemed a while. He was a thick-set man, with a peaked hat, K.D. uniform and a row of medal ribbons.

When he saw French was no use to me he tried Kiswahili. He said, "What were you teaching the natives?"

I said I wasn't speaking to them.

"So you do understand Swahili?" he asked. I told him I did.

"I thought so," he said, with a lot of meaning in it. "Have you been to Kenya?"

"Yes."

"I thought so," again heavy with meaning.

He then demanded my revolver. He took it, broke it, spilling the ammo on the ground, and handed it back.

"Now you have your gun and I have mine", he said, waving his own to draw my attention to it, meaning his was full.

Looking at my tent and camp and seeing I had no servant he said,

"Why do you live like a 'maskini' – poor person, a down and out?"

I didn't bother to answer that. I was feeling hungry and was more bored with this interview than worried. I hadn't eaten since yesterday at lunch time.

He asked for my papers. I got my passport, etc. and lit a candle. But he wouldn't examine them then. No doubt he feared a trick from a dangerous agitator such as I while his attention was so occupied. He put them in his pocket and ordered me to report to his office in the morning. He called to a policeman and ordered him to stay and guard me with instructions to 'Chungu Luyu sana' – Guard him well.

He went away and I got going with my soup making. But before it was ready the police officer returned with a man in plain clothes, who I took to be the Administrator.

He was a more sociable person, though perhaps more dangerous. He talked a while, in a friendly way, but all the time sounding me as to why I was travelling. Presently they went away.

It is a queer coincidence that I borrowed the book *Facing Mount Kenya* by Jomo Kenyatta, from Monsieur de Munck and it is in my pack. Had they found that, it would have taken a lot of explaining away.

By now my fire was low, my soup half cooked and nearly cold. I was so fed up I had no will to go on cooking, even though I was famished. I drank my partly cooked soup and went to sleep.

The guard had deserted his post. He had no blanket so he pushed off. He sat for a while after they had gone and the night's watch looked a bleak prospect with no blanket or covering and not enough wood to keep the fire going. Lubero lies high. It was very cold and damp at night time.

This morning, my guard was back and had the fire going before I was up. It was still misty and cold so I was almost grateful to the police for supplying him. I had him take a couple of jigger flies out of my toes. The jigger gets into feet usually under the nail and lays its eggs. They swell up in a few days. When you dig it out you must be careful not to burst the little sack or they may spread over your foot. They leave quite a hole when they come out. They are as itchy as hell when they are there. I didn't bother to make breakfast since I wanted to catch this truck to Mambasa if possible. I struck camp as quickly as I could and packed up my kit.

I had to walk the length of the town to reach the office. The shops were just opening and the first batch of street loafers had already shuffled into the day's position. It was rather humiliating being escorted passed them. At the Territoire I had to wait till the Administrator arrived. He returned my passport and papers and apologised for the incident, but said I must in future ask permission from the local authorities to camp. But, by this time I had missed my truck. I got on the road. It seemed a good one for a lift. I felt very hungry but didn't want to start cooking in case something came along. I walked all morning then got a lift with a farmer and his wife who were going halfway between Butembo and Beni. Butembo is quite a big place and growing fast.

The farmer invited me for lunch to his farm. I thanked him. He didn't know how grateful I was to him for it was now forty-eight hours since I had eaten, except for the half-cooked soup last night. The farm was a little one, growing coffee. The farmhouse was low and rustic. We sat on stools that wobbled on the beaten floor round the table and I tried not to show how hungry I was. Only the woman spoke a little English.

I got on the road again and walked another five or six miles then got a lift from a Catholic missionary going to Beni. He invited me to spend the night at his mission which was a few miles outside the town. Like all missions it is a hive of industry. Even at 6 p.m. when we arrived, the buzz of an electric saw could be heard. I have a room, bare but comfortable. There were about ten sat down at the evening meal, the White Fathers with their hillbilly beards and long white habits. We had hot milk – "Only one cow, we mix water with the milk" – with bread in it. Then we had meat and rice and mugfuls of black coffee. They said no grace at the beginning, but at the end of the meal they all stood. I hung my head expecting a solemn thanksgiving, but instead they did a chant and nobody seemed to be very pious about it. Some rolled up their napkins as they chanted, others rattled chairs, had a puff at their cigars – locally made at a mission, but not this one – in between the choruses, or coughed and blew their noses. Yet, that way they seemed to have more of a natural sincerity. But anyone who visits a mission cannot fail to be impressed by these people and, though I am not a Catholic, I think the Catholic missions are the best and most practical. I had a walk round the grounds and the school.

I walked all day today with no lifts. It was a lonely road. It was good to get the pack off and the camp made. Food is a bit short, but I had some packets of soup and I made some. Then I made a scone in the ash of the fire and brewed a mug of coffee.

Another day walking. Two trucks passed but didn't stop. I got some meat from natives along the way, which I will roast on a spit. I have just entered the Ituri forest.

Next day I walked all forenoon. It's strange walking through the forest. At about noon a truck came along and stopped. There was a Greek in it with an African driver, going to Stanleyville. It's a long truck haul from Beni to Stanleyville, well over 400 miles, but these trucks do it continually as Stanleyville is the nearest point to collect supplies.

At the Ituri River we were held up for a couple of hours. It's one way traffic from there to Mambasa and our way was closed. The Ituri is wide. It is something wonderful to see a great river under a darkening sky with the jungle on either side – something that gets inside you.

At 6 p.m. the barrier was raised and we went through, but when darkness fell we found the lights wouldn't work and there was nothing to do but pull into the side and wait for daylight. And, as darkness fell, so the jungle awoke you could feel it grow alive – sounds in the dark, the incessant whirr of the insects, the scream of a monkey, the thrashing of the branches as something moves. It felt cosy and secure in the cabin of the truck.

It was midnight when a small car came along. The Greek hailed it and asked the driver to take us to Mambasa. I said I'd sleep in the truck but the Greek insisted I come and stay at the hotel with him. So I went. We got into Mambasa at about 1 a.m. We woke a sleepy native who showed us to a room. In the morning we had some breakfast in the little dining room. Before we had finished, the truck arrived with my kit. I thanked and bade goodbye to the Greek and went to find the Administrator to ask the best place to go to see the Pygmies. He advised me to come to Putman's camp. Pat Putman was an American who came to study the Pygmy years ago. He got so engrossed with them he stayed. He was the greatest expert on these people. Unfortunately for me, he had died six months ago, but his wife was carrying on the hotel. It is a queer place. It must be one of the strangest European hotels. At night a huge fire is lit in the middle of the lounge floor. There is no chimney. Africans run the catering and live off the profits and Mrs Putman lives from the lodging side of the business.

Of course, I can't afford to live there. I made a camp further down the way, but I went up to spend the evening in their lounge. I hope to go deeper into the forest away from the road tomorrow.

CHAPTER 20

LIFE WITH THE PYGMIES

Since my last entry in my diary I have lived with the Pygmies: how strange a world it has been! Africa has often been described as a land of contrasts, and I've seen some of the contrasts in the eastern Congo and in Rwanda Burundi, where the Pygmies with light, golden brown skin and only averaging about 4ft in height live side by side with the Watutsi who are dark-skinned and 7ft tall.

Here, too, by the Epulu River – where the animals are more ferocious than anywhere else in Africa – is the elephant station, the one place in the world where African elephants are tamed and trained for work. In the morning, at 6.30, I went along to see the new elephants begin their training. At the word of command from their keeper – each one has its own boy – they will put their head to a tree and push it over. The elephants, when fully trained, will understand twenty-two different words of command.

After their half-hour training, they are led off to the forest with their keepers to feed all day. At sundown they are brought back to be washed and shackled for the night. I went along to see them doing their ablutions. The line of elephants, each with its keeper on its back, went down to the water. The keepers threw down the mats they sit on and the elephants wade out into the river. The keepers stand on their backs and at a word of command, the elephants completely submerge and leave the men ankle deep in the water.

On leaving the water each elephant picks up its master's mat with its trunk and lifts it up to him. Then in line again they go back to camp where they are tethered by a chain round one leg attached to a stump in the ground.

The elephants when trained are ready for lumber work or even ploughing. They are hired out to anybody who wants them, or sold abroad.

In charge of the elephant station is a tough little Greek who shot many forest buffalo, until one got him. He walks with a limp now. He was telling me how they capture the elephants. Only very young ones are captured since it would be impossible to train a fully, or half-grown one. They are always captured on the plains up near the Sudan border.

The hunting is done on horseback. When a herd with young is sighted, the rider lets off a few shots into the air to frighten them. Once on the move, the riders harass them with more shots, speeding up the chase. Eventually, the young ones fall behind and the riders speed the herd on even faster till the young are well behind. Then the one to be captured is selected and ropes thrown round its legs and the two old tame elephants trained for the work, move up on either side of the captured one. The presence of these two old monitors calms down the bewildered and frightened baby. It is then easily led back to captivity.

But the camp at the Epulu River is not wholly confined to elephants. Many other animals captured alive are caged there waiting for shipping abroad to zoos or circuses.

A lion claws at its bars when a visitor goes too close. Chimpanzees sit with impassive, wrinkled faces and vacant eyes like old elders at a tribal court, and many other animals are there too. But the most important of all are the okapis, the rare animals that are only found in this area by the Ituri River in the Congo, and are held there until someone comes to buy them.

**

But, while the Watutsi have been only recently 'discovered', and trained African elephants were almost unheard of, the Pygmies have been meat for travellers' tales ever since travellers have been going to Africa. They were known to the ancient Egyptians and were depicted in carvings in the tombs of the Pharaohs. But, as so often happens with travellers' tales, many inaccuracies have been spread regarding these little people.

I had come to the Ituri forest believing that the Pygmies were mysterious people who lived in the heart of dense jungle and were rarely seen. I had been told that they built liana suspension bridges over rivers and that they dug pits to trap animals and killed elephants by dropping heavily weighted spears on them. I found that none of this was true, all such feats of engineering being the work of the big Africans. An example of how wrong impressions are spread was shown when a few years ago a famous television team went to photograph the Pygmies building a liana bridge. When they found that the Pygmies do not make bridges, in order not to disappoint their public, they had the big Africans teach a group of Pygmies how it was done and photographed the fraud.

The Pygmies do live in the heart of a great forest, but when I was there the colonising Belgians had cut a road through the middle of that forest and, to streamline their administration, they made all Africans live near it. All Pygmies are slaves to the larger Africans, and although they roam the forest at will, they stay within a few days' radius and report back to their masters at frequent intervals. The slavery seems to be voluntary, the Pygmies supplying meat to their masters in return for bananas, plantains, yams, cooking pots and other produce of the more settled mode of life led by the big or 'real' people, as the Pygmies refer to them. Nevertheless, a Pygmy must obtain permission from his master before he can marry.

Unlike most African tribes the Pygmies practise monogamy and have a fairly high moral code. They have no language of their own and speak that of the Africans to whom they belong. Legend has it that at one time there was a Pygmy language and, every so often, someone claims they have found the lost language. But to date all such claims have been refuted.

But now the Pygmies were ready for the hunt. How small they looked! How incredible to think that they were going to hunt where they might meet some of the world's largest and most ferocious animals! Their miniature weapons – arrows no bigger than knitting needles – looked like toys and emphasised the deception. Standing beside them I felt like a giant. Indeed, these past few weeks with them had been like living a chapter of *Gulliver's Travels*. Here in this Congo forest was Lilliput in reality.

We left the cluster of little huts and filed off down a path in the forest. We had barely gone a hundred yards when we came on a man sitting beside a fire. Although they had just left the fire at the camp, the hunters squatted beside this blaze for a few minutes to chat and laugh. This practice of lighting a fire only a short distance from the camp just before the main party left was a ritual with every hunt for which I could never find an explanation. What superstition lay behind it? Was it a fetish to ward off Esamba–Esamba the evil spirit, which meant death to anyone who saw it?

Presently, Faizi the leader rose, crooked his left arm into his side and slapped the hollow thus made with his right palm, making a sound like clapping with cupped hands, but louder. He led the way into the bush. A woman picked up two burning brands from the fire and took them with her. Since the Pygmies cannot make fire, it was this woman's job to keep the sticks alight all day, which she did by holding them together or swinging them to and fro so that there would be fire for warmth and protection should we accidentally be benighted away from camp.

Off the path the jungle is as dense as coconut matting. The trees grow close together and from the branches dangle liana vines, which are laced into a mesh at ground level by thorny creepers that tear at clothing and skin. While I struggle along as if caught up in a never-ending spider's web, the Pygmies move with ease. They are silent too. There are over a dozen in the party, yet, except for my blundering, scarcely a sound is heard. When I get caught up in snags, they melt away and by the time I have freed myself there is not even a snapping twig to guide me. Then, like a wraith, one appears by my side smiling patronisingly to lead me on.

No one speaks. All communications are made with special whistles, calls and clapping. This hunting language is effective; the people back at the village always know if we have caught anything, and if so, which kind of animals, before we get there

When they decide to cast the nets they play them out at an incredible speed, never getting them tangled. There are four nets, each about 100 yards long and four feet high. One man is left to hook them up to the trees while the others circle round to beat the game into the trap. By the time the last few feet are being hitched up, the beaters have started hooting and catcalling.

Sitting behind a tree beside the net I wonder what, if anything, would fall into the bag – antelope, wild pig, buffalo, leopard, perhaps even a rare okapi, the antelope with the giraffe-like neck and zebra stripes, whose existence when referred to by natives was scoffed at by white men until one was killed some years ago. The forest buffalo is smaller and even more cunning and aggressive than the plains type, and will not only charge if met but stop to gore and trample. Its horns, unlike those of the buffalo, are straight and sharp.

How tall the trees are – how solid the roof the knitted branches form! High up in the fan-tracery, a family of monkeys swings away from the approaching din. As the shouting and threshing draw nearer, the tension mounts. Moisture dripping from the trees, drums louder and louder on fiddle-string nerves.

It rained last night. How it rained! Great sheets of solid water that came with a roar so that a shout was barely audible. Yet the little beehive-shaped huts made of leaves piled shingle fashion on frames of criss-cross sticks, which the Pygmies throw up in an hour or so, kept one almost dry. But what the rain misses, the humidity finds when the sun rises. Dampness finds its way into everything, spreading mildew, rotting clothes and boots. Here sugar is always in a lump, and salt never pours.

It is hot and sticky. The tattoo of raindrops quickens in tempo. Louder. Louder. The beaters are almost on us. Anything lying doggo must break now. Anticlimax! The beaters arrive and nothing is in the nets. Nerves twang loose and legs jelly momentarily with the aftermath. Roll up the nets and claw a way through the barbed entanglement to another pitch. Hook up the nets. Wait. Anticlimax again. And again and again – then success.

A little grey antelope is caught in the net. Its squealing slips an octave then fades away pitifully as my Pygmy companion stabs it with his spear. On to the next pitch and more success. Two antelopes this time. And at the next stretch another one and to round off a juicy pig. Each time the animals are skinned and cut up at an astonishing speed, sometimes even before I have groped my way to the scene.

The hunt over, the women bent with laden baskets, the Pygmies sang and capered their way home. There was no need for silence now. As we went, Faizi showed off his jungle to me as a gardener would his garden. That plant was good to eat, this one was poison. If you dug up this bush the roots were succulent, but that one was bitter. Suddenly, a man shouted and pointed to a honey bird. It led them to a beehive high up in a tree. The fire carrier handed the man one of her sticks. He shinned up the tree with it and stuck it in the nest. He wore no protective clothing and yet he did not appear to be stung. When the bees were gone the man tore off great lumps of honeycomb and threw them down to the people below. There is nothing more refreshing than fresh honey on the comb when you have had a hard day.

Back at the village when the meat was divided up there was time to rest. A 6ft long pipe, made from a hollowed banana leaf stem, was lit and passed round. Everybody, men, women and children, took a few puffs and handed it on; I had a feeling it was not tobacco, but Indian hemp that burned in the bowl. The plant from which it is made grows wild in the forest.

Faizi sat on a stool made with three sticks lashed together with bark thongs and told me how he had killed an elephant. He spoke Kingwanna, which was near enough to Swahili for me to get the gist of the story. The other Pygmies gathered round to listen, though they must have heard the tale many, many times. In Africa storytelling is an institution. By it, folklore and history are handed down. It is heady entertainment, and a good storyteller is always sure of an audience, no matter how hackneyed his tales.

Faizi was no mean raconteur. With actions and dramatic pauses he carried his listeners with him, and before long they were clicking their tongues and shaking their heads in acknowledgement of his deeds as if it were all new to them. Faizi, eager to prove his bravery and skill as a hunter, had tracked the elephants alone. When the time was ripe, using the wind astutely, he had crawled right up to one and run under its belly, stabbing it in the bladder with his spear on the way through. He had followed it for two days until it died.

The story finishes, the dancing started. They formed a circle and pranced round in time to impromptu songs and clapping. The singing had charm, the dancing a rhythm of abandon that epitomised the Pygmies' attitude to life. Yet they make no musical instruments. Sometimes they borrow the drums of the ordinary natives, but on their own in the forest they dance to their own singing and clapping. They clap their chests and also bend their left arm into their side and clap the hollow made with the right palm. And just as Faizi did previously, from this they produce a loud carrying sound like clapping cupped hands, but louder.

While dancing they form a circle, at the same time singing and clapping. As they sing the circle moves round, then they stand and one or two move into the middle, do a few turns and join the circle at the other side. When a young belle is in the dancing, she is seldom out of the middle. No sooner does she join the circle than she goes into the middle again. They take their dancing seriously, the men carrying their bows and arrows, the young girls, glad of the opportunity to show off their wares, all with serious faces as they prance through their mad fandango or shuffle round the ring. All ages joined in, revelling in the spells they cast with their flashing bodies, old crones with puckered faces and leathery breasts flapping, elders who tried to inject some dignity into the fandango.

On and on they danced, whirling and stamping. Far away the drums of the 'real' people talked. The night closed in and with it, the rain. The dancing ceased, the drums fell silent. Above the swish of the rain a bush-baby cried pitifully. This was Africa.

***

From the Epulu River and the Pygmies and elephant station, I made my way to Stanleyville, via Bafwasende. At Bafwasende they told me of a strange secret cult the natives practise in the forest. They heard the details from boys who have been converted. The movement has a name which means 'Ruling'. Their belief is that its members after death will come back as white men. When one dies, they leave the body in the river until the skin rots. They then rub off all the black skin, leaving the white flesh, and bury the body. Now comes the bit which is amazing! The members are told that when they die they will see a straight road ahead of them. If they follow this it will lead them back to life as a European. If they deviate and take any of the side roads they will come back as a Greek!

Most of the traders in eastern Congo are Greeks and in the western part they are Portuguese. It is strange that the African regards them as something less than European.

On the way to Stanleyville, I passed the great rivers of the area. There is something about these forest rivers which hold your attention. What do they see as they wend their way into the jungle far beyond the haunts of man? Most of the rivers are bridged, but two must still be crossed by about a dozen dugout canoes roped together with a platform over them to take trucks and cars.

I had to walk on and off for a week over the last stretch. It was late when I dropped off the truck that had brought me the last 100 kilometres. I just had time to collect my mail at the post office before it closed. A crowd gathered round the post office when I went in and the police had to break it up. Most Africans are interested at seeing a kilt and a European carrying a pack, but I had never seen anything like the Congo natives for gathering in crowds just to stare.

It was over three months since I had received any letters so all else was forgotten till I had read them. There was quite a pile and also some magazines and newspapers from Mr Lanning. I took a chair on the verandah of a hotel and proceeded to read. I didn't realise how the time passed until the lights were switched on and I noticed the sun had gone down and heavy clouds were drizzling rain. Also the looks of the management were, by now, downright hostile, for I had occupied a place far too long without ordering any food or drink. But the prices were far beyond my pocket, and although I could not give them custom, I was much obliged for the chair and table.

I realised it was time I looked about for a billet for the night. By now the rain had got down to it in earnest. With the rain was a hot steamy oppressiveness. In my pocket I had a list of about half a dozen names I had received from various people of friends of theirs in the town, who they said I should look up and would be sure of a welcome and a bed. Over the past years I had received many such addresses and letters of introduction which I had never used. To me it always seemed like begging charity to go to a perfect stranger and say 'Here I am. What are you going to do for me?' But this time I decided to seek the hospitality I had been assured would be mine.

I looked up the first of the list. It was the house of a merchant behind the shop where a native watchman dozed over a fire. A fleshy, bald man with rimless spectacles leaned out of the light to peer closer at me when he answered my knock. I told him why I had come and who had given me his address. He asked me into the enclosed verandah and told me to sit. I could see his apprehension as I approached the chairs in case I sat on an easy chair and wet the cushions with my damp clothes. I sat on a hard chair. I could hear the family talking in the lounge.

The man, Monsieur Dupré I will call him, after a few questions gave me a lecture on wasting my youth wandering as a tramp. Had I no ambition? Did I not want to build up something for later years?

"When it's too late you will find yourself left behind by your generation, then you will always drift for you will fit in nowhere."

He spoke fairly good English and went on and on. When I tried to defend myself with, "But perhaps in my wandering I will find something more valuable than the money I might have made had I settled in one place." He made a 'humph' which said plainly 'Don't be ridiculous'.

When he had finished he said he was sorry, but he had no room for me. I had not realised I was in no fit state to enter a home. My boots were muddy and my shirt was sweat dirty where the straps of my rucksack had rubbed. I needed a haircut and I was wet. I felt low as I went out into the night again. I was angry, not at him for refusing me but at myself for asking. I tore up the list of names. Perhaps I had struck the worst of the lot at the first go, but I couldn't afford to be humiliated like that again.

I walked around the streets looking for a place where I might find shelter. They were deserted except for people who crowded into the pools of light of the hotel verandahs, like flies around a lamp. The buildings stood out against the sky like tombstones. I was downhearted and wasn't paying very much attention to what I was seeking. Occasionally, cars passed with dazzling lights, sloshing up mud and water from the deep pools in the dirt roads. Along the beams the water-filled ruts glinted like steel rails.

I passed a furniture shop window with a bedroom suite displayed. A rich carpet was on the floor. A table lamp by the bed splashed soft light from under a frilly shade on a pink, satin bedspread. The setting was inviting. My boots squelched as I went by. A military band swung past with trumpets blaring and drums beating, with petrol torches flaming on the end of long poles. I learned later that it was the band of the Leopoldville contingent which had arrived for the regimental gathering two days hence.

Now I was wet through. I had some coffee in a little Greek café. It had a verandah that ran round two sides of the building, one of them away from the pavement. I asked if I could sleep out of sight at the far end. For an answer he said, "Why you no try other hotel?" He wouldn't take the money for the coffee, which made me feel more like a tramp. I wandered around a while after that, not really looking for anything or anywhere in particular. I remember the strains of an accordion from a lighted window tugged at me and I stood and listened.

A watchman who had seen me passing a couple of times asked if I was looking for somewhere. When I told him why I was walking around, he told me where to find the B.M.S. missionaries' house they kept for their use when they were in town. Acting on the watchman's instructions I found the house down on the canoe wharf. It was a good place with bedroom and bathroom and I was thankful. But then I saw a notice on the wall that visitors were requested to pay 75 francs (about 11/-) per night for sleeping there. That was cheap compared with local prices, but too much for me. My small fund had to be saved for necessities and a bed was not essential to me, even on such a night.

I put on my pack again and told the caretaker I would not stay after all. I went down the drive and stood among the trees and watched the old man lock up and go home. Then I crept back again and unrolled my sleeping bag on the concrete floor of the porch. It was good to rest. If my bed was hard I had long since forgotten to notice such trivialities. Except for the rain that was occasionally carried in with the wind, my place was dry. I was grateful to the missionaries for their house and hoped they would not be offended at this liberty I had taken.

I stayed a week in Stanleyville. It was a city in embryo. One day, they said, it would oust Leopoldville as capital and commercial centre of the Congo. But it had a long way to go yet and even then, it would always be 15 miles from the sea, which made communications with the outside world difficult as there were no roads between Stanleyville and the Atlantic. The Congo River was the only means of reaching the town coming from the west. The prosperity that came to the Congo with the war and the post-war boom that mushroomed Leopoldville, swept up the river into the interior and reached Stanleyville about 1950. About then the little jungle town woke up and rubbed the country apathy from its eyes.

Even so, you could not do much window-shopping in Stanleyville, for there were not many big windows. But they were on their way. New dirt roads had pushed their way out into the jungle clearings and new buildings sprawled along the river's edge. The town had outgrown the single strip of tarmac that defined its old limits and concrete skeletons, swarming with workers like bees in a honeycomb, hummed with activity and showed a new town in the making.

Before I left Stanleyville I looked in to the Central Post Office and was delighted to find some mail awaiting me in the poste restante. Among the few letters was one from Andrew Sneddon, a Scottish friend with whom I had shared several hiking trips in the Scottish Highlands. It was a surprise to hear that he was now married and working in Kano in Northern Nigeria. Since that was one of the places I intended to visit on my way to the Sahara, I resolved to look him up and renew our acquaintance. (Little did I know then how propitious this piece of news would prove to be.)

***

The next few weeks' section of my travels are recounted purely from memory because my diaries for the period were lost in a disastrous accident, the details of which are explained in the following chapter.

On my way northwest of Stanleyville heading for Bangui on the Congo/ French Equatorial border, I tramped for three weeks through tropical rain forest, camping each night by the track side. That experience in itself was wearing enough, but what ensued made it positively nightmarish. In hindsight, even to me it has acquired a kind of perverse drollery, but at the time it was most certainly not funny.

As my trek began, the local bush telegraph went into action with the news of a strange, bearded man coming through the forest. Most of the natives had never seen a white man before, far less one wearing some kind of skirt and, naturally, they were fascinated – so much so in fact, that several dozen of them, mostly women and children, decided to follow me and watch my every move all day and for most of the night. When I say every, I mean exactly that.

As the little procession progressed, each particular group would reach the limit of its bailiwick – so to speak – but the "telegraph" ensured that a fresh batch was ready to maintain the vigil. And so they watched, and watched as I walked, rested, cooked, ate, washed, camped, slept and – well – need I say more?

After a week or so of this, my nerves began to fray and I was given to pause occasionally and bellow at them to go away. Of course that had little or no effect; even drawing my revolver and firing two shots in the air gave only temporary respite.

Those were the three longest weeks of my life.

In retrospect, I take some comfort from the thought that for weeks – or perhaps even years – afterwards a few hundred Africans probably derived some merriment in telling the story of the strange creature who passed among them, carrying all his possessions on his back.

CHAPTER 21

FRENCH EQUATORIAL AFRICA

Two days ago I suffered the biggest set-back I have ever had. I will try to put it down as it all happened.

On Monday morning, the 15th September 1954, the convoy was ready to leave. How pleased I was! The four weeks of waiting for it had been so very monotonous. I must write about these four weeks. There had been the 300-mile walk in the rain and mud with little food, coming up from Fort Sibut to Archambault. I was glad to arrive. The Administrator said it was impossible to go any further for the whole area was underwater. However, there was this company "Unifac", which ran barge convoys up and down the Chari River between Fort Lamy and Fort Archambault.

When I arrived there was a convoy ready to leave, but the engine of the little tug was out of order. They thought perhaps three or four days should see it right and the convoy on its way. I was elated when offered a lift on it free of charge. Of course, I had to provide my own food and the journey should take eight days.

I arrived in Archambault with £4 (2,000 francs). All the way up from Bangai I'd been a Scrooge with the money, rationing myself to a rather severe diet considering I was doing some heavy walking. I knew what I had must last me until I reached Kano and that was an awfully long way ahead. I wondered how I was going to provide food enough for the eight days voyage. The days passed and there was no sign of the boat getting ready. The mechanic was not very energetic and without the manager there, he had long siestas in the afternoon until 4 p.m. As time passed he would always say the boat would be ready tomorrow or – his favourite – "after tomorrow". The result was I never knew where I was. I was left hanging on all the time.

Fifty miles from Archambault is a tribe where the women put enormous wooden discs in their lips like duck bills. This dates back to the slave-trading days, when the men of the tribe made their women do this so as to make them so ugly the Arabs would not take them.

I wanted to go to photograph them. The road was closed to traffic and the only way was to walk or go by bicycle. Since two or three days was all the notice the mechanic – Monsieur Robert Beonec – ever gave me, I thought the only way I could go was by bicycle. It was impossible to borrow one and the lowest price I could have hired one was 1,500 francs and that was out of the question so I had to give up the idea, although I was very keen to see them. I was angry, for had I known I was to be so long waiting, I could have easily walked.

Robert proved how French we imagine the French are, when he brought in his native mistress and proceeded with his business while I was sitting eating, only a few feet away from the bed. Both seemed quite unconcerned by my presence, which I hastily removed.

He was a spineless character and could never bring himself to say how long he would be. He kept putting off my questions of when we would go. His three or four days passed into a week. That week I didn't eat very much. I cut myself down to a very spartan diet to conserve my meagre funds. I considered the waiting lost time and therefore couldn't allow much of the remaining funds on it.

Then, at the end of the first week, I had nearly all my money stolen, leaving me about 500 francs (£1). I suspected the house boy or the sentinel, but it was impossible to pinpoint it. Since I couldn't speak any French or Sango – the native language – I was stymied from questioning the boys. Even if I could have, it would have been impossible to get it back. I didn't bother to tell Robert about it. I knew he could not get it back anyway, and he would always have the suspicion that I had fabricated the story so as to court pity. Perhaps I was wrong; it was hard to put these little fears into words, but I felt that a person such as I must be cautious. If you have no money, the people were so ready to stamp you as a nuisance or undesirable. Had I owned the world I could have raised hell and nobody would have doubted my story.

So I just had to take it, and wonder what I was going to do for food over the next few weeks. The frustration, the hopelessness on top of the monotony and melancholy of the past week, which the lack of food and lack of anything to do and someone to talk to had brought on, knocked the stuffing out of me for a time. I wrote in my diary then, 'There's one consolation in being at rock bottom of the world, the future must be better, it can't get worse.' I didn't know how wrong I was, or at least, how wealthy I really was then – I still had an awfully long way to go down. Little did I know that I would not wait long before I learned this.

I didn't eat much for the first week; I ate even less during the next fortnight. I had one meal of manioc – the cheapest native food – per day. That kept me going, but didn't stop the hunger. When food is down to starvation diet you can't build up much mental resistance – your mental resistance suffers as much as your physical. After a time I didn't feel the intense hunger I did at first. It settled into a continual gnawing craving for something and a listlessness that made life heavy.

Once, M. Schalbart, the father-in-law of the Manager, invited me to dinner. To me the meal was a banquet. There was soup and fresh salmon, tinned caviar, steak and chips, then meat and vegetables and sweet and coffee and, with the meal, three different wines. But all this on a stomach which had forgotten such food was too much. I suffered acute pains and diarrhoea afterward and ate nothing for the next two days. So the meal lasted me three days – four actually, for I ate nothing on the previous day knowing I was going to get a good meal the next day!

The situation was worsened by the fact of my having nothing to do. There was nothing to read, everything being in French. There was nobody to talk to. I saw very little of Robert, the mechanic, and indeed had little desire to see more. He ate out at the hotel so we had no common meeting ground. There was nothing to take my mind off the fact that I was hungry. Also aggravating the situation was my impatience as Robert's 'tomorrow' and 'after tomorrow's passed into weeks and my money dwindled on useless waiting.

At the end of the third week I sold my watch for 2,000 francs. It was worth at least double that, but I was at the thin end of the bargaining wedge. With that money in my pocket I felt like a millionaire. Funny, three weeks before with the same amount I'd felt so poor. The first thing I did was to buy myself some better food for a good meal. It was fine, but like the meal with M. Schalbart, it gave me pains in the stomach afterwards though not so bad, since what I bought wasn't such rich food.

The next day I was joined by two Swiss men who were hitch-hiking their way home. They hoped to be home for Christmas. They are good fellows but are deplorably equipped. They had big rucksacks packed with souvenirs, but they don't have any pots, mugs or plates. One of them has a broken spoon. That is their total accoutrements for eating, so they are dependent on all they meet.

They both speak quite a bit of English, especially Mark, who speaks five languages well. We pooled our food and what little money we could spare to buy more. They were quite low.

Robert was still leaving 'after tomorrow', so they were quite happy to have arrived in time. Ten days after their arrival the boat was ready to leave. That was last Monday. We should have left on Sunday afternoon, but Robert had to have his usual siesta and slept too long and then said "tomorrow". Typical to the last.

Monday morning was wet with drizzling rain. The date was the 13th. There were twelve barges and the tug. If I were superstitious I'd say two 13s were too much for luck's sake.

I was so happy when we cast off. After the weeks of miserable existence and these four awful weeks from Bangai, this was a good day. To the surprise of the boys, I let out three resounding cheers. Ten minutes later the accident occurred. Perhaps the barges were overloaded. Maybe the convoy was too big for such a small tug. Or it could have been that the engine was not running well enough to have started on such a journey in the first place. It could also be said that the lines were cast off before the engine was ready to take over. But all that is not for me to say. The inquest to be held later would prove who or what was at fault.

We swung out into the midstream and the whole convoy turned broadside on to the current. The engine spluttered and started but seemed too feeble to do much about controlling the huge mass. The barges swung about helplessly. The current took us across the river. One barge hit the bank and the other slowed and piled up against it. Pandemonium broke out. Cargoes toppled and were swept away. The horde of native passengers were screaming and jumping overboard. There was the crashing and splintering of wood and the splashing of crates and boxes as they slid into the water. Chaos reigned!

Three barges sank, one of them loaded with salt. The one I was on listed at an acute angle and I went overboard in between it and the next one. I heard the two smash together after I went through. I swam back to the wreckage and climbed aboard to search for my kit as all our stuff had been on top of the engine housing. Everything was gone.

Out in midstream, Kurt was standing on a load of boards which still held together forming a raft. He was carried out of sight. Mark was sitting in a barge that had grounded. I shouted that all the kit was gone. He answered that he'd managed to save his own. He had seen them go and managed to grab his rucksack.

I took stock of my possessions – one pair of shorts and sandshoes – in my pocket was one handkerchief, my spectacles and exposure meter and 210 francs (eight shillings and five pence)! My kilt, revolver, boots, hat: everything was gone. Later, I made a list of articles lost and found it amounted to £130.00. It was even more formidable than I had expected. In addition, my £100 I carried for immigration purposes in travellers cheques had gone. I should be able to reclaim these but it will take time.

But cash values in this situation are useless. The problems confronted by the lack of the items are more formidable than the price of them: first the question of where and how to buy them with no money; how to manage without them; how to cope with the trouble to be faced by having no passport or money and, because of that, the fact of being a destitute person in a foreign country? What trouble would I meet in trying to enter Nigeria when I had no money to put down as the immigration bond? Perhaps among my losses was the right to enter the next country. Who knows, they may repatriate me as destitute and I would hate that. I suppose it is impossible to really assess what I have lost in those grim five minutes.

I think most of all I regret the loss of my camera and the films I had taken and the photos I won't be able to take. I will have no pictorial record of French Equatorial Africa or the Belgian Congo from Bosoko on: all the photos of the Gwaka girls of Budjala, the circumcision and ceremonial dress for that occasion – gone! My diary too; that is a big loss. I will never be able to remember all the details. Who knows what I have lost in that.

Of the most sentimental value, I feel the loss of my old, battered hat which has been through everything with me since being issued to me in 1947, while with the army in Kenya. A real old friend lost.

My rucksack and boots – what will I do without them? Kano is the nearest place where I might pick up replacements and that is weeks, perhaps months, ahead and in the meantime I haven't even a pot to cook with or a plate to eat from or a change of clothing.

But, to take up the tale from where I left off. As I said, Mark had been lucky enough to save his kit and Kurt went down the river on a raft of boards. The other Unifac boat which had arrived from Fort Lamy on Sunday, raced down stream in an attempt to head off some of the flotsam.

We sat in one of the barges. A strong, cold breeze had sprung up. I didn't have a shirt since I had taken it off to keep it dry when we embarked. I was cold. Mark loaned me a jerkin. It was soaking wet, but it shielded me from the wind and I was thankful for it.

Presently the other boat came back and took us back to the Unifac office. Kurt's rucksack had been picked up also and brought back by a native in a canoe. Mine was never seen; it was so heavy it would have sunk straight to the bottom.

Kurt came back later. He brought with him my sleeping bag, water bottle and the small bag I keep my writing case and letters in. He had seen them floating and at the risk of his life had dived into the river and retrieved them. A native with a canoe had rescued him and then he'd been picked up by the boat.

So in the accident, no lives had been lost and nor was anybody injured. But thousands of pounds worth of material had been lost.

Now the three of us began to plan about food. We didn't have a pan to cook with and our funds were considerably lower. Mark gave me a pair of socks and Monsieur Schalbart gave me a shirt and a mosquito net, so the first of my immediate needs were seen to. He also loaned me 2,000 francs.

He wanted to give it to me, but I only accepted it on the basis that I could pay it back into his bank in London when I reach there.

We borrowed a pot from the natives and cooked some pumpkins and ate out of basins and lids or tins – whatever receptacle we could find. I had already given up worrying about my loss. One must be resigned to such things when travelling. But I did feel sorry about my camera and revolver having gone.

The Manager returned by air from Fort Lamy the next day to look into the incident. In the afternoon we had a pleasant surprise when some Nigerian boys working for Sedec brought us food. This was the kindest action we had experienced here. The Nigerian boys heard about my plight, and considering themselves British, felt they had to do something. They brought bread and tinned food which we could never have afforded to buy, even before the accident. Such kindness from Africans when Europeans had been apathetic touched us deeply.

I had written to the British Consulate at Brazzaville reporting the loss of my passport. Also I wrote to Blacks to ask them to re-equip me with rucksack, tent, boots and cooking canteen, on the understanding that I would pay for them later when I got home. I hoped they would agree. If not, it would have been difficult. Even so, it was Kano where I must pick up the equipment and that was a long way to go yet.

I also wrote to the *Courier* newspaper which had in the past been interested in my journey, to ask them to contact a local newspaper in Kano to provide me with a camera and debit the price to them (the *Courier*), also on the promise that I would repay them when I got home. I hoped they would agree. Yet again, even if they did, to go from here to Kano without a camera was a big loss.

We got a job diving for the Company to try to retrieve some of the lost cargos. The food we were given was perhaps as good a payment as we could get, but later we were given some pay, one thousand francs (£2.00) each, for our diving in addition to our food.

The river is about 18 feet deep and the current very fast. At first we tried ordinary diving, but the current carried us away from the place before we touched bottom. Then we got a long iron bar from the boat's side and went down hand under hand that way. The pressure was very great and made my head pound terribly. We plugged up our ears, but it didn't help much. However, we carried on. We located two of the three barges, but they would have to wait till the dry season, when the river is low, to raise them.

This was a new job for me to add to my list of various occupations. We found we could outlast the natives underwater. Kurt was the best with 33 seconds to his credit which, at that depth with the heavy pressure brought on by the strong current, we all thought was very good.

Next day we were diving all day. It was good work and good exercise but gave you a bit of a headache.

We found and put ropes round and hauled in a huge new winch in a great crate. The company was very pleased. The winch was valued at 200,000 francs (£400) so it was a profitable day for them.

It was not Robert who said it this time, but Monsieur Alex Delacroix, who said we would be leaving next day. It was he who brought up a convoy of barges from Fort Lamy on Sunday and he would captain the combined convoys going down again. He seemed a man of firmer character than Robert and had six years' experience of navigating this river.

The manager of the company came down before we left and gave me some of his clothing. It was all too small for me, but he said that perhaps at Fort Lamy I would be able to exchange the two shirts for one new one that fitted me.

Also before we left, the Nigerian Africans brought us more bread and tins of sardines for the journey. Really, words fail me about these people. They were the only people who came forward to help, except the manager and his father-in-law, who must have thought they were duty bound to give the few articles of their clothes they gave me. These Africans were certainly way ahead of others I had met, being so sensitive in giving food and clothes and aware of the trouble I was in. One of them even gave me a new hat (valued at about 400 francs (16/-), which was so necessary, for the sun is very strong, another made me sandals out of rubber tyres. All the food as well as the hat must have cost them a few thousand francs and that must have been quite a sacrifice for them with their small salaries. I only hope they realised how much we appreciated their kindness.

***

It was on Saturday 18th September that I finally left Archambault. Five weeks I was there. Five weeks of monotony, hunger, disaster and general bad luck. To me that place seemed to hold a curse. We left in the afternoon in convoys. The convoys were joined together further down the river into one big one. We stayed that night 20 kilometres from Archambault at the village of Helibongo, a little native settlement.

We didn't go so far the next day. Some engine trouble held us back. The convoy was not anchored at a village, just in the bush. On the bank where the barges stopped, a puff adder snake was lying sleeping. Delacroix killed it with a spear and Kurt, Mark and I ate it. Everybody was aghast at us for doing so and all the boys stood around watching as we ate, as if waiting for us to drop dead. It was the first time I had tasted snake. It was very good. If all snakes are as good as this very poisonous variety then I hoped to get more of them. Inside the snake was a whole rat, which it must have just swallowed whole a short while before. The snake meat is white and there are a lot of small rib bones, but it made an excellent meal.

The scenery on either side of the river was flat and uninteresting. The Nealim hills made a welcome change. They are low hills, but on the flat land they stuck up like a sore thumb for the whole forenoon before we reached them.

In the early morning we reached Bousso. We should have reached there yesterday, but the little engine broke down. We almost made it but had to anchor only a mile away. M. Delacroix preferred to anchor rather than go the last mile and risk the dangers of landing in the dark.

Yesterday, while the convoy was going on only one engine, there was almost a repetition of the Archambault disaster. The wind and current swung the huge convoy towards the bank. The engine was switched off and it was only at the last moment and by expert handling of the rudders, that the barges were swung round in line again. He was a first-class captain.

Two days ago he went ashore and shot a waterbuck, so there was plenty of meat on board.

Bousso was a small native town with a few European officials and missionaries. I went along to the Protestant Mission to see if they had any old English magazines or papers that I might read. The missionaries, Mr and Mrs Price, were an Australian couple. They were very friendly and nice, so different to the American ones at Archambault and Sibut. I only wish I could have had the time to accept their invitation to breakfast.

I was struck by the rows of streets in Bousso. Although each hut or group of family huts was enclosed by a high mat fence, there were distinct streets between the rows. All, or most of the huts, had rambling pumpkin and native cucumber plants growing over the thatched roofs and the big vegetables were ripening. The convoy left Bousso about 11 a.m. That night we were anchored by a reedy swamp which was as near the edge of the river as we could get.

River travel in these cramped conditions was rather monotonous: all day the phut, phut, phut of the engines, the river sliding placidly by, the flat banks rarely changing in scenery. Occasionally there were single or herds of hippos splashing merrily like Blackpool bathers, or a basking crocodile, or the antelopes that stood drinking on the bank watching as we went by – they don't seem to attach any danger to us. These things broke the monotony, but through time even those became commonplace.

Sometimes a wind came up and the river became like a choppy sea and splashed in the barges. Then the rain came and it wasn't so good for there was no proper shelter.

We made tea on a fire in the pointed prow of the barge and we rationed out our sugar to make it last out the voyage. Kurt had the biggest appetite of any thin man I had met. He was always hungry. At times, his desire for more and more food was almost obscene. He got angry at the sight of the small ration and seemed to have the idea it would be best to eat everything at one meal and then let tomorrow look after itself. Unfortunately that philosophy can hardly be put into practice on a boat. He was a good chap, but immature at 26 years old. Twenty-two year old Mark was a much more sensible person.

So the days went by: the grey mornings, the P.T., lighting the fire for the tea, then lying about, the yellow, blistering sunshine that makes the shadows black, the constant noise of the engines, the evening and the mosquitoes, the rain and wetness, the hot sultry sticky nights, the morning hustle to get the barges roped in place and be off – so there was another day..

We tried to break up the inactivity by doing some P.T. morning and afternoon, but there were two things which never became stale with their familiarity. To me the sunrise and sunsets never lost their spell. It is said some people are affected by the moon. Similarly, if there is a form of lunacy attributed to the rise and decline of the sun, then I am afraid I would be one to be affected. Here on the river, the sunsets in particular hold a charm which never failed to hold me. Each morning and evening, unless rain shut them out, I paid homage to the rise and fall of the sun by giving it my whole attention.

Another day passed with nothing much to break the monotony. The convoy consisted of 24 barges. It was like a small floating village. Behind, at the back of the convoy, were the two boats pushing. At the helms, working in unison, stood Quassi and Nana, the tall, proud Sava tribesmen, their faces carved with the tribal markings. When the cuts are made, they rub crude latex into them so that, when they heal, the scars stand out in relief like embossed leather. How they stood the sun all day in the same position beats me.

We were nearly at Fort Lamy and expected to arrive the next evening.

Now, as we continued on the river, the temperature was hotter and more unpleasant. The river had lost a lot of its force. We had heard that in the dry season the water would barely cover your knees if you walked across the river. Yet it was a quarter of a mile wide and the bottom couldn't be touched with the sixteen-foot pole they have.

We passed many villages perched on the banks of the river. Some of them had buildings like castles with embattlements and keyhole-shaped Moorish doors. I think they were mosques, but they looked strange these mud castles here in the heart of Chad. At sundown the convoy still had 18 kilometres to do. M. Delacroix was very ill with malaria and heart complications. He had to stay in bed but, partially recovered from his illness, decided to do the last bit even in the dark

In the evening we berthed at Fort Lamy. The light of the town was a welcome sight; so long had I waited to get there. M. Delacroix proved how good a captain he was when he brought his convoy in by the light of a torch and nosed the barges, grouped in a rough four abreast formation, in between the other boats with only inches to spare on either side. It was too late to go ashore.

Fort Lamy at last! Mark and Kurt had gone to stay with a Swiss man in town. I strolled around the company grounds. The road to Kano should be open in a few days. No word from the British Consulate regarding my passport and entry into Nigeria.

I met a Scotsman (born in Malaya), a Mr Macdonald, who lived here and worked for Sedec (Lever Bros) He did the transport between here and Nigeria. He said he could fix me up with a lift when the road opened. He lived in one of the two-storey, mud buildings in the village. He lent me his camera so that I could take a film of the place.

I've been roaming around photographing today. Fort Lamy is quite a fascinating and picturesque place. The houses are square with flat roofs, many are double storey. They looked like something out of *Beau Geste*. They are made of a mortar consisting of mud and straw and from the roofs fantastic arrays of gargoyles jut out into the streets. The balconies of the two-storey ones are walled with embattlements, giving them a fort-like appearance. Most of the doors and windows faced westward so that they only catch the setting sun.

In the sun-baked dusty streets one mingled with a motley of interesting and, in many cases, exotic people. Arabs and Islamist Africans dressed in voluptuous, brilliant coloured gowns and cloaks, with knives carried in a strange fashion, strapped to the inside of their upper arm.

There are the ordinary natives and the westernised ones in European dress. And there are the women of the black Arab tribe that bring in the milk to the market. This tribe owes the colour of their skin to the coming of the Muslims. Prior to this there were brown and black tribes. Those Africans who would not take the Muslim religion were slaughtered and the women taken by the Arabs who came as invaders.

All dress in the same way, a kind of tribal uniform. Their hair is done in a multitude of plaits like rope that dangle down nearly to their shoulder. They all wear a blue cloth wrapped round them as a dress. A brass ring through one nostril completes the outfit. They bring the calabashes of fresh and curdled milk from as far as 20 kilometres away, doing the 40 kilometres on foot. I am told that to keep the fresh milk from turning sour they put a few drops of their own urine into it. All Chad and especially Fort Lamy bears the look of strong Arab influence and Arabic is the general language.

Donkeys are used a lot. Sometimes one sees a single native, sometimes a dozen, sitting on the hindquarters with their legs almost touching the ground, jog-jogging along, many wearing the big, pointed straw hats with great wide brims that drown the owner in a pool of shade.

The temperature is terrible. It is not so much the heat which is so unbearable, but the humidity which is high now, with the rains finished and the land drying up. It is stifling and even the nights are seldom cooler. You just sit and the sweat rolls down. It is impossible to concentrate on anything. Also the insect life at night is formidable in their numbers and variety. Yet they say in a month all that will disappear and one could dispense with a net at night and the climate has no humidity and is comfortably hot. October is the worst month.

On the first day of the worst month, I went to see Khalifa Faraj. I had heard interesting rumours that everyone knows he is a slave trader, capturing whole villages and transporting them by caravan to Egypt for sale. Nobody has been able to pin anything on him. I thought it would be interesting to meet a real live slave trader. As an excuse, I decided I would ask if I could travel on one of his caravans, feeling sure he would refuse me, but at least I would have met him.

His house was a whitewashed, double-storey one at the end of the main street, one of the elegant mud houses. A big, new, American car stood at the door. Kalifa was a small Arab with a wiry, twirly moustache. He wore the usual long white gown and had a colourful waistcoat and an embroidered skull cap. He spoke no English, but one of his nephews did. To my surprise they said I could go on a caravan if I came back in the season, about December or January. But I was sure the one I was allowed to go on would be a legitimate trading caravan. Also, it was all very well them saying that now. Perhaps if I had gone back then, they might have changed their mind, but it was interesting to see him.

The next day I did receive word back from the British Consul in Brazzaville in response to my request for information regarding my passport and entry into Nigeria. It didn't make any difference: they said they couldn't do anything to help.

I was invited to go with the manager and his friend to the latter's concession away in the bush. We got bogged down in mud and it was late when we got back.

This was the day I was supposed to leave. I went along to Mr Macdonald who said a Sedec truck was leaving in the afternoon. I went along again but was told it would be tomorrow – British territory again! I thought it would be fun trying out my English again after the spell in French territory. It would give my hands a rest!

CHAPTER 22

TURNING NORTH FOR THE HOMEWARD JOURNEY
NIGERIA: BRONZES AND JUJU

The immigration officer was a Scotsman, McDonald by name and Chief of Police in Maiduguri. He had received a letter from Andrew Sneddon claiming me when I entered the country and it made quite a difference. I had no trouble and was granted a fourteen-day permit to get through to Kano where I could see about getting it extended.

The Police Officer invited me to his home should I want to spend some time and also lent me his camera so that I could photograph some of the local sights. I moved over to his place that afternoon.

How good it was to be handling British currency again and to be able to use English as a general language instead of fumbling with French. How much we do take for granted in life! I appreciated now even hearing the radio speaking English and listening to the news in English. The only fly in the ointment was that the main news was of a dock strike which had paralysed shipping at home. It brought home the reality that was Britain – strikes and more strikes.

Maiduguri was a wonderful place, a perfect photographers' paradise. In Bornu province, it was famous from time immemorial as the Bornu Empire; to walk down the street was to walk into the past. A thousand years were lost when you stepped through the gate into the town. In the narrow alleys between the square mud huts, people walked who seemed to have stepped from the Biblical world. People in flowing robes, donkey men in high-painted straw hats with wide brims and ugly hags with broken teeth, red with betel nut, croaking to all who passed to buy their wares.

But perhaps the most interesting and picturesque were the Bornu horsemen, with their high-pummelled saddles and great swords. Sometimes, there was one in a richly embroidered cloak who had two servants running at either side of the horse, the harness decked with gaily coloured tassels, the high saddle plated with metal ties on rich cloth, his sword ornamented, the scabbard covered with red cloth. The horses were of fine Arab strain, thin legged and aristocratic. I am no judge of horse flesh, but the sight of them made me think of high, white-flecked waves – wild, high-spirited and powerful but graceful and smooth in their movements.

And there were the Fulani women who rode great bullocks – riding them as others ride horses. These were the cattle Fulani. How can I describe all I saw in a walk through these streets?

I wanted to see the market on Monday and also get some more photos of the place. I went to see Mac to see if it would be alright to stay over. He was happy for me to stay till after the market.

Market day was quite formidable. The two things that impressed me most were the sale of ironstone for making mascara, and the barber shaving heads in the shade of the great tree with tethered horses around and saddles with big, flat metal stirrups like ash cans and swords lying about.

I left Maiduguri on Tuesday. Mr McDonald had arranged a lift with a friend of his and I went along to where the trucks were standing. All were carrying half a load and the back portions were set with seats for passengers. They were known as 'mammy wagons'. Some of them had mottos or slogans on divine thoughts painted on boards across the front. The two that struck me most were one saying "Trust in God" – the driver took too wide a turn and missed a wall by a hairs breadth – and another saying "Nothing without labour" – it was broken down and the driver and mechanic were head and shoulders deep into the bonnet!

It was a long wait. I had some tea and nuts from a little boy who carried a huge kettle and a charcoal brazier, and sat with the Arabs under the tree. We chatted the time away until the truck was ready to go. It was 5 p.m.

I asked the African owner how long it would take to reach Kano and was surprised when he said we should arrive the next forenoon. 370 miles! He said there were two drivers so we could go non-stop.

The truck moved through town stopping here and there, sometimes just so the driver could talk to someone. At one stop a light-coloured Arab joined the driver and sat with me in the front cabin. The town was crowded, as always, in the last hour before the sun went down. As the truck crept through the narrow streets, dipping wheels into pot holes and bumping over mounds of earth and rubbish, the stream of pedestrians clad in voluminous robes parted to allow it to pass. Many cyclists careered dangerously along through the crowds. All the bicycles seemed new and the frames, most of them, still had the brown paper wound round them. Here and there men drew their robes about them, loosened the tapes which held up their spare loose trousers and squatted at the edge of the street to urinate. The truck barely missed the gargoyles on the houses which jutted out into the streets like hedgehog bristles.

It was almost dark when we ran out of the town. The tarmac ran out at the airport a few miles out and we were held up there for some time. I dozed for a while. When I woke I tried some conversation with the Arab at my side, but we hadn't a word in common so I dozed off again, only semi-conscious of the rattling from the road corrugations. There was life in all the villages we passed.

The driver stopped at a village, which appeared to be a recognised night halt. Already many other great freight trucks lined the roads and even at that hour the market square was alive with activity. The moonlight was hazy with wood smoke. Lanterns twinkled. Vendors sat over their single trays of kola nuts, sugar, guavas, etc., each with a lamp at his or her side. Some would be lucky if they sold a few pence worth for their night long wait. The driver said he would wait there for the night. Evidently, the chance of a chat with his cronies, the other drivers, outweighed his intention of driving all night.

I spread my sleeping bag out under a tree and went to sleep. At about 3 a.m. the driver wakened me. He had changed his mind again and wanted to go on. The merchants were still there when we left, huddled over the pitiful little quantities of nuts.

We arrived in Potiskum with the first light of dawn. The town was just beginning to wake up. I bought three pence worth of tea from a boy who poured it into my billy can. It was too heavily scented to be enjoyable, but I was thankful for it after the long drive. The drivers seemed to be in no hurry to leave Potiskum. Some stores were unloaded and more taken on, some of the passengers were also exchanged for new ones. The driver had an endless stream of people whom he must visit or stand and talk and laugh with. It was 10 a.m. before we left and I was bored stiff with hanging around.

But now the progress was even slower. At every village we would stop and wait while the driver drank bottled beer at the native 'hotels'. These were grass hovels and only the name 'Hotel', blatantly displayed on rough boards, resembled their European counterparts. The day dragged on. He continued to fortify himself against tiredness with beer. Darkness fell. At about 11 p.m. we entered the gates of Kano. I slept under the truck.

Kano! How glad I was to be there. With daylight this morning I made my way to the Trade Centre to find Andrew Sneddon, my great friend from night school days. It was grand seeing him again after all these years. And now he is married with little Linda to occupy his time. Margaret, his wife, whom I met for the first time, also made me feel welcome. So, after all these months of looking forward to getting here, I had finally arrived.

After a few days settling in I went down to Bompai, the district where the police are. I made arrangements regarding obtaining a new passport, but I was refused permission to work, which was a big blow. I was pleased to find there was some money waiting for me at the Post Office for a couple of articles I had had accepted.

After a couple of weeks in Kano the Harmattan began to blow. This is a dry, cool, dust-laden wind which comes from the desert. It brings the temperature down to bearable degrees, except at around midday when the heat still gets oppressive. But the Harmattan pushes dust in everywhere. It dries up the skin so that you feel it crack when you laugh, you feel it in your nose and you hair goes like straw. When it blows, visibility is reduced and houses at a hundred yards seem hazy.

I had been in Kano for four weeks enjoying normal home life and the social contact with friends of Andrew and Margaret. One night when I had agreed to babysit for them while they went out to dinner, a knock came at the door. A friend of theirs had come to see me and invited me to dinner at his home. I was disappointed not to be able to go, but the solution was obvious – the baby must come too. That night went down as baby Linda's first outing with a young man and my opportunity to take out a charming companion.

I had never seen a more enchanting place. Kano, a walled city here in this twentieth century existed like a throwback from some distant past. Within the walls life had remained unchanged for a thousand years. What I wrote about Maiduguri could be said for Kano, but on a much bigger scale. It was a fascinating place with horsemen in long robes and pointed straw hats.

Andrew and I hired bicycles one Sunday morning and cycled round the perimeter of the wall. A week later, on a Sunday also, we hired bikes again and cycled around the city for a while and, on the next Sunday morning we walked along the top of the wall for about half the circumference of the city. It got quite exciting in places where it had worn away to a razors edge, with a drop of perhaps 40 feet on either side. In many places I had to go barefoot as my old sand shoes couldn't grip.

At the half-way stage, we cut back across the centre of the city and headed for Kofar (gate) Nasarawa one of the main gates of the old city. It was an eventful walk through busy streets free of vehicular traffic. We passed a fine specimen of a man with a pointed hat and flowing robes and mounted on a great bullock (how I regretted that I had lost my camera); we stopped at a street-side stall to buy a pennyworth (a large handful) of ground nuts, freshly roasted and hot off the griddle. At one point we were aware of a commotion ahead, the cause of which, we discovered, was the presence of an African holding one end of a thick chain some ten or twelve feet long. The other end was attached to the collar round the neck of a large spotted hyena which he goaded into charging at members of the crowd, causing them to scatter in fear. Powerfully built and standing about three feet high at the shoulder, this hyena was a formidable beast, but not surprisingly, its fearsome jaws were encased in a strong leather muzzle. On reflection, one wondered how this muzzle was removed at feeding times!

The kilt, which Alec was going to send me, had still not arrived because, no doubt, of the awful dock strike at home. I supposed the equipment from Blacks wouldn't come before Christmas either due to that hold-up. I was so lucky that Blacks had agreed to supply these things with the agreement I pay when I get home. Andrew's friend from Lagos, Mrs Macnab, who was in Scotland on holiday, had agreed to bring out a camera for me which I had arranged with a relative to buy for me and send to her in Perth. She was due to arrive in Nigeria the following morning.

Andrew and I cycled up to the airport at 5 a.m to meet the plane. Mrs Macnab had brought the camera, but she had it packed in her luggage and couldn't give it to me then, so I had to wait till I got to Lagos before I picked it up. What a nuisance! I still couldn't take photographs. Still, I was lucky that she had been able to bring it.

It seemed strange seeing Mrs Macnab and hearing her say she had left London only yesterday. A strange thing distance: it would take me the best part of a year to do what she had done in a day.

Next day, Andrew received some newspapers which had come by sea mail. I wondered if my kilt and kit had come also and I went down to the post office to see if they were there. But they still had a mountain of parcels to clear yet and it might be days before either was delivered, even if they were there.

I resolved to leave the next day and start out for Lagos. I was very ill-equipped but would have to cope for the next month. At least it was slightly better than it was during the time I travelled from Archambault to Kano. Although I had no tent or boots or proper pans, I could manage.

I went down to the market to see if I could get a blanket to use as a ground sheet. What a seething place Kano city market was! It was the largest market in all Africa. What an atmosphere to be caught up in as you wended your way through the crowds, the vendors shouting to you to look at their wares, the children pestering you with the inevitable "Baturi (white man), gimme dash". 'Dash' is the local Nigerian term for "Baksheesh" or money for nothing.

I got the blanket for five shillings after quite a lot of haggling. How they liked to barter! It was almost like a game and the longer and harder you bargained, the better they seemed to like it. But, woe betide the man who made fun by bargaining with no intention of purchasing anything. The object of the game was for the buyer to beat the price down to what he thought was a fair price, while the trader tries to wheedle the last penny from his customer's pocket.

It was 11 a.m. before I left Kano. I had said my goodbyes to Andrew and Margaret and the lovely little Linda, and had agreed to get back from my wanderings round Nigeria for Christmas. As I left the town I came on some vultures tearing at the body of a cow or horse and, seeing their hatred when I went near, I went on my way. I walked only a couple of miles out of town when a mammy wagon stopped and agreed to take me free of charge. I sat up in the back on some bags of flour.

At one village, I went with the driver to an eating house – a small shelter with a low table and tins for chairs – where I had some very hot rice with red pepper. At villages we stopped at, there were always the little boys selling titbits – peanuts with syrup, sugar candy, oranges, etc.

At Yashi, where I had to branch off for the Zaria road, the driver of the truck actually went and spoke to the driver of another truck waiting there and arranged for me to go with it to Funtua. So I transferred from one truck to another. But this one had only wooden seats and four hours on them along a bumpy road almost brought one to a 'dead end'.

It was interesting travelling in the back of these mammy wagons; there were so many different types, Hausa, Beri-Beri, Ruling Fulani, and Southerners, Ibos, Yoruba and more.

At Malin Fashi, a little village, it was market day. Here I saw the local cattle, Fulani and their owners. Strange people with their waist cloth caught up between their legs to form a tight pair of trousers. They wear little caps like Spanish matadors and carry swords which are usually carried slung by a loop over their shoulder with the hilt downwards. Their features are finer – different from the other Africans. Two of them boarded the truck and travelled some distance.

It was about 8 p.m. when the truck arrived in Funtua. The street was dark except where there were fires burning or the open door of a shop. I passed the little police station and decided to seek shelter there. The office was filled with police men dressed in their tight trousers and loose fitting, thigh length blouses. The constables have a wide 'V' of light blue against the darker hue of the rest of the cloth, from the shoulder to the waist. For the N.C.O's the 'V' is of red cloth.

There was little of the fuss I expected. They received me as if it was a normal occurrence to have a European asking to spend the night in their station. A native in a 'riza' (a loose fitting garment worn over trousers) whom I learned was the N.C.O. in charge, but off duty, showed me to the end of the verandah where a pallet was laid on the floor for me. He brought his own primus stove for me to cook with and later, to my complete surprise, produced a small portable radio. This in a small town where I thought there were no Europeans. I tuned in to the BBC news and then heard the last ten minutes of the commentary on the Wolves-Spartak football match. It was a pleasant surprise, the Wolves beating the Russians by four goals to nil. Considering three of the goals were scored in the last five minutes, it could hardly have been more exciting. It was a pleasant nightcap.

The police were extremely helpful. They said they would instruct any passing truck to pick me up. I set out walking and sure enough, about an hour later, a truck loaded with passengers stopped and the driver said he had been told to convey me to Zaria. It was a very old vehicle and broke down several times within a few miles. At one of these halts a native-owned private car stopped and the owner offered to take me.

While driving along he asked if I knew where he could purchase a revolver – never mind about permits, etc. – because he carried large sums of cash, sometimes for business reasons. He was a timber contractor. It was almost impossible to obtain a permit to carry a firearm in Nigeria. I had to deposit mine with the police at Bompai before I left Kano.

At Zaria I was accosted by a man, Dick Bubb, who, after some conversation, invited me to his home to spend the rest of the day and the night. His wife was expecting a baby at any time, but they made me very welcome. They told two good stories of the stupid things the native servants do even after years of service. Once Mrs Bubb found the boy splitting firewood with the best carving knife and on another occasion another boy put her dirty tennis socks to soak in the filter for drinking water. Also, the servant of a friend of theirs, after finishing the floor, continued to polish the furniture with the red floor polish, spreading it liberally over the table, chairs and cabinet.

Kaduna is the administrative capital of Northern Nigeria. Soon after leaving Zaria I got a lift with a P.W.D. truck. Sitting up in the back I got in conversation with a road gang foreman. He spoke quite good English but tended to get his words mixed up.

"Where do you come from?"

"Port Harcourt."

"Do you prefer the north to the south?"

"No, but the wages here are more beautiful."

At Kaduna I went to an army camp and asked if I might stay there. They were very willing to help. I am staying in the Nigerian Regiment N.C.O.'s mess – how they drink these fellows!

Next day, I was stopped by an African Police Inspector who asked for my passport. A nuisance!

I was invited to lunch by an army couple at their married quarters. Lunch was supposed to be at 2 p.m. However, the afternoon session got under way, the women vying with the husbands in drinking, and so we sat down to a dried up lunch at 4.30 p.m. In the evening I went with them to tombola at another mess, but it wasn't pleasant seeing the married women drinking themselves stupid. They had to be helped out at 3 a.m.

I was back in Zaria again and had to get back to Funtua to get on the main road south. Before I left the army camp they were very generous with wangled kit. I had acquired a new bush hat and two great pairs of 'cobble-crushers' (boots!), also a cape groundsheet and some other odds and ends.

On the road again I got a lift back the 50 miles to Zaria with a mission doctor. I was back with Mr Bubb who had made a warm invitation that I stay with them again when I returned. It was very kind of them to have me at this time when Mrs Bubb was so near her time. I supposed Mr Bubb was glad of some male support!

It had to happen! The doctor had to be called at 3 a.m. for Mrs Bubb. I felt awkward at being there at such a time, but Mr Bubb insisted he was glad I was there so he had someone to talk to while he waited. Although the doctor said 10 a.m. for the event, it was now 9 p.m. and still nothing had happened. The waiting was very trying for all concerned. I went out for a walk round to lose myself for a while.

Mr Bubb was telling me of an awful local practice in childbirth. In many of the houses he had seen special beds made on raised mud platforms. These platforms were hollow. A fire was lit at the end of the bed which heated the whole place in the same way as a baker's oven. The pregnant woman was laid on top of this. The heat forced the birth, but some women got horrible burns in the process.

The baby was born at 5 a.m. this morning. I saw it at about 8 a.m., the newest baby I had ever seen. Mrs Bubb had a very bad time, but now she was fine and both were doing well. The baby was a boy, about 8 lbs and Mr Bubb was very proud.

I left at about 9 a.m. and walked a few miles, then got a lift with a radio engineer to the turn-off for Lagos. There was a notice on a board stuck in the road telling me the road was closed beyond Birnin Gwari. I hung about there most of the day. There is a Native Administration Office near the turn-off and presently I was joined by some more natives, the leader of whom, John Obagu, was a businessman.

He and his beliefs are worthy of a word. He was a true product of the modern Nigeria. He spoke good English, wore thick horn-rimmed spectacles, was loquacious and, like people with inferiority complexes, liked to touch on themes. He was on a tour of all Nigeria to look for new fields to expand his transport business and to date he owned ten trucks and one pickup van. It was the first time he had been to Northern Nigeria and regarded it almost as a foreign country.

I turned the conversation to religion and the subject of Juju (witchcraft), and I got a shock. This man, who seemed so near to being a European, firmly believed in the tribal witch doctor.

"My own cousin can change himself into a leopard. Once, while at my house, he went behind a bush and a few seconds later a full-grown leopard jumped out at me. I was very afraid and covered my face with my hands, expecting to feel its teeth biting me. But the growling stopped and I opened my eyes. But there was no leopard. There was only my cousin standing laughing at me."

I think this is a good example of the fact that no matter how fast we push our civilisation on these people and no matter how westernised they seem, underneath, very near the surface, is a primitive African. It will be many generations before education changes their beliefs.

Later in the day a District Officer, on a visit to the Native Administration Office, saw me and asked my business. He invited me to his place for the evening. He is very busy. The new elections are using up all these Administration Officers' time. He firmly believes that they are not ready for elections yet, and that London is pushing them far too fast.

It was very unlikely anything was going down the new road, but I felt I had to go back to Kaduna to check. However, the District Officer arranged with a colleague of his, who was going to Zaria, to take me along as the Resident was due to visit his part of the country that day.

I arrived in Zaria about noon. The person I travelled with was a naturalised Pole who was the Co-Operative Officer for this region. His job was to organise the local business men and farmers into cooperatives to protect them against speculation sharks. His conversation was interesting and I learned a few ins and outs of the commercial world as it is in Nigeria. I learned that the shop traders, mostly Syrians, made as much as £8 extra profit on a £15 bicycle if it was sold on the instalment scheme, which most of them were.

While walking through Zaria I was stopped by a plain clothed native policeman and asked to produce my passport for examination. That is the second time. The last time was when I was leaving Kaduna. This time I was very irritated at having to undo all my kit. The policeman, or detective, seemed almost afraid to look at it by the time I found it, airing my views of him as I raked inside my bundle. I think he regretted having stopped me!

I had to walk a couple of miles beyond Zaria before I got a lift in an army truck going to Kaduna.

Outside Zaria on the way to Kaduna were great pinnacle boulders as big as six-storey blocks of flats. Some were perched precariously on a mere point or corner, and others were built up on one another in queer balancing acts of nature. They reminded me of Southern Rhodesia just outside Salisbury.

I had decided the best way was to take a third-class ticket – unheard of by Europeans in Nigeria – to Minna, about 100 miles away, which would take me past the break in the road. I hated the idea of going by rail. But I didn't have time to walk this bit if I was to get back to Kano by Christmas. I walked out to the station, about three miles, and learned the train was not due till 11 p.m. It was then about 3 p.m. I decided to look up Dick Scruby,

Andrew's friend. I went back into town and, after some difficulty, at 5 p.m. I located his house. He made me very welcome.

We were driving round town when Dick saw a friend, an army officer and his wife. He stopped to talk and of all the luck he told him that in the morning there was an army truck leaving to go right to Lagos. What a pinch! Saved by the bell from going by train! We went along and saw the N.C.O. who was going with the truck and it was arranged he would pick me up outside Kaduna. It seemed the new road was open now. That night I stayed with Dick.

In the morning at about 9.30 the truck picked me up out on the aerodrome road. It was a great ten-ton breakdown wagon that was going to Lagos to be written off. In charge was Sergeant Harry Sachse, a big, portly cockney in his forties. The 70 miles of new road cut across dry bush country to the Funtua to Zunguru road: no natives lived there; there was no water, just dry, dusty grass and trees. Once on the main road we passed an occasional village.

We camped in Mariga, a little village by the side of the river of that name. I had a dip when we arrived to get cooled off. Travelling up on the back of the truck there was no canopy so, between the sun and dry wind caused by the motion, I felt dehydrated. The natives here were not so hospitable as in other parts of Africa. They seemed quite apathetic towards us, whereas in East Africa we would have been welcomed by the headman.

We breakfasted early. I had a large, flattish pan made at the Trade Centre in Kano. It was my washing bowl. My billy can was my shaving mug, cooking pot, frying pan and plate. Off at about 7.30 a.m. we reached Kotongoro two hours later: a fairish-sized town with a mediocre market. After that, the hundred mile stretch to Jebba!

We crossed the Niger at 5 p.m. It was an impressive bridge that spanned that great river, really two bridges with an island in between. The approaches to the bridges were deplorable, narrow and steep and really dangerous. On the eastern bank one got a most impressive view of a jammed, huddled mass of conical thatched roofs; on the western bank, a horrible collection of rusted corrugated iron. The African private travelling on the back with me said, "These people don't know how to build. If there was a fire it could never be stopped." They are learning! He comes from near the Cameroons. The truck had been parked in the railway station. We slept beside it, of course.

In the nude as usual, I had a dip in the river while half the population looked on. I got eaten alive by little fish. They kept nibbling at my feet as soon as I stood still. All along both sides of the streets were stalls with women selling oranges, bananas and bread. Their bread is made with sugar instead of salt. The natives like the sweetness and usually eat it dry.

Continuing on, I thought that day the most interesting of this journey. Nigeria was divided into three provinces – you could almost call them states, for they were completely different units, each with its own governor. Kaduna is the administrative capital of Northern Nigeria; Enugu, the capital for the east; and Ibadan for the west, with Lagos as the Federal capital. Going south, Ilorin is the border of north and east. But it is more than just a division on the map. It is a natural border.

As soon as you pass Ilorin, the country changes: it is more lush and green, with the road winding between palm trees. The dryness is gone from the air. Rain is more frequent. The countryside had just been laundered by a shower and after the dry dusty north, it looked as green and crisp as fresh lettuce.

The people are different too: shorter and stockier. Also at Ilorin was the start of the tarmac road, tarred all the way to Lagos. A hundred miles south of Ilorin is Ibadan, the town with the third largest native population in all of Africa, after Cairo and Johannesburg respectively.

After Ilorin the villages came quicker compared to the long empty expanses of the north. The villages were mere semi-circular groves where the bush receded from the road for a few yards. As a warning, notice boards herald a village and before you approached each one, a notice tells you to "Go Slow through LADIKUN" or "Go Slow through ONDUNDU" or "ILE-ABU" and so on. Travelling at 25–30 miles per hour it would take perhaps five seconds to pass through. We stayed at Ibadan that night at the barracks and arrived in Lagos about noon. I was welcomed at the R.E.M.E. NCO's mess and stayed there.

Greater Lagos covered quite an extensive area. The barracks were in Yabba suburb, about four miles from the city. It was all built up. Lagos city is actually on an island, connected to the mainland by the Carter Bridge. There was a social dance in the mess put on by the married lads and I and the partner I danced with won the statue waltz. The prize for me was a car key ring with a miniature dummy attached. All I needed now was a car to attach to it!

I went and collected my camera from Mrs McNab. I thanked her for her kindness in bringing it from Scotland and was pleased to hear that she had not had to pay Customs on it. It was a fine camera and I was so pleased to have one again. Being without one had been like being without a right arm.

I moved from the barracks next day to stay in Apapa and spent a hectic day in Lagos city. Today I saw the sea again for the first time since Cape Town. There was so much to do while I was there. My visitors pass had to be extended; I must apply for a visa for the Sahara and scout around for odds and ends I wanted to buy. This was the last real shopping centre I would see until I reached North Africa.

Lagos was an awful place. I had never seen a place where mass hysteria reigned so mightily, and I had seen Cairo! The traffic was the most unpredictable, the most impatient, the maddest and the most dangerous mass of moving metal I had experienced – from a pedestrian's point of view. Shop assistants were apathetic or just plain rude to customers. The clerk in the French consulate who dealt with me was the most dumb and insolent man I had met. Even in the city centre the sidewalks were cluttered up with junk heaps of rusted corrugated iron that passed as fruit or haberdashery stalls and looked as beautiful as open, festering sores.

Few, if any, of the narrow streets had pavements. Traders cluttered up the edges with their stalls and motor cars hurtled through the traffic lane left with complete disregard for life. The past couple of days had been quite hectic. I seemed to have been going all out the whole time. I now had my visitors pass extended till 15th January. The French visa for the Sahara had been applied for at Dalcar through their Consul here. I hoped to get the reply at Kano soon.

I bought lots of odds and ends I would be needing on the journey ahead and spent much more than I should have. But this was the last opportunity before getting to North Africa and then I would be in French territory so the prices would be high. I enjoyed the cafeteria in the Kingsway, the largest department store in Nigeria and later had coffee in the closed-in courtyard of a hotel "The Bristol" – where the waiter tried to charge 2s6d when the price was really 6d – he chose the wrong man!

I bought myself a cheap, extremely portable, flash unit for the camera. Though expensive for me at the time, I would be able to capture images of the life I had hitherto missed and after all, most of the atmosphere, the life in the city, happened at night. Wild dances, the tinker trader huddled over a tray of kola nuts by a tiny flame lamp, tea by open fires, streets animated as they never were during the hours of daylight and heat. Now maybe some of that was in my grasp.

I planned to leave Lagos next day and was on the road early, but it took some time to get out of Lagos, or Greater Lagos. As I walked, I thought of conversations, information I'd been given by the people I had stayed with who have been in the country working for some time. I think all of this is worthy of note.

At the dinner table with Mr and Mrs Bubb and friends of theirs, including the Education Officer and the Trade Instructor, the debate was heated and divided. The Education Officer felt that the dominance of strict, inflexible religious practices was holding progress and development back.

This was contradicted by the Trade Instructor, who countered that it was wrong to try to change a people's religion and with what justification? Besides, he argued, the same could be said about some of the Christian missionaries in Africa.

My observations as I travelled through Nigeria were these. Nigeria is made up of three provinces or states. The north and south were as extreme as any two foreign countries could be: climate, people, religion, history, social outlook, mode of life, customs. While the south was still pagan and savage, the north had a civilisation of books and culture for hundreds of years. Their civilization was Islam and didn't run along lines like ours.

Then the British came. The Christian missionaries were rejected in the Muslim north so they concentrated on the south. The southerners were bulldozed into western ways and Christianity, but the northerners were lazy. They hadn't the drive, the initiative, the southerner had learned from the European.

But to me the northerner was the better type, a deeper, steadier type as far removed from the savage as many European people. I saw the southerner as a better worker, more business-minded, nearer to our ways, but he was shallow – just a thin fifty-year veneer of western civilisation over the barbarity and superstition that could or would break through at any time.

I had never seen a country so politically minded as Nigeria: this mad rush for government, these high-pressure politics, the puffed-up, self-important politicians. Then in Nigeria the natives had become so self-important they would not hesitate to take anybody to court who even swears at them. One man I knew was taken to court by an ex-employee, whom he had sacked, charged with calling him a 'lazy bastard'. Oddly enough, although he had called him this many times, this particular time he hadn't said a word, but plenty of the natives were willing to swear they had heard him say so. The judge threw out the case, but it cost the company £10 for lawyers' expenses.

***

Out in the open I got a lift with a European textile traveller to Abeokuta. I was dropped off at the bridge. On the bridge was a hold-up. There were two men with a bullock. The bullock had decided it had had enough and just stood without moving. One man had a rope round the animal's neck; the other man had a rope round one hind leg. When the man pulled in front and the bullock tried to charge him, the man behind pulled on its leg. When the bullock tried to turn round on the man behind, the man in front pulled on his rope, a kind of tug-o-war ensued between the two men with the bullock in the middle. They were still there with an irate line of traffic on either side waiting to cross when I left.

Abeokuta is built on a series of hills. A narrow street threaded rows of rusted, corrugated-iron shops. In places, there was no room to walk while a motor passed. I was hot with climbing the hills and sat at an orange stall and ate three or four (4 for 3d). I was feeling hot and sweaty and my back was uncomfortable. The pack I had been given, after I lost my own in the river, was not very good. The army valise was too small and I had an extra roll with my sleeping bag on top, which made it top heavy and pulled it away from my back. I was wishing the new rucksack from Blacks would come soon. I missed my kilt too.

I was a few miles outside Abeokuta, when a mammy wagon stopped. When I said I couldn't pay, they said it was alright and I climbed up the back and wedged a space in the sardine-tin crowd. My companions were a heterogeneous crowd: on my left was a bespectacled native whose thick lips hung open as loose as the end of an empty sack, on my right was a man in the traditional dress of the Yoruba tribe.

I got talking to them and got on the subject of Juju. Funnily enough they opened to it and chatted away. Then one man at my back broke into the conversation when the other had been explaining one point in the belief. This man stated the other was wrong. He knew, he said, because he was a Juju priest. Only then did I notice the coral necklace he wore, the rank of office.

The conversation went on till we arrived at Ibadan. No doubt the priest could not remain aloof any longer and had to submit to the opportunity of being the authority on the subject in question. At one village we stopped at, the other passengers brought me some yams fried in palm oil, and bananas. They refused payment saying I was their guest. Yams are 1d a slice, bananas 4-5 pence.

I arrived in Ibadan and got straight on the road for the Yoruba city of Ife (pronounced *ee-fay*). I soon got another lift from an African of the agricultural department. The lorry was loaded with fowls in hutches going to the government farm at Akule. The driver chatted away about the farm and how it was run.

***

At Ife I walked round until I found the government rest house. These were good places, providing a furnished house for the charge of 6d per night. A caretaker was there to provide water and firewood. You had to provide bedding and all cooking utensils, etc. I wanted to see the Ife bronzes. Ife was steeped in Juju. Here in Ife was a mystery: who made the Ife masks?

I went along to the local museum where the bronze heads are. There are seventeen of the known twenty Ife bronzes there. These are bronze effigies of the heads of past Obas and gods. One of the heads, Olokun, is used as an insignia on the 6d stamp in Nigeria. Olokun is usually the god of the sea, but in Ife mythology is the wife of Odudua, the creator or father of the Ife and also the Yoruba tribe.

Ife legend has it that Odudua descended from heaven by means of a long, long chain. At that time all the world was covered with water. He brought with him a chicken and a calabash full of sand. The fowl scratched in the calabash and scattered the sand over the water which became dry land. The children of Odudua subsequently went out from Ife and founded the various Yoruba kingdoms.

So the beliefs are that Ife is the cradle of the Yoruba tribe and Odudua was the first Oni, or king.

But to get back to the bronze masks or heads. Nineteen of these bronzes were discovered in 1939 when excavations were going on for the foundations of the new Afin, or palace. The twentieth one had always been in possession of the Oba. These masks are accepted as masterpieces of art. The masks are hollow shells, the bronze at no place more than an eighth of an inch thick. Some, like Olukun, the one of the stamp, have no top to the head. Others have holes round the mouth and it is thought these could have been to fix hair for beards.

There is nothing crude about these masks as in most other African art. These are fine and the features are perfect. Had Ife had a lost civilization of people so accomplished as to produce these fine works of art? Who were the original Ife people? Local history says a light-skinned people came from southern Egypt about 600-1200 AD and settled in this part. Were they the first of the Ife tribe? Were their descendants the people who made the masks?

Yet there is no trace of a lengthy development, nothing to show a gradual rise in standard until perfection. No, suddenly they are there, perfect, nothing after, for the art has been lost now. It has been thought that perhaps the art was learned from the Portuguese. But in Benin they say they learned the art of bronze casting from Ife hundreds of years before even the earliest Portuguese penetrated into the country.

All the bronzes found are in perfect condition. One is Oluwo, a queen who ruled with a very stern and cruel hand. It was she who introduced the pattern known as 'Luwo' in making roads. This is created by small flat stones placed on edge, forming a series of fan shapes which is very decorative. Also in the museum are many terracotta heads and fragments of what must have been whole statues of people, all very finely made.

The museum was small and not officially open. I obtained Christopher Abebourale, a nephew of the Oni (King) of Ife, as a guide. At the museum we found the native curator. He pulled on his trousers before showing us round, but I was disappointed because I was not allowed to take any photographs of the bronzes.

Also in Ife was a tall monolith, about 20 feet tall, which was called 'Oranmiyan' – walking stick. Oranmiyan went from Ife to be the first Oba of Benin. Benin, in search of a leader, had asked Odudua, the Oba of Ife, to send someone to rule them. Odudua first sent seven lice to the chiefs of Benin to be cared for and returned to him in three years, before he would consider sending them a ruler. The lice were returned in the prescribed time to Odudua and they were bigger and fatter than when they had been sent. He then said, "The people who can look after such minute pests could surely take care of my son."

So Oranmiyan, his son, left Ife and became the first Oba of Benin. Oranmiyan had a son and later left him to be Oba in his place and Oranmiyan returned to Ife. When he returned he stuck his staff in the ground and there it stands to this day, turned to stone. Copper rivets have been hammered into it in lines in the shape of a trident. These, the story goes, were put in when it was wood.

This stone was reputed to have great Juju powers. It was believed that great evils would befall the city if the stone falls, and if it does then it must be women who erect it again.

Later in the day while sitting in the C.M.S. bookshop, I asked some people about Juju. They were not of Ife but called in a local man. When I asked about the subject he became very cagey and said he must see someone at the Afin (palace) before he could answer any questions. We went off together and he consulted one of the court messengers and was given answers, at least to some of my questions. Incidentally, these court messengers have a special hairstyle to signify their post. Half their head is shaven, leaving the other half still thick and woolly.

After some time my guide said he could show me the place of the spirit of Odudua, but no man could see the place because it was guarded by a swarm of bees which would sting the eyes of anyone who came near and great evil would befall them. I said I would like to try and he agreed to show me but would not go near.

We walked through the town. One big, double-storey house I saw on the way had a number and letter '£4,000', worked with a cement mould into the fence round the garden. Also, in the cemeteries on the headstones under the engraving was inscribed "This grave cost £…" and a figure quoted.

My guide took me to see Chief James Olusinmi, a Juju priest, the representative of Odudua and guardian of the spirit. At his house, a crowd of women were singing over a great calabash of beer. Chief Olusinmi explained that someone had died and the women mourners were feasting. He waved us inside because it was difficult to hear one another speak above the noise.

The house was like most of the type common in Ife. The rooms were built in the form of a rectangle with a courtyard in the middle. In this courtyard was an oblong pit about a foot deep with a hole for drainage. The courtyard was roofed over except for a square opening in the tin above the pit. The Chief regarded me with obvious suspicion and hedged when I asked any questions regarding Juju and about Odudua in particular. He would not give my guide permission to show me the place of the spirit, but gradually he did melt a bit and showed me the Juju altar with the staff leaning against the wall, which was in memory of the first Oba.

Then he showed me a stone in the pit. It was about two feet six long and 18 inches across and roughly 6 inches thick. One face had been rubbed smooth. This, said the Keeper of the Spirit, was the pebble Odudua carried around in his pocket to sharpen his razor. Outside he showed me what was Odudua's shield. This was a high slab of rock jutting from the ground. The exposed part was more than six feet long and about three feet wide, and one foot thick.

So much for the Juju Priest, the Keeper of the Spirit of Odudua, the father of the Yoruba tribe! I left the place with the crowd of women doing a special dance in my honour in the hope of getting 'dash'. But, before I left, I visited the courtroom. This was a great hall with raised dais, where the Oba sits on a high-backed carved chair. The doors were heavy ones, deeply carved showing hieroglyphic figures and objects. Carved totem poles stood all over the place. They portrayed grotesque figures in peace and war. Some were copies of old designs, Portuguese soldiers in ancient dress with rifles and pistols.

On the floor was a chain which, I was told, was the original chain by which Odudua descended from heaven. Anyway, it was representative of it. During court, the chain is formed into a circle on the floor. When the plaintiff is required to plead, he must do so standing in the circle.

Another place of interest was a new entrance to the Afin. The gates had been newly carved. These were extremely thick and the carving very deep on both sides. The pictures on each panel seemed to tell a story, but the theme was hidden to my inexperienced eye. However, it seemed to tell something of the history of Ife, for in some the figures were dressed in old Portuguese uniforms and in another was a man on a bicycle. The carvings were quite good but very crude compared with the art in the museum. The gates were enclosed in a long, open hall, the roof supported by wooden pillars carved into totem poles, on which great heavy, grotesque figures and faces were depicted.

There were many market places in Ife. In all the markets of Southern Nigeria I found a new innovation to those found in the rest of Africa – namely the Juju stall. Here the medicine for the witchcraft was sold. To a layman's eye it consisted of heaps of rubbish – old bones, skulls, teeth, claws, skins, dried monkeys, dogs, snakes and cats and some bits of odd junk. I waited to have the stall holder tell me about it and learned that a person wishing to

274

possess the Juju magic would consult the local practitioner and the medic would prescribe the medicine required. The patient would then go to these chemists and buy the required ingredients which he took back to the witch doctor so that he might perform the magic.

There were dried snakes to be crushed to powder, which was strong Juju by which no snake will bite the owner. Claws, with the addition of the medic's mumbo-jumbo, were a talisman against wild animals, the owner of which would never be attacked should he be going on a trek through the bush. The stiff carcass of a cat was used to provide Juju so that a man might never be thrown by any assailant, for the cat possessed the power always to land on its feet.

I saw and photographed a team of wandering drummers in town and their drums were the shape of an hour glass. Skin, or hide, is stretched tight by raw hide thongs attached to both ends. The drum is held under one arm and beaten with a small, bent stick. I believe there are three tones in this drum language compared to two in the Congo. The pitches of the notes are varied by the drummer squeezing the strings with his elbow, thus changing the tension of the skins.

As I was writing in the rest house high up on the hill, the rumble of drums being beaten in the town rolled up from the valley. I wondered what they were saying. The drums speak here in this part of Africa. The talking drums here were small, portable things and did not have the range of the drums in the Congo. While in the Congo I met an Englishman, a Dr Carrington, who had made a study of the African drum languages. He recounted an incident when his and his wife's knowledge had come in very useful. They were in a hotel and his wife had gone ahead of him to their room. He had been out in the evening and came back late to find the room had been changed. He set out along the corridor whistling in drum language, "Where are you, where are you?" Thankfully, the answer finally came, also in drum language, "In here, in here".

***

It was very late, almost noon, when I left Ife. I had a walk round about again, as I wanted to have another look at the Juju stalls and chat to the sellers.

I got a lift to Ilesha then walked all day. I spread my sleeping bag under a tree by the side of the road and my thoughts went over the events of the day. Before leaving Ife, I had walked round, stopping here and there asking about this and that, when a boy asked if I would like to see a Juju shrine. He took me into a compound and there, covered by a crude shelter, was what I thought was an ant heap about five feet high. But then I saw that it was apparently hollow and had a wooden lid, the shape of a basin, on top. This was their idol. Into it was put the blood of the sacrifices, chicken, goats, etc. and the bowl was for catching the blood. The boy who took me was a Christian, he said, but he went almost pink with fright when I made to lift the lid to look inside. He said a sacrifice had to be made first before it was opened. I also saw natives spinning their thread from cotton in their own crude way, and weaving the narrow cloths seen in this part of the country.

I woke with the sleeping bag sodden by a heavy mist. It was hardly light, but the wetness made me uncomfortable and I was glad to be up and walking. The mist was thick and heavy and seemed to hang on me like a cloak. It stayed long into the forenoon.

In this part of the country there is the curse of midges. They were worse than any slave driver could be for they forced you to go on walking, even though you longed to sit down for a rest. Sit, and in a second you were tearing at the lumps they raised on your legs and arms.

I came to a village where, beside a big fire with a pot on it, a woman was pounding yams. I joined her and brewed myself some tea on her fire and sat by it sipping it from my blackened billy can.

On the road again I was soon picked up by an African driving an open truck. This man was a demon at the wheel – Toad of "Wind in the Willows", had nothing on him. On a road which under the best conditions was not made for speed, in one frightful hour we sliced 50 miles off the journey in almost solid mist. The driver seemed oblivious to the screaming of the tyres as the truck swung round whiplash bends, blind jack-knifed corners and shot out of the mist, while I prayed silently that no other vehicle would meet us coming the other way as we screwed round them. I held my breath when he aimed the missile at razor-edge bridges and hurtled over them with bare inches to spare on either side. Sometimes, there was a bump at the beginning of the bridge, which threatened to pitch the truck over into the river. Luckily, on each flip, the truck touched down with a four-point landing and continued on course.

The climax came with a blowout in the right rear tyre. I couldn't bear to imagine the scene had it been a front tyre. The tyre was in tatters. There was no spare wheel, so I could do nothing to help. I gave my thanks and walked on. Later, I got a lift to Benin in a mammy wagon. I hunted round for a non-catering rest house, but there was none, only a catering one which, although cheap, was beyond my purse.

I saw the District Officer, Mr Mackay, in charge of the rest house to see if any arrangement could be made whereby I could stay at the rest house without buying meals. However, he said it was full anyway, but he and his wife invited me to stay with them for the time I was there – really decent of them. Both came from Perth and attended St. Andrew's University.

I packed a lot in the next day. There was something sinister about this town. Step into Benin and you glimpsed the black heart of Africa which remains the same as it was before the white man came. I had never seen so much witchcraft in all Africa as there was in Southern Nigeria and Benin was the worst I had witnessed.

The witchcraft and gross superstition which bubbled just under the surface of the rest of Africa and was usually visible under the transparent veneer of civilisation had broken through here in Nigeria and was plainly visible. The Oba of Benin was the first African ruler I had met who was a professed pagan. He worshipped the Juju gods, he was the High Priest and his Juju was the most powerful in the land.

I began the day by going along to the museum with Mac, the District Officer. He introduced me to Jacob V. Egharevba, the old African curator, a mine of information in local history and author of many books on Benin folklore. The old African was a grand character but was quite an egotist. Mac had advised me to oil the wheels with a 'dash' of 5/-, which I did. He rambled on about Benin's ancient history, too fast for me to digest it. It was obvious, or should I say he made it obvious, that he was well 'clued up' on the subject.

The bronze work of Benin was interesting. There were heads and scenes of Obas sitting in all their regalia. The work differs from the Ife masks in that Benin's was fiercer, heavier and more elaborate. The work in Ife was the Greek; in Benin it was the Roman. But, like Ife, the modern carving was vastly inferior to the ancient. The Oba told me it was because the carvers nowadays could not afford to take the time that their ancient colleagues did. In olden times, the carvers and moulders were kept by the state and months would go into one piece of work. But now the bronze and wood carvers must sell their goods to make a living, so commercially the art had been killed.

I visited one carving shop in a Benin street. Four men sat carving heads out of ebony. One man had made a head in four days. They were quite good as far as native art goes, but no better than I had seen turned out by Congolese, East African or Barotse tribes, whereas the ancient arts of Benin and of Ife especially, would have held their own in any part of the world.

Before leaving the museum, old Jacob brought the visitors book for me to sign. I wrote a short note on my views in the 'Remarks' column. I was surprised when the old man suddenly became quite cold after reading it, for my remarks had been entirely complimentary to the museum. When I asked more questions he hardly answered. Then he said, "You didn't mention anything about the curator." I said, "Oh sorry," and laughed it off. But still he remained distant. Finally he added, "There is still room at the last of the page to add a word of praise." Seeing he was going to close up like a clam, I added under my signature, "I am reminded by the curator to add that his services are entirely satisfactory and his knowledge of local history and folklore remarkable and in this I entirely agree with him."

That seemed to please him. I don't think he saw the humour in the remark. I arranged to come back later when he could show me some of the shrines in the private homes.

I had a walk round the town after that. At one place I visited a Juju shrine, an altar to the Spirit of Iron. The Ohon (priest) was there. He wore a cloak with pieces of metal, including pennies and halfpennies, sewn all over it. To the layman, the shrine looked like an old blacksmith's anvil piled high with scrap metal, but I was assured that whatever impressions I had, this was powerful magic; at least, through this the priest could speak to the god in question.

Outside the thatched shelter that housed this shrine was a clay image draped with grass. It was the idol of the ESU (the Devil). Sacrifices to it kept the evil spirits happy. Another shrine I saw had old knives, etc. leaning against the wall. This was a place of offerings to the departed warriors.

In the afternoon I went back to see the curator. He obtained a bicycle for me and we toured part of the town and visited several houses. Most of the houses are built in the same design as in Ife, with the rooms built in a rectangle enclosing a small courtyard. In the middle of the courtyard was a shallow square pit with a drain in one side. It was roofed over except for a hole above the pit. Most of them could not really be called 'courtyard', the area being about the same as a small room.

Most of these private shrines were simple, crude altars with plates and sticks and other odds and ends displayed. Most of them were idols to the departed spirit, but some were to other special gods – god of the sea, god of iron, god of water, god of the fields, etc. One place was a sort of recess with plates set into the mud-cement of the altar. But it was the floor that caught the eye. The whole place was laid with cowrie shells, embedded in the beaten mud, set in intricate designs. In some houses a chain was nailed to either door post and lay on the ground across the threshold. This was to bar the passage of any evil which may try to enter the house.

We returned to the museum whereupon the old man said, "People usually give me a good 'dash'". This after the 5/- of the morning! Perhaps I should have explained my situation, but when I made no move to give him more money he walked away and never listened to my spoken thanks. Egharevba was an intelligent man by any standard. He was a historian of no mean standing and could hold his own on local anthropology with any man.

From the museum I went over to the palace. I had made an appointment to see the Oba at 5.p.m. The palace was a rambling, mud building with a corrugated-iron roof. The Oba received me in the long narrow room he used as an office. As I entered he came from the far end to welcome me. We shook hands. He spoke good English. There were some natives sitting on the chairs arranged along the walls. Most of them left when I entered, but a few sat still like wallflowers at a dance.

I was shown to a seat by the desk. A servant brought an iced drink from the refrigerator. That was a contrast, for from the moment I entered the door, I had an uneasy feeling that I had stepped back into pre-British rule Africa – a land full of magic and evil spirits. As I sipped the refreshing drink I scanned the row of framed photographs on the wall. Some were of past kings, but most were of the present Oba in various fantastic, ceremonial dresses for Juju worship.

Akenzua II, the Oba, had ruled the Beninese since 1933. He was dressed in a long white gown and cap, which resembled clerical attire. This, I believe, is a very ancient dress of the Beninese and its origin may be from the Portuguese priests.

The first Christian missionary to visit Benin was John Alfonso D'Aveiro, a Portuguese Roman Catholic, at about the end of the fifteenth century. He returned about ten years later and persuaded the then Oba, Esigie, to be a Christian. The Oba sent an ambassador to the King of Portugal, asking him to send priests to teach him and his people the faith. By 1515 the missions were installed, for it is recorded that the European missionaries went with the King to a war at that date.

The mission made progress. But the climate was bad and owing to the frequent deaths amongst the priests, the European fathers were recalled and the mission was left in charge of Ohensa (native fathers). The Portuguese came to inspect the work every five to ten years. Under these conditions Christianity carried on for nearly two centuries. But by 1695, when two White Fathers came to inspect the mission, they found the Ohensa and all the other Christians had lapsed into idolatry and had converted the churches into Juju shrines, in which they made sacrifices. The emblems of Catholicism, the Rosary and Crucifix, may still be traced, with slight modifications, among the Juju paraphernalia. The long white cloak and mitre-type hat the Oba wears were also legacies from the bygone Christian era.

We chatted for some time about this and that. I remarked at the marked decline in the standard of workmanship of the Benin carvers and brass workers. I said I had visited the carvers in a shop this morning and although the carving was good, I felt it was in no way of the standard of the old carvings. The Oba said in the old days the carvers were maintained by the state and if they turned out faulty or inferior work they were punished. Now the state no longer provides for them so they have had to commercialise their industry. Because of the increased production necessary to bring in a liveable income, a lot of the art has been lost.

He told me about the Benin year. There are 13 months in an ordinary year and it is known as a female year, *UKPO NAMWEN*. But when the *OHEN UKPO* (year priest) predicts the coming year to be full of misfortunes which will befall the people, then that year is declared *UKPO NOWE* (male year) and it will be 14 months long. The *OHEN UKPO* of that time had predicted the great 1918 flu epidemic.

About this time there was a great shouting outside the door. A group of people were awaiting audience and, at the Oba's consent, they filed into the room. As each man entered, he went on his knees and putting his one clenched fist over the other, he raised them as if he were running his hand up a stick until it was over his head, saying as he did so 'dum'. The 'dum' is long drawn out, like 'dum-m-m-m-m' ending when his clenched fist was over his head. This was the royal salute.

When the crowd had settled down, a queer little man entered. I learned that it was he who had made the original shouting and warbling when the others had wanted to come in. This was the court jester. He wore a comical black hat and carried a long stick with a flat disc on the end like a bat. He stood in the centre of the floor and started a singing chant, twirling this long bat all the time and raising it up and down. The Oba explained he was singing praise and also news of the day from the city. If, by chance, the jester had heard someone speaking against the Oba or making fun of him, he, the jester, would repeat what he had heard and say the name of who said it, even though a crowd had gathered such as now, in their presence.

The jester's clowning antics over, the crowd got down to the business they had come for. One man spoke on their behalf. They were all from the Native Administration Office. They came to offer their thanks to the Oba for his guidance over the previous years. The spokesman said that previously the clerks, etc. had been on a much reduced wage standard, with various scales for the different peoples. But now there was no discrimination.

I was surprised that the whole thing was conducted in English. The orator spoke well and his speech was well composed.

When the office had been cleared again the Oba said he would show me the rest of his palace, whereupon two small boys, who had been squatting all the time on the floor, brought the King's sword so that we might proceed around the palace. These two little pages were the royal sword bearers. One was completely naked save for some anklets. The other wore a cloth round his middle. The sword they carried was made of brass and ornamented with engraved scrolls; it was broad and curved like a scimitar. It was the custom that wherever the Oba goes, this sword must accompany him.

The walls of the palace were of mud and very thick. The mud plaster on the interior was finished in a corrugated surface. Many of the rafters were carved with an intricate spiral design in patches. The roof was corrugated iron and very high. The doors were large and heavy and weighted by a chain with a heavy weight – odd pieces of scrap motor engines – attached from the wall above the door and hanging down behind it so that they were self-closing. The doors were hinged in a simple way, with a knob of wood projecting from the top corner of the door into a socket in the wall and a similar one at the bottom corner rests in the ground.

It was interesting and, in a way, eerie not to mention rather exciting, being led along the dark corridors and having the huge, creaking doors heaved open by servants whenever we approached.

The Oba showed me several of his Juju shrines. These included three main ones, one for each of the three societies in the royal household – *IWEB, IWEGUAE and IBIWE.* Only people who have been initiated into one of the societies can enter that part of the palace. Children and the uninitiated, if invited, could worship there also.

The Juju shrines or altars in the palace were similar to the ones in the Chiefs' houses but more elaborate, i.e. carved wooden heads, sticks and bells, etc. When he had showed me round, the Oba ordered the two little sword bearers to show me the Great Shrine of the departed Obas. He didn't accompany me.

The Great Shrine is situated some distance from the palace. One of the little boys brought a huge key and ran on ahead to open the gate. The key consisted of two pieces of bent iron rod, each over a foot long and joined by a short piece of chain. One piece of metal was pushed through a hole in the door and dangled on the inside until the hook on the end had engaged the bolt. All rather complicated and requiring not a little skill in fishing. I would reckon a novice would take quite a time to hook the bolt.

The Great Shrine was in a huge quadrangle surrounded by a high wall. Along the wall where the altar was, a corrugated-iron roof projected. I was greatly impressed by this huge altar. It comprised three piles of carved heads, bronze masks, cast bells, and carved elephant tusks. Along the back was one huge slab of wood carved in heavy relief. At the foot of the centre pile was a small stone trough. This was to catch the blood of the sacrificed animals which were ceremoniously slaughtered over the altar after which each article was touched with the blood. There were runs of blood down the side of the dais.

There were altars to *OSAONBUA,* the chief god. Offerings of white cockerels, pigeons, chalk and peeled wands, all made to this. Other altars were to *OLOKUN,* the great god of the sea, son of *OSAONBUA.* He was the god of good luck and weather and *OBEWEN,* wife of the earth and goddess of breeding.

In the old days, pre 1897, there were human sacrifices. At the ceremony the slave to be sacrificed was brought in. The Oba whispered a message in his ear which he, the slave, was to take to the dead Obas when he reached the other side, and then the slave's throat was cut. When the British punitive expedition stormed Benin in 1897, they arrived in the middle of one of these Juju ceremonies. Eye witnesses wrote of the bodies of sacrificed slaves hanging from almost every tree.

One last item of interest on the Yoruba tribe. It was the custom to bury the master of the house in his own house. They buried him two or three feet down in the middle of the floor of his living room or, as many of them preferred, across the threshold of the door.

The following morning I went along again to see the Oba as I wanted to take a photograph of him beside the Great Shrine. At first I thought he was going to refuse, but then he called his two little pages to bring the royal sword and we went over to the Shrine. Two Juju priests also accompanied us. They were Chief *EHONDO*, high priest responsible for killing the royal sacrifices, and Chief *OGIEMWENSE,* high priest of the medicine men.

Also this morning, the Oba showed me the anklets of coral beads he wore. These and the necklaces of the same were several hundred years old. I thanked the Oba for all the time he had given me and knowledge of the Juju customs and left to have a walk round the city. It was interesting to see a gang of prisoners cutting grass in the charge of a warden. Two of the prisoners were keeping time with long nails tinkling on glass bottles, while the others swiped away with their *langa-langas* to the rhythm. The tinkling bottles were very musical and demonstrated how much better these people worked when there was music or singing, or some other medium for keeping rhythm. The *langa-langa* was very like a scythe – a strip of flat metal bent and sharpened at the end to cut the grass. When I went over to photograph them they insisted on a 'dash' – money or cigarettes. The warden was quite indignant when I said prisoners were not supposed to have cigarettes or money.

CHAPTER 23

CHRISTMAS IS COMING

I left Benin in the morning. I was sorry to say goodbye to Ian and Isobel Mackay. There were a fine couple and had been very generous in giving me such hospitality.

Some way out of Benin I got a lift in a private car owned by an African who stopped and asked if I wanted a lift. Looking inside, it seemed impossible that the car could accommodate me. The front seat had been pushed so far forward that the driver had to sit straight backed behind the wheel. This to allow space for three women, children (I didn't know how many) with cases and trunks and even some fowls in a basket. The native who was obviously in charge sat beside the driver with a bottle of beer and a glass in his hands. He insisted that he could still make room for me and my kit. He did!

I was surprised when he introduced himself. He was U.O. Ndem, Hon. Member of the Federal Government for Calabar. He was going to Enugu. I spent an interesting few hours with him until we reached Onitsha, a 90-mile journey. As we went he had great difficulty in drinking his beer without it slopping over.

Ndem was of the N.C.N.C. party (National Council of Nigeria and the Cameroons) which was quite pro-British. It was opposed to the Action Group which was very nationalistic and wanted all Europeans out of the country.

"We of the N.C.N.C. don't like this plan of the country being split into three regions and the Cameroons. If we get in with power we will do our best to abolish that and, instead, divide the country up into many little regions. As it is, each region is big enough to think independently and say 'to hell' with the rest of the country. In other words, we would have three states or countries. If the country were divided up into smaller groups, each would feel more dependent on the Federal Government and so they would hold together better as a country."

That was one of the points answered by Ndem. To my question, "Do you still want Europeans if you get self-government in 1956?" he said,

"When we started actively working for self-government about five years ago, we wanted rid of all Europeans. Then we expected the government to hinder our progress. We were very surprised when the British government not only agreed to our self-government but assisted us in every way. If anybody had prophesied then that such things as are in practice now could take place, we would have said they were silly. But now we have African Ministers of State who have European secretaries working for them. The white men do their work well and give every assistance necessary and pay their superiors due respect."

"So you will still want the Europeans to stay?"

"There will always be room for the right European in Nigeria. The white man who comes prepared to work for the good of the country will always be welcome. If he comes with ideas of lording it over the African, then he will be made to leave."

I got the impression that Ndem, like most other Africans, had got some inflated ideas about the Europeans working for Africans. Yes, at Kaduna or Ibadan and, I suppose, at Enugu too (the three Regional Government seats) and at Lagos (Federal Government there), there were the Europeans who acted as secretaries to the African ministers. They saw that everything was prepared for them, that the car had petrol etc., and addressed them as 'Sir'. No doubt the Africans and especially the Ministers, themselves, revelled in this new turn of events. But I wondered if the Ministers realised (I was sure all of them did) that without the European beside him, advising, pushing, showing by example, he would be lost.

It was so galling to see how these politics were disrupting the country. It crept into everything. Men, Africans, were appointed to posts for which they were totally unfit, simply because the country wants to see Africans there. "When the railway (now government) is changed to a Corporation," I was told by a senior railway official, "there will certainly be an African General Manager." In fact, I was not sure that they hadn't one already. He, this official, said there was no African in their employ who was fit for the post, but for political reasons the job would have to go to one. Without any previous experience on which to draw, I suppose this was only to be expected and therefore any judgement was to be tempered with this salient fact in mind. However, on a practical level, it did little to mitigate the feelings of frustration and resentment such appointments caused. That's how it was in every department. But, let's get back to the road!

***

At Asaba we came on the Niger. Here it is wide and majestic. We had to wait over an hour for the ferry. It was quite a big boat that ran back and forward.

Crossing the river, we passed the great sand bar in the middle where the old slave market used to be. In the exceptionally heavy rains it was covered over and had been covered this year. I paid 6d to cross on the boat.

Onitsha is on the opposite side of the Niger from Asaba. Now I entered the Western Region of Nigeria. The government seat was Enugu. On crossing the Niger, I also left the Yoroba and entered Ibo Land. I thanked Ndem and left him; I could have gone on to Enugu with him, but I wanted to have a look around here.

Onitsha is one of the oldest settlements in this part of the country. It was one of the first, if not the first, places where the European missionaries, I think, or maybe traders, settled when they came up the Niger. Its market was extensive and quite famous. To walk through the shouting, jostling crowds, sample the wares and smell the odours was quite an experience. Now in Ibo Land I could see the difference in the dress from the Yoruba. The Yoruba wear a dress like a smock, open down the sides, like the Hausa of the north, but not so long and less voluminous. They wear long trousers underneath this.

The Ibo had no special dress, but many wear the Yoruba style. Some are elaborately embroidered and are quite expensive. Walking down the street in Onitsha you saw places like the 'Hope Rising Mechanic' shop, and the 'God Given Bakery'. There were coffin makers busy planing and sawing with rows of their finished articles on show along the pavement, each decorated with fancy gilt ornaments, lightly tacked on so they could be removed before the coffin is buried. And the orange sellers, as in all Nigerian towns, with their fruit piled into a pyramid beside them. They sit and strip with a knife half the thickness of the peel. The Africans liked them like that so they could suck the juice.

Later, I went up to the rest house. It was a long pull up the hill and with the humidity my shirt was soaked with sweat. I saw the District Officer and got in, although it was full up so I slept on the sofa. Nobody was cooking so I had the kitchen to myself. In the evening the District Officer came along and asked if I'd like to join him and some friends whom he was visiting. I went along and spent a pleasant evening. There was a black District Officer, born and brought up in the U.K. Funny to hear him talk – a black man with the tongue of a European.

***

Next morning I got a lift to Enugu and the person driving was going back to Port Harcourt the next day, so I decided to go with him. It was away back the way, but it was a chance to see that port.

From Onitsha the road starts to climb. The vegetation grows thinner and thinner until you are rolling through undulating, open grassland with trees dotted here and there. Grand country, after the oppressive closeness of the south. It was dry too with very little humidity.

Enugu is impressive in its setting. The road climbs to the top of a ridge and at the first clearance you see the town nestled down in the bottom of a circular valley, 1,000 feet below, like a miniature in a saucer. To descend into the bowl you go down Millican's escarpment, a tortuous road cut into the face of the cliff. Blind bends, with scarcely room for two vehicles to pass and nothing to stop the outside one from going over the edge to an almost sheer drop of several hundred feet, made the journey impressive.

Arriving in the town I scouted around for a place to make camp. Finding no place suitable after rooting about the vicinity for a couple of hours, I decided on the railway station. I parked myself in the yard and, gathering some rubbish, I prepared to make a fire. The usual crowd had gathered round me. A native policeman came along to see what the commotion was about. His house was quite near and he asked if I would like to use his fire to cook on. I was grateful. At his house his wife brought fuel and water. I have spread my sleeping bag on the cement floor of his little verandah.

That night I slept without a net and was only wakened once with mosquitoes biting. In the forenoon I had a stroll round the market which was quite extensive.

The fellow with the car was ready to leave at noon. It was a little car, but we made the journey down to Port Harcourt in six hours. He only came out about six weeks ago and his conversation was interesting with all the latest news and trends from the U.K.

I met a very interesting, intelligent and also outspoken African. I was on the road again walking between Oturkpo and Makundi when a car stopped, a large American make. The owner was an African and he had an African chauffeur.

Down the winding road into the steamy lowlands again, through Onitsha once more. As in all Africa, cyclists made the roads dangerous. But here in Southern Nigeria there was an added liability ... the palm wine carriers.

The bicycles are festooned with calabashes of all sizes, draped round the handlebars or spindle projections at the hubs and in long wicker baskets that project on either side of the carrier. When a car passed they tended to wobble and their movements were entirely unpredictable. One capsized and sprawled across the road with gourds rolling hither and thither, almost on the bumper of the car. It was only the quick action of the driver who threw the car to the side of the road which averted a serious, if not fatal, accident, even though it was touch and go with the car in the skid that followed.

Near Aba we came on a crowd of people dressed in grass skirts and ornaments as for a Juju meeting. In the centre of the crowd was the Juju priest. Wearing a huge, hideous mask with long straw hanging from it which completely hid his body, he looked grotesque. I had great difficulty in photographing him and it was only when I got angry when one grabbed my arm that they yielded. They are so avaricious. It was not fear of the camera that made them unwilling, but they wanted 'dash', a fabulous amount (10/-), before they would allow their photos to be taken. For me, of course, that was out of the question. They said they were on their way to bury a man who had died. I got a good photograph in the end.

We arrived at Port Harcourt about six o'clock. I found a non-catering rest house and was staying there.

There was no colour bar in Nigeria. If there was then it worked in an opposite way to the other countries which were condemned for it. In the rest house there were three suites. I was in the centre one. On either side Africans occupied the accommodation. They rolled up in their cars and it was I who was in the lower living standard. In the hotels – I went to a couple for tea – you only saw the odd European. The hotels are all rather shabby in furnishings, but they serve their purpose.

The European commercial area (shops and offices of big companies) is over a mile from the town. It was a nuisance having to walk between them. Being Saturday, half-day, I was going flat out back and forward, getting some things I needed. It was hopeless to do everything in one area, then over into the town. I thought I'd do that, but got referred from one to the other for anything particular.

I had been looking forward to seeing the sea in Port Harcourt but, of course, it was well away from the open water, lying well up the delta. There was only the creek where ships went their way at high tide. I had a walk round about, but the tide being out, the place looked muddy and unattractive.

The climate down here was most trying with the area getting something like 300 inches of rain per year. That's some rain! The humidity was 100% and the sun was blanketed by a layer of thin cloud cast up with the constant evaporation and was just a dull glow. This lid of cloud shut in the land with its heavy, sultry, suffocating atmosphere. In this oven you slowly baked!

I left the rest house in the morning. It took me a long time to clear the city and suburbs. How I hate walking in these places. The crowds come to gaze and follow me as if I were some animal. I try to make myself oblivious to them, but when you are soaking with sweat and tired from the load, your nerves are more on edge. Hounded by the laughs, the jeers, the mocking of attracted crowds like a dancing bear, my temper worked up to seething pitch. Yet I don't know why. They had done nothing to me. I thought I'd grown immune to all that, although it was the same in the Congo. But these things seem to try me more. Maybe it's time I was back in the U.K. Four and a half years under these conditions are probably beginning to tell.

One man drew in to me, his bicycle broadside and stopped so that I almost stumbled.

"Hello, Johnnie," he said and I all but struck him. Pushing my face within inches of his I said through clenched teeth, "Where did you get the idea my name was Johnnie?" At the same time I grabbed his bicycle and threw it out of my way. A policeman was on the spot in an instant as if he had been waiting for just such a move.

"You must come to the police station," he said. My look to him must have been of forced tolerance as I stepped passed him to be on my way, eager to be away from the rabble.

"Don't bother me," I said. The policeman was insistent and stepped in front of me again. "You must come to see the Inspector," he ordered.

At that I blew up. I was in no mood to be played with. I threw my kit to the ground and exploded with, "You people are all the same. Give you a little bit of authority and it goes to your head. Listen! If your Inspector wants to see me then he will come here. I'll run about for no man." So saying, I sat on my bag.

"Go on, run along and bring him," I told the policeman.

Met with resistance his self-confidence flagged. He dithered, obviously at a loss. His arrogance fled from him.

"All right," he said meekly. "You can go on your way."

It was wrong of me to lose my temper and say what I did, but who could remain diplomatic under such conditions? If they would only leave me alone, my temper has been near the surface for some time now.

A little later a very breathless man ran up to me and said, "Excuse me, Sir". Angry at more interruptions but unable to throw his politeness back in his face, I stopped and waited for him to explain himself. He was the leader of the district ex-servicemen's league. He could not believe I was not in the army. Like all the others, they could not understand why anybody should walk and were convinced, even when I denied it, that I was in the army and on some kind of scheme. He said he had heard about the trouble with the man with the bicycle and the policeman and regretted it for the trouble it had caused me.

This keeping up of the ex-serviceman's spirit I found was very common in Nigeria. They seemed very proud to have been in the army. This man took me into the compound of another member of the league. A folding chair was provided for me and a basket of oranges brought and pressed on me. Later when a lorry came along they stopped it and persuaded the driver to give me a lift. I was most grateful.

Africa is a land of contrasts and Nigeria more so than any other country, I think. Primitive and modern, the sumptuously rich and the miserably poor, the healthy and the diseased, the kind and the cruel and many other opposites live cheek by jowl.

Thus, this kindness in the midst of the abuse … how can you judge a people one way or another? The longer I was in Africa I realised I knew less and less about it. How soon we form opinions when we come to a country! How stupid and how wrong. How harmful the fixed ideas we bring with us.

In the truck my shirt soon dried on me. It took me about halfway to Owerri, on the road now less frequented by traffic than the other but a longer way round by Aba.

The village we stopped at seemed almost too typically African to be real. Graceful palms lent over on curved trunks, shading the compound clearings. Stately women in floral dresses balanced calabashes on their heads as they walked. In a few compounds native women watched over huge bowls of palm nuts on a fire, boiling out the oil.

It was well into the afternoon so I prepared to stay in the village. Selecting a compound, I went up to the fire and dropped my load. My arrival, as usual, caused some excited chatter among the women and quiet speculation amongst the elderly men. No questions were asked. A chair was brought and, later, some oranges which they wanted me to buy. I refused them.

I was surprised when a motor came along and pleased when it stopped. It was a government truck. It took me the 30 miles into Owerri. Also, in the back of this small truck was an African, smartly dressed in an immaculate, but dusty suit and brown brogues and fancy stockings, he carried a briefcase. He was a barrister, he told me, returning to Owerri after the weekend in Port Harcourt. Now, we all know that briefcases and attaché cases are for the prime purpose of carrying a businessman's lunch, together with – that is, if there is room – a few papers or letters. This one looked odd with the neck of a beer bottle sticking out of the corner.

I didn't go into Owerri but dropped off at the turn-off for Onitsha and north, and walked on. I passed a stream where some Africans were washing. Like all the streams I've seen down here, the water is crystal clear, four or five feet deep and you could see pebbles on the bed.

Passing a huge building standing on its own like a misplaced block of flats, I was hailed by a Catholic priest. It was a mission school. After some conversation he invited me in for the night. It was very good of him. I had to acknowledge how lucky I was. Lucky this should be here, lucky the priest should be wandering about in the grounds saying his evening prayers.

It was a new building with hot and cold running water, carpets, easy chairs, a Frigidaire and flush lavatory. All modern conveniences and … the food was good. In the evening I went with four of the Fathers to a film show in the camp of Shell D'Arcy, the company which was prospecting for oil in this part a few miles away.

The following morning I got a lift into Onitsha in a mammy wagon. I'd walked a few miles before being picked up. That three-hour journey was one of the most uncomfortable journeys I've had in a motor. I would not have believed that people could be jammed in so tightly. The seats were along the walls and down the centre. We were sitting back to back in the centre with barely room to catch your spine on the edge of the seat. When more people crammed aboard loud shouts of indignation went up from the passengers. Surely it was impossible to get more on. Then the conductor would jam himself in between two tightly compressed people and wiggle his backside to force a space between them. He'd rise quickly and the newcomer would wedge himself into the place. The conductor would shoe-horn as many places as new passengers. I was most thankful to arrive.

The face of one of the passengers was horribly mutilated, criss-crossed into a chequered pattern with tribal scars. He was from the village of Umudioka, 12 miles from Onitsha. In this village, this was done to a man when he becomes an elder. A man with such a face was greatly respected by the younger villagers.

Walking through Onitsha I met a man I had met before and had lunch at his home. In the afternoon I got on the road to Enugu and soon got another truck going all the way there, a journey of over 100 miles that day. Arriving in Enugu and walking down the street, a European stopped his car and asked if he could help in any way. He could see by my garb I was tramping about. On hearing I was heading for the railway station to sleep, he insisted that I came home with him. He worked on the railway and he and his wife were a fine couple.

I was lucky enough to get a truck out to the Jos road. I had to walk a couple of hours then, but later got a lift from a Shell d'Arcy prospector up to his turn-off, near Oturkpo. It was dark and I decided just to sleep by the side of the road. I scraped around in the dark and collected some brushwood to make a fire. I was sitting beside my blaze with a meal half-cooked when a native truck came and stopped, surprised at finding me there. He agreed to take me into Oturkpo. Once there I made for the police post and asked to sleep there and made my bed down on the verandah. From there it was a striking scene, common in all these towns, with just the flares from the open lights of the vendors, the smoke from the fires and the evening crowds milling about.

I was on the road very early next morning and got a lift in a ramshackle old truck which broke down more often than I care to remember. I don't know which was worse – a long walk without a lift or a truck which continually broke down. It was going to a small market village. I carried on walking and after a while a private car came along. It was owned by an African who had a chauffeur. He was a trader on a large scale and his conversation was very interesting, even though at times not very agreeable. He talked about the difference between Africans and Europeans. He was more outspoken than most Africans you meet without being abusive like the agitators who are too outspoken. For my part I said little, content – no, eager – to hear his side of the business.

"You know, you Europeans were wrong right from the beginning. You tried to make us like yourselves. You sent your missionaries out to us. They came with fixed ideas. Because our way of worship did not conform with yours, they called us heathens and worse and did everything in their power to break up our religion. We did have a religion, we still have. We call it Juju as you will know. The missionaries didn't stop to learn our ways. They condemned us out of hand. How can you condemn a thing if you know little or nothing about it?"

"But you can't tell me that the practice of making human sacrifices is not an evil and hideous thing," I felt I had to put that in.

"Granted," he said. "But you know, you Christians also used to make human sacrifices. In the old testament of your Bible, we read of similar ways of worshipping."

"But that was thousands of years ago before Christ, therefore before Christianity," I said.

"Yes, but had you not stopped us from making these sacrifices, we would surely have come to learn it was wrong through time."

"But your idols, your clay images, your altars of rubbishy offerings to your many gods – do you believe that these are necessary?"

"No, I don't. But like everything else, religion or the way we worship needs time to advance, and in time these things will die away. You speak of our many gods. Well, you know, like the Christians we also have one Almighty God. He is the creator of all things, the giver of life. He was never worshipped with human sacrifices. All other gods we worship are lesser gods. Most of all, we worship past ancestors. Do you Christians not also believe in an afterlife? Then is it wrong for us to try to speak to our departed ones? The offerings or sacrifices we make at present will one day cease. Do not condemn our beliefs because of these trivialities. After all, in your churches you have wooden images of your Christ and clay models of your saints. You have rituals with candle burning and incense, are these things so different from ours?"

I wanted to tell him that what he spoke of was mostly Roman Catholicism, that in our Scottish churches we had few things of that sort and little paraphernalia. But I thought it was only hair-splitting, for we were speaking of Christianity in general and I had no desire to bring up our internal differences.

"As I said," he continued, "your missionaries set out on the wrong foot. Before they came they had already decided we were bad. We needed to be saved. Perhaps we did. But if, when they came, they had taken time to learn our ways first before denouncing them and doing everything they could to break up our social structure – for remember, our lives revolved round our religion – they may have done some good. Had they taken time, they may have seen that fundamentally our ways were not bad, that in our own way we had a religion. If they had taken that and built on it they may have been more successful. They could have still taught us to love and honour our neighbour, to give without expecting anything in return, to be good. Through that we would have learned that some of our customs were wrong, human sacrifice, for instance, and would have given them up instinctively. But no, the British wanted to do everything at once. They cut us off from our customs by law before we had time to realise why they were wrong. They humiliated us into being ashamed of what we were."

Again, I wanted to add that many Europeans are humiliated when they come face to face with the realisation of their past life, but held my tongue.

"The missionaries set about browbeating us into believing about the white man's god, the Christian God. They taught us to read so that we may be able to read The Book. They made us discontent.

"I went to a mission school. I grew up a Christian. I forsook my own people and their ways. I married my first wife by Christian ceremony. But I was wrong.

"I went to England. I go every three years for business and pleasure. The first time I went there I learned many things. Why did your missionaries not tell us that it is not your Bible which says you cannot have more than one wife? It does not."

I was ashamed of my ignorance. I could neither confirm nor deny this.

"It is your civil law that restricts a person's natural tendencies. That is what I find in England. I found all my teaching, all the rules I restricted myself to and had been unhappy with, were marriage laws, but inside your civil laws. Men had many wives and the women many husbands. Your civil law drives the people to make a mockery of your marriage ceremony.

"But that was not the only thing I found in Europe. Few, very few, live by any of the Christian ideas I had been taught. I came to realise there was something wrong where children could grow up without any code other than your civil law to live by. Now in the old days, our religious, social and moral laws were intermixed. No child grew up without a thorough knowledge of these and would not dare to break them. They respected them. Call it fear if you like, but with Christianity were we not taught to fear God also? But whereas Christianity fails to control a nation, our religion did, and controlled it very effectively … and without a police force. We had no need for police.

"Many, no, most Christian converts," he said 'converts' with an ironic smile, "have or are doing the same. As we Nigerians are coming more and more into our own, nearer to self-government, Christianity is declining. More than three quarters of the Christian converts revert, like myself, back to our own religion and ways."

I didn't know where he got his statistics or what they were based on, nor do I know if they were correct. I put this conversation down for what it is worth. I do not know if it is the general feeling abroad among the Africans, but somehow I believe it is. The theme of the conversation went more into a general strain then.

"Why do you to go Britain every three years?"

"I do some business, buying, mostly, and shipping the stuff out here. But I go for pleasure too. I find I can have a good time in Europe."

I had a feeling his "good time" was one of the European habits he had picked up and which was too good to lay aside like the others! Later he confirmed it. He got on about the different European characters.

"I find the Continentals, the French, Germans, Dutch and all are more realists than the British. The British are more idealists than the others, but sometimes this idealism takes the shape of pretence behind which they hide. For instance, in London a woman who is more than friendly in Hyde Park will not recognise you in the street. But on the Continent, if she knows you at night she will recognise you by day also."

I don't know if that was much of an example of idealism, but it made me mad.

"Mind you," he went on, "I admire the British dignity and diplomacy. In difficult situations that self-control will carry the day where, with others, the baser instincts may come to the fore and make a situation impossible."

At about this time the car was stopped by two native policemen who asked to see the driver's licence. As the one took the licence he had a better look inside at the occupants. Suddenly he pulled open the door and climbed in and abruptly ordered, "Take me to the police station."

We were just outside Makurdi then and in a few minutes we were outside the station. When the policemen got out he suddenly said, "I want the European."

"Me?" I said in amazement.

"I have orders to take you to the Commissioner of Police."

"But ..." I began to protest.

"You'd better go," said the African trader, eager no doubt to be rid of me if I were a criminal.

I was angry at being so rudely turfed out of this comfortable and interesting lift. But I could not fail to commend the policeman for his astuteness. First I gave him full marks for being so observant and recognising me. Then to grasp the situation so quickly and wait until we got to the police station in case I should make trouble.

I went in to see the Commissioner of Police, a European officer. I asked, rather abruptly I fear, if he had given orders for me to be brought in. He said he had. The police at Oturkpo had phoned through to say I had stayed the night there and gave my description. The Commissioner gave a general order to have me brought in should I be seen in the area. He no doubt thought I must be a Communist since I did not travel in luxury.

I was tired of being stopped and questioned as if I were a criminal and I'm afraid I was rather short. He asked for my passport so I fished it out. He asked me if I had had a meal, and I said I hadn't, which was true. He said he would phone up the Guest House and order a meal for me at his own expense. I thanked him but declined the offer. I wanted to stay independent. Being picked up and questioned made me feel a hobo and to have him offer me a meal made the feeling even greater.

I left then and walked through Makurdi and over the great bridge that spans the Benue river, then up the long hill at the other side. I bought paw-paw for a penny halfpenny and found a shady tree. I took off my shirt, which was saturated, and hung it up to dry. I enjoyed that paw-paw. It was really too much for one person, but it was the first I'd eaten all day.

However, as I sat there in the shade and thought about the incident and the Police Commissioner's kind thought that I might need a good meal, I regretted I had been so brusque. Perhaps he would have been pleased to hear a little of what I had been doing in Nigeria and the rest of Africa. Most District Commissioners, where I had to present myself, had not treated me like a hobo and had been interested to hear of my travels and of my plans to write a book one day with the aid of the diaries I have kept in the years I have been travelling. I thought, perhaps, I had been a little ungracious and was sorry.

I got a lift then with a Roman Catholic missionary for 30 miles. I continued walking when he left me at the turn-off.

I met an African hunting with a bow and arrow. He had something I hadn't seen before. I tried the bow and it had quite a hefty pull, but I was surprised to see he pulled it back between thumb and forefinger. Then I saw how he did it. He carried a small hunting knife with a metal handle in the shape of a loop. He inserted his fingers through this loop and held the metal on the inside of the bow string and pulled it back with that.

Further on I met another hunter carrying the unique throwing knife which I saw near Lake Chad. It was shaped like an "f". The arm was pointed and the inside of the curve was sharp. The idea is to lame the animal with it.

Later, I got a lift on a truck which took me into Lafia. It was dark when I arrived and I bought some tea in a native restaurant. The place smelled so badly, I went outside to drink it.

294

I walked about the street, down the rows of flares looking for bread, shouldering my way through the idlers. I got some and went along to the police station to sleep. But the African sergeant said he'd have to see the District Officer, which he did. The District Officer came down to see me. He was very surprised and said I must come to stay with him. I said I appreciated his offer but I didn't want him to feel he was under any obligation to put me up, but he insisted so I am at his house.

Next day I got a fine lift in another private car belonging to an African trader which took me over 100 miles to Bukuru.

After Karshi, the escarpment forms a wall which seems insurmountable. The road finds a way up and suddenly you were on the plateau 4,000 feet up. The change was quite dramatic and on the top it was wonderful. After the lowland and the south, it is like fairyland. Wide open orchard country with short grass and distant views. It was so dry and bracing with a breeze always blowing – it was wonderful. Up here you felt you were on top of the world.

At Bukuru I walked around for a bit, having a look at the tin mines. I made some tea by the side of the road and a car came along going into Jos. The road was tarmacked between the two towns for about ten miles and plenty of traffic used it. It was dark when I arrived and went along to the police station as usual. I slept on the floor of a room which seemed to be used as a first aid lecture room. There were no lights about and no place where I could cook. I was quite hungry not having had anything to eat since 7 a.m. Still, that's nothing unusual.

That night I slept in a native village. In Nigeria they called them 'pagan' villages. Actually it was not really a village – mainly one family and just three huts. Over on the other ridge there was another one.

I spent the day in Jos. Quite a biggish place and a good shopping centre. It must have had more Europeans in its vicinity due to the tin mines than any place in the north. At about 3 p.m. I collected my gear and headed out of town. It was grand walking up there on the plateau. You could walk all day and never sweat – so fresh and bracing.

I came on this village and wanted to take some photos, but they wanted money so, since it was getting on, I decided to camp there thinking perhaps in the morning, when they had got used to me, I would get my photos. It was strange. Up there where the climate was the coldest in Nigeria, the natives wore the least clothes. The women wear only bunches of leaves fore and aft, the young men wear a piece of rawhide around their middles. The old man here had a blanket.

Last night at that village I slept outside. They offered me a hut, but I declined. Outside it was bitterly cold, but dry. How different from the south where the nights are humid and sticky. Even on a verandah in the south, my sleeping bag was always damp in the morning. But last night was different. The stars overhead were crisp and bright, and the stream where I washed in the morning was icy cold and refreshing. After the south I relished the cold.

The natives had no wood for a fire. Last evening and early this morning when they arose, they made a fire from dried grass and the dried stocks of the guinea corn. I got my photos that morning before I left.

I walked most of the forenoon. At one place I passed what I thought looked like a European farm, although I knew that no European is allowed to farm here or any place else in Nigeria. I went in to have my water bottle filled. My surprise when I met the owner! He was a Fifer. He was in tin mining. Mr Haley was studying a sample in a test tube when I happened along. He explained some interesting facts about tin mining.

All over the plateau around Jos, apart from the big mining companies, hundreds of little 'one man' mines were being worked. Twenty-one years was the longest any European was granted for mining. But even this was very rare. Seven was the normal time allowed. At the end of the seventh year it was possible that it could be renewed. No European was allowed to farm on any piece of land leased. Thirty to forty pounds per acre was paid to the local farmer as compensation and all the pits had to be filled in and the land left as before when the time was up.

With all these restrictions and controls was it worth mining? For tin, perhaps not. But … With the tin was the mineral columbite. They used to throw it away as useless; then it was discovered that this mineral was the only metal to withstand the pressure of the jet engine propeller. It suddenly became of fabulous value. Miners went over their old slag heap reclaiming what they had recently discarded as useless. Tin took second place. It would be more proper to say the mines were now columbite mines, with tin as a bi-product. At present, columbite sells at £2,500 per ton. Of this the government claims £500. Tin draws a mere £500 per ton.

"Of course," said Mr Haley, "you have to shift a lot more earth to get a ton of columbite than you do to get a ton of tin. This year I have only collected seven tons of columbite."

Well, it didn't need a mathematician's brain to know he'd made £17,500 on columbite. Running costs were high, there was labour and a European manager and the land compensation. But supposing the running costs took all the profits of the tin, which I was sure it wouldn't, even £17,500 clear was a fair whack for a year!

With my bottle filled, I carried on walking. I got a short lift from a lands surveyor then walked on.

About noon I was picked up by the District Officer who was on tour. He invited me to lunch. He and his family were staying in a school. The school stood isolated on the moorland and served all the surrounding district. Later that afternoon, I walked further then had the good fortune to get a lift from a rather high official in the agricultural department, going all the way to Kaduna. It was so interesting meeting so many people of such varying professions and occupations.

We arrived at Kaduna at about 11 p.m. Mr Wilson – it was a double barrelled name but I didn't get the first part – invited me to stay the night in his home. I gratefully accepted. People are really kind! In future years I would have a lot of leeway to make up in the world in the kindness line, for all I had received in these years I had travelled.

Next day, in the forenoon, I got a lift from a Syrian to Zaria, 50 miles in 40 minutes! After Zaria, I got a lift from a botanist after I'd walked a mile to Funtua. It was almost dark by then and I was preparing to camp, but a car came along and stopped. It was a man going all the way to Kano, but I dropped off at Malin Fashi because I wanted to photograph the local cattle – Falaxi.

I was staying in an old disused rest house. There was not a particle of furniture in it. I could hear some rats running about. Since I'm sleeping on the floor, I hoped they wouldn't make any trouble.

The date was 20th December, 1954, and I was back again in Kano. Oh, but it was good to be back in the comfort of a regular home! Good to know I didn't need to move on the next day, nor the next, nor the next. Good to feel settled for a time. I arrived here after a series of lifts, mostly in mammy wagons.

So, I had made it in time for Christmas. I had tried hard to keep within time, and Andrew and Margaret made me feel very welcome. It was good to see them again and to hear that my replacement kit had arrived. I was thankful to receive it and how trusting it was of them to send it on a promise.

***

Kano, the walled city, on the fringe of the Sahara, like a great port on an ocean it stands, ageless, timeless. To enter one of its gates and wander through its streets is to walk back a thousand years. Yet, amidst the age old buildings were the modern innovations of telephone and electricity. In a land of contrasts, Kano took its place.

I set out to write a long essay on Kano, but I found it hard. I had been there too long; I should have done it when I first came, putting down everything I saw when it was all new. Now I had been there so long the sights were common place and it made heavy work of writing about everyday, commonplace things unless I was weaving fiction around it. I had to wait till I had left for time to lend Kano the enchantment to make me feel like writing about it.

All the things I knew were so romantic and picturesque, but how humdrum they were now: the crowded streets, the horsemen, gaily dressed in exotic robes embroidered with silver thread – silver beaten from Marie Theresa dollars brought back from Abyssinia by the pilgrims returning from Mecca; the people riding bullocks; the picturesque donkey drovers dressed in their high peaked conical straw hats; the men with the great straw bowlers that fit over a head cloth or turban; the vultures that line the walls – they were royal game, nobody could kill them – and who were the city's cleansing department for they kept the streets clear of waste. There were the dye pits most of which were over ten feet deep. They are handed down from father to son.

And the Emir and his palace with the chamber room decorated in Hausa art – a hotchpotch cross between Picasso and the immature scribbles of a child – painted in black and white with crushed mica mixed with the mud cement so that it sparkled like tinsel. In that council chamber was a huge and beautiful glass topped jukebox. Perhaps the Emir played it when his councillors' speeches got too long-winded.

There were the various sections in the old City inside the wall: land given to the Tuaregs; Sabon Gari – strangers' town – allotted to the foreigners, southerners mostly, who came in an influx since the British took over; and Tundan Wadi – the Place of the Rich Men – where the traders lived when they arrived too late at night after the gates had closed. Some of the original gates still existed and were closed at darkness. They were made of strips of metal riveted together.

In the streets you saw the veiled Tuaregs. I saw the Emir and his procession leaving court. His bodyguard, the Doggero, dressed in vivid red and green striped cloaks, the man with a ten feet long horn, blowing it to warn the people of the Emir's approach; the Emir's horse with fancy harness with silver trimming and inlaid saddle and coloured tassels.

There were the prison warders with their distinctive blue on white striped cloaks. The great pits in the city where they dug the clay to build the houses. The beggars – I had never seen so many and such horribly diseased and mutilated specimens, many of them came from professional begging families and were crippled or maimed at birth so their deformity might be part of their stock-in-trade. You couldn't go far before you were accosted with "Dash, Baturi – gimme dash".

There were the ground nut pyramids due to the railway's inability to cope with the export, each bag costing £1 and there were 30,000 to 40,000 bags to each pyramid. In Sabon Gari, the natives' liking for flowery language and slogans – there was the 'Live and Let live Hotel' and the herbalist shop called 'The University of the Invisibles'.

298

I put the notes down as they came into my head. There was no cohesion to them now, but I vowed to sort them out some time and add to them as I remembered them.

The police in Kano – no Kalsina province – complained about being issued with short trousers because they had to change into longs when they prayed. The great carts hauled by natives that menaced the streets of Kano and made traffic dangerous.

Antimony, looking like shiny lead, was selling in the market. They used it to make the black substance to put on their eyes.

To telephone in Nigeria was to bring on the first stages of insanity. The crippled beggars, wearing their begging bowls made from half a calabash as hats while they dragged their mutilated bodies along by their elbows, or on hands and knees. The Hausa salute – the right clenched fist held up with the thumb along the side of the forefinger and not across the knuckles. The greeting was "sanu", said with the fist held up.

All these things made Kano a magical place which would forever stand out in my memory.

***

At last, it wouldn't be long before I could be away. During the last month I had lived from day to day, waiting for my visa from Dakar, fretting all the while as the season for desert travel and my chances of finding camel caravans all the way across the Sahara whittled away. I wrote a reminder to Dakar and sent cables to the French Consul at Lagos, but nothing seemed to do any good in hurrying up the French authorities.

At last it came. Now I could get away by Monday. I had been a long time in Kano When I came back from the south I was bothered for weeks by fever, a slight but malignant dose of jaundice and stomach disorders. None of it was bad enough to put me to bed, although I had to fight to stay on my feet. I think it had been hanging on me for some time, perhaps months. Perhaps it was that which made me so ill-natured at times when in the south.

Now I was well again with my appetite back with a vengeance. Andrew and Margaret had made me so welcome and I enjoyed their home and hospitality, but I had been there too long. I was reasonably well equipped again and I loaded up with as much of everything as I could carry, because experience told me that things would be at least double the price in French territory.

It was not without apprehension that I started out on this lap of the journey, but I expected that would go as soon as I was on my way – like the tension one gets before a fight or as when a game begins then is lost as soon as the action starts. I was told by the Karouni Company that I could have a lift on one of their motors up to Zinder. They said there was one due to leave at anytime and that I should be ready to go. All day I had been on edge waiting for it but nothing up till now. Another day, Monday, passed and the message was that the truck would most likely leave the next day, but still no news. It seemed to be going to pass the same as the day before. It was late afternoon and still no word. Andrew and Margaret had gone into town. Then it came. The phone call said to be down in 15 minutes, the truck is leaving. That was at 4.30 p.m. and a friend, Sid Wren, offered me a lift to the truck depot. It was most unsatisfactory for it meant not seeing Andrew and Margaret to say goodbye. Still, I couldn't miss the truck. They would understand. By a stroke of luck Andrew decided to go up to Karouni's to see if there was any word of the truck leaving and it arrived at the same time as we did. But the panic was unnecessary. The truck was not leaving for another couple of hours! We went home and Andrew took me back at 7 p.m. It was a huge 10-ton truck with a trailer carrying steel girders, the overall length being more than 50 feet. It was having trouble with its lights and it was 8 p.m. before we left.

I felt strangely on my own when I wished Andrew goodbye and the truck pulled away. I don't know why this was, for this was just like any other parting on the journey. Perhaps it was that while in Nigeria, where English is spoken so freely and at the Trade Centre with so many Scots people and Andrew and Margaret coming from Kinross, I could lapse into old dialect, it was so easy. Local house names were in everyday use and the home papers, *The Peoples Journal*, *The Mail* and *The Post* all helped to make one feel as if home was just around the corner. Yes, who could imagine one was far away from the doorstep when you went up to the airport and wished so many people goodbye as they went off home, knowing they were only a couple of meals away from their firesides. You could even go up to the bookstall and buy yesterday's home daily papers.

And above all that, there was the comfort of the home, the things you began to take for granted and even grumble about like the 'boy' who was long bringing the potatoes or if the bath water was cold.

Yet why should I look to these things? I had them before and had been glad to be rid of them after a time. Maybe I had been away too long and it was time to go home.

CHAPTER 24

FRENCH OCCIDENTAL AFRICA
On The Road: Zinder and Tanout

Thursday 10th February, 1955.

The bucket seat I had in the truck was only bare metal and had no padding. The road is badly corrugated. In the headlights with the ridges casting shadows, the road seems like a long scrubbing board or a ploughed field and, after a day on that seat bumping over corrugated roads, one felt more than a little sore. Still, that was a minor detail, although I felt so stiff it was an effort to sit anywhere, but if I suffered no worse on the way I'd be very lucky.

It was quite cold when we left Kano and the cold grew more intense the further we got from the city. It was bright moonlight, but the wind blew and increased in volume as the temperature dropped. The trees thinned out and the grass gave way to sand. In the headlights sand powdered into mist and was swept in gusts.

About midnight, the driver stopped to sleep. The truck was loaded with bags of cement and I climbed up the back and unrolled my sleeping bag. I was glad to bury my head inside and let the wind and sand whistle over me.

The wind was still blowing when I awoke and we got on the move again at 7 a.m. The land was in monochrome – a grey, flat, drab colour. Between the few trees, the sand ruffled into wrinkles and was whipped away in clouds by each gust of wind. Natives here and there bent into or lent back on the force, their mouths covered by their head cloths, their rigas streaming out like thin curtains at a draughty window.

It was still early when we arrived at Daura on the Nigerian side of the border. The native policeman had a fire burning in the corner of his mud house and I was reluctant to leave its smoky warmth after he'd checked my passport. The mud house was the usual type with the mud buttresses running up the walls and over the ceiling in a thick arch.

It was a couple of hours before we left there. The next part of the road from Daura to Matameye – the first town inside the French Niger Colony – was dreadful. Along most of the 40 miles the road was a river over 18 inches deep in places, with high banks on either side. Rocks had been thrown in haphazardly to give it foundation and the vehicles a grip, which added to the realism of a rocky bed. It was swamp land and the waterway continued right into Matameye. There the Customs held up any advance for about three hours – a typical French easy-going attitude.

While waiting, I got my canteen and went into one of the grass mat-surrounded compounds. A woman was sieving meal. I pointed to the fire place and shook my pan. She sent a little girl to make up the fire and bring water and I made some tea. Outside in the compound, a good-looking horse was knee-haltered and in the cooking hut, a high-pummelled saddle lay with a pile of gaily coloured saddle blankets and flat stirrups.

It was about 4 p.m. before we got moving again. The driver stopped at Takieta and waited for hours. He seemed in no hurry. That was the worst of African drivers. Even the best of them would stop whenever he felt inclined and time meant nothing to them. It was too cold to wait outside so I hunched myself in the seat with my legs wound up over the engine and dozed, but I awoke sore and horribly stiff. At last we got going again. The narrow bucket seat was a torment. I had now been in it over twenty-four hours, except for the few hours' sleep in the back.

At last, Zinder! The wind had sprung up again or perhaps we'd just moved into it. I got up into the back of the truck, unrolled my sleeping bag and was into it in a flash. Alas, I was not allowed to remain. The policeman wanted to check my passport. No, he couldn't wait till morning. He had to see it and he wanted to get away home. The sand was cutting, the wind extra cold after the sleeping bag. The native policeman was in a mud hut. He wore a long blue cloak with a hood which came over his head. It seemed just the thing for the wind and the sand. The shelter shook and the wind howled as he bent over his lamp to examine my papers. I was soon back in the bag again and didn't bother to cook anything.

That was last night. This morning I saw the Commissaire du Police. He was a genial and friendly person. He couldn't speak any English and was highly amused when I said I wanted to join a caravan. To my delight and surprise I found no opposition to that idea. I had imagined all sorts of restrictions and controls in case I came to harm. In fact, it seemed ridiculously easy. The Commissaire said, through an interpreter, I should go down to the market and, if I got a caravan to Agades, I must come and inform him. No more than that. It was as if I was going for a bus! He asked if I would be leaving that day or the next.

I went down to the town. Zinder was a stirring place. In the streets were caravans of camels: the light skinned, veiled Tuaregs riding camels with their saddles with the high pummels in the shape of a cross. Were they really Christians? Are they really the descendants of the old Carthaginians – Hannibal's people – driven into the desert with the Arab conquest of North Africa, over a thousand years ago? Their slaves, or workers, the 'buzu' – the dark-skinned people seen in Kano – walked in front with the pack camels.

I couldn't find anyone who could speak English and was advised to see the manager of the bank. He said he would phone an Arab who was extremely wealthy and influential and a customer of the bank, and see what he could do for me. I had to go back in the afternoon.

Unfortunately, it turned out to be not as easy as I had been led to believe.

There were no caravans going to Agades. They wouldn't go until towards the end of the season in another month's time. At present they were all working south taking the ground nuts to Kano and would only return to Agades at the end of the season.

I could if I wished, he said, hire two camels and employ a Tuareg guide which would not be expensive and go that way. But my idea was to join a regular caravan and see how they lived.

I decided to see the wealthy native myself; Alhezi Muktar was his name. The bank manager had said he was a millionaire. I got instructions on how to find his house. It was down a narrow alleyway between mud houses, just wide enough to allow the passage of his large, Ford American car. That was his only show of wealth. He lived in the same austere way as any Hausa native who had taken Arab ways. He showed me into his house and then drove round to a friend of his who spoke English. You could see he was the local Tsar by the way everybody was so servile to him. At his friend's house, a chair was brought to him first – very unusual when a European is there – and a stool for me. Muktar remained standing until the stool was brought, then took it and offered me the chair.

I asked him about the salt caravans to Bilma, but they left from Agades so I must look there for them.

Did Muktar, the Millionaire, have trucks going to Agades? Yes. Four thousand francs (about £9.) Expensive? But no! I was a European. Why even a black man would have to pay 1,500 francs. Still, one must pay for the privilege of being white! Rather a discrepancy, I thought!

Back at the Commissariat de Police, where I had left my kit, the Commissaire agreed that I could cook and sleep in the backyard. Later, he invited me for supper. He even allowed me to use the kitchen, an awful, soot-encrusted mud hovel with one window. But wood was provided and that was something, since it was very scarce. He asked where I would sleep. I said under the tree. I had noticed it earlier and, in fact, it looked very inviting and fresh. But he showed me to a little room over in the workshops and said I could sleep there. It was an awful place, no window of course. It was a native style, mud building. I would much rather have been outside, but thought I had better accept since he had offered it.

The meal was very plain, but I was most thankful for it. The Commissaire said he would get me a free lift to Agades. I intended going there and then trying to get a caravan going up through the Hoggar Mountains.

It was the day of the big market so I went along to see it. The whole hill was black with people. Visibility was very low; there was so much sand in the air. It was remarkable how near things began to drift into the blue haze. The market was interesting in the amount of camels and horses, all decorated with fancy, colourful harnesses, which were tethered all over in any piece of shade there was, and even in the sun where the shade was overcrowded. But that day, the sun hadn't penetrated in force through this haze barrier.

I bought three small 10-franc loaves of bread for a Nigerian shilling, which was good value, then went to the local café and ordered a coffee – my usual feeler to the cost of living. They agreed to accept Nigerian currency. It cost 2/- for one cup, not a pot, just one cup. And that was reckoning a shilling at 30 francs. I would be lucky if I got 22 francs to the shilling when I came to change my travellers cheques. The bill was 60 francs. At the latter rate of exchange it would be almost 3/-. It was not very strong coffee either and only tepid. I reckoned it cost 6d a mouthful!

I visited the old fort; it was a real Foreign Legion affair. The original old turret was still there and the old gateway still in use.

In that old place I slept in, there was a hole in the floor. Thinking it was rats or mice I paid little attention to it and the corner of my sleeping bag actually covered it. I was sitting in the next door place where there was a lot of junk, but it was more open than the room. The Commissaire came in and told me not to stay there as, without a doubt, the hole in the floor of my room was a snake's. To think! I did not sleep in there again. I went to my tree where I had originally planned to take up my abode.

The truck for Agades was supposed to come today but didn't, and I had been hanging about all day. In Zinder one would know they were in French territory even if they were ignorant of the country. It was full of the angry-looking, military-type motor cars which the French seem to like so much, flying about at full speed, taking corners on the brakes as is the French style of driving. Gears are only there to help you to get up to top speed, and once there … hold it.

All the houses were flat-roofed, mud buildings, even the European one. I can't help thinking that, if this were a British colony, there would be better houses and the streets would be tarred. The French seem quite content to live in rather primitive conditions, whereas the British colonist sets out to make his living conditions as much like his home as possible. Which is better: the French free and easy way or the British? I haven't, or can't, make up my mind.

Sunday and, of course, no truck today. When I asked the Commissaire he shrugged his shoulders, his arms dangling with his hands open, fingers apart, the palms towards me, and his mouth drooping at the corners. A typical French way of expressing that they don't know anything. He speaks no English so I have little or no communication with him. Apart from the few words with the bank manager and Muktar the Millionaire, last Thursday, I hadn't spoken to anyone since leaving Kano. Anything I did have to say to the Commissaire or anyone else had to be said in my very, very limited French, aided by much gesticulation.

Yet I am not complaining. I'm beginning to find pleasure in being alone again. I've found my feet again. The little twinge of tension, the apprehension I felt on leaving Kano had gone, as I thought it would now that the 'fight' has begun. I felt complete master of my situation again … and to hell with tomorrow.

The lavatory. This was in a tumbledown mud hut with not enough headroom to stand up straight. One must move in and out like a half-shut knife, a posture which makes the arranging of one's dress rather difficult. The actual site was two raised bricks for each foot where one squats. There was no pan or hole, merely a hole in the wall at the back through which the boy pushed his shovel to remove the day's debris. There was no door and one could wave to the passers-by or pass the time of day with Madame while she waits her turn. There was quite a through draught from the hole in the wall and the paper rarely lay long where it was dropped. Indeed, it was sometimes quite a job to get it down to the ground if the wind was blowing strongly and creating an updraught from the shovel hole. So the papers flew about the yard. I had a morbid fear of catching one across the face. My only satisfaction was that any matter, other than the paper, was too heavy to be blown about by the wind; if it were otherwise, we would have been in real trouble here!

It is strange that the French, who lead the world in elegance and who have perhaps a more subtle taste for the finer things in life than any other nation, should be so lackadaisical, so crude about their sanitation. Things are much the same in this present day!

For the past few days prisoners in blue uniforms, guarded by an armed policeman who wears an army greatcoat and sits with his rifle across his knees, had been replastering the walls of the Commissariat. It was looking very fresh and new with the red mud plaster over it. The men spread the mud with their hands. After each rainy season the outside of the mud houses were fissured with surface cracks which would deepen if left. So, at the end of the rains, a fresh ply of mud was smeared over them. This way these buildings lasted for generations, even centuries.

At noon today, the Commissaire said I must go for the truck. It was waiting down in the town. I went down and found the truck in the yard of some Arabs and they asked me into the house. They were just about to have lunch and they asked me if I would like to eat. I agreed, gratefully. There were about a dozen sitting on the floor mat. They were all Algerian Arabs, their colour ranging from quite a pale skin to almost black.

A piece of sacking was laid over the centre of the rug and a long, low table brought in. A whole side of a very large goat was brought and laid on the table. They began eating and motioned to me to join in. I was starting from a handicap, having first to take off my puttees and boots before I could move onto the carpet. I was in time to grab three or four ribs before it all disappeared. After the meat a basin of sliced tomatoes was laid. The idea was to break off a piece of bread and dip with the fingers into the basin. Many of the hands, especially of two greasy-looking mechanics, didn't seem very clean. Next, two basins of stew came. Spoons were provided for this. These were the only cutlery used with the meal. After each communal basin the native servant brought a basin of water and soap and a kettle of water to wash the hands. Each man, as well as washing hands, took a mouthful of water, rinsed his mouth, put in a finger and cleaned his teeth then spat the water into the basin. I was third on the list and would not have liked to have been near the end!

The table and sacking were removed and the men sprawled out on the floor. A charcoal burner was brought with a very small tea pot and a bunch of fresh lime leaves. When the water boiled, the man the tray had been put beside put a handful of leaves in the tea pot. That must have been half full for it seemed ludicrously small for such a great company. The water was poured in. The man filled a big glass, poured it back in the pot then filled little whisky glasses with the linden tea and passed them round. The tea maker was kept busy making potful after potful, each time putting in fresh leaves. The glasses were filled repeatedly and the tea was very strong. It was the first time I had tasted linden tea made from fresh lime leaves instead of them being dried first.

By then it was about one o'clock. At 2.30 p.m. the truck moved off. Every inch of the load was covered by passengers. I was up on the back of the truck this time, but was allotted a good position in front with my legs over the end and my feet resting on top of the cab. I liked it there. So high you got such a fine view of the countryside and the wind in my face was refreshing, but it dried up my eye and made it clog up and stick and was uncomfortable.

It was 145 kilometres from Zinder to Tanout. Along the way we passed many single travellers, sometimes with just the camel they rode, but others led a spare one along. All of them had the look of veteran travellers. Calabashes for water dangled at their sides, bundles wrapped in skin in many cases were piled so high that, instead of a hump, the camel was flat along the top. On this the man sat. The truck travelled fast. Hung over the side was a whole goat skin. The animal had been skinned without slitting the belly. Only the neck and legs had been cut and the whole lot peeled off and the skin filled with water. The neck, tail and legs were tied with thongs.

It was dark when the truck arrived in Tanout. They dropped me off at the 'campement'. I found the night stay would cost me 200 francs (about 9/-). The native in charge agreed that I could sleep on the floor. I had to pay 100 francs for the campement. I felt I was tricked into that. Had I known they would charge I would have gone outside and camped, although I did get the use of the kitchen and firewood.

It was so difficult not knowing the language. I thought the Arab on the lorry had said he would call for me in the morning, but I think he must have said I should come to the truck in the morning at the village about half a mile from the campement. But where I was supposed to find the truck I had no idea, since the place was like a rabbit warren. Its labyrinth streets were passages of six inch deep loose sand, which went nowhere in particular or, at least, they twisted this way and that in tortuous endeavour to find a way out of the huddle of mud houses; the alley merely ending in the compound of a house where the stranger who followed it startled women beating corn into flour. The young ones ran giggling into their homes, the old women, turning wrinkled faces murmured "sanu!".

When the truck had not come by 11 a.m. I decided it must have gone without me. I went down to the village, had a look round and found it. They were leaving in the evening. Time means nothing to Arabs – morning, evening – they are all the same.

But, last evening, about 6 p.m., the truck left Tanout. I was up at the back. It was cold and became biting as the night wore on. At first it was possible to look into the wind and see the land as the headlights picked it out. But, as the time passed, the bite in the wind was honed to a fine edge and I was forced to rake out my sleeping bag, wrap it round me and turn my back to the lights.

On, on, on through the night. The road was a track through the sand. Off the track the sand was loose. Once, when the driver swung off the road to follow a gazelle with the lights to have a shot at it, the truck stuck. It was over an hour before it was back on the road again, even with the aid of the long, flat, irons every vehicle carried here to put under the wheels in just such a situation.

The way was very bumpy and, in the back, myself and the natives who were huddled there were rattled about a great deal. Sometimes, from the void beyond the truck would come a shout, a greeting, and as we drew level a shadowy camel rider would appear dimly in the darkness, waving courteously before he was swept away into the night. Sometimes there were solitary night riders, sometimes in pairs or groups and sometimes whole caravans with over 100 camels.

At about 1 a.m. we stopped at a village, the first since we left Tanout. We slept there until about 5.30 a.m. then, with a rush, the Arab owner appeared from a house, climbed into the truck and blew his horn, the warning that we were off. There was only time to bundle up everything and climb aboard. Everything was in turmoil in the back when the truck moved off. The cold was worse even than last night after sleeping. We huddled, miserably waiting for the sun; then, when it appeared, wishing it would hurry and put heat in its first pale rays. Eventually it did get warmer – then really hot.

CHAPTER 25

THE LAND OF THE TUAREGS

Wednesday 16th February 1955 – Agades.

Well, here I am, Agades! Home of the Tuaregs, the veiled, pale-skinned desert nomads, perhaps the most mysterious and interesting people in all the Sahara.

Agades first appeared on the flat horizon like an island in an ocean, the tall minaret of the mosque sticking up like a spike. As we drew nearer, houses broke the even rim of the skyline.

It was rather strange entering this town. There were no straggling huts to form any suburbs. Suddenly, you came from the emptiness of the desert into a tightly packed, mud town. There were very few trees about. The town, or oasis, lies like a pimple on a bald head, completely at the mercy of the sun.

I disembarked at the market square in the centre of the town and from where the streets radiated. A crowd gathered round and a native policeman with a Sam Browne type belt and revolver at his waist tried to question me, but gave up when he could not make himself understood. I asked for the Commissairiat and a small boy was told to take me there. It was about a mile from the town on the site of the old fort. The Commissaire did not speak English. I was hoping he would. He stamped my passport.

I was rather at a loss what to do. At Zinder the bank manager had said one Doadezi, a Swiss, spoke English so I could look out for him. I decided to look him up and see if he, being acquainted with the place, would know how I should go about getting a caravan to Tamanrasset. It transpired that Mr Doadezi had a small shop. He was the only white trader except for the U.A.C. company stores. I supposed he did transport and importing as well. I found his place, but by then he was indisposed – lunch, siesta, etc. – until 3.30 p.m. Between these times nothing stirred in French Africa.

Not wanting to make any move until I saw him, I sat on my pack at the door of his shop until that time. A few of the locals came and sat with me, having nothing else to do apparently other than helping me to do nothing. It was rather a long wait.

At 3.30 p.m. Mr Doadezi appeared from his house. I stood up and greeted him. He didn't answer. He looked me up and down and, as he drew close, I said in English, "Do you speak English, please?"

"No," he said without stopping, and passed into his shop.

Since then three different people had told me he did speak English. In fact, one man said Doadezi's mother was a Scot.

The abruptness of this interview after such a long wait and since I was depending so much on speaking to someone, left me rather bewildered. I felt quite lost. Now, what to do? I felt so frustrated at not being able to speak the language when the only person I could turn to had just turned his back on me. I heard there was a campement here, so I asked if I could camp nearby so that I could get water. I went in the direction I was told, but not finding it went to a house to ask directions. Luckily, it was the house of the magistrate, although I didn't know it then. He spoke some English and he asked me in and offered me a drink. His wife brought a huge piece of cream tart. I hadn't eaten since the previous morning and it was very good. I told the magistrate I was intending asking permission to camp beside the campement. However, he drove me round to the court. Many of the natives who worked there also lived in the compound. He said I could camp there and the natives would see to my fuel and water needs . I didn't bother putting up my tent, it was so dry there.

For three days I made enquiries at every place I could and there seemed to be no caravans going to Tamanrasset. It was the wrong season. It always seemed to be the wrong season! Apparently, the rains failed in the area and all the caravans were heading south and Tamanrasset had no produce to make a trading caravan worthwhile. So! No caravan from here to Tamanrasset. I would have to get a truck going that way and perhaps at Tamanrasset I would be able to get one going further north.

I had landed myself in trouble by being very foolish at Zinder. At Zinder I changed £1 note of Nigerian currency and decided not to change any travellers cheques till I got here in Agades. Now I found there was no bank here. The shops were too small to accept a cheque so now I was left with just a few francs. Luckily, I had quite a stock of stores from Kano. I got 435 francs for the £1, but now I was left with about 100. I spent it in small doses in the market: 5 francs worth of tomatoes, 5 francs worth of dates, 15 francs for meat bones to make soup and 5 francs for vegetables, 10 francs for bread – a loaf which was not much bigger than a big roll. That kept me going for about a couple of days, at least the meat did. But I had given up buying it and was baking scones now, though the flour I had wouldn't last too long. I wasn't sure if there was a bank at Tamanrasset either, so I was in a bit of bother. I thought I might have to sell something, a jersey or something, to get some money.

It was getting extremely difficult to get a lift. Transport through the desert was quite a business and few, if any, of the transporters were willing to give free lifts. I had to hope someone would take me otherwise I knew I would be in a fix. Thinking positively, I decided to make the most of my enforced stay here to find out as much as I could about the caravans, information which would be useful if, in the last resort, I had to make it alone across the desert.

The great Bilma caravans left during October and November. They wait until the crops are ripe, then load up with these to take to Bilma and bring back salt. The journey takes seventeen days and November is the best month to go. It is cool then with no, or at least very few, sandstorms.

Caravans also went at the same time to Fachi, a very ancient town in the desert, not far from Bilma. I had been told it was a very interesting place, the people living exactly the way they have done for a thousand years. The caravans go from Agades, Zinder and even Kano, although Agades was the nearest, and according to my information, it was to Agades that my data applied. If I decided to go alone it would be necessary to hire a camel, or perhaps two camels, and one man to look after the animals and me, also.

According to my calculations:

Hire of camels – 60 francs each per day

Hire of a man – 60 francs per day

3,060 francs

Food, perhaps 10/- per day – 4,250 francs

At a total of 7,310 francs the journey would cost me approximately £15.00. Food may not be 10/- a day if one was living simply, taking a bag of native meal instead of expensive tinned or other European items. However, it may be necessary to hire an extra camel, making three, for carrying water. I had been told that it was better to use aluminium bottles and not glass for carrying cooking oil. Broken oil bottles could ruin or at least spoil other food.

One itinerary I thought of was going to Kano for the Salah in September. I could then go to Fachi by caravan in October or November and from Fachi to Bilma, even if that last bit necessitated hiring an extra camel after leaving the main caravan. Then it might be possible to return to Agades or Zinder or Kano by the caravans returning with the salt or, if one way was enough for camel travel, return to Agades by Trans African trucks. It may be possible to hitch a lift back, but I thought this would be difficult as they were not keen on hitch-hikers. The fare, I estimated, was 7,000 francs (£14) each way on the trucks to Agades. The trucks, at that time in February, were running three times a week to Bilma from Agades.

To make your own caravan needed four camels and one guide. One man I spoke to who had done a lot of camel travelling in Algeria, said for the four camels, the guide and food, you could reckon on £1 per day, all in. That would easily cover it all, in fact that was allowing for extras.

But that was if you were making your own caravan. If you were joining one, such as the Bilma or Fachi ones, the cost would be less. After the caravan, it would be interesting to return to Kano for the big Juju festivities around the New Year; then one could proceed to Congo, to Budjala, for the Qwaka circumcision ceremonies in January or February.

And another itinerary might be: to Aden, to work for some time and learn Arabic properly, then to Jibuti, through Abyssinia to Kenya and on to Uganda and down the Nile from Lake Victoria to Egypt.

And a third: Cape Town up through South-West Africa and Angola.

And, lastly: in order to complete the whole of Africa, round the west coast by Dakar, Gambia, Sierra Leone and the Gold Coast, returning via Goa and Timbuktu.

I had plenty of options!

***

This desert town of Agades is a quaint place. In the sandy, narrow streets one passed veiled Tuaregs, heavily robed, many carrying swords and innumerable little leather cases, no bigger than lockets some of them, dangling round their necks. How mysterious and fascinating they seemed with only their eyes glinting above the cloth that covers their faces.

In the market square were some double-storey mud houses with fancy architecture, which lent a sort of grandeur to the place. Most picturesque of all were the Tuareg Camel Corps police, their dress was no different from the ordinary Tuareg, but they had crossed bandoliers with the tips of the bullets glinting in the sun. They rode magnificent camels and had rifles slung at their saddles. How statuesque they looked sitting high up on their camels, veiled, armed and mysterious.

Agades is the place P.C. Wren immortalised with his book *Beau Geste*. It was here the siege, which he wove into fiction, actually took place. There was nothing left of the old fort which was besieged by the Tuaregs for three months, before being relieved by a column of the Camel Corps and troops force-marched from Zinder. The officer who led the relief party still lived here. He was a lieutenant in the Camel Corps when he won the place. Now he was in his seventies and in many ways he looked on the place as his.

I went to see him yesterday. I was warned he spoke no English, but I found a native of the W.F.A. Company who spoke some English and Hausa. Commandant Beau Geste, as the old man is known, speaks Hausa.

The old man, stout and frail and wheezing with bronchial trouble, laid down the pot he was eating from and rose from the table as I knocked. He lived in a native mud house, no different from the Tuareg, except he had chairs and a hat rack at the door.

I had been warned that he was sometimes very short with visitors, but I was lucky enough to catch him in a friendly mood. He brought me in and agreed to answer any questions I asked. My interpreter was a Southern Nigerian and perhaps his Hausa was as sketchy as his English. He could not follow what I was saying, and had no idea of words such as 'fiction', 'besiege' or 'relief'. After a lengthy discourse between the old man and him, I received a completely different answer to the question I had asked. But, gradually, with this very unsatisfactory medium and my little French posed directly to the Commandant, I pieced together his story, and with it, an idea of the Sahara before the French tamed it – wild, ruthless, hard; a land beyond even the powers of fiction to describe.

When I saw signs of fatigue in my host I bade him farewell. He moved in a bent stoop with me to the door and wheezed an asthmatic 'au revoir'. It had been a thrill to meet the man who had taken the lead in such a memorable event.

A couple of days ago I climbed the minaret of the mosque, a ninety foot high, mud tower. Wide at the bottom, it narrowed to a point at the top and all the way up were little openings, windows into the stairway. It was nearly 400 years old. It had no geometric shape, and all over it, the ends of the building poles jut out like the bristles of a hedgehog. A crude mud tower that has seen four centuries of desert sun and wind, I wondered how many muezzins have shattered the morning silence from the top of this ancient monument? How many silent caravans have welcomed the sight of it from the empty desert?

When I entered the compound adjoining this mosque, I was greeted with a feeble wave from a wizened ancient who looked older than time. The loose skin on his face was wrinkled and lined deeply like the bark of an old oak tree, his hair downy white. Was this the muezzin? I didn't know. Could he really climb up that tower to call the people to prayer? On wide-splayed, shaky legs he led me to the door into the tower, but made no move to follow me.

Inside I had to stoop. It was dark and pillars broke the place up into a maze of sections. I had difficulty in finding the doorway to the stair. This was an opening barely three feet high. For the first 20 feet or so the stairs had long since crumbled away and there was only a steep passage about four feet in height that curled upwards. Further up, the steps took form and the headroom increased until it was possible to stand upright. At each little opening in the wall you could see the ground grow further away. Near the top, the passage narrowed and the twist in the stairway tightened. The last part of the stair was barely a foot wide and it was necessary to wriggle upwards sideways.

At the top the platform was about four feet square with a low parapet round it. From there Agades was a drab group of mud cubes, each with its little walled-in compound. Beyond the houses on all sides stretched the desert, empty, limitless, like looking at the ocean from a small island.

The afternoon was far gone and the shadows long. I waited a long time, just watching the silent town below. From the desert a camel train arrived. I watched it grow from a dot till I saw them. They passed below me and carried on down the street, half a dozen camels and two riders. How satisfied they must be to have arrived! Then I squeezed through the hole in the floor of the platform and wormed my way down the dark stairway again.

The afternoon was nearly gone as I wrote in my diary. I just made up my dough and put it on the ashes to bake. There was water on for coffee too. Small, plain fare, but very welcome. The 100 francs I have in my pocket was very little to go on and it would have to last goodness knows how long. I had the coffee and the scone when I finished writing, after it got too dark to write.

Where I was camped was under a flat-topped thorn three. I didn't bother using the tent since it was so dry. In the morning I lay and watched the birds flitting about the branches above me. Not many people could have had such wonderful decorations on their bedroom ceiling.

Later on, I watched as one of the wives of the native caretaker arrived back from the town. Her four children ran to meet her with glad, animated cries. The eldest took the bundle from her mother and put it on her own head. The three smaller ones hung on their mother's arms and skirt. It was a happy little scene. Funny how that is the same all over the world.

The next two days were hell. A sandstorm. It started but didn't really get into its stride until the second day. It blew out at darkness in the evening and the night was calm. Then it came back with a vengeance in the morning and it was tearing the place to bits all day. Caught in the open as I was, it made life grim. The wind was a howler. It screamed through the trees and picked up anything loose and hurtled it as far away as it could. Sand got in everywhere. Buildings twenty yards away were blotted out by the yellow cloud. Occasionally, a woman holding grimly to a water jar would drift out of the fog and pass into it again like a shadowy figure in a dream.

Sand gritted in my teeth. It clogged up ears and nose and turned eyes into red running pools. Cooking was out of the question. I tried, but the

314

wind took the heat from the fire before it could rise to a pot on the stones. In a sudden brutal gust, the pot was thrown to the ground, its contents lost, the light aluminium lid carried off like a leaf of paper.

On Sunday I heard there was a truck for Tamanrasset. I went along to Mohammed La Harech, the owner. He was sullen and dour but reluctantly agreed to allow me to go in his truck. He said 'apres dima' – that meant Tuesday. So, in the middle of the storm, I packed and made my way to the town. Packing was a problem. It screwed the sleeping bag to knots when I tried to roll it. Sand was everywhere in my pack. However, I managed and made my way against the sand-choked wind up to the town half a mile from where I camped. I found the truck and, seeing it already packed, put down my pack and waited for it to go. It was about 1.30 p.m. and I thought it would go about 2 after siesta. But 3pm. and 4 p.m. came and went and at last, I looked in at M. La Harech again. I should have done that before, but he had been so uncooperative the last time I didn't want to approach him again. He said the truck wasn't leaving until tomorrow morning. He had seen me sitting there when he returned to his shop at 2 p.m. and had not told me. He hardly bothered to look up to tell me it was going the next day. I seethed at his attitude, but indignation was something I could not afford. I supposed I should be grateful for the lift. I was, very grateful, but I would have liked to lean over the counter and wipe the sneer from his face. If I hadn't been indebted to him …!

I slept beside the truck that night. The storm had died down again now that it was night. I hoped it didn't start again the next day. I felt humiliated that I had been taken for a bum by Doadezi and the Arabs. It made me feel low.

Two days out from Agades: 435 kilometres – 272 miles. It's 911 kilometres to Tamanrasset – 570 miles. The truck was averaging just over 100 miles per day the journey should take another two days, making four in all. We started out in the morning. Up in the back of the truck I had two Tuaregs as travelling companions as well as the lorry boy, a curly haired Arab youth, dirty, but very cheery. In the cab four Arabs, including the driver, were crammed.

The previous day the storm had died down to a powerful wind. It was going our way, so when the truck moved, there was no breeze to temper the sun's heat. I had secured a place on top of a steel petrol drum. I thought that bucket seat from Kano to Zinder was uncomfortable! This one was alive and bounced about continually with the rough road – and it was rough – and the rim cut into my thigh.

La Harech must have passed his contempt for me on to his driver. I could see in the way he scarcely looked at me during the stops. All forenoon we rode through a wilderness of scorched bush and tinder dry grass. All the vegetation lacked colour, the green had been bleached from it. After seven hours driving we arrived at Teguidda n'Tacem, a few mud houses forming a village below a long hill, conspicuous in the surrounding flat country. There, the Arabs made a meal and one of the Tuaregs stayed. Having so little food with me, I wished to conserve it for the evening and used the time to lie in the shade of the truck, gloriously cool after the frying pan that was the exposed back of the open truck.

We were off again by 3 p.m. The bushes were thinning out now. About 5 p.m. the driver stopped and he, with his boy, went over to fell a dried tree to be used as firewood. I went over and carried an armful of wood to the truck. For the first time the driver seemed to notice me. The other passengers had remained by the truck.

When we stuck in the sand later, I took my turn with the shovel and heaved the metal boards into place and afterwards ran, carrying one to the slowly moving truck to hook it on the side again. Once out of the hole the truck kept moving slowly so that it would not sink and the workers must pick up the metal boards, shovels etc. and run to catch up and climb on.

When we stopped at night, I was no longer the punk European or the bum. I was asked to join in the meal while the driver nodded and laughed and joked to me, his eyes dancing with friendly merriment.

We spent the night at an Arab camp, miles off the track. After dark, the driver left the track and struck a course across the virgin desert, zigzagging round patches of dangerous looking sand. How he took his direction beats me. There was nothing to follow, except perhaps the stars.

At length we arrived. For the last mile we were guided by a light. There was one tent. One tent! And he had found it. The tent was made of skins and was merely a low wall to the prevailing wind. Some camel saddles lay about and, from a distance, camels bawled occasionally. Some children ran to the truck. Their heads were shaved except for a ridge down the centre of their crown. One of the Arab passengers disembarked here and another joined us in the morning.

As I said, I was 'in' when they made their meal and was even given the honour of having my food served to me on a plate instead of dipping from the communal basin. I had been accepted.

Travelling the next day was through real desert. Sand, not a blade of grass or a bush. Flat sand, rippled in places. No dunes or rises to break the monotony. I lost count of the number of times we had to dig the truck out of the sand. Sometimes it just ran the length of the boards then sank in again. This happened half a dozen times before it finally got going again.

After hours of rolling over a flat void, a house appeared. A single house, like an apparition. How strange it seemed to find it! There was nothing else, no tree, no other building. It was an empty ruin, no one lived there anymore.

This then was In Abbangarit, so importantly marked on the map. But it was not the ruin which warranted the mention on the map – there was a well fifty yards away. On the map it said "l'eau très bonne". The water was dark and musty. Still it was water and the goatskins were filled. These skins kept the water remarkably cool.

We stayed there just long enough for the Arabs to pray. Four lonely figures standing looking across the desert to Mecca. What does that religion have to make its believers so devout?

On again, hour after hour, with the sand and the sun as the whole world. Could there really be other places outside this? Were there really towns and other countries, other people? This emptiness seemed so vast it must fill the globe. This loneliness – so intense in such solitude: could there really be other people alive? Was it possible you dreamed of these cities and people you thought you had seen?

In Guezzam was a tiny oasis. A few trees – so welcome – with the ruins of past building under them. In the centre of this group of trees was the office of the local administrator. There was a small walled-in courtyard and a rest house, I believe, and looking so strange, a petrol pump. There was a well in the courtyard with a pump attached. I enjoyed a wash, the first in two days.

CHAPTER 26

ALGERIA

Tamanrasset – those four days were over! What an interesting journey! And, how uncomfortable! But that was soon forgotten in the satisfaction of having arrived.

Tamanrasset lies over 3,000ft up in the Ahaggar Mountains. These last couple of days from In Guezzam had been across the desert. In many places the way was marked by small cairns of stones, in others by petrol drums sunk in the sand. But mostly there was nothing except old wheel marks and these, in places, were almost obliterated by drifting sand. Yet on many occasions, the Arab driver, like on that first night, would strike off the beaten track into the blue, cutting off or going round parts he knew from past experience were difficult. There was something exciting about seeing nothing but our single tracks winding back over unmarked sand.

So much emptiness! Not a dune or bush to break the smooth rim of the horizon. Look all around and you always seem to be in the centre of a huge, flat disc.

There was one part on the map marked 'très difficile'. The whole way was difficult, but this part was exceptional and fulfilled what was written about it. When the times the truck just ran the length of the boards then sank again, numbered nine or over, I got to call this 'a bundle'. Sometimes we'd have a bundle, go a few miles then have another, then not much further and have another one. It was all very trying and I had a pair of very skinned hands to prove it. The number of 'solo's' and odd ones and twos we had when we dug it out came with monotonous regularity.

Yesterday, we travelled from 6 a.m. till 10 p.m. It was a long day sitting on that petrol drum. Four days on that drum had given me an intimate knowledge of them. I never knew these things could be so human, or inhuman. This one developed great bumps and ridges just where it could hurt me most, and with the most devilish accuracy. With fiendish glee it sharpened its rim so that it cut into my thighs. It and the box in which the boy kept the cooking utensils, united in an endeavour to make my journey as trying as possible. It was perched above me and was tied with a string to the side of the truck. At the most inopportune moments, for example, when we were bumping over ridges or squirming through loose sand and when my drum had started up its usual jig – it had the queerest sense of humour – the box would break its bindings and spew pots and pans and bags of meal over me while I was doing my damnedest to ride my merry drum. I was continually tying the box up.

Aiding and abetting these was the sun. The open truck provided no shelter and the sun worked its way into a blind fury, trying to fry all on board, but the wind in its turn was more insidious in its ways. Slowly it dried up the skin, eyes, lips and hair till they cracked, at the same time covering everything with a thick layer of dust.

The nights were very cold and it was necessary to sleep with most of my clothes on, but it was fine and dry for sleeping out.

At night and morning and during the midday stop also, we would sit in a circle and sip linden tea. The brewer concocted his mixture in two ridiculously small teapots which he filled almost a third with sugar and the leaves. There was the usual ritual of pouring out the tea into a glass, waiting for a minute or two, then emptying it back in the pot again. Then the little whisky glasses would be half-filled – less than an egg cupful – and passed round. You sipped it – it tasted good! – and passed the glass back to be filled with the next making. You rarely got the same glass back and they were never washed. Each potful was made separately, not just by adding water. I have seen over half a dozen brews made at a sitting.

On approaching the Haggar, black rocks jut out of the sand and break the billiard table surface. The mountains are strange. Many are half buried by sand with only the ridges showing like the skeletal vertebrae of some prehistoric monster. There is no vegetation, just grotesquely shaped mountains of naked, burnt rock and sand – a dead world.

Tamanrasset is in Algeria. No visa was required for this country and I had no trouble. The Haggar is an annexe of Algeria, something similar to the Cameroons being a protectorate under the administration of Nigeria. It was governed by the military with no police there.

The truck was going all the way to Algiers. The driver only told me this that day and said if I liked I could go on with him. In fact he would like me to go, he said. At least my efforts in joining in the work had been appreciated. Quite a difference to the sullen attitude they had towards me on the first day. However, I wanted to explore around Tamanrasset for a few days so I refused the offer, although I would have been in Algiers in five days. With hindsight, perhaps I was a fool to turn down such a good offer. Lifts were very hard to come by and with it I also got my food. But it was not my idea of seeing the country just flying through it like that.

Tamanrasset had tree-lined streets and tilled land with a good irrigation system. I wandered around, made a fire beside the water furrow and brewed some tea. The water wasn't too clean being only a foot wide and a few inches deep and in which the natives washed their clothes, etc. After that I found a place to make camp near the main street and where a water furrow ran nearby. Firewood was very scarce; it was brought in on the backs of donkeys by the Tuaregs from 20 or more kilometres away. I had to pay 150 Algerian francs (3/-) for a bundle of just a few pieces. Some men of the Civil Airlines were camped nearby.

In the morning I was told there was an English woman living here. I wish I had known before and I went to pay her a visit. I had been told she was a 'bit queer' having been here for twenty years without ever being away. Her name was Frances M. Wakefield, sister of Dr Arthur Wakefield, a member of the 1922 Everest expedition when six or seven porters were swept away in an avalanche.

She was a missionary and lived in a native type house. I went along a narrow alleyway, stepped over a long ditch and climbed over a refuse mound to reach her door into the compound. Her living room was a deck chair surrounded on three sides by a pile of papers. She was a small, grey-haired lady of 76 years, who had not left Tamanrasset for over 20 years.

She was first attracted to the Tuareg by a pamphlet written by Dugald Campbell, the Scottish travelling missionary, where he said the "Tifinagh", pronounced Tiffinaff – the Tuareg script – needed recording. She came here and had translated stories from every book of the Bible into the hieroglyphics of this Tuareg writing, a magnificent achievement. She finished in August 1954. She had just started a Roman or Latin translation.

I found her a fascinating old lady. Far from being queer, she was remarkably sane. Her 'office' was another little mud room crammed full of papers and books with a rough table at the little window. Round her seat were seventeen different open Bibles from which she was working. There were three different French Roman Catholic versions, an Arabic edition (Van Dyke's), a Hausa one (Miller's), three English translations, two German – Revised Luther and Allioli Roman Catholic ("an awful loose translation but, oh, what beautiful German!"), others in Italian, Hebrew, Greek – she had difficulty in writing Greek, but remembered Hebrew well – Septuagint, Latin and Spanish.

She said the Tuaregs must have been Christians at one time – it was Greek Orthodox Christianity they had. It was remarkable how many Tuareg words are the same as Greek. For instance, the Tuareg word 'Angelus', (Angel), is the same as the Greek 'Angelus'. She wrote the word in the

320

Greek script. She had been forty-eight years abroad in Muslim countries. At one time in Arabia, she lived for four years as an Arab with Arabs.

She appeared to overestimate me as a person. When she was writing out the Greek words she would say, "Now, what is the Greek for 'to make'? I don't remember as well as I used to."

It was a direct question and not just said in a musing way. She seemed to take for granted that I must be able not only to speak Arabic, Hebrew and Greek and so on, but also to write it. She was showing me the books she had written in Tifinagh. She would pick up a book and say, "Ah Daniel", or "And this is Ruth".

What terribly poor conditions to be living in for a lady of her age and ability. I wonder now what happened to all her invaluable work when she died – was it all lost?

***

I left Tamanrasset this morning. After leaving there was very little sand, just a wasteland of stony rubble and peaked, mountainous piles of loose rocks, as if they had been poured from a huge tipper. Tit is a green patch with some water running through it, 40 kilometres from Tamanrasset. It was here in 1902 that a company of the Meharisti, the Camel Corps, were attacked by Tuaregs. They formed a square with their camels and killed over 200 Tuaregs. Only one soldier was killed and two wounded. But the interesting part is, the French left the bodies where they fell as a warning to the Tuaregs. The skeletons were still lying there, bleached white with the sun, grinning skulls and bones littered the sand. The Tuaregs, putting their faith in the amulets they carried round their necks, charged again and again, believing nothing could harm them. One talisman in the bones of a skeleton had a bullet hole through the centre of it. Rotten luck!

We passed the little oasis of In Amguel, another patch of greenery in the sea of sand. Green corn was growing in little squares of earth divided by irrigation channels. I was interested to see little mud viaducts, four or five feet high, that carried the channels over dips and ditches.

The truck I was travelling in was a monster and we arrived at In Eker at about 2 p.m., making a short, easy day. The driver shot a gazelle on the way. In Eker, which looks formidable on the map, was one building surrounded by a turreted wall. The turrets and loop-holes had been an addition to the original wall. I wondered when the necessity arose. It was most picturesque there. On all sides blue mountains – they were mauve then with the sunset – looked over wide, empty expanses of desert.

The people I was travelling with were of the company "Direction de l'Aéronautique en Civile". There were a dozen of them. They gave me the feeling they thought I was a tramp. All of them, except one, completely ignored me. When I appeared they would look up to see who it was, then when they saw it was me they turned away, not perhaps deliberately to avoid me, but just as you would turn from something worthless. It didn't make for a pleasant atmosphere. To generalise, the French en masse I had found were not quick to friendliness. Not all of them, for some odd ones had been more than pleasant and very helpful.

We left In Eker by first light. The road led through pink mountains that changed to purple as we drew near them. There was little sand, just miles and miles of pebbled stones. It was very picturesque country.

As we came on to Arak, the mountains came nearer and became weirder in shape. There were great boulders with holes through them. The mountains at Arak were the most impressive I had ever seen.

Arak was a hotel. A single place in a little oasis that lay at the foot of a great buttress, split and hewn into castle-turret-like shapes. We were to stay there that night. The others had a meal in the restaurant. I just had mine ready when they came out and the Captain had decided to go on. That was 4.30 p.m. We went on through the mountains and, when we left them behind, through the sand. We in the back dozed. At 1.30 a.m. we arrived at In Salah. They dropped me off when they arrived, and went off to their camp.

I spread my bedding and slept. In the morning I found myself in a wide open square in the centre of town. I hunted round for a place where I could camp but couldn't find anything; then I found the swimming pool and was there when a sandstorm blew up. They are a nuisance. The sand whipped up by the wind cuts like a lash. I huddled in the latrine, the only shelter I could find. It smelled as only French latrines can – the drainage floor was littered and was foul. I don't know which was worse – to be out in the storm or in that revolting place – but I stayed there for three days. There was barely room to stretch my legs. I had to clear part of the floor to sit and I had been cooking there too.

In Salah could almost be called a beautiful place. There were many fine mud buildings done in the fancy architecture common in the area, but usually badly worked in the Sahara. It was a little oasis where the sand dunes came right up to the Moorish arched gates of the town. Sand carpeted the streets and filled in corners like snow drifts.

Meat was more expensive here than in Tamanrasset. The mutton was 110 francs a kilo and camel meat was 60 francs. Here I paid 90 francs for a bone with some meat on it for soup.

I enjoyed swimming in the pool before the sandstorm started blowing. It blew all day again the next day. It was awful. I was too late in crossing the desert – this was the month for storms.

I spent all day in the latrine. I was getting used to the stench, the cramp and watching where I sat and where I put my feet. When I was cooking, the fire increased the smells. Luckily the sand doesn't blow at night time, but a strong, cold breeze kept up every evening, which made it very uncomfortable for me for I had no heavy clothes with me, coming from the south. The Frenchmen wore duffel coats, air force jackets with fur collars or the long, heavy cloaks with the hoods on them common in the Sahara.

Wood was extremely scarce. I had to pay 50 francs (1/-) for three pieces about a couple of feet long. I had to conserve them for cooking and, although I could come out of my hide out after dark and breathe in some sweet, fresh air, I could not make a fire for warmth so I got chilled to the bone with the biting wind.

The market here was pitiful. In the great space, about half a dozen old hags sit over baskets with hardly anything in them. That night the wind dropped to a cool breeze. The moon was bright so I decided to climb the sand dunes and look down on the town in the moonlight. The streets were quiet. There was only the muffled shuffle of my feet in the sand carpet. Out through the arched gate and along the avenue of trees that ended abruptly in the desert, the wind played with the trees as a child plays with a rattle. The sand of the dune was tightly packed and firm, but my feet made deep prints.

At the top I lay and looked down. The town was not very distinct, but a few of the main buildings stood out in the pale moonlight. Here and there a fire twinkled. Now and then a camel sobbed loudly and pitifully and donkeys carved up the silence with their occasional braying. I lay there a long time. The sand was soft and comfortable and, with my two jerseys on, I was warm.

In the silence and solitude my mind drifted hither and thither and I made no effort to control it. I thought of home. So near now, a few months, two or at the most three. What would it be like? Five years I've been gone. How many changes? I thought of the little things I would do, the things I would like to see again: the sea breaking over the shore dyke, the car tracks in the snow in winter, digging the garden in the spring – such a bind, but even that had its attractions. I'd miss the last bus home from Dunfermline, and curse, then buy some fish and chips at the shop in Pittencrief Street as I walked home. I'd step down into the dark interior of Drummond's wee shop and hear the doorbell clang and I'd do the Sunday round of Drumfin, Sunniside Road and home by Gilanderston Toll.

I thought back to where I had been. I looked on myself as a detached person. It was quite easy, as there I could look down on myself as a different being. I could see the person that worked on the Cory Freighter and travelled through Somaliland and the Ogaden. I saw the boy who came to Kenya in

1951, remembering the thoughts, the ideas, the illusions he had. I saw him grow older, much older as he wandered further south and more so while there and on the way back.

There was no continuity in my thoughts and dreams. I remembered the letter from a girlfriend I received after the ambush with Davo up in Kipiperi – married! Maybe she thought I would be sad about that. And Pam, the girl I met in Nairobi as a young soldier, and again on my journey … And Caryl – happy times walking on the beach and on Table Mountain … Let bygones be bygones!

It was quite late when I retraced my steps into the town and next day it was windy again but not as bad as before. I met some people from the oil drilling company and spent some time up at their canteen.

***

To my great surprise the next night, an Arab came looking for me to say I could go on a truck to El Golea, 260 miles further on from In Salah! The truck was leaving at dawn. This was strange for this truck belonged to a merchant who had overcharged me 20 francs on candles. I had been to another shop and bought one more candle just to see the price. When I saw I had been overcharged, I went back to reclaim my money. Now, it was this Arab who had sent a man looking for me to take me to El Golea. It was a surprise to get a free lift from these people and to have them go out of their way to give me it. I wondered, perhaps he was trying to make amends for trying to swindle me, although I didn't think so for that wouldn't worry him.

Anyway, I slept beside the truck and we left at first light. It was a big oil tanker. There was only the driver and a boy, so I was in the cabin. It was the first time I had been inside a truck since Kano!

The desert was terrific! The road followed the stony, hard ground and spectacularly shaped mountains lay along the whole route. Round table mountains that rose sheer on all sides from conical mounds of scree, like great columns that have sheered off halfway up. I thought at one time these pillars of rock must have been twice the height they were now and had been eroded with the weather. The sloping mounds at their bases grew as the pillar crumbles. You could see it in various stages: some of the mountains were high and the mounds at their base low. There were others where the solid rock had disintegrated and only flat-topped mounds remained.

Away from the mountains stretched the sand dunes, wave after wave as far as the eye could see, like a great sea petrified at the height of a storm. Sometimes these sand mountains came near to the road then suddenly stopped; a wall of sand rising straight from the stony hard ground.

It was almost dark when we arrived at El Golea. 420 kilometres from In Salah to El Golea, with the emptiness only broken by the lonely, little Fort Miriba, now with the tents of an oil drilling company clustered round it.

The character of the town had changed from the Saharan type further south. The influence of the north had crept this far into the desert. Here there were Arab coffee houses, unheard of further south. I went into one and from the cries and welcomes, even taking into consideration my kilt and rucksack, which is strange to them, it seemed that a European entering their café was an uncommon event.

The room was arched. On the sandy floor Arabs sat in groups playing cards or dominoes, each wrapped in his hooded cloak. At the end of the room was an open fireplace where the coffee pot steamed. It cost 5 francs for a small glassful – in a hotel it would cost at least thirty. A small boy said he would show me a place to camp. He did, and it was a grand place in a grove of date palms. There was an irrigation furrow running by and even taps and a shower room built. The small boy returned with a friend the next morning. Had no food to give them but gave some clothes to wash with the promise of some pay. My guide stopped calling me 'Monsieur' and I became 'Patron' now as he hurried off, eager to have the job finished.

This town lies between mountains on one side and the rolling sand on the other. I climbed one of the hills to get a panoramic view of the town and beyond. At night it was cold as usual. The ground where I was camped was white with salt – the water here had a very salty taste and where I lay the night before I drew the dampness from the ground as if there had been a frost in the earth. So last night, while foraging for firewood, I came on an empty house. The door was barred but a window was open. I slept there, but in the morning the man who owned the house made plenty of trouble and went to the Chef de Région and had me ejected, even from the camping site. It appeared the site was private ground reserved for the Touring Club of France. I went to see the Chef and afterwards he gave me permission to return to the camping site. However, by good luck I met a man who was talking to an army officer. He had been in the Canadian Air Force during the war and, seeing the kilt, no doubt wanted to air his English. When I said Ghardaia, the army officer said he had a truck going there next day and I could go with it. It was leaving at 4 a.m. What luck, to find one just like that! At the barracks where I accompanied the army officer to find out what time the truck was leaving, French non-coms in the army in the Sahara were in very picturesque uniforms and were walking about in wide black pantaloons with white scroll patterns embroidered down the sides.

***

325

It was 320 kilometres (200 miles) to Ghardaia. The truck left just after 4 a.m. There were no doors on it and it was cold. Oh, but how cold! We arrived just after 12 noon.

Ghardaia was the biggest place yet. It seemed the widely spaced towns or oases were bigger the further north one travelled. The Mediterranean look and atmosphere sensed at El Golea is apparent in Ghardaia. The narrow cobbled streets filled with little shops, the town, a tightly packed huddle of square, flat-roofed houses that covered the side of a hill, could be any place along the Mediterranean coast. I camped in the Gardens of the town where there were tennis courts and a swimming pool.

It was a fascinating place, and it was fun to wander and get lost in the maze of streets, no wider than alleyways, that climbed up the mountainside.

It lies in the valley between the bald mountains. Nearby, on the top of one of the mountains, lies another little walled town, which looking from below, appeared like a small hat on a very big head, and in two other valleys lie two more walled towns. I climbed one mountain to look down on all of them.

I also visited Beni-Isguen, one of the walled towns. I was not allowed in without a guide or chaperone and was not allowed to take photographs inside. Most definitely so. Everyone was most adamant in their refusal and at 1 p.m. I was almost forcibly ejected from the town when the gates were closed, lest I walk the streets and disturb the siesta. It was a quaint little place with streets of stairs and overhanging buildings. I was most disappointed at not being allowed to use the camera inside. I tried all three gates, and at each one a gate keeper turned me out.

All day I burned at not being allowed to take the photos in Beni-Isguen. Like most things in life, that which is denied you takes on an added attraction. I resolved that somehow I would enter the town without the guard and take the photos. I knew it was wrong to try and buck these native taboos, for most of them are founded on religious grounds and no matter how silly they appear to the European, it can cause no end of trouble if they are broken. Still, I make no apologies for my actions. I wanted these photos and was determined to have them. (I learned later that Beni-Isguen is the town of the Mossadecs, the 'puritan' Muslims.)

I set off early and soon was along at the town. I skirted the gates and climbed the hill. The town covered the side of one of the hills. The road and main gates were at the bottom. At the top was the mosque with its minaret, sticking up like a sore thumb. The wall enclosed all.

The day before I had noticed that at the top, the streets were almost deserted. It was there I wanted to try to break in. Outside the wall at the top was the cemetery, with its mounds of rocks and vases and jars, which were laid with the dead when they are buried.

I looked around there a while waiting to see if anybody had followed me up the hill. All was quiet. I scouted around to find the best part of the wall to climb and chose a corner where a square turret jutted out. I built a three foot high tier of stones so that I could reach up to the first row of oblong loopholes. After that, it was as tricky a piece of finger and toe nail work up the rest of the fifteen-foot wall as I have come across and, at one place, I had to jam my knife into a crack to use as a pinion. Several times I thought I must fall, but at last my skinned fingers gripped the top edge. With heart beating loudly from exertion and fear of being detected, I heaved myself up till I could see inside. There was nobody about. In an instant I was over and had dropped into the loose sand.

I felt in high spirits, although I might still have to answer as to how I entered this forbidden town. I wandered through the streets feeling strangely free at not having my 'tail' as I had yesterday. I took the photos I wanted and, when someone looked long at me, I hurried down another street before he could recover from his surprise and raise the alarm or question me.

At last, when I had seen most of what I wanted, I ventured into the market square. I had the camera ready and whipped off a couple of shots before someone came running across and stood close in front of me so I couldn't take more. He was joined by others and the air was thick with their shouts. The man who had come first poured rapid Arabic, then French, over me, no doubt asking me where I'd entered the town and what had I done with my guide. I played for time with my ignorance, tying them in knots with my abortive French and making myself look a fool who had just wandered in there. At last the main gate was in front of me. The crowd had increased to a mob that moved with me. The gatekeeper came to meet us and, while my captors were vehemently explaining how they had found me, I slipped out and beat a hasty retreat. I felt as happy with my photos as a boy eating stolen apples!

I spent all morning roaming the streets of Ghardaia. I never grew tired of them. The narrow streets, the men on donkeys, the women wrapped in white, coarse blankets with only a small eye-hole showing, the children, so wrapped with clothes that they waddle.

There are as many or more branches of Islam as with Christianity. It was interesting to see the little changes here and there. Ghardaia was the first place coming north where the women cover their faces and it was quite different from the towns south, apart from being much bigger. They have fruit and vegetable stalls as in any French town. Also I watched brass workers making fine trays. The craftsmanship was far advanced from the crude work one saw in Kano. Here it was excellent, especially the intricate wire inlaid in the brass.

In the afternoon I watched a wedding celebration. The son of one of the rich merchants had just taken his first wife. In the market square, groups of Arabs were armed with muzzle loading rifles and short blunderbusses. First the rifle squad would run into the centre of the clearing and, at a given signal, fire off their weapons at the ground. The guns were only loaded with powder and no shot. When they had finished they ran back to reload hurriedly, while the blunderbuss squad went in and blasted the ground. It went on like that for the whole of the afternoon, non-stop. The air was thick with gun smoke and the smell of the burnt powder was heavy.

It was funny to see these old, bearded gentlemen – some of them so fat they waddled and puffed as they ran – act like small boys slamming off these guns and hurrying back to reload, their eyes twinkling as they jammed in the ramrods, as if there wasn't a second to lose. Even though there was no shot in the guns, the blast was sufficient to send little stones from the ground shooting in all directions. I feared one might hit the camera and break it.

At about 4 p.m., I was in a shop buying some bread. The shopkeeper asked me where I'd come from and where was I going. When I said Quargla, a man drinking at the counter turned and said he could take me to Zalfano, half the way there. He was leaving in an hour. What luck, and for the second time in so few days.

I hurried back and struck camp and returned to the shop at 5 p.m. The man came at 8 p.m. – it was a long wait. While waiting I wandered into a coffee shop and had a glassful, it cost 10 francs. I drank it rather quickly, not wanting to miss the lift and hurried back to the place where I had to meet him. When he hadn't come in another hour I took another walk to warm up and went to another coffee house on the opposite side of the street from where I'd been before. The coffee here was 20 francs. I wondered at the difference until I saw some women without veils dressed in bright coloured silk dresses appear through a door. I had a look that way. There was a courtyard enclosed on all sides by small rooms. Most of the doors were closed, but where the doors were open a woman sat. The courtyard was crowded with men. The coffee house was a brothel, hence the double charge on the coffee.

At 8 p.m. the fellow arrived and we got on the way. We had a puncture. The knife-edged night wind sliced us into small pieces as we changed the wheel.

By going to Quargla, I was leaving the direct route to Algiers. But it was that way to Biskra. The trouble was with the Arab nationalists and the fighting was in the hills there. I thought perhaps it would be interesting around there, so I went that way.

I slept in the garage of the farmer who gave me a lift before setting off for Zalfano, which was a military post and a roadhouse. The man I was with had a farm there. He started three years ago sinking boreholes and irrigating, but although water was two metres down it wasn't good, yet, through time, he thought he would have some palm trees!

I got a lift to Quargla last night in a military truck driven by a French officer. A typical French driver, very fast and very jerky and had all on board bouncing about. After finding a place to camp, I met a French couple who spoke English and went with them to the Annual Fete of the Engineering Regiment of the French Army here.

Stopping for coffee at a hotel in the afternoon the proprietor got talking and, when I got ready to go, said I must stay for lunch. Very decent of him!

I visited the Saharian museum here and it was very interesting. One thing that struck me was a mounted crocodile, an eight footer, which was caught at Tamanrasset. Quite fantastic: crocodiles in the middle of the Sahara. It was thought to have come by subterranean streams from the Niger. That shows the extent of the water that runs under the sand. It is strange that in Africa the water is nearest the surface in the areas where there are deserts. The Kalahari, for instance, as well as the Sahara: both average 49 feet down, though in the Sahara many places are much less. At Zalfano, the farmer was getting water at one and a half metres.

Quargla is not as interesting as Ghardaia. It is interesting how at each oasis the customs and the people are quite different. Still, this is not to be wondered at, each place being as much cut off from each other as islands in an ocean. In Quargla the people are darker, more like the Sudanese and not as Arab-looking. The women are not so strict in the veiling and the young, unmarried girls are without any covering of their faces at all.

Here they have a peculiar thing which I haven't found in any place else. In the narrow street there are little arched recesses in the walls. You find them here and there in every other street or so. Around most of them are finger marks, as if someone had wiped dirty fingers round the edge of the alcoves. From what I can gather, the recesses are put over the grave of some old revered person. They are for women who go to pray for fertility. They make offerings of oil made from crushed dates and this is smeared on the wall with their fingers. In some of their little places – the arch rarely exceeds eighteen inches in height at its highest point – a stone cup is left.

The couple I met yesterday say they have a lift for me to Touggourt tomorrow, but the man seems unreliable and I am not too sure of it. Still, I will go and see.

CHAPTER 27

TOUGGOURT TO BATNA

Sunday 20th March 1955.

I reached the square before 6 a.m. in the morning as instructed but, as I thought, there was no truck. When I went to the house of the couple I couldn't get much sense from the man, so I left it at that. I thought I would try my luck on the road and got a lift within half an hour. Still sand and nothing else between places! But, this must be about the end of the desert now.

I asked where to camp and got put into an awful place in an open garden by the main street, where I was bothered with howling, goggle-eyed crowds of the local population hanging round me all day. There were civilian police here. This must be the dividing line of the country. All land to the north has civil administration and all to the south is military. Even the road maintenance and all public engineering is done or supervised by the military.

Here in the native town were long, narrow streets roofed over with palm trunks and mud. They were as dark as mine runs and the donkeys you bumped against could be pit ponies. This was for coolness to shut out the sun.

I tried to take some photos in there, or I should say, I did take some, but it was doubtful if they would come to anything. Still, it was all interesting. Here and there, the light coming through openings in the roof was like solid yellow pillars in the darkness. Children playing under these openings were spotlighted by the beams like actors on a stage. A man wheeling a square, two-wheeled barrow of native food called to all about his wares, his voice echoed down the tunnels. Women wrapped in blankets with one eye showing, shuffled silently along.

I moved my camp into the grounds of the hospital and got my water from the treatment room. I had never seen such unsanitary conditions in any medical place. At about 12.30 when I went for water, the Arab orderly was wrapped in a blanket on the floor having his siesta. The sink was dirty. Blood-stained bandages lay on the floor where they had been dropped during the morning treatment time. Flies swarmed over them and also on the blood stains on the chair and the piece of flesh cut from a wound which was lying on the sink board.

In the afternoon I met the resident doctor, a Frenchman. He talked of Scotland, having spent some time there on his last leave.

I spent the latter half of the day with a French family. Madame Jean D'Esparbes came to my camp last evening. She was the teacher of English at one of the schools and, on hearing there was a British person camping at the hospital, she wanted to talk with me to check her accent as it was six years since she had mixed with English-speaking people. She invited me to tea that afternoon. She had six children, the oldest of whom was a girl of twelve. She had not been working that day, as the schools all over France and Algeria had been on strike for one day for some claim about salaries. The morning paper had announced the one-day strike.

The schools in Algeria – Touggourt anyway – were open only eight months of the year, as the four summer months were too hot for school. One month out of the eight – a fortnight for Christmas and another at Easter – were holidays, so school existed for only seven months of the year. The four months were paid holidays for the teachers, so they did well.

Madame D'Esparbes had spent all day baking. Although she had never been to Britain, she had heard the British had a great tea at 4.30 p.m. with masses of cakes and scones. She said she had learned to bake muffins recently, but she was so sorry she hadn't had time to bake any for me.

It was all so good and I am afraid I overate all these fancy things – such a sudden change after my own fare. The children seemed delighted with this strange but wonderful meal. All six of them were there in force with a few of their friends. At times, Bedlam would have seemed like a tomb compared with the eruptions at the tea table. But I enjoyed it. It reminded me of home when we were all children.

I did appreciate Madame's efforts in doing so much to provide the legendary 'tea' of the British people. Not only in that, but in many other ways she was kind as only a mother of a large family can be.

Monsieur D'Esparbes came in at 6 p.m. He was a clerk in the local Town Hall. He refused the tea and drank a glass of 'Anis' instead. He smiled as he refused the tea, as if it were a joke to be offered such a drink.

I had got to know a couple of Italian tourists in Touggourt. They hired camels and a guide to go into the desert. I went along with them, but I walked while they rode their camels. We went a few miles in the dunes and it was almost dark when we returned. How lovely it was at sunset – the vivid colours, the rippled, curved, knife-edged sand ridges, the camels, the Arabs who accompanied us, the black silhouettes of the little, domed burial chambers against the red sky, the peace, the solitude. We came on a stone stairway that rose from the sand. What had been there, the remains of a town? There was something awesome in the spectre-like masonry alone among the dunes climbing to nowhere but the sky. The sand had formed a circular dune round it and it lay as if in a saucer, the last remains of a long dead town, perhaps.

I spent a day roaming about the town with three of the D'Esparbes children, as eager – sometimes too much so – guides. We visited the Kings' graves, the domed tomb where there were nine stone slabs over past Muslim chiefs. We wandered about, the children keen to show me every nook and cranny of the old town. They took me to the little musty shop crammed with 'sun roses', the stones found in the sand, of quartz and mica fused together into intricate and beautiful designs. I bought a few small ones for 10 francs. They ranged from little ones the size of your finger nail to great, massive ones which were difficult to lift.

In the evening I was invited for a meal by the other teachers of Madame D'Esparbes' school, the single ones, three men and three women, at the house of one of the men. It was a good evening. They made a present to me of a two-kilo box of choice dates and they had all autographed the box. One of the men, the Arabic teacher, was Muslim, an Arab. He did not eat the boiled ham nor drink the wine we others did. He had goat meat and water. His skin was white, he dressed as a European and, except perhaps, for his eyes, it was difficult to tell him as different from the others.

The following morning, at Madame D'Esparbes invitation, I went along to the school to speak to her pupils. Some of the brighter ones could speak some English. I spoke for some time, but I don't think they understood much of what I was saying. Even Madame D'Esparbes' English was not very good, so her pupils could hardly be expected to be better.

I had lunch with the family; then Monsieur went with me to the market and spoke with one of the merchants there and got a lift for me to Biskra. It was the main market day at Touggourt, so there were many trucks from the north there.

The truck left at 2 p.m. It was very slow. I walked around El Djemaa, a village where the truck had stopped. An Arab policeman stopped and made me go to the Administrator to have my passport checked. How they all love to do that! At about 1 a.m. the driver stopped to rest. It was very uncomfortable trying to sleep up on the back on the empty baskets. My sleeping bag got torn and feathers flew about. The truck started again at about 5 a.m. and we arrived here at 9 a.m. That slow truck made the 220 kilometres (137 miles) seem like a marathon run.

At Biskra, I was practically through the desert. Ahead lay the Saharan Atlas Mountains, where the fighting with the rebels was going on. Biskra was exactly like a southern French town. All traces of the Sahara were gone now, except for the Arabs who dress in their own way, but most of the local 'indigènes' dressed as the French and looked like French peasants. On a scale of size, Biskra was the biggest town yet and followed the general run in size increase I had noticed as I had come north.

It had a tightly congested population that filled the streets and lolled round the many cafés. Gramophones blared out Arabic music and every small boy was a boot black who pestered you at every turn for 'service'.

I camped in the Town Gardens, known as 'The Garden of Allah'. I believe someone wrote a book of that name about Biskra. It was a fine place, with leaning palm trees and flowers. I had some trouble getting permission to camp because the military – French paratroopers – are occupying the place. I had been warned not to move my camping spot after dark or I would be liable to be shot by any of the many sentries who patrolled at night.

The town was teeming with soldiers and I noticed at least one of the biggest hotels had been commandeered to billet them. They walked about in groups of three or four and were not allowed to go singly. All French troops wear American uniforms and carried American equipment, so it looked like the Yanks were in occupation.

I visited old Biskra one day. It lies a mile or so from its modern counterpart and was the native style of village. While on my way there a jeep driven by a French officer with three Arab soldiers drew up. The French officer snapped, "Papiers!". No 'please' or 'Monsieur'. It was evident his approach was meant to intimidate. It made my hackles rise. I said in my pidgin French that I had not got my passport with me. He started to shout at me in a torrent of French, which I couldn't make head or tail of. But he finished his burst again with his request for my 'papiers'. I replied in a pained, exasperated air that I hadn't got my passport, but if he'd like to drive to the camp I would willingly show him them. He went into another fit of abuse and his hands sliced the air. With this I assumed I was supposed to be a cringing wretch. I assumed a look of what I considered to be martyred patience and, when he again demanded my passport, I said as slowly and as tersely as I could in English, "I haven't got it with me."

Now that his first curt demand and the following outburst had not brought about the effect it normally produced, he went into even more fearsome convulsions and pushed his face within a foot of mine.

It was stalemate … he kept asking for my papers and I had none. In the middle of his apoplectic discourse I made a gasp of uselessness and, turning my back on him, I made to walk away. Behind me, after a pause, the stream of words broke into spluttering and gasps of incredulity as I heard him climb out of the car. He came in front of me with his revolver drawn. The three soldiers were round me with their sub-machine guns covering me. One came and took my knife from its sheath and searched me with patting hands for other weapons.

He ordered me into the vehicle and his "Allez's" to hasten me on were in a tone which suggested "I'll show you'. When I was in and the soldiers and I settled, he suddenly told the Arab to give me back my knife, ordered me out and, just as quickly, drove off. It ended like that – the French! Unpredictable!

How this town teems with loafers. The cafés in the centre of town that filled almost every pavement with their chairs did endless trade but became packed after about 3.30 p.m. when siesta had finished. It was useless to ask directions from anyone in the street. He and a few more would not only tell you, but walked with you to show you where you wanted to go and, of course, demanded payment for their work. Being Muslim, it was men who crowded the streets; women were rarely seen except along the streets of brothels where the harlots, in their fine, pink clothes, sat at the doors or on the little rickety wooden balconies that lean out into the narrow streets from each house. There they seemed like cattle in their pens. Each called you 'Chéri' as you passed. The streets are in the very centre of the town and had a sickly, depressing atmosphere about them. The filth did not stop with their morals, but extended to their houses and to their streets. Looking about you as you walked under these balconies, some might just be emptying a pail of muck into the street as you passed.

These were the Arab prostitutes. The French ones were in the hotels and nearly every hotel and bar had its licence prominently displayed outside beside its signboard.

All Arab prostitutes in the whole of Algeria, I was told by the butcher in the market who spoke English, came from one tribe between Ghardaia and Djelfa. Contrary to the normal custom, with that tribe a female child is welcomed with rejoicing, while male babies are unwanted. The girls were brought up to enter the trade and travel into every town in the Northern Sahara and Algeria.

I had my boots mended and a couple of rents in my rucksack sewed. The rucksack Blacks sent me was too small and, being overloaded, it was giving way very soon. It was only a couple of months since I had received it.

I met a German tourist who was there for a few days. He was the only tourist in town. The terrorist war here had killed the tourist trade. We sat at a café for a time. When the bootblacks pestered us with such deliberate persistency so that conversation between us was almost impossible, he gave them a few francs so they would go. They plagued every stranger in town.

If they would only take heed when they had been refused 'service', it would make the life of other travellers more agreeable. The German was an elderly man and very pleasant. I believe he was Director of Music for Children at the BBC in Hamburg.

I set out next morning hoping to get a lift to Batna. I walked all day, but no lift. The road was busy with traffic but nothing would stop. I suppose it was due to this being a danger zone and most drivers were afraid to stop and many, no doubt, were dubious of picking up a stranger with so many terrorists about.

My worst fears realised, I had to spend a night out on the road alone. I cleaned up the .25 and made sure it was in good working order. Also, I had the spare ammunition handy. It was still desert and there wasn't a drop of water about, so I had to rely on my only bottle. I hoped to get a lift next day.

I spent an uneasy but uneventful night. I heard or saw no one and didn't hear any gunfire or anything which might have indicated that fighting was close.

A storm blew up in the morning and the mountains disappeared. The choking sand once again made existence awful. How glad I was to be through with all that sand now, at least I hoped I was finished with it.

Midway through the forenoon a truck stopped. I could hardly believe it after so many had passed. I had long since ceased to bother even to look around when I heard one coming and just kept walking, so I was surprised and exceedingly pleased when this one stopped. It was going to Batna. The puzzled driver – I couldn't make him understand why I was walking in such a remote and troubled area – agreed to take me.

It was 117 kilometres from Biskra to Batna. From the beginning, the road began to climb into the Aurès Mountains which are part of the Atlas Saharan chain. In those 117 kilometres the Sahara desert ends. Beyond Biskra it was still a rocky, sand-swept wilderness. Then you came to a little oasis and further on another and then, nearer there, was another and another until the stunted grass from the one barely ends before you entered the area of the next. The road plays snakes and ladders with the railway, crossing and recrossing it on the way up into the mountains. You pass through the awe-inspiring El Kantari gorge and enter the little town of that name. You are on top of the plateau now and from here, the land looks strange after the endless sand. For miles and miles now, the ground had the green sheen of new corn just breaking surface and there were little, red-tiled farm houses dotted here and there, looking very isolated after the congested oasis of the desert.

The truck arrived at Batna about 1 p.m. Now the towns were monotonous in their similarity to European ones. Batna had wide, well laid out streets and was even more European looking than Biskra. The same kind of trees grew out of the circular gratings in the pavements as in Paris. Here, as in Biskra, carriages and cabbies with pairs of horses and sometimes three in harness, clip-clopped through the streets with harnesses jangling.

The rest of the day since I arrived was spent with the police. Now, every place I arrived in seemed to bring its debacle with the police. It was quite a session, the worst yet. I was picked up while sitting at the pavement tables of a café. A plain-clothed policeman ordered me to come with him to the station. In a room there, they searched me and, after examining my passport, turned out my kit. As an explanation for this treatment they said they had a war on their hands and had to be careful of all strangers, and they hinted, although didn't say, especially wanderers such as I in case they were communist agents.

They went through my kit carefully, paying particular attention to all my papers, photos and the contents of my writing case. One, a captain who spoke good English, even took my diary to read through parts of it. I told them I had a gun before they found it. No, I didn't have a license for it! The Arab detective who picked me up said proudly to the captain something which I took to be, "I told you so, I can pick them out a mile away".

After everything had been examined and returned to me there remained the question of the pistol. I thought at least they would confiscate the gun, at the worst a fine or even jail sentence for carrying an unauthorised weapon.

I was taken from one office to another and questioned over and over again by a different plain-clothed officer. The same questions: where did I get the gun? Why did I not have it licensed? Why was I here? How much money do you have? Why have you been travelling so long in Africa? Where do you get money from? Why did you go to Kenya? Why were you so interested in the Mau Mau? Do you speak to the Arabs here? And many more. I had my answers off by heart before long.

After a time, I was left on my own. When the next person questioned me I sensed they had had a parley and, it seemed, decided I had no ulterior motive in coming here. I was no spy or agent to stir up trouble. This last one also settled the last question on hand. He picked up the telephone and I got enough to know he was telling someone that I wasn't a vagabond either. I had money – not much for what he says he is going to do. I caught the word 'economist'! He does his own cooking. Yes, there were "pommes de terre" and rice, etc. in his pack.

I was left on my own again. Then to my great surprise the captain brought in my pistol and ammunition and gave them to me saying, "You are in a very dangerous area. Keep this by you at all times. I advise you not to go to Timgad; it is in a very bad area."

Then he said I could go. They didn't give me a licence or permission to have the gun. It was all very strange.

I found a place in the public gardens to camp. It was very cold, this place being in the mountains. Over the wall from where I was camped was the cemetery. It was raining when I awoke in the morning. Luckily I had pitched the tent last night. I swithered about whether or not to bother putting it up. It was cold and sometimes it is better wrap it around like a blanket instead of erecting it. I wonder why? I hadn't been in the habit of using it lately. Funny, I get these premonitions sometimes and there was nothing to suggest a break in the weather last night.

What a miserable day today. I had planned to go to Timgad, the old Roman city 36 kilometres out, but it was useless to go as photography would have been impossible.

A small bivouac is an odious place to live in when it rains. It is like living in a hole, only worse as you must always be conscious of your movements in case you touch the canvas as the rain would come in then. It was very muddy outside. It clogs up boots and I must be most careful to keep my feet outside the tent, or at least at the edge. All day I have been cold and wet. This is the first rain I've seen since French Equatorial seven months ago and I am taking ill-out with it. How miserable it makes life when you haven't a home to go to.

But I am lucky I am in a town. This afternoon I went into town to buy some bread, etc. I had some coffee in a café that jutted out onto the pavement. How cold it was outside. The rain splattered the glass by my table. A cabby rattled by on the road, the horse breathing steam, its head drooping …who'd be a horse on a wet, cold day? A great mixture of pedestrians passed my window: Arabs with peaked, hooded cloaks pulled tight about them; old bearded men; young street urchins wet and cold looking, with jacket collars turned up; Arabs, many of them in European clothes; boot-blacks with their boxes under their arms … who wants wet shoes polished? Arab women, veiled – some wear the 'yashmak' here instead of wrapping a blanket round themselves; elderly French ladies with umbrellas; slick Parisian-like models in shiny Wellingtons and plastic coats. An Arab woman pounded a door across the road and got no answer, her blanket flapping like clothes on a line. I pulled my cape on and went 'home'.

My tent is in the middle of a quagmire. I was sitting in it, wet and sorry for myself. I looked out and near the dying embers of my fire were three small Arab boys, their heads buried in their hunched shoulders, their hands deep in the pockets of ragged trousers. They were soaked. It made me realise how well off I was. There is always someone worse off than you.

I am a fool, a silly, sentimental fool! This morning I found my waterproof cape had gone. Stolen! That's what you get in return for kindness. It makes one so bitter and hard. I'll see them in hell now before I help the next Arab, child or adult.

This morning the rain had stopped. The sun danced about among the watery-looking clouds that swept across the sky. A stiff, cold breeze blew. I decided to try and risk going to Timgad. I expected a soaking, especially now I have no cape. It was rather late in the morning before I decided to chance it and once on the way, I realised I'd been a bit foolhardy. The chance of making the return journey before dark didn't seem so good. There is a curfew in Batna. After dark, anyone who walks in the streets is liable to be shot.

How cold it was. I wore my kilt round my shoulders and even with two jerseys I felt cold.

I got a lift first to Lambese in an Arab truck. The Arab driver said the French and Americans were no good. But the English were good. I suppose the countries would be reversed if I were French or American.

At Lambese I went to see the museum. It is a little old building standing in the middle of what looks like a graveyard. All around are the remains of Roman ruins; stone blocks with Latin inscriptions carved on them, decapitated statues of the gods and men in togas, and broken pillars. The rusty iron gate creaked loudly as I opened it. It was a grey day, windy and cold. I pulled my kilt tight round my shoulders – I was wearing long trousers.

In a little cottage next to the museum I found the curator, a little woman who was either French or Arab. Hard to tell which. She showed me around, reciting the name of each article or statue in a sing-song voice. There are some wonderful pictures in terrazzo work from the floors of the ancient Roman town. After leaving the museum I crossed the ruins of Lambese to reach the road. In the middle of some ploughed land stood a great stone arch, gaunt and lonely.

On the main road the rain came on heavy. I took shelter in a little farmhouse. The owner kept talking in Arabic to me, unable, it seemed, to grasp the fact that I could not understand. Again on the road after the shower, I got a lift for a few kilometres in a police truck. They warned me against wandering about on my own. They dropped me at the fork of the road where the other road goes to Arris. More rain came; I sheltered behind a haystack. The wind was very cold. This part of North Africa, with its little farms, haystacks, red-tiled farmhouses and indigenous white people, belongs more to Europe than to Africa.

Later, I got picked up by a French family in a Citroën car. They took me right to Timgad, although it was past where they were going. The first sight of Timgad one gets on approaching is two pillars silhouetted against the sky. This is the first Roman ruin I have seen. I have read so much of the

Romans, but it is not until now that I realise what a great civilisation they had then, and how far advanced they were.

How real the life seemed in the paved streets, still with the chariot wheel ruts worn into the stone, the magnificence of the buildings, the planning of the city and the excellence in the workmanship, the carvings, the statues, the writing. In these things they were so far ahead of us even now. I wandered around, fascinated. The amphitheatre, so silent and empty now; what crowds, what scenes have you witnessed? Best preserved and most impressive is the arch like the Arc de Triomphe in Paris. At times the sky provided a theatrical backdrop, black and wild. Standing out white against such a backdrop, the old stone seemed to live.

There were many French soldiers stationed on the edge of the ruins. In the main streets are the marks of caterpillar tracks on the flagstones. Tanks must have passed through. That would have been a sight worth seeing. The old and the new. So much a contrast to the Roman legions which once walked those same streets.

Occasionally, the sun found a hole in the clouds and then I ran about taking the photos I wanted. It was 3.30 when I decided to head back to Batna. Already it seemed to be growing dark and I feared that I had little chance of making it back. I walked to the main road. Looking back, the broken pillars, the arch, the silent ruins seemed like a gravestone to the dead empire that was.

While walking, an Arab passed with horse and cart. He told me to climb up. I did, and travelled with him for four kilometres until he branched off to his farm. I walked some more then, to my relief, a truck came along and gave me a lift into Batna. I arrived at 5.45. Just beat the curfew by a couple of minutes.

CHAPTER 28

ALGIERS AND... GERALD

Algiers at last! That was a big milestone. It is a great, throbbing city, like another Paris. I was very lucky getting a lift first to Setif and then another straight into Algiers. Over 300 kilometres in one day was good going.

The Kabylie Mountains are wonderful, like great masses of crumpled brown and silver paper. I can think of no other way to describe their beauty than to say I'd like to come back and spend longer there some time. The driver of the car was armed with a rifle and revolver. He had come through Aris and Timgad where the nationalists are active. Also he said it is very possible to run into trouble in the Kabylie Mountains because there are many Fellagha (bandits) there also.

Big changes! I had decided to go through Tunisia to Sicily and Italy instead of Morocco and Spain. It was going to take too long to get the visas and also was going to be too expensive. And yet I would still have gone on with all that, but have taken a notion to see the ruins of Carthage at Tunis. Since Timgad, I have thought I'd like to see more of the old ruins. My mind was more than half-made up and it only needed that – the delay in getting visas – to make me really decide to head east instead of west. I will go to Sicily and Italy and perhaps Switzerland.

I bought myself a waterproof jacket, ex-US army stock. It ran away with a lot of my capital, but I needed it. The continual cold was making me feel miserable at times.

It was April and Easter Monday – the end of the Easter weekend. A year ago to the day I was at Mubende in Uganda. These few days since arriving in Algiers, I have stayed at Dar Naama, the Headquarters of the Algerian Mission Band, a Protestant mission. Arriving in the city with nowhere to go and camping impossible, I decided to take the advice of Dr Wakefield, the old lady at Tamanrasset, and seek out the mission. I had to swallow a lot of old convictions to do that as I had always told myself I would not take advantage of any mission where they were obliged to accept you, even if you approached them uninvited.

Since I arrived, I wondered if I was slipping, if I was being weak. So often I imposed restrictions on myself to see if I could carry them out, banning some little pleasure or luxury for a time – I will not take sugar in my tea for one month, or I will not buy anymore cheese until…, or I will not eat fried bread with sugar until I arrive at some place, some hundreds of miles in advance – (I was partial to the latter, which was an expensive luxury being made with cooking oil) – and deriving a sort of austere pleasure from this. I can't remember ever breaking a ban having once imposed it on myself. Yet I came and sought a place in the mission. It was all so comfortable. The bed was the first I had slept in since Kano, two months ago, the simple but welcome meals were the first regular ones I had eaten in that time also. But I wished I hadn't come.

Although I still had some things to do in town which would keep me another couple of days, I determined to leave the mission and look up the youth hostel, although that place, cheap as it was, would strain my purse.

In these past few days here, I had come under a strong spiritual barrage from the missionaries. Being Easter, all the missionaries from the outlying stations had come into Dar Naama. All at some time have witnessed in a word or outspoken wish that someday I might find Christ. One particularly, Alex Porteous, a Scot, had tried to convert me. I liked him and admired his work, but I couldn't find it in my heart to believe – but really believe, I mean.

During walks and talks and the car run to the beach, Alex has tried hard. He has done one thing, however – he has made me think. These people were ordinary people once, living normal lives I suppose, sinning nonchalantly like most men and women. But now, without exception, they had something: a passion. Not the emotion that burns up the fanatic, but a serene force. Could there really be something in what they believe?

I am no atheist. But I cannot bring myself to accept blindly the miracles of the Bible, the Immaculate Conception and the infallibility of the words so ambiguous in meaning. To the questions which twisted my logic they could only answer that we are not capable to even ask these questions, that man is unable to understand the ways of the Lord, and that it is wrong, sinful, to even question the words, to try to bring them to materialistic ends. But that didn't help me for I was still left groping, wracked with indecision. With so many conflicting thoughts, I tried to be truthful and not voice any prayers I couldn't believe in, even though it would have pleased the missionaries immensely if I had.

I put into words to Alex what I had only thought before. We are told to ask the Lord in prayer when all else has failed. There have been times, many times, when I have felt finished and could have willingly asked God to help me. But then I always thought, 'If there is no God, then it was a

341

waste of time to pray. If there is a God then you had no right to ask for help, for in times when you don't need him you refused to believe in him. If you only believe when you need help, then you don't deserve to receive it." So I don't pray. I can't remember, even in my most dire moments, ever having prayed.

One day a group of young student missionaries, mostly American, but also including Canadian and English, stopped me in the street on seeing the kilt. They invited me to their mission for supper. I went. I wondered. These young girls, so vivacious, so fresh – would they grow into the sexless, sweet old dears of Dar Naama like the missionaries I have met elsewhere? Would these men of around my own age and younger grow into angelic, virileless males brimming with benevolence? Yet all, young as they were, held the same force I saw in any of the believers. While I hovered over an abyss of indecision, they had decided and have received something I did not have.

While at this mission the Minister, Mr Brown, a man I thought to be an Anglicised American, but who turned out to be an Americanised Anglican, asked me if I had ever thought of going to the Lord, really giving myself up. Do you want to become a Christian? I'd like to be. Right now? He asked the last lady in the room to leave and join the rest in the other room.

This shook me. Did he really mean me to make an outspoken vow just like that? Surely this had to come from within.

"Are you ready?" he opened his Bible. I felt trapped.

"No, I'm not ready. Not yet."

We went in and joined the crowd.

***

I had been twice to the Casbah. I was warned repeatedly not to go alone. When the last British ship came in, three sailors went in and never came out again. I carried the pistol though I knew it would be of little avail if the situation arose. In such confined, crowded quarters, I would be swamped.

The Casbah was a city within a city. The 'Rue de Casbah' branched off from one of the more modern streets. It was a narrow, cobbled street set at an incline, which made one lean well forward on the way up. Dive off this 'Rue' into the even narrower side streets and one was lost in bygone centuries.

The Algiers Casbah was a living, thriving hell: an open, festering sore that leaked evil. Down in its dark streets, where the sun had been lost for untold centuries every vice, from murder to the petty thefts of the dishonest merchants, was rampant. In the narrow stairways which tunnelled under the leaning houses and which served as streets, one could purchase anything from stolen odds and ends at bargain prices, to the 'my sister, just fifteen'

342

of the little boy who claimed to speak English – that was the only sentence he knew.

This casbah was a caricature of the others I had seen, almost comical in its exaggerated features. The houses on either side of the street leaned over from the first storey and barely touched each other. This was said to be in case of earthquakes when they would buttress each other. On the steps of the streets, where the width permitted, hotchpotch collections of stalls were set up. Here was a fruit stall, its vivid colours a welcome splash in the gloom, there a man lying asleep over his table of remnants he was selling and, further on, a shoemaker with rows of sandals on view, then a peanut vendor and a haberdashery stall. Here the crowds jostled each other. The small streets were empty, save for an occasional woman dressed in a black cloak who padded silently passed, her eyes flashing with curiosity at you from above the white veil that hides the rest of her face.

In the Rue de Casbah, the main thoroughfare that flows through this living cesspool, the 'indigènes' had borrowed the French idea of open air cafés. At the tables sat Arabs and Berbers in their colourful and picturesque cloaks – known as the burnouse – and headcloths, looking almost too theatrical to be real.

A century ago this was still the den of pirates and smugglers. Piracy, with ships operating from Algiers, lingered long after it was stopped in most other places, until here it was also smothered; smuggling still goes on but was not as present here in the Casbah as in the elegant modern part. Each time I went to the Casbah I was thankful when I came out unharmed. Even the police left well alone there. I never saw one there, yet in the modern streets they patrolled armed with revolvers.

I moved into the youth hostel. I told the missionaries I was leaving town. This was a lie, but I hoped a white one, as they would not have allowed me to go to seek another place had I not said I was leaving. Before I left I put 500 francs in the mission box. It was nothing compared to what I had received, but at that moment it was one third of my total capital until I got to Italy. I was left with 1000 francs (£1).

The hostel was a fine one. Large and spacious, it had gas cookers and a fine common room. There was a Swiss fellow there I met at Constantine. He spoke good English and he had spent a year up till now travelling around France and Morocco. We were talking in the afternoon. He started out at the same age as me, but unlike me he had no set place to go. He said he might go to Tripoli or try to get work in Senegal. He didn't know where. Then, as we had so much in common, we got talking of why we were travelling. As we talked, I could see he had the same ideas, the same desires, the same fears as I had when I started. He was as I was four years ago when I started out. And, as we talked, I realised I was putting into words the pieces of the jigsaw of life that separated us. Knowing myself, I could see what was in his mind perhaps better than he did himself.

When I was asked in Rhodesia by the old Colonel at Lialui "Why" I had answered, "Adventure, interest, to see the world." But within myself I knew there was something lacking in that definition, yet I couldn't think what it was. I didn't realise why I was travelling, although I had then been wandering for three years. I was looking for something, yet I didn't know what.

While we talked I suddenly realised I had crystallised into words what I hadn't been conscious of even thinking. And yet it had always been there, subconsciously, turbulent. Although it was to the Swiss I was talking, I was as much a listener as he. It was as though the words were not mine, as if a third person was telling us what we hadn't realised we were thinking.

I thought I was looking for adventure, for interest, studying the natives, but all the time I was looking for something else. The other reasons I put forward materialised. I had found adventure, I had seen enough of the natives to satisfy my curiosity, but I had to wander the length and breadth of Africa before I found the main thing I was looking for, yet it was always the nearest but the most elusive of all my quests. I had set out to prove myself to myself.

Although I didn't go into the matter further then, looking back I can see where my search ended, although there again, like the unconscious quest, I didn't realise it was over. It ended somewhere in French Equatorial Africa, after the walk in the rains, the trial of being so short of food, the realisation I could carry on after losing all I owned. But, as I have said, impossible as it was to put what I was looking for into words, neither could I have said, "Well, that's it," when I found it. Yet subconsciously, I knew I had and French Equatorial Africa was merely a climax. I had been building up that way slowly, for a long time.

Now I could see it all. The slight lessening of interest since then; the feeling I thought was apprehension on leaving Kano; the desire to be home again, all grew from the fact that now I had proved myself and to continue the rest of the journey was unnecessary. What I thought was apprehension was not the fear of going through again what I had done, but merely the realisation that there was no need for further privation.

***

There was a French school teacher at the hostel who told me he would be driving towards the Tunisian border. He offered to take me. He was the slowest, dreamiest and most procrastinating person I had ever met. A year younger than I, he was as dithery as an ancient, rotten with senile decay.

344

And yet I liked him in a way. Perhaps what irked me was that I saw in him some of my own failings. I must admit that I am given to dreaming occasionally. Sometimes I wake to the fact and curse myself for a lazy fool, weak-headed because I cannot control my mind. Of course, there are times when dreaming is permissible – beside a campfire, on railway journeys when your mind automatically goes clickety-click to the wheels. There's a time and a place for everything. But yet, from this fellow I drew some comfort of mind also. I realised how far I had to go to be as bad as he; like the man who indulges in an occasional drink compared to the drunkard.

Gerald Bucknell was his name. We were supposed to leave early in the morning – "We leave early and do many kilometres". 'Early' meant rising at 8 a.m. Then, when I thought we were ready to go he said, "I must just go to town to buy a book I saw, then we go". Town, or the centre of the city, was about five kilometres away. He had a little Citroën two-horsepower car. So he went off and I waited in the hostel. He came back at noon and said he would go to the café to eat and be back in an hour, so I cooked myself something. He came back and we loaded the baggage into the car. Then he stood for a minute with his chin in his hand, thinking. Coming to a snap decision he said suddenly, "I go to eat at the café. Then we go."! I thought he had just come back from there. Where had he been for an hour? Already I'd got used to accepting his ways. He went to eat and came back in half an hour. Now, we are ready to be off? But, no!

"I just run into town for a book I saw yesterday. Then we go"

I thought he'd spend all afternoon doing that. The man seemed to go through life in a stupor all the time, so this time I went with him. He got lost in the traffic and did a couple of turns round a roundabout. Eventually we got to town. He looked for a parking place in the shade.

"There's a place." It was on the other side of the street. He swung into a U-turn but, halfway round, he stopped and for seconds just gazed into space while traffic from both directions was raising Cain with their horns. Then another one of his lightening decisions.

"No, we try another place."

So off we went, passing twenty shady, empty spots ideal for the purpose. He seemed to have forgotten he was looking for a parking place for he drew up abruptly in the sun and got out. An idea had flashed into his nimble brain. He paused with his hand on the door handle, gazing down at the pavement for a while; then quickly snapped it shut, locked it and, although I was inside, walked away.

He came back in about three quarters of an hour and I was pleased to see he was carrying a book. Now we could get on the way for Constantine. The time was 3.30 p.m. But... we must pass the youth hostel again on the way out...

"I just go in to play some music on the piano. Then we go."

Luckily the door was locked and he couldn't get in so, after a reasonable time standing weighing up the door, the handle and the street, he returned to the car and we actually left the city.

Bouira, in the Kabylie Mountains, is 120 kilometres from Algiers. We arrived at 8 p.m. Gerald drove to a hotel and I prepared to go to find a place to camp. The hotel had a great cobbled courtyard with a horse trough down one side. It was cold and there were many Fellagha (terrorists) there and camping wasn't very safe. It would have been difficult looking about in the dark too. Then the proprietor came, a fat little man whose legs twinkled under him so fast when he walked that his barrel torso appeared to run on castors.

Gerald had a double room for which he paid 400 francs. The proprietor said I could have the other bed for 100 francs and I accepted as he also said the police would not allow me to walk out of town to camp now it was dark. The door of our room opened directly onto the main street.

Gerald gets more exasperating as the time passes. He is likeable because he seems so helpless. But I couldn't stand too much of him, living in contact with him depending on him as now. He writes music and he played me some of his stuff on his accordion. One of his waltzes was particularly mellow and catching. I wondered what his world was like. He seemed not to live in this world but to be wrapped in an invisible cocoon. Normal conversation with him was impossible and seldom were two sentences coherent. When asked a question, it took a long time to penetrate and, if he gave an answer, it was impossible to follow it up as the curtain would have dropped again and by the time you managed to get your second question through, he had forgotten about the first one. Yet he was quite academic. He understood Greek and Latin and his music was good according to my ear.

When driving, he would sometimes rest his elbow on the wheel and cup his chin in his hand, then pull out a scrap of paper and write down a few notes of music. All this while his car was going. His abstractness almost cost our lives. We missed a train at a level crossing by seconds – oh, less than that! – a second or two at the most. Neither of us would ever be so near to it again. If the train had been that one second earlier I would not be writing this now. The road crossed the track on a hill we were coming down, so even if the train had crossed the road seconds before us, it would have been impossible to stop at the speed we were going to have missed the wagons. Gerald, a devout Catholic, crossed himself several times after that.

I had never met anyone who did so many incantations as Gerald. When he woke, he sat up in bed and muttered a prayer and crossed himself a few times before rising. He prayed and made crosses before he ate any food, even though it was just a piece of bread. He crossed himself if we passed by a cemetery and prayed at all odd times of the day. It was rather trying at times. Often I spoke to him and, after the normal wait for it to sink in, I would receive no answer. I would ask again, but often the reason for his silence was that he was in the middle of a prayer and then I must wait till he had finished and crossed his chest before repeating what I said, or leave it unsaid as I usually did.

In the morning I rose, washed, dressed and went out to the bakers at the other end of the street for bread, came back and ate it before Gerald had opened an eye. Again we were supposed to be starting early. He rose at about 8.30 and, without washing, he dressed, flattened down his sleep dishevelled hair with his hand, put on his beret and asked if I would go with him to church. I said I would walk with him, but I wouldn't go in. We went to the chapel and I waited outside expecting him to be only five or ten minutes. He was 35 minutes. Several times I was on the point of going but I had said I would wait and didn't want to go back on my word. But I was thoroughly fed up with him.

After that, he dottered about the room before we at last got away at about 10 a.m. But we had only gone half a dozen kilometres when he suddenly remembered he wanted to see someone back in town to take their photo. So we went back. He went into the house to see whoever it was while I sat in the car for two hours waiting for him. At last, at 12.30 p.m. we made our early start. I had hoped we would go straight through to Constantine today, but it was impossible with half the day gone before we started. With the few francs I had left, I was living on the minimum possible and each day longer I took to get to Italy made it harder for me.

As we climbed through the mountains, I endorsed my desire from my previous journey through them to return there some day. One day to come back with my own transport and wander at my leisure among the Kabylie Mountains. The day was as soft as a shy maiden's kiss; the sky billowy white and blue. The mountains rolled away in green waves; the road in a gay, frisky mood twirled and capered in a devious dance through one pass after another. In the fields men ploughed with two, four or even six horses or donkeys in harness, scarring the contours with straight furrows. The hills looked comfortable in their ploughed cardigans. The soil was rich, the best I saw in Africa. It was dark brown, moist healthy-looking land when it had been turned over.

To each plough there was quite a team of natives. Apart from the one handling the implement, there were at least two more encouraging the animals in their efforts and usually a few children running round also. Here and there a tractor merrily tore away at the land, denoting a French farm. The Berbers rarely, if ever, go in for modern ways of farming.

Setif was 180 kilometres from Bouira. We arrived about 6 p.m. Gerald went to a friend of his, a school teacher also. We had coffee there and I was

347

interested in the decoration. The walls were papered and the woodwork grained in similar fashion to houses at home. Since it was a small house and barely enough room to put up Gerald, I went to look for a place to camp. They suggested the railway station and sure enough the station master agreed to my sleeping in the waiting room.

Gerald was going almost to the Tunisian border and said he would like me to go with him. I knew he liked company but also, when he stopped so often at cafés he had me to watch the car while he was inside. It was unsafe to leave a car unattended even in a main street, for thieves were always watching for just that chance.

Last night in the railway waiting room at Setif was an uneasy one. Arabs came and went most of the night. Some were drunk and made plenty of noise. I had to be wary about my kit in case some of it went.

In the morning I started walking on the road. I hoped I'd get a lift before Gerald came along, since I was tired of his time-wasting ways. But I walked for a few kilometres and anything that came along didn't bother to stop. Then along came Gerald. He seemed pleased to find me and, for a brief time, seemed to be alive to this world while he bundled in my kit. Then he turned the car and headed back for Setif. He had come out looking for me. That's the part of him I felt mean about. I cursed him and fume at him, yet he was so simple and kind in his own way I couldn't help liking him. We went back to his friend's house and had coffee and pastries his wife had baked. That is as near to a breakfast as you can expect to get in any French home and I appreciated it.

Then Gerald started talking of going and half an hour later managed to make the car. Then he lingered over the wheel while the family stood on the pavement. Finally, his friend, no doubt knowing his ways, took the initiative and more or less told him to get on his way. He went.

Some distance out of Setif a road leads off the main one to the old Roman ruins of Djemila. Gerald, on seeing the signpost, decided to go there. I was very pleased and felt that he went for my benefit, because he had already been there twice before. The ruins are some 30 odd kilometres from the main road. All the roads, even secondary ones, are metalled in North Algeria.

On the way we stopped at a school. The teacher was a friend of Gerald's. The school house was a lone building in a sea of green rolling waves. Its remote loneliness made it seem strange why it should be there. Yet in the folds of these green hills live hundreds of farming communities. Attendance to the school was spasmodic according to the season, for if the season required the children on the farm, then school was neglected.

The French had an interesting family allowance system. My facts were hearsay but maybe quite accurate. For each child the government paid 7,000 francs per month. To receive this, the children must attend school. There was no difference made for race. French, Arab, Berber received the same.

This system showed that social machinery made for Europe cannot be used with efficiency elsewhere. The family benefit system was evolved in France to increase the declining birth rate. But in Algeria there was nothing deficient in their birth rate – among the Berber and Arabs I mean – rather the opposite for the good of the country. You found natives drawing up to 100,000 francs a month – procreation was a good business under the French. Yet since Algeria was no longer a colony and was now regarded as part of France, any differences made between French and Arabs would be regarded as racial.

But the allowances did make the people find employment and the parents sent their children to school. Yet I wondered always when passing through the innumerable little villages and towns in Northern Algeria, why there were so many idlers in the streets. Early morning till late evening every café – and there were many of them even in the smallest villages – had crowds sitting at its tables, crowds of people with nothing else to do thronged the streets.

The French said the people are extremely lazy and have no desire to work.

The African did not regard working as permanent. He looked for a job to accumulate funds for some particular desire – a new bicycle, a fancy shirt, a slick suit to wear all the time, to look like the dandies one sees in the street, to earn money enough to buy a wife, or simply to buy liquor. By raising the wages it only allowed the worker to realise his ambition sooner and leave, thus increasing the employment problem even more and reducing the efficiency of the industry, for with a constant changing of labour no man could learn to do a job well.

But, to come back to this little school house...

There were two classrooms downstairs. The husband taught in one and the wife in the other. Their home was upstairs. They were granted so much land round about to cultivate but did not find the time to do it, so they had leased it to a local farmer; and went shares with the profits.

Gerald said he would look in for five minutes. That turned out to be more than a couple of hours and we had lunch with them before we left. The drive up to Djemila was magnificent. Truly I wanted to come back to these mountains, unless of course my appetite was satisfied with my own land, but just now after these years in Africa, this land of quiet pastures, green hills and solid country folk was like a cool drink.

To know anything we must have comparisons; we would not know beauty if we had not seen ugliness. We take for granted the green fields unless we have seen the desert, and a drink would bring no pleasure unless we had known thirst. Immediate comparison lends enchantment or the opposite to whatever we see, more so than a long past memory. So perhaps I was seeing these lands through desert-tainted glasses. But, at the time, it all felt magnificent.

The ruins of Djemila, although not so extensive, were even more interesting than Timgad. Their effect was probably enhanced by the fact of a guide in this case, who lifted the curtain of time here and there, for a glimpse of the buildings as they were in their heyday, whereas at Timgad I wandered about alone and anything beyond the broken masonry had to be supplied from my quite inaccurate imagination.

Here were the two rows of broken columns of the Christian church of the fifth century and there the restored ruins of a church of the fourth century. The domed roof of the chapel where people were baptised had been replaced. Set in the circular wall were arched recesses where the people sat and above each was a little stone ledge where lamps were placed.

Further down the hill was the Temple of Septimus, the walls and great columned portals still in good condition. You climbed a wide flight of stairs and the doorway towered above you. Two semicircular stone ruts showed where the mighty doors rolled back on wheels.

At the bottom of the hill was the oldest part, dating from before the Christian era. In the temple was a great stone block engraved with characters in the act of preparing the sacrifice. One in relief of a man with raised axe over a tethered bull was exceptionally clear, considering it was over a thousand years old when the Norman conquerors landed in England.

There was the flagged floor of the great hall of sports, where the Romans held their gymnastics and the place where the carved wall ornaments left nothing to the imagination that it was the men's place of pleasure. Here was the Temple of Jupiter with the great headless torso still standing.

In the market place were stone troughs with a hole in the bottom, where grain was measured and sold. The streets were paved. It was an unforgettable experience to wander through this silent, dead town.

On the walls of the nearby museum had been set whole floors of mosaic. These had been lifted piece by piece and set into the walls. What a jigsaw! The pictures depicted were magnificent. What pigment did they use, I wondered, that endured with such vividness to this day?

It was already late afternoon before we got on our way again. The rest of the drive to Constantine was uneventful except for the hundred and one things that caught Gerald's eye and made him turn and look out the rear window for seconds at a time, while the car wandered about the road, impervious to any oncoming traffic.

On arrival in Constantine I found the youth hostel office locked, and since it was about 9 p.m., it was too late to look up anybody for the key.

Gerald went to a hotel and booked in but refused to leave me until I had found a place to sleep. At times his simple faithfulness really touches me. You would think it was he and not I being assisted. We looked about trying to hunt down the key to the youth hostel but being Saturday night, it was hopeless to find anybody. The streets were even more packed than normal. There were some local elections coming up and crowds were going about shouting slogans. At length at 11 p.m., Gerald said I must come to his hotel and sleep in his room. The place was quiet and the receptionist had gone so I got in unobserved. I slept on the floor and left in the morning before anybody was about, although I had a job missing the doorman.

I looked up the address of the holder of the key to the youth hostel office and dumped my kit there. I cruised round most of the day and decided that tomorrow I would go with Gerald to Tebessa.

In the Rue de France, one of the narrow but main shopping streets in Constantine, on the stepped pavement of the steep street, letter writers slept stretched out or did their business, if they were lucky enough to get a customer. They ranged from the Arab in European clothes and red fez, who had a deck chair with a sun canopy to the old, ragged man in a faded and patched burnouse, who wrote Koran sermons on a board covered with sand.

***

Gerald was in excellent form and we got away at the most unearthly time of 9 a.m. There were no villages along this road and little to attract his attention so we made fine time, arriving at Tebessa by noon. Once over the mountains, we were into the fringes of the desert again. Camels plodded here and there or nibbled at the tufts of dry grass. Again I met the wind and the sand and was not happy with it.

Tebessa is an old Roman town and most of the modern building still lies within the high wall which still stood complete with ornate gateway.

I was in a way sorry to say goodbye to Gerald. Although the most aggravating person I had ever met, he was also very likeable. I thought his abstractness was due to an overactive academic brain and perhaps it was. But, yesterday in Constantine, he proved to be a mere mortal when he insisted on going slowly by the crowds that were just leaving a cinema so as to admire the girls in their Sunday dresses, and indeed, he was even more detached than normal when I tried to say anything to him if a particularly beautiful girl went by.

He was supposed to be back at his school to open it, but since he was the only teacher, he was nonchalant about losing a day or two. He still had 200 kilometres to drive to get to his school in the desert. He would not get there until the next day since he had to find someone to go with him. The police would not allow a lone traveller in case he got stuck in the sand.

I had written before in my diary about comparisons. What better way was there of learning the value of food than when you hadn't got it? Now my main interest in the world was food, and a loaf of bread was one of the most valuable things on earth. When I was obliged to spend anything, I reckoned it in bread not in francs.

True to form, before he set off, Gerald kindly gave me a loaf of bread which I was most grateful for. Thank you, Gerald.

CHAPTER 29

IMPRISONMENT – ARAB STYLE

I camped in a clump of trees. Some Arab farmhouses were scattered nearby and some of the locals came to join me for some time at my fire. One brought me some firewood which was scarce and asked for food. He would not have bothered had he known my situation having only one precious loaf, but I shared what I had.

What a day! Another one wasted with the police. I had just struck camp and was crossing the fields to the road, when two policemen on bicycles appeared and, on seeing me, waited until I reached the road. Whether they had come specially or not, I didn't know. The fact I was camped among the people was enough to stamp me as a suspicious character. They asked to see my passport, studied it and then searched me and found the pistol. They stopped a passing taxi and ordered the driver to take us all to the station. They gave their bikes to two of the crowd which had gathered, with orders to take them to the station.

At the gendarmerie I went through the old routine, answering the same old questions. They turned out my kit on the floor. Then I had to wait until the captain came and it was noon before he arrived. By then they seemed to have come to the conclusion that I was all right. Once again, to my surprise, the pistol was returned to me and I was allowed to go, with the advice and warning not to camp outside a town again in Algeria or Tunisia.

After that, since I'd been taken to Tebessa, I thought there would not be much chance of a lift on the Gafsa road and decided to head for Souk Ahras instead, and cross into Tunisia from there. But I found hitch-hiking in north Algeria, away from the main Constantine–Algiers road well-nigh impossible. Half the people didn't want to stop and the other half were afraid to pick up a stranger in case the police pounced on them.

I drummed up some tea by the roadside. The wind was a force that tore the flames away from my mug and bent them flat. Eventually a car stopped. The driver thought I was a soldier and finding I was not was reluctant to take me. It was only when I walked away that he decided and came after me. He was going to the next village, Morsatt, 30 kilometres away.

The road went by queer-shaped and very picturesque mountains. At Morsatt there was one that was like a hand sticking up, the pillared rocks as fingers. After Morsatt it was the same as before, with the few cars that came past, some even slowing down to have a better look at me. When it became evident that I wasn't going to get any further by car, I made my way back to the village and camped on the outskirts. I pitched the tent beside an old tumbledown affair where an old woman lived. These villages were very similar to those in Europe – the houses with their gardens were very like those in Scotland.

I was sure the police would look me up again. I couldn't get turned for them now. It seemed if you didn't travel by your own car or in luxury, it was evident you must have some ulterior motive to live among the people and soon I was in real trouble.

I got on the road next morning and, after half an hour or so, a car stopped. It was going to Clairefontaine, the next village 30 miles on from Morsatt. But before we arrived there, a cordon of three gendarmerie armed with tommy guns stopped the cars. It was immediately obvious what or who they were looking for. Ignoring the driver, on seeing me one pushed the muzzle of his gun through the window and ordered me out. Without bothering to ask for my passport, the others grabbed my kit and transferred it to a police car waiting at the side.

Someone in the cars which passed me must have informed them of the suspicious character tramping the road, as the police recognised me instantly, obviously from a given description. Angry at another delay, I felt confident of my release this time. I knew they would search me and the revolver was the only thing they would have against me. I even said humorously to myself when the car turned and headed for Clairefontaine, 'Thank goodness, we are at least going in my direction. I would have been most annoyed if they had taken me back the way I had come.'

But to use the saying, I was riding for a fall. 'Third time lucky?' No, not this time.

At the station it was obvious they meant business. With hardly a word the door was closed; two gendarmes covered me with machine guns while another searched me. The revolver was found, of course. They went through my kit reading all private letters and looking at the photos I had. As on the previous occasions they realised they had drawn a blank as four of the secret agents went and became even friendly when they learned what I was really doing. But, whereas before each case had been confined to the station and the officer in charge turned a blind eye to the revolver, this time they had phoned headquarters before they had checked up. So now it was out of local hands.

At midday I was given a meal of Arab food, couscous. It was apparent I was there for some time and the day dragged on, but all the time I thought

I would get away. But towards evening the Sergeant told me I must go to prison at Guelma, 160 kilometres away. They would take me the next day. This was a nuisance just when I was hurrying to get to Tunis.

That evening I was given a couple of eggs and some bread to eat. Then I was led to the cell. The policeman flashed his torch around to give me my bearings then closed and locked the door. It was pitch dark. My kit had been taken from me. I felt my way around. Half the room was filled by a board about ten feet long and six broad. This was the command bunk. It was on a slope with a ledge along the bottom where you put your feet to keep you from slipping down. As far as I could make out, the only other article of furniture was the urinal bucket in the corner.

While on my finger tip voyage of discovery the door was opened and a man catapulted into the cell and sprawled on the floor. His means of propulsion had been a kick or push from the Sergeant. He and a policeman stood laughing at the door. The man picked himself up. He was an Arab and he was drunk. The Sergeant said he was a regular customer. When he stood up the Sergeant slapped him hard across the face. The Arab just stood in the torch light, a silly grin on his face. The Sergeant slapped him again, then told him to kiss me. I find the French habit of men kissing, even on the cheeks, repulsive, and I strongly objected to this wine-soaked idiot kissing me. But it was obvious the man meant to do what he was told, and he certainly had strong reasons to know not to disobey. The policemen laughed at their two prisoners struggling. This was their fun. Without being really offensive to the drunk and it was difficult to keep him at bay, so bent was he on obeying the Sergeant's command, he eventually managed to press his lips somewhere about the back of my neck.

The Sergeant then made him take off the string round his waist and with his hands engaged holding up his trousers, he was told to kiss me again. This was even more fun to the onlookers than before. The Arab would make a pass and have to stop to pull up his loose trousers. Eventually I grew sick of being a puppet and pushed the man away, hard. His trousers went down, he tripped in them and clattered down on the cobbles. The police laughed as they banged the door shut.

In the darkness I found two blankets on the bunk. The Arab had had another two thrown in with him. They were big heavy, prison blankets, coarser than army ones. It was cold and the two, one above and one below me was hardly adequate.

That night was a terrible one. The cell provided no comfort, but to share the communal bunk with the wine-crazed maniac made the night a nightmare. When I went to sleep he was still on the floor where he had fallen, giggling away to himself. Eventually he found the bunk and climbed on, talking loudly all the while. Several times during the night he woke me with his giggling. In the still of the night in the confined cell, it seemed maniacal. Twice I was wakened with him crawling over me and each time I wondered what devilry he was up to. But it seemed he didn't know what he was doing. All the same, it was not very pleasant.

At 4 a.m. while it was still dark, the policeman came and wakened me. By 4.10 a.m. we were in the car on the way to Guelma. I had an officer with one bar on his epaulette and a police corporal as guards. It was the first time I had had a special car and travelling companions laid on for me. It was obvious that they trusted me for at one time they both left the car while I was still inside and their tommy-gun was lying on the seat. I felt, if I won the judge over to that way of thinking also, I'd be in the clear.

The road wound up and over the mountains. The morning was dewy wet. In the mountain villages and farms, Berbers wrapped in their hooded burnouses were leading cattle out to the fields and starting the farming day.

We arrived at Guelma at 7.30 a.m. I had some coffee with the policemen at a café then they went to look up the judge. We sat in one of the courtyards and had to wait a long time. At one time, six Arabs were brought in to face a Judge. They were all handcuffed together, a chain passing through the three sets of cuffs. These were unlocked at the courtroom door while a policeman covered them with a tommy gun.

At last my turn came and I was led into an office. A man sat at a typewriter, the judge walked back and forward and an interpreter sat at the end of the table. I was formally charged with having a firearm in my possession. After that most of the talk seemed to be more or less irrelevant to the actual fact of the revolver. The judge asked about my journey. My kit was brought into the room and all my writing material laid on the table. The judge looked through the photographs.

Presently, they typed out a statement which I couldn't read, but which I signed. Then I was told I would have to wait three or four days before I knew the verdict. In the meantime the judge kept my diary and notebook to study and I was granted freedom on oath that I would not leave the town. I asked for a place to camp and was taken to the 'Marie' who showed me to a vacant square in the centre of the town and told I could camp there.

Being made to wait was punishment in itself. Every day lost made my situation regarding finance more precarious, for I still had to eat. I had tried to eliminate this failing as much as possible, but even at the edge of continual hunger, my few remaining francs were dwindling fast. And now four days just sitting about was going to ruin me.

The place where I camped was the front door of hell. Scores of children tortured me to within a hair's breadth of madness. And not only children. The Arab adults came along also to stand and stare.

356

These Arab children were the worst I had met. That might also go for the adults also. I like children, but these little toughs were the most loathsome I have ever had to deal with. They had no home life. Living in the streets, their education came from the gutter and even when grown up it rarely rises above that level. They swarmed over my camp – literally hemming me in so I couldn't raise an elbow. They tramped on my pot and fell over my guy ropes, breaking them. When I asked them to leave or go back a bit they only mimicked what I said and stayed there. When I became harassed and cleared them away forcibly, they threw stones at me. When I returned to cooking or whatever I was doing they crowded in again. This went on from first light until dark, and even after dark. It was very trying for I couldn't even leave my tent to attend to nature or everything I owned would have gone.

I had made up my mind to go to the police and ask if I could go to prison while I awaited the verdict. That would have surprised them. But after two days at the mercy of these hooligans I was ready to go anywhere. However, help arrived. The wife of another judge, not the one dealing with my case, asked me if I would like to camp in their garden. She was also an English teacher and wished to converse in English.

Madame Minod also invited me to join them for meals in her home. That was my biggest worry solved. But she had such a small appetite and I was embarrassed at eating on after she had finished, so I was still always hungry. Madame Minod, like Madame D'Esparbes in Touggourt, wanted so much to show me she understood the English customs and way of life as well as the language and I studied, with amused appreciation, her efforts to make me feel at home. In the morning she said, "I have cornflakes specially sent from England. They are impossible to get here." The French never eat cereals. She promptly gave me them in a plate, dry, with neither sugar nor milk. I ate them and sang my appreciation. She beamed her pleasure.

But sometimes her idea of giving me a 'home' meal backfired.

"The English don't eat bread at meals, I know." So never offered me any which I could fain have eaten plenty of.

She had a French maid who was married to an Arab. This was the first personal contact I had had with mixed marriages. They have one baby. The maid and her husband sat at the table at the meals also, but when Ramadan started the husband did not eat with us. During Ramadan, the 30-day fast, Muslims must not eat between sunrise and sunset. It is a system completely out of date with the modern way of life, for it means they get little or no sleep during the night and not eating or drinking or smoking during the day, they were too tired to work.

The women, especially the elder ones, were much more conservative than the men. This Arab's mother wanted his French bride to wear a veil and live the Muslim way of life. She rebelled against it and continued in her own way.

Monsieur Minod also has an Arab maid servant, also a married girl, who comes in her black cloak wearing a veil. She takes these off on arrival. She wears normal European dress underneath. After her work at about 4 p.m. she dons her Arab garb again and goes home. The French maid – she seems more a companion to Madame Minod than a maid – and her Arab husband live in the house.

One day I was invited by Monsieur Blance, the interpreter who I had met at the court house, to his home for dinner. He and Madame Minod, being the only two teachers of English – both take private pupils – in Guelma are bitter rivals, although they have never met. So I went from one camp to another. Monsieur Blance lives in a modest room. He had laid on a special meal, having engaged a woman from the island of Corsica to cook for him this night. What a meal! The kind I dream about. There was roast beef, rich brown with a crisp crust and potatoes, excellent soup, green peas served by themselves as a course, and wine, white and red and, afterwards, coffee and of all things chocolate cream cakes and pastries – four each!

Monsieur Blance said he had been sorry to see me in trouble with the police. He had wondered what type of person I was. During the hearing of the evidence he had decided I was not a bad character and, later he decided he wanted to have me as his guest for a night so that I may carry with me from Guelma more than just memories of police and court action. As it is I will have many memories of kindness from Guelma. Even the police, I don't feel sore at. In fact, I have grown to respect the French police very much.

Today, I went back to the court office to see what they were going to do with me, prison, a fine or both. At the office the judge handed me my diary and notebook and said I could go. I asked for the revolver but he merely shrugged his shoulders. This I took to mean they had confiscated it. They gave me no receipt or anything to indicate what had happened to it. So that's that. They took no action against me and I was never really in court. Still, the loss of my revolver is quite a blow. I had had it for so long and grown attached to it. And travelling and especially camping at night in the country and Tunisia with the 'fellagha' on the rampage is no joke if you are not armed. Still, I suppose I should be glad I got off without a fine or imprisonment. I would have had to do time, for they would have found it difficult to get money from me. What a nuisance it has all been but, at last, I was a free man, even though I had lost my revolver.

I start tomorrow for Souk Ahras. Everybody warned me not to go that way because it was a hotbed for 'fellagha'. But I had decided to go that way before I was warned and couldn't let myself be intimidated into going by the coast road. They did not realise it, but the more they told me how dangerous that way was, the surer it was that I must travel it. I would never have forgiven myself for being so cowardly had I let that trouble put me off, but I realised it was just foolishness on my part.

I left Guelma and had walked all day without a lift. The few cars that came along, passed me by. It was very difficult getting along this road, and it was very disheartening when cars didn't stop. I believe there were two reasons for the difficulty of hitch-hiking there. One was the terrorist war, people were afraid to pick up a stranger on the road, and the other was the national character of the French. When in a car, a Frenchman liked to fly along at full blast and didn't stop for anything.

I pitched my tent near a big farm. It was owned by a Frenchman. It seemed just like a farm at home with big plough horses that came in sweating, the cattle being watered at a trough and the red-tiled farm buildings enclosing a square courtyard. It rained in the night and in the morning the French farmer asked me in for coffee and bread. His kitchen was very modern which seemed strange out in the wilds there. I thanked him for his hospitality, it had been very welcome.

CHAPTER 30

CARTHAGE AND FAREWELL TO AFRICA

Wednesday 27th April, 1955

I was very lucky and got a magnificent lift right into Tunis. It seemed it was going to be a repetition of the previous day, but then I met some soldiers. They asked me where I was going. I told them, saying hitch-hiking was almost impossible, then a car came along and they stopped it. No doubt the driver thought it was something official for, once stopped, he accepted me.

They were a Dutch couple in the car and, luck of all luck, they were going direct to Tunis, about 300 kilometres. I asked to go to Souk Ahras, but once started and in conversation I said I was also going to Tunis, they said I could go all the way with them if I wished. I was only too pleased. Had I not met the soldiers I am sure it would have taken me days to get there and God only knows what I would have done for food. As it was I arrived with about 100 francs (2/-) and I wondered what I would eat after tomorrow. I hoped I would get a boat over to Sicily or Italy straight away.

It was a grand ride. The road through the mountains was unbelievably twisted. I had seen some devious mountain tracks, but there was none that surpassed that road over the last of the Atlas Mountains and into Tunisia. Then, from the cold and mist of the heights, you corkscrewed down into a lovely fertile valley.

We had our passports stamped at Ghardimaou and passed into the mountains again. The couple deviated from the road to visit the Roman ruins of Bulla Regia. The ruins on the surface were not so much to see, but there were the best preserved basements I had seen. It appeared that all the houses were constructed with basements below ground level. These were designed and ornamented as much as the upper storeys. The people lived the summer in the basement where it was cool, and in the winter above at ground level. Many of the basements were intact, the arched roofs only allowing light through the square opening. The mosaics of the floor were fantastic. One of two men and a woman was as good as when it was done two thousand years ago.

After the ruins we went back to Souk el Arba and swung towards the north, making it a long way into Tunis. We touched the sea at Tabarka, then headed east again to Mateur. At one point there was an extraordinary sight. On the north side of the road were rolling sand dunes, on the south green pastures, with only the strip of road separating the two.

It was almost dark when I was dropped off at the outskirts of Tunis. The address the Dutch couple were going to was on the fringe of the city. By the time I had walked into the centre, the lights were half an hour old. The cafés were crowded. Tramcars rattled along their rails. I had been writing sitting on a bench under a lamp in a tree-lined boulevard, but now I had to search for a place to sleep. I had no idea where.

I found a large house, like a tenement where there was a big open stair. There was a space in the twist of the stair where I bedded down. Nobody bothered me. I was keen to see Carthage and in the morning I hitched my way there. Carthage was about 17 kilometres round the bay from Tunis. The Americans were building a Memorial Cemetery to their war dead there. I asked for and was given permission to camp in their grounds.

The ruins of Roman Carthage were scattered over an extensive area. It must have been a great city for those days. There was little left of the pre-Roman Punic city. Over the ruins had grown a village which still bears the illustrious name and an electric train ran through what was the centre of the ancient city. What a bridge in time!

There wasn't much to see of the theatre. The bowl in the earth still existed, but there was no semblance of steps or columns there. However, I was told a French Dramatic Company came every year and acts there. The audience sit on the grassy slopes which were once stepped and paved. People said that the acoustics of that amphitheatre were fantastic. A whisper from an actor could be heard at the furthest top of the slope.

Looking across the bay to the twin-peaked Bon Kernine was the Bey's Palace, the provincial governor's residence. I happened to be near there when, with a fanfare of trumpets and a tune by a brass band, the royal car swept out of the gate preceded by three motorcycle police and followed by a jeep full of more police. I was asked to back well out of the way, by one of the many foot police in attendance. I thought it was a special occasion, but learned it was just normal routine. The pantomime is acted every day each time the Bey leaves to go for a drive.

The Bey's special soldiers who guarded the palace wear red serge trousers and little embroidered jackets with red fezzes. With these they wear white American gaiters, which struck a modern discord to the quaint, picturesque uniforms. They carried extra-long rifles and marched with bayonets fixed.

Apart from Carthage, there were many other little villages around this area. The most interesting was Sidi Bou Said, a quaint little Arab village. Anyone wishing to build new property there must build according to the local architecture. By government decree, nobody must mar this little museum piece by planting a modern type house in its midst.

I went down to the harbour to see if any ships were going to Sicily, asking if they would take me, but there were none. There was only the regular passenger ship that went to Palermo every Wednesday. It was going to be difficult.

Next day, I realised one of two ambitions I have hankered over for a long time. I was walking along the Avenue Jules Ferry. The sight of my kilt had caused the usual interest. A crowd of Arabs followed me, laughing and mocking me. I was long since used to this and had always treated it with the contempt it deserved, although I had long wanted to retaliate. With the Africans it had been like childish fun and I always consoled myself with the fact they knew no better. But the Arabs were different, because they had more intelligence. Their scorn was more galling and much more detestable. As I was walking, one stepped out in front of me and pointed at my kilt and doubled up with forced mirth.

Too long I had held myself in. This time, even before I realised it myself, I had caught him across the face with the flat of my hand. The blow straightened him up and carried him out of my arc of vision. I neither stopped nor turned to see how or where he was. The momentary self-satisfaction was intense. The sight of the sardonic laugh wiped off by one of surprise was enough. But it was really a silly thing to do. With relations between the Arab and Europeans strained as they were, it only needed a spark like that to start a furnace. For an instant after the blow there was silence from the mob. Then more laughing. But this time the derision was for the one I had struck. His derision had boomeranged.

But immediately after that, the crowd overtook me. I kept on walking until they stopped in front to bar my path. One said in French "Why did you strike this man?" I was pleased to see the red weals on my victim's face. I answered in English that I didn't understand. This stumped the spokesman for a bit. He turned to the crowd that was gathering to ask, I believe, if anyone spoke English. I saw it was now or never. Every second increased the ring round me. Hemmed in by such a mob, there was no telling what retaliation they would make. I pushed forward. A man hunched his shoulder to keep me in the circle without actually making an issue of it by putting his hands on me. I hunched mine, harder than his; then I was through. I walked faster through the interested pedestrians. I saw two white hats of Foreign Legionnaires and knew then I had company, so I slowed down. I had no more trouble.

My other ambition was to decapitate a hen or cockerel when it was at the height of its cackle. Ever since lying with jaundice and malaria in Tanganyika with the hens wracking every nerve in my body with their racket, I had hated them with deep conviction, Even now, a hen screeching grates on my nerves, but I have never satisfied that craving!

The entrance to the Medina, the Arab quarter, was through the Port de France, the giant gateway with the enormous metal doors. I wandered through the Souk, the shopping streets. It was after dark and to see it during Ramadan after dark was to see it at its best. All day the people have had nothing, but at 7.15 p.m. a gun boomed announcing the end of the day and then all can have breakfast. Cafés were in full swing, people were happy. It really was worth seeing.

The Souk was extremely interesting. It had an atmosphere all its own, quite different from the casbahs of Algiers or Constantine. Here the little shops had an elegance lacking in the others. The commodities were found in sections. There was a whole covered street of shops selling sandals and shoes. Then there was the carpet section, the beef section and so on.

I wandered around the ruins of Carthage the next day and climbed up to Souk Ahras and looked down on the bay. I also went out to the American Cemetery and I got a job! I started next day at 7 a.m., working as an Arab, drawing the same wage, 750 francs per day, and working straight through until 2 p.m. The job was opening crates of marble. The marble for the memorial was cut and each stone numbered in Italy. Here it was unpacked and fitted like a huge jigsaw.

This job was the lifebelt thrown to a man overboard – like the answer to a prayer, only I hadn't asked for it. I reckoned if I worked for a week I could just make the 4,000 francs for the boat for Palermo, Sicily.

I finished the first week working. I thought I would never have to ask for an advance from an employer. But I asked and got 1,000 francs on Wednesday. That hurt my pride a lot. But I was completely out. Even so, 1,000 francs (£1) for a week's food isn't so much to go on for doing a hard day's work and then I wanted to have some change over to get some groceries before I left Tunis.

I wondered if the time I have been going so short of food this week on such meagre rations for working, had anything to do with lack of concentration. I found myself putting things off and even to write my diary required a mental effort. My thoughts kept wandering away. My diet had been porridge in the morning and potatoes and bread in the afternoon. I had three potatoes each day and I drank the potato water.

The Arabs were not good to work with. It was Ramadan and, during Ramadan, they were physically unfit for heavy work. But I thought they played on the idea. They ate after dark and did a lot of visiting, so they had little sleep. During the hours of daylight no food, not even water must cross their lips. By 11 a.m. they were finished as far as work went. But I felt that a lot of it was malingering. At night, I was quite sure they had far more and better food than I had. I felt very tired after 11 a.m. also but I made myself go on so that I would not be classed with them.

I finished work on Monday. They paid me one day's wages extra as bonus for my work. So I drew 5,100 francs. I paid back the 1000 francs advanced to me, which left me 4,100 francs. The boat fare to Palermo was 4,025 francs. So it was all very neat. I had 500 francs left from the 1,000 francs to buy some things to take with me to Sicily. That was 500 francs (10/-) I spent in the one working week for food – not very sumptuous living.

On Sunday I was invited to the home of the people who gave me a lift out to Carthage from Tunis. That was the best of hitching; you did meet so many people.

Monsieur Brun spoke good English and he gave me information and a new way of thinking regarding the colonies. It seemed that Tunisia might have self-government and the local settlers were very indignant. I could imagine that the Kenya settlers would be the same if the Africans in Kenya were given self-government. But Monsieur Brun was one of a small group of progressive thinkers who believed that nothing could be gained from eternal antagonism between the peoples and that the Frenchmen there must stay and associate more with the Africans, whereas many were saying they would leave, for in their opinion the country would be finished for them.

Now that I had been round Africa, many of my views had changed. I was beginning to see that the old ways of life in Africa must be finished: self-government, something new, a different way of thinking was needed. And also, it seemed the French too were realising this. The ideas they thought were new were the ideas that had been abroad in many of the British colonies for many years.

With those thoughts in my mind the next day, Tuesday, 10th May, 1955, a momentous day, was my last day in Africa. It was virtually the end of my journey. Although Europe lay ahead, the adventure of Africa was ended. What I had done, seen, learned about and loved in that most wonderful of continents, would be with me in memory for ever.

THE WAY HOME

The ship sailed at 6 p.m. heading for Sicily. Although there was still Europe to cross I was going home, back to Scotland. My thoughts roamed over the past five years and I contemplated what I had achieved. I had learned so much of the history of that great continent, made friends along the way, experienced fantastic hospitality and done things I might never have expected to – not all good, I have to say. Being imprisoned didn't come high on the list and neither did almost starving, not to mention almost losing my life falling through the crust of an erupting volcano! But it taught me to be self reliant and unafraid of what the future might bring.

I landed in Palermo, Sicily, at 8 a.m. in the morning and spent the day in town. It was wonderful to change my cheque from the job in Carthage and be solvent again. It was a long walk out of town in the afternoon, as the town trailed on in long suburbs. However, I got a lift part of the way in a horse and cart. The Sicilian carts were very interesting. They had pictures, landscapes, etc. painted on their sides which were very artistic and well done. At night, a man gave me permission to sleep in his garden and I made my way across Sicily next day via the centre road. It was very beautiful and the road was, if anything, even more twisted and looped than the one over the Atlas mountain border between Tunisia and Algeria.

Hitch-hiking was much easier here. The Sicilians would stop and even if they could not take you, the driver would stop and apologise. I think the national character was the first thing one noticed on landing; the people were so friendly. A worker, a bricklayer would shout his greeting to you and if you replied would come over to shake your hand and immediately return to what he was doing. Perhaps quick friendship is not lasting friendship, but to a stranger in a new country it felt very nice. Compared to these people the French seemed so cold and distant, although I grew to like them very much.

I left the town of Catania to make my way out to the open country before camping. I asked where I could camp and two men on a motor scooter – I think every male in Sicily owned a scooter – accompanied me to a place where there were forty Germans camping. They made me very welcome. The camp was in a beautiful setting where little islands rose to peaks just out of the water.

Most of the Germans were from Munich in the American sector and spoke English, which was very welcome. That night I went to a dance with them at a local night club and next morning went goggle fishing with them. Although the water was colder than at Mombasa where I last swam with goggles, I thoroughly enjoyed it, although I twice hit my hand against sea urchins and had some spikes in my fingers which I couldn't get out.

After another day at the beach I hitched down to Messina and got the ferryboat across to Villa San Giovanni. So, at last, I was on the mainland of Europe.

I cleared the village and looked for a place to camp. Wandering through a dilapidated trellis gate in a garden, I found an empty hovel. I was going to camp outside but the neighbours, who soon gathered, said I should go inside. The street pump where everybody draws water was just down the steps. The Italians were very friendly – one of the neighbours brought me firewood, another brought me a plate of macaroni.

After San Giovanni I made my way up to Cogenza, Castrovillari and Sorrento, and then crossed from Sorrento to Capri. Italy south of here is very mountainous. The road twists unbelievably all the way. The Italian drivers risk certain death every minute as they go along at speed, swirling round the bends apparently oblivious to the fact that other vehicles may also be using the road coming the opposite way. My experience with them told me their reflexes are remarkable. Perhaps it goes with the quick Latin temperament!

And on to Capri – what an enchanting isle! It was one of the few places where one wasn't disappointed after all that has been said and written about it. In the town and Anacapri, everything was laid out for the tourist. At first I thought it was so artificial, but now I know that this was the character of the place.

I found camping impossible. Every inch of the island was owned and fenced off. At least, any piece where it would be possible to camp. The rest was too far away from water. I met an American who was going to be a missionary. He was staying at a little pensione for 300 lire per night, so I decided to join him. Senora Ferrari, the proprietress, was not a pleasant person, but it was a place to stay.

A couple of days ago we walked over the island to the Blue Grotto. A small opening in the rock at sea level opens into a great cavern. We swam in. I thought it would be a better experience than being rowed in like many of the thousands of tourists. Swimming in the Blue Grotto was an unforgettable experience. Looking from the back of the cave towards the opening, the water seemed as if lit by a blue fire, as if all underneath was phosphorescent. In the water our bodies gleamed with a most unnatural whiteness. Looking away from the opening, the cave was dark except where the ripples reflected on the uneven ceiling high overhead.

We visited Villa San Michele too and spent an evening at a little night club 'The Casa Rosa'. As we ate a dish of Spanish mussels, chicken and rice, the male dancer and his partner with guitar were wonderful. Like most places, the magic of Capri was best seen in the evening or early morning. To look across the water towards Vesuvius in the morning, before the sun had dispelled the veil of mist which joins the sea to the sky, was unforgettable. The translucent monochrome blue of the scene, the delicate touch of nature's hand, made it seem like a Japanese painting, soft, hazy and unearthly.

Sorrento was idyllic. I have a memory I will always carry of looking over Fisherman's Bay at a red sunset.

In mainland Italy, I was lucky to get a lift on a truck going to Rome. Walking in that fascinating city, always a romantic, I was transported in my mind to a time of Caesar, Cleopatra and legions of Roman soldiers. At the Colosseum as darkness fell, with scenes in my head of gladiators fighting to the death, I lay down on a stone bench to sleep. I was wakened by the awareness that someone was leaning over me with a knife, sawing through the straps of my rucksack. Instantly alert, I twisted his arm behind his back and he dropped the knife and fled.

With still so much to see in Italy I was anxious now to be home. However, I had promised to spend a day with Mark, in Switzerland, who was with his friend Werner at the Chari River when the barges collided and sank and I lost all my gear. They had supported me well at a time when I was very low. He was delighted to see me and laughed when I gave him back a T-shirt of his that he had given me. Apart from that, I took advantage of lifts in trucks across France to the ferry at Calais. Arriving at Dover my luck continued and I found at the port a truck heading for Edinburgh! The driver dropped me very close to home.

I walked the last few miles to my village, Torryburn in Fife, and as I approached the house that was my home, a neighbour standing at her door jutted her chin and greeted me with, "Aye, Davie", as if I'd just been down to the baker's for the rolls and not been travelling for five years! After all, this is Scotland, where nobody is allowed to get a big heid. This is the land o' 'Och, Ah kent his faither'.

But Isa didn't have the last word. What emotion she lacked or preferred not to show was made up by my family: the tears of joy and the welcome fireside said it all!